The Alcoholic Family

THE ALCOHOLIC FAMILY

Peter Steinglass, M.D.

with

Linda A. Bennett, Ph.D.,

Steven J. Wolin, M.D.,

David Reiss, M.D.

BasicBooks

A Subsidiary of Perseus Books, L.L.C.

Library of Congress Cataloging-in-Publication Data
  The alcoholic family.
  References: p. 365
  Includes index.
  1. Alcoholics — United States — Family relationships.   2. Children
of alcoholic parents — United States.   3. Alcoholism — Treatment —
United States.   I. Steinglass, Peter.   [DNLM: 1. Alcoholism.
2. Family.   3. Family Therapy.   WM 274 A35285]
HV5132.A44   1987   362.2'92   80–47741
ISBN 0–465–00097–5 (cloth)
ISBN 0–465–00112–2 (paper)

Designed by Vincent Torre

97 98 99 00 01 CC/HC 9 8 7 6

*To the many families who,
by sharing their stories with us,
have taught us about alcoholism and
its consequences for family life.*

Contents

PART V
The Late Phase of Development

PART VI
Treating the Alcoholic Family

Acknowledgments

LIKE OUR SUBJECT, the Alcoholic Family, this book is the product of multiple influences. It has been nurtured by the guidance of many teachers, and the support of many colleagues and friends. Its developmental roots are in the dual wellsprings of family therapy and alcoholism research.

For two of us (P.S. and S.J.W.), an early exposure to family research and therapy during psychiatric residency training at the Albert Einstein College of Medicine first taught us the power inherent in the family system. Albert Scheflen was a most important influence during those early days, especially demonstrating to us the feasibility of research with whole families as a tool for seeing what is not easily made visible. For another of us (D.R.), this same lesson was learned at the Massachusetts Mental Health Center, under the expert guidance of Eliot Mishler.

When P.S. and S.J.W. later received postgraduate training at the Laboratory of Alcohol Research of the National Institute on Alcohol Abuse and Alcoholism (NIAAA) under the leadership of first, Jack Mendelson, and later, Morris Chafetz, a crucial step occurred. We were encouraged by both to pursue the notion of examining couples and whole families with alcohol problems, even during episodes of intoxication. Our research perspective has never been the same.

With colleagues David Berenson and Donald I. Davis, we studied our first Alcoholic Families at St. Elizabeths Hospital (where the Laboratory of Alcohol Research was located) and developed the underpinnings of what was to become a series of funded research projects, supported by NIAAA, the Rehabilitation Services Administration, and most recently the Still Water Foundation of Austin, Texas. We owe much to our supporters in the Psychosocial Research Branch of the Division of Extramural Research, NIAAA, and especially want to thank Tina Vanderveen for her confidence in this work.

Since 1974, our alcoholism studies have been carried out at the Center for Family Research (CFR), a multidisciplinary research group we founded within the Division of Research of the George Washington University

School of Medicine's Department of Psychiatry and Behavioral Sciences. It was in 1974 that the fourth author (L.A.B.) joined the other three at our Center, bringing her special perspective as a cultural anthropologist to our investigations of alcoholism and the family.

A number of people at George Washington have been particularly important in supporting our work at CFR. Tom Webster and Jerry M. Wiener, in their role as Chairs of the Department of Psychiatry and Behavioral Sciences (Tom during our initial years at GWU; Jerry since 1977) have provided invaluable and consistent encouragement, not to mention a reliable base from which to grow and experiment. John Naughton and Tom Bowles, the two Deans for Academic Affairs, and Fred Leonard and Michael Jackson, the two Associate Deans for Research at the medical school during the past decade, have lent comparable administrative support both for CFR and for our programmatic alcoholism research in particular.

We also want to note, with special affection, our appreciation for the support received from Professor Atara Kaplan De-Nour, Chair of the Psychiatry Department at the Hadassah-Hebrew University Medical School. The initial drafts of our manuscript were prepared during a sabbatical year the first author spent in Professor Kaplan De-Nour's department.

Now we move on to a particularly important and special group of people—our research colleagues and staff at the Center for Family Research who participated with us on the research projects and clinical programs that provided the data that forms the substance of our book. Janet Moyer and Lydia Tislenko served as Project Directors for the Steinglass studies and lent their remarkable and prodigious organizational and intellectual talents to these projects. They have proven invaluable colleagues. Martha Ann Teitelbaum, Denise Noonan, and Katharine McAvity have been equally important contributors in the Bennett and Wolin projects. Marion Usher, Jeffrey Jay, and David Glass deserve special thanks not only for their contributions to the development of the clinical treatment model discussed in our book, but also for their constant intellectual and emotional support for our work. Em Sause, the CFR Administrator, was the overseer of the countless tasks and details that need attention and solving in the running of a multidisciplinary research program. Margit Holdsworth was the key person in the final steps of manuscript preparation, and her attention to detail and unflagging good humor were critical in shepherding the book project through its final stages.

No one has been more important to the successful completion of this project than our editor, Jo Ann Miller. As can be imagined, when four authors write a book together, many unforeseen difficulties and delays arise. Jo Ann's consistent faith in the project has therefore been one of those ingredients that, in retrospect, was essential to its successful completion. She has unusual gifts for seeing how a manuscript can be sharpened, reorganized, brought alive. We hope the reader will agree with us that our book has benefited immensely from her applying these talents to our work.

We have also made generous use of the creative talents of Abbe Steinglass, who designed the illustrations for the theory chapters.

Behind this long list of colleagues and mentors sit the two most important groups of people without which this work would never have happened—the families we are part of and the families we have studied. Both deserve our gratitude and affection.

Preface

IN THIS BOOK, we explore the complex world of alcoholism and the family. It is not our purpose, however, to present an exhaustive review of all that is known about this subject. Instead, we want to introduce the reader to a particular viewpoint about these families, the viewpoint of the systems-oriented family clinician-researcher. The book thus tells a selective story, a story that focuses primarily on data about the relationship between alcohol use and family interactional behavior.

In telling this story, we are sharing what we have learned as the result of a series of systematic studies of families with alcoholic members, studies that were carried out over a ten-year period. We describe the visits we made to these families in their homes. We report what we learned from talking with them at length about their past, about their family rituals, about the families they came from, about the heritage they feel has been passed on to them from prior generations, and about their intentions regarding the legacy they intend to pass on to their children. And finally, we discuss what we have learned about psychotherapeutic treatment of alcoholism, in the process describing a family-oriented intervention program combining family therapy principles with an understanding of the specific needs of the family with alcoholism.

As our story unfolds, it becomes clear that although our topic is alcoholism and the family, our interest is focused on a particular type of family with alcoholism, the family in which chronic alcoholism has become a central theme of family life. In these families, alcoholism is no longer a condition of an individual family member. Instead, it has become a family condition that has inserted itself into virtually every aspect of family life. These are the families we will subsequently be calling "Alcoholic Families."

In the course of the book, data from three different sources are integrated in the service of telling a coherent story about Alcoholic Families:

- Clinical interviews, including both research and psychotherapy interviews;
- Quantitative data from a series of studies of families with alcoholic members; and
- Selective data drawn from the literature published by other researchers and clinicians.

The book is divided into six major sections:

I. In an *Introductory* section, the core issues associated with alcoholism and the family are delineated (chapter 1), along with problems of determining prevalence rates and accurately defining alcoholism when the focus of interest is the Alcoholic Family rather than the alcoholic individual (chapter 2).

II. In the *Theory* section, a family systems model of the Alcoholic Family is spelled out in detail. This model sees family life as a product of the dynamic interplay between two sets of processes—one set associated with regulation of family life (described in chapter 3); the other associated with family growth and development (discussed in chapter 4).

(Although the model focuses explicitly on chronic alcoholism and the family, it is intended to be a model of broad applicability. That is, it starts out by describing in detail the normative regulatory and developmental processes in families, and then describes the types of alterations in these normative processes that can occur when the family organizes its life around a chronic psychopathological condition like alcoholism.)

Briefly summarized, the model is built around a developmental construct we call *systemic maturation*. This construct posits that all families, regardless of composition or age of members, proceed through a developmental process that can be conveniently divided into three different phases (early, middle, and late) based on the sequential emergence of a set of developmental themes. These developmental phases are assumed not only to be universal, but also to be epigenetic in nature. Overall, therefore, it is possible to describe a characteristic life cycle for the modal family, a life cycle that is surely influenced by the unique personality, past history, values, and so forth, of the family, but that nevertheless takes its most fundamental shape from the process of systemic maturation.

The second major construct in our model is that of *developmental distortion*. This construct refers to those changes and alterations in the customary shape of systemic maturation that are the consequences of specific unique experiences with which the family is forced to deal. One such experience is chronic alcoholism in a family member. Here is it useful to ask the question—are there certain characteristic changes that families make in priorities, in behavioral style, in distribution of energies and family resources when chronic alcoholism becomes a major organizing theme for family life? We believe the answer to this question is yes. The next three sections of the book therefore attempt to illustrate how these developmental distortions occur in the Alcoholic Family. The sections deal, respectively, with the early, middle, and late phase of systemic maturation.

III. In the *Early-Phase* section (chapter 5), attention is focused on the critical developmental challenge of identity formation. Regarding alcoholism, the issue is whether or not family identity is to be built around alcoholism as a central organizing principle. In other words, is this to become an "Alcoholic Family?" Most new couples, upon joining in marriage, set in motion a life course that in retrospect seems to have been highly overdetermined. That is, most early-phase families are strongly influenced by experiences from their families of origin as they embark on their own careers. Further, as the new couple draws on its past to weave the fabric of the new marital relationship, traditions from one side or the other will predominate. Which family of origin is to become the principle transmitter of its own identity, now passed on to the newly formed next generation? Which spouse's past relationships are to provide the model for new family rules, choice of friends, patterns of communication, and so on?

It is at this time that patterns of alcohol use may also be decided. Although alcoholic-level behaviors may not emerge for many years, rules and attitudes toward alcohol use are laid down at this early stage, establishing the fertile soil for the subsequent development of alcoholism. If predominating traditions are drawn from a family of origin that was itself organized around alcohol, the new family also has a high likelihood of including alcohol in its life. Thus chapter 5 concentrates on research and clinical data that bring into focus the struggles of the early-phase Alcoholic Family as it deals with identity formation issues.

IV. In the *Middle-Phase* section, attention switches to an examination of family regulatory behaviors in the Alcoholic Family. Our model suggests that as the family moves into the middle phase, it becomes increasingly specialized in its areas of concentration. One such area of thematic concentration can be chronic alcoholism itself. This is what occurs in the Alcoholic Family. Concomitant with this process of thematic specialization, the family must also place greater emphasis on the maintenance of a stable family environment conducive to orderly growth. Paramount in this regard are the regulatory behaviors the family uses to order its own life.

Insofar as these regulatory behaviors are influenced by the family's need to accommodate the vicissitudes of chronic alcoholism (especially daily and monthly cycles in drinking patterns and the consequences of behavior while intoxicated), developmental distortions inevitably occur. For example, the family becomes inordinately concerned with the maintenance of stability within the family in the face of wide fluctuations in behavior secondary to drinking. The consequence is often the imposition of increasingly rigid and dictatorial regulatory behaviors, behaviors geared more toward maintenance of the status quo than toward promotion of individual or family growth. And a corollary of this emphasis on day-to-day stability is a gradual flattening of the family's growth curve.

Thus in the section devoted to the middle phase of development, we turn our attention to three types of regulatory behaviors that reflect the above process—short-term problem-solving strategies, daily routines, and family rituals. Each type of behavior is the topic of a chapter in the middle-phase section of the book—short-term problem-solving in chapter 6; family daily routines in chapter 7; family rituals in chapter 8.

V. Finally, in the *Late-Phase* section, we move on to an examination of the two critical questions associated with this phase of development—the family's final distillation and clarification of its unique identity; and the process of transmission of this identity to future generations. The late-phase family, often stimulated by the major changes in family membership that typically initiate this phase, goes through a process of consolidation and concretization that brings into sharp focus key themes in its life. It is a kind of summing-up procedure, and its core dynamic feature is the dual process of concretization of the family's sense of itself (its identity) and the transmission of this identity to the next generation. The family has now come full circle in its life cycle, in that the generation the late-phase family is attempting to transmit its identity to is, of course, participating in the early phase of a new (but connected) family.

For the Alcoholic Family, the process of summing up its family identity invariably means making a statement about the alcoholism issue. The various options available to the family are discussed in chapter 9. Transmission, of course, means whether or not alcoholism is to be passed on as a legacy to children in the family. This issue (which is also addressed earlier in chapter 5 when the early-phase alcoholic family is discussed) is approached in chapter 10 from the perspective of the late-phase family.

VI. Finally, the book concludes with a *Treatment* section. This section is not intended to provide an exhaustive discussion of family therapy approaches to alcoholism. Such texts are already available (e.g., Davis, 1987; Kaufman and Kaufman, 1979; Lawson, Peterson, and Lawson, 1983; Steinglass, 1976). Instead, we outline the most important parameters of treatment as they evolve from the clinical and research data previously presented. Emphasis is once again placed on a developmental perspective, and a detailed description of a typical course of family therapy with an Alcoholic Family is provided.

This book is being written at a time when interest in the Alcoholic Family is finally beginning to blossom. No longer are such families thought of as the clients exclusively of alcoholism specialty clinics. No longer is research into alcoholism exclusively focused on the alcoholic individual (especially his biomedical status). At the same time, our understanding of the Alcoholic Family is far from complete. As our story unfolds, there are many junctures where available data remain painfully superficial and our thinking about these families becomes, by necessity, largely speculative. Even when specific research data are available to us, studies in this field are still at an early stage and often raise as many intriguing questions as they answer.

But the broad outline of the story is nevertheless beginning to take shape. And it is this framework—the developmental history of the Alcoholic Family—that we attempt to construct for the reader as the central task of our book. Perhaps at some points the emphasis appears too technical for the reader interested primarily in clinical issues. At the same time, the reader expecting to be able to evaluate specific research findings may find the voluminous case material provided in the book a distraction. But our own goal is to subordinate both clinical and research data presentation to the telling of a consistent and organized story about this most interesting group of families.

PART I

A FAMILY SYSTEMS
APPROACH
TO ALCOHOLISM

This book accurately reflects the clinical facts and family dynamics of the families described but all names and identifying details have been changed while preserving the integrity of the research findings and conclusions.

CHAPTER 1

Setting the Stage:
The Core Issues

Two Case Histories

WHEN NOAH emerged with his family from the trials and tribulations of the great flood to resettle the land, one of his first acts was to plant a vineyard. Shortly thereafter, we are told, in the first biblical reference to intoxicated behavior, "he drank of the wine, and was drunken; and he was uncovered within his tent" *(Gen. 9:21)*. A family drama of no small consequence to the participants involved then proceeded to unfold.

Ham, Noah's youngest son, noticed his father's condition and brought it to the attention of his two brothers, Shem and Japheth, who took a garment and laid it over Noah while taking care to avoid looking at their father in his drunken condition. "And Shem and Japheth took a garment, and laid it upon both their shoulders, and went backward . . . and they saw not their father's nakedness" *(Gen. 9:23)*. When Noah awoke from his wine-induced stupor, he immediately recognized "what his younger son had done unto him," and reacted with fury and outrage: "Cursed be Canaan (Ham); a servant of servants shall he be unto his brethren"; but to Shem and Japheth, Noah said, "Blessed be the Lord God of Shem . . . God shall enlarge Japheth, and he shall dwell in the tents of Shem; and Canaan shall be his servant" *(Gen. 9:24–27)*.

The second biblical reference to intoxicated behavior occurs in the story of Sodom and Gomorrah. The wicked cities are destroyed shortly after Lot escapes with his wife and daughters. But Lot's wife has been turned into a pillar of salt; tired, confused, and frightened, Lot retreats to a cave in the mountains west of the Dead Sea with his two daughters to await the next turn of events. They are in a wilderness, totally alone, and despairing of their future.

In this desperate situation, Lot's daughters talk together about their future and define the central problem and its solution: "Our father is old, and there is not a man in the earth to come in unto us after the manner of all the earth: Come, let us make our father drink wine, and we will lie with him, then we may preserve seed of our father" (Gen. 19:31–32). In this they shortly succeed. "And they made their father drink wine that night: and the firstborn went in, and lay with her father; and he perceived not when she lay down, nor when she arose. And it came to pass on the morrow, that the firstborn said unto the younger, Behold, I lay yesternight with my father: let us make him drink wine this night also; and go thou in, and lie with him, that we may preserve seed of our father. And they made their father drink wine that night also: and the younger arose, and lay with him; and he perceived not when she lay down, nor when she arose. Thus were both the daughters of Lot with child by their father" (Gen. 19:33–38).

These passages from the stories of Noah and Lot are among the earliest "case histories" describing what can happen when alcohol is introduced into family life. The dilemma faced by Noah's son Ham, on seeing his father lying naked in a drunken stupor, has a poignant and familiar ring to any clinician who has listened to the struggles of an adolescent trying to decide how to behave in the face of a parent's drunken behavior. Should it be ignored or should it be confronted? Or, to use the metaphor from the Book of Genesis, should it be covered up or left uncovered? Ham is not the first son to attempt a strategy of "covering up" to protect his family's public image, only to have a parent's wrath visited upon his head. Alcohol consumption and the subsequent resulting behavior seem, in this circumstance, to have few redeeming features.

The second story is also familiar. As "modern" students of human behavior, we are aware of the close association between alcohol consumption and incest. But the story of Lot and his daughters has an unfamiliar twist. Lot's intoxication is used as part of a conscious strategy to solve a major problem the family faces, the conception of the next generation. For the moment, let us ignore the possible long-term negative consequences to the psychological health of the two daughters who solved the problem in this particular manner. Also put aside skepticism about Lot's ability to perform sexually, given current scientific evidence about the effects of alcohol ingestion on sexual performance. (The significant point of Lot's story is that intoxication is used to solve a family problem.)

If we view these two biblical families as if they were part of a research study, what generalizations could be made about them? What are their shared characteristics? Clearly, neither question is easy to answer. Alcohol apparently played a very different role in the lives of each family and had very different consequences for the individuals involved.

Even the most basic question—is alcohol good or bad for family life—defies a straightforward answer, given the data encompassed in the biblical cases. For one individual, Noah's youngest son, the sequence of events initiated by his father's intoxication, proved devastating. (For Lot and his daughters, otherwise forbidden behavior became socially acceptable at least partially because it was carried out under the influence of alcohol.) The family survived and succeeding generations were guaranteed, presumably because the family was able to act during periods of intoxication in ways that would have otherwise been unacceptable. If one of the primary tasks of the family is the propagation of subsequent generations, then alcohol permitted this family to solve a major dilemma in an inventive fashion. What might have been an irreconcilable clash between two culturally determined mandates—the task of propagation and the incest taboo—was averted and a positive outcome obtained. Thus, the question—is alcohol good or bad for family life—seems not so simple after all.

These two case histories describe, at least in particular situations, how alcohol use affects family life. Since we do not know whether the dramatic accounts of the consequences of alcohol use in the Noah and Lot stories presage a continuing history of alcohol abuse in the families, we cannot assess what the impact of chronic alcoholism might have been on them. Yet even when we move forward in time several millennia and ask the same "good-bad" question about the relationship between alcoholism and modern family life, we find that the answer is still complex.

For example, suppose that the question is rephrased in terminology that a sociologist or a psychologist might use in studying the relationship between alcoholism and the family. (A typical research question might be—how *stressful* is alcoholism for the family? This appears to be a simple, easily researchable question, likely to yield clear-cut results. Researchers might find, for example, that alcoholism is very stressful, or particularly disruptive of family life in the areas of financial affairs and social relationships, or only moderately stressful compared to a chronic physical illness in a child (the latter compares one chronic condition with another). For each of these possible findings, the hypothesis is one-dimensional: Alcoholism appears to have only one type of impact on families—a negative one. All that remains to be elucidated is the target area and amount of negative impact.

Some research findings are compatible with this view. For example, if alcoholism is, in fact, universally stressful for families, we would expect to see, as one consequence, evidence of elevated family disruption and dissolution (divorce rates). A number of studies suggest that this is, indeed, the case. Chafetz, Blane, and Hill (1971), in a study of the effects of alcoholism on children, found that 41 percent of the parents in alcoholic families in their sample were divorced or separated, as compared with 11 percent of nonalcoholic parents. (Furthermore, 60 percent of the parents in the intact alcoholic families were rated as having poor marital relationships, compared with 11 percent of the nonalcoholic couples.) Vaillant (1983) reported comparable differences in divorce rates of alcohol abusers versus moderate drinkers (for both a college-educated and a "core city" sample).

However, the overall picture is not as uniform as the above data might suggest. Although divorce rates (indicating marital instability) might seem higher when one or both spouses are alcohol abusers, in fact only a very small percentage (perhaps 3.5 percent) of the total adult alcoholic population live alone (Whitefield and Williams, 1976). The vast majority continue to live in intact family situations (with parents, siblings, or spouses). Thus, alcoholism is, clearly, not so overwhelmingly stressful that it automatically leads to the expulsion of the alcoholic by the family. There is also reason to believe that even in Skid Row populations, many "homeless" alcoholics are still engaged in enduring relationships with one or more important family members (Singer, 1985; Wolin and Steinglass, 1974).

Similarly, although increased incidences of family violence or incest are associated with chronic alcoholism, we posit that many, if not most, families with alcoholic members are relatively quiet types. By quiet we mean that, despite internal family distress, to the outside observer such a family's condition repeatedly escapes detection. Professionals as well as lay people are often surprised when they discover that a seemingly stable and untroubled family has one or more alcoholic members. Thus it is just as likely now as it was when the Bible was being written that alcohol abuse in one family leads to the kind of negative consequences suffered by Ham, while in another family it becomes part of the fabric that the members use to structure their lives, including the solving of important problems.)

Professional Attitudes—Negative to Positive

In our society, alcoholism is such a common problem that it eventually touches the lives of almost everyone. It may do so via personal experience with alcohol or through contacts with alcoholic individuals at work, or in an embarrassing incident at a party or a restaurant, or even because of an automobile accident. By the time one reaches adulthood, one's contacts with this condition have been multiple and one's attitudes about alcoholism tend not only to be sharply defined but also ingrained. This is as true for professional clinicians and researchers as for lay people. And, as we all know, for the most part these attitudes have been negative.

The Family Seen As A Negative Force

A negative professional attitude toward alcoholism has often extended to families with alcoholic members.* By and large, professionals have taken a rather pejorative view of these families. Clinicians, hearing from their patients about life in such families, have tended to conclude that they are enemies of individual growth. The family comes to be thought of as a negative force in the individual's life—at the very least an impediment, a blockade, a hurdle that the patient must overcome; at the worst, the root cause of the patient's psychopathology. Researchers have called attention to disturbed communication patterns, rigid role distributions, and dysfunctional coping behaviors evidenced by these families.† A look at earlier clinical literature on alcoholism and the family reinforces the view of negative research attitudes.

In an article by Whalen (1953) for example, discussing the possible unconscious motivations that lead a woman to marry an alcoholic man, four categories of wives are described, each with its own pejorative title: "Suffering Susan"; "Controlling Catherine"; "Wavering Winifred"; and "Punitive Polly." Whalen's article, described in one of the classic texts on

*See, for example, the reviews of the clinical literature by Bailey (1961), Paolino and McCrady (1977), and Edwards, Harvey, and Whitehead (1973).

†A recent review by Steinglass and Robertson (1983) provides ample documentation.

the alcoholic marriage (Paolino and McCrady, 1977, p. 37) as "an excellent example of a specific application of the psychoanalytic concept of defense mechanisms," is also an excellent example of attitudes that existed in the 1950s (and perhaps continue to exist) toward wives of alcoholic men.

In extensive descriptions of common interactional "games" used by alcoholic individuals and their spouses, Steiner (1969) includes as titles of game "scripts" such phrases as "Drunk But Proud Of It" and "Lush." Some of the names of characters in these scripts also reveal the underlying attitudes toward alcoholic marriages reflected in the Transactional Analysis approach: two examples—"Persecutor" and "Patsy."

Thus alcoholism researchers and clinicians have often projected a picture of families of alcoholics as having a ready capacity for cruelty, tyranny, boredom, and disintegration. In our own discussions of our research data and clinical findings, it may at times appear that we are in agreement with this pejorative view. But don't be misled. While it is true that the families we describe here tend to have very low tolerances for uncertainty and to emphasize stability and predictability to the possible exclusion of inventiveness and novelty, it is a mistake to conclude that they should, first, be saddled with negative labels and then be isolated and ignored (either by clinicians treating alcoholism or by researchers).

A More Complex, Empathetic View

In recent years, a more empathetic view of families with alcoholic members has been emerging. Family-oriented clinicians and researchers have drawn on the burgeoning interest in family systems theory and on findings from family interaction research to suggest that families with alcoholic members constitute highly complex behavioral systems with remarkable tolerances for stress as well as occasional bursts of adaptive behavioral inventiveness that provoke wonder and admiration in observers.

Along with this new family perspective, there is an increased awareness of the multidimensional nature of the relationship between alcoholism and the family. For example, we have been urged to consider cultural factors (Bennett and Ames, 1985), the intricacies of drinking behavior (Jacob and Seilhammer, 1987), and family behavioral characteristics (Ablon, 1976) to understand what happens when alcoholism and family life mix. The main message seems to be that these families vary greatly and do not fit into simplistic formulas or uniform explanatory concepts.

Since families with alcoholic members are most likely highly heterogeneous groups, there is every reason to believe that they vary widely not only as to the usual sociodemographic characteristics (social class, ethnic group, composition) but also that they differ dramatically in the dynamic and behavioral aspects of life. Alcoholism in one family may be associated with a coping style centered around an attempt to isolate the alcoholic individual, to protect other family members from possible consequences of his or her behavior while intoxicated, and to emphasize values of self-reliance and lowered expectations. In another family, alcoholic behavior may go virtually unnoticed by other family members. A third family might view alcoholism as inevitable—a predetermined and built-in feature of life closely linked to the family's cultural or ethnic values. In yet another situation, a family might be fully aware of the dreadful consequences alcoholism imposes on its life, but still be helpless to construct an effective strategy for coping with these challenges. In some instances, families do seem, either wittingly or unwittingly, to make matters worse, to behave in ways that amplify, rather than diminish, problems.

Yet if alcoholism can have very different consequences for different families, we still would like to know if these are patterned and predictable, or purely random and idiosyncratic. Vaillant (1983) examined a similar set of issues from the perspective of the alcoholic *individual,* effectively arguing that alcoholism is a condition that has a a describable "natural history." This natural history, elucidated by his data, is not uniform for all alcoholic individuals. But one can nevertheless identify a series of critical way stations—points of choice—that are faced by all individuals who develop chronic alcoholism. The options they choose at each of these way stations determine the subsequent course of their condition. Although different choices mean different courses, the challenges faced are similar ones—hence, there is a structure that emerges in the natural history of the condition.

Is there a comparable natural history of alcoholism if one takes a family, rather than individual, perspective? Or are the number of solutions attempted by families so large and diverse as to make the picture hopelessly vague? Not surprisingly, our answer to these questions is a positive one: A family perspective adds substantially to a clinical understanding of the natural history of alcoholism and, by extension, to its effective treatment.

The basic thesis of this book is that for many families, alcoholism is a condition that has the capacity to become a central organizing principle around which family life is structured. When this occurs, alcoholism becomes an inseparable component of the fabric of family life—the family becomes an *Alcoholic Family.* * Because their lives are organized around alcoholism, these families have a unique developmental his-

*The term *Alcoholic Family* is used when we refer to families in which alcoholism has become a central organizing principle. Families in which this systemic reorganization has not occurred will be designated either "families with alcoholic members" or "families with alcoholism."

tory. The central focus of our book is this life history of the Alcoholic Family.

Five Core Issues

If families with alcoholism demonstrate heterogeneity rather than homogeneity in their structural and functional characteristics, what then is the best approach to this subject? Rather than focusing on one-dimensional factors like specific personality disturbances, physical addiction, abnormal metabolism, or genetic predisposition, we need to make sense of the many ways that alcoholism affects families and that families affect the condition.

Of the many aspects of alcoholism that have attracted the attention of researchers and clinicians, five are particularly relevant to any study of the interplay between alcoholism and family life. Each family with an alcoholic member must contend with a condition that (1) is chronic; (2) entails the use of a psychobiologically active drug; (3) is cyclical in nature; (4) produces predictable behavioral responses; and (5) has a definable course of development. Other aspects of alcoholism may eventually prove more important for the alcoholic individual. For example, the medical consequences of alcoholism may endanger life. But the Alcoholic Family's behavior is an attempt to contend with these five specific characteristics and, therefore, they are of particular interest to family-oriented clinicians and researchers. Clinicians want to know, for example, how family behavior has been shaped by the chronicity factor associated with alcoholism and what impact the use of alcohol has had on patterns of interactional behavior within the family.

If we look more closely at each of these five existing aspects of alcoholism, a complex range of additional issues and questions arise.

Chronicity

Alcoholism has both an insidious onset and a long-term course. Although this course may include periodic crises, often explosive in nature, alcoholism is by definition a chronic condition. From a life-span perspective, therefore, the Alcoholic Family is a family that has somehow managed to maintain its long-term structural and functional stability, despite what might be assumed to be a destabilizing condition. The family researcher-clinician thus wants to know not only how this relative long-term stability has been achieved but also what price the family pays for incorporating a chronic condition as one of its life themes.

The Use of a Psychobiologically Active Drug

Alcohol is a powerful drug whose psychopharmacological properties include the ability to produce both transient stimulant and subsequent depressant effects, as well as major disturbances of memory function, mood, cognition, sleep, and verbal interactional behavior.* The introduction of a psychobiologically active drug into a family system cannot help but alter interactional behavior as well, presumably changing affective tone, sexual behavior, and aggressive and other behavior. Long-term central nervous system depression produces lethargy, somnolence, and withdrawal. Cognitive disturbances in an alcoholic will often force the family to communicate in nonverbal ways. Investigations of nonverbal physical communication, affective feeling tone, interaction rates, as well as the content of verbal interaction, therefore, become important in understanding the impact of alcoholism on the family system. (In many of the studies described here, we incorporated measures of these family behavior parameters.)

The Dual-State Pattern of Behavior

Most alcoholic drinking patterns are cyclical in nature, exhibiting off-on cycling periods of intoxication ranging from several hours to several days interspersed with periods of sobriety. In dealing with the individual alcoholic, the often sharp contrast between behavior when intoxicated and when sober is as striking as the manic-depressive cycling of bipolar affective psychosis. A major clinical discovery described at length in this book is that a comparable duality or cycling exists for interactional behavior patterns within the Alcoholic Family. Off-on cycling of drinking behavior is paralleled by alterations in behavioral patterns within the family.

Behavioral Response Is Predictable

Individual alcoholics display remarkably consistent patterns of behavior during periods of intoxication (Tamerin and Mendelson, 1969). Further-

*Readers interested in these aspects of alcoholism should consult the comprehensive review articles by Mello and Mendelson, 1978; Mendelson, 1980; Sharma, Ziedman, and Muskowitz, 1977; Birnbaum and Parker, 1977; Freed, 1978; and Pokorny, 1978.

11

more, behavior during a drinking episode can be predicted from a knowledge of prior responses to alcohol, which implies a high degree of patterning. If this phenomenon extends to the family, one would then expect to see predictable patterns of interactional behavior associated with alcohol use. For the family-oriented clinician or researcher, therefore, those aspects of family behavior that are characteristically highly patterned—for example, problem-solving, daily routines, and family rituals—may logically be connected to drinking patterns as well. These behavioral patterns are particularly likely to be shaped by the impact of the predictable individual response of the alcoholic family member once drinking has started. Because these family behavior patterns are amenable to systematic study, they become convenient "windows" for the family researcher studying the relationship between alcohol use and family behavior in the Alcoholic Family. Not surprisingly, therefore, we will be detailing studies that focused on exactly these aspects of family behavior.

The Life Course of Alcoholism

Alcoholism was long thought to be a condition with an insidious onset and a life course of generally steady deterioration (Jellinek, 1960). Recent epidemiological data has challenged this perception. The national probability surveys of drinking practices carried out by Cahalan, Cisin, and Crossley (1969) and colleagues (see chapter 2) document either substantial "spontaneous remission" rates (even in cases of severe alcoholism), or stabilization (leveling off) of drinking behavior and of associated alcoholism-related difficulties in many subjects. These data strongly suggest a variable rather than a steady life course for alcoholics.

Although it is as yet unclear whether these patterns reflect different "types" of alcoholism or are attributable to other factors, it is reasonable that different long-term patterns of individual drinking behavior will result in different life histories for Alcoholic Families. A family systems clinician or researcher would attempt to determine how closely and consistently the drinking pattern of the alcoholic individual fits with the pattern of family organization. In the "stable" family situation, a reasonable and probably complementary fit exists between the characteristics of the alcoholic's variable life course (i.e., steady state drinking; alternating periods of months to years of sobriety with months to years of drinking; spontaneous remission; treatment-associated remission) and specific organizational characteristics of the family (e.g., daily routines; relative tolerance of uncertainty; family developmental characteristics).

From this brief description of the five existing conditions of alcoholism, it will be obvious that they are of special relevance to a family clinician or researcher working with the Alcoholic Family and are central to the discussions of clinical and research study that follow.

The Impact of Alcoholism on the Family: A Representative Study

The history of professional and lay attitudes toward alcoholism is complex. Our view is that the best approach to the subject of the Alcoholic Family is a conceptual framework that acknowledges the complexities rather than one that insists on reducing them to simple dimensions. Our approach is to view the family as a set of interconnected individuals acting together to produce a unique social unit that changes in a predictable fashion over time—that is, a *family systems* approach that emphasizes the developmental properties of families.

We began this chapter with two "case histories." The examples of Noah and Lot made one of the central hypotheses of our book immediately clear—that alcohol use will have very different implications from one family to the next. The use of alcohol may in one instance act as a divisive force (e.g., in causing the rift between Noah and his son); in other circumstances, it may serve a cohesive function (as in the use of alcohol illustrated in the story of Lot and his daughters).

We also suggested that a comparably complex set of conclusions would emerge if the question "Is alcohol good or bad for family life?" was asked and the answers systematically studied. Let us therefore examine the findings from one such study at this point.

We conducted a study that addressed the question posed earlier in the cases of Noah and Lot, that is, what is the impact of alcohol abuse on family members? Or, more simply, how stressful is alcoholism for families that have to deal with it? This sample study's findings also illustrate three major conclusions that set the stage for our discussion of the Alcoholic Family: First, the psychological and behavioral impact of alcoholism is often far greater for nonalcoholic family members than for the ones actually doing the drinking; second, the magnitude of alcoholism's negative consequences is often unrelated to biobehavioral aspects of drinking (e.g., the actual quantity and frequency of alcohol consumed, or the presence or absence of physical problems such as evidence of addiction or medical pathology); and third, the impact of alcoholism may be largely determined by characteristics of the family environment.

The Study Design

The study we have in mind asked a sample of thirty-one adult alcoholics and their spouses (a total of sixty-two) a set of questions about their drinking histories; the degree of physical, social-behavioral, and treatment consequences associated with the alcoholic's behavior; and the level of the alcoholic's psychiatric symptomatology (anxiety, depression, paranoia, and the like). Each subject completed two standardized questionnaires and responded to structured interview questions about his or her drinking histories.

The first questionnaire, the Self-Administered Alcoholism Screening Test (SAAST), has been used extensively to identify alcoholism in a general population (Swenson and Morse, 1973). Subjects are asked a series of alcoholism-related questions, and their responses to these questions provide a good general guide to what might be called *magnitude of alcoholism* experienced by the individual and his or her family. In our study, answers to selected items were used to calculate three separate subscores for the potential physical, social-behavioral, and treatment consequences of alcoholism.

The second questionnaire, the SCL–90, has been widely used as a self-administered symptom checklist (Derogatis, Lippman, and Conti, 1973). It provides reliable measures of the overall level of psychiatric symptomatology currently being experienced and separate subscores of the degree of symptomatology in nine traditional psychiatric dimensions: somatization; obsessive-compulsive symptoms; interpersonal sensitivity; depression; anxiety; hostility; phobic anxiety; paranoid ideation; and psychoticism.

The drinking history interview, the third source of data for this particular study, provided information about current level of alcohol consumption (known in alcoholism research as a quantity-frequency index of alcohol consumption) and about longitudinal patterns of drinking behavior.

The sample population, divided into three main groups, was particularly interesting because a wide variety of drinking habits were represented. Some of the alcoholic individuals were steady drinkers (e.g., they had been actively drinking for a period of at least six months prior to this particular study). These drinkers included those whose heavy drinking was primarily restricted to weekends and holidays, as well as daily drinkers. Another group, although currently drinking, had not been doing so on such a consistent basis. These individuals tended instead to follow an alternating pattern of wet and dry periods, a pattern that included, but was not restricted to the one we call "binge drinking" (an intensive but circumscribed period of drinking extending over days or several weeks). A third group in the study were not currently active drinkers. Some had been dry for substantial periods of time and were, in all likelihood, recovered alcoholics. Others might return to drinking in the future. But all of these nonactive drinkers had, at some time in the past, gone through a period of at least five years when they were drinking at alcoholic levels)

The Research Findings

The findings that emerged from this study provided an unusual picture of the patterns of stress experienced by members of Alcoholic Families.

The first research question was do these people seem to be experiencing *significant* levels of distress? The most direct means of answering was to examine psychiatric symptom levels—first, of the alcoholic spouses as a group and second, of the nonalcoholic spouses—and then to compare SCL–90 levels of the two separate groups to two comparison groups studied by Derogatis and his colleagues: a sample of normal subjects and a sample of psychiatric (presumably nonalcoholic) outpatients.

These comparisons revealed that both the sample of alcoholic spouses and the sample of nonalcoholic spouses experienced levels of symptomatology somewhat greater than the average experienced by normal subjects, but lower than the symptom levels of psychiatric outpatients. On average, the people studied experienced some degree of distress, but not an amount that we would consider statistically significant. However, the distress when it was experienced, was experienced by both the alcoholic and the nonalcoholic spouse. This finding was our initial evidence that stress attendant on alcoholism is spread uniformly throughout the family rather than being restricted either to the person who is drinking or to the nonalcoholic spouse.

The study's findings took on greater interest, however, when comparisons were made between magnitude of alcoholism, on the one hand, and subjective experience of distress as measured by psychiatric symptomatology, on the other hand. Magnitude of alcoholism was measured in two separate ways: by a quantity-frequency index of current alcohol consumption and by the longitudinal consequences of alcoholism as reflected in the physical, social-behavioral, and treatment history subscores of the SAAST.

For quantity-frequency data, logic would dictate that the higher this index, the higher the magnitude of experienced distress. Yet data from this particular study did not establish any such relationship. An attempt to correlate quantity-frequency of alcohol consumption with levels of psychiatric symptomatology was not significant for the correlation coefficients computed, and the levels of these coefficients indicated that the relationships were almost wholly random. Amount of drinking proved to have absolutely no associational relationship to levels of psychiatric symptomatology. One might argue that this would not necessarily be surprising for the alcoholic spouses involved, since drinking could be hypothesized to be an attempt on the part of these subjects at symptom reduction. (It has been argued, for example, that alcoholism in men is frequently the result of an underlying depression (Winokur, 1974; 1979). But for the nonalcoholic spouses, one would assume that the more their alcoholic partners drink, the more these people would be prone to anxiety, depression, and similar feelings. So the lack of a relationship between alcohol consumption levels and symptomatology was the study's first interesting finding, although a "negative" one.

The second intriguing finding—this time a "positive" one—emerged when SAAST scores were correlated with SCL–90 scores. Highly significant relationships were found between social-behavioral consequences subscores and a variety of symptom indexes. But these relationships were found to exist only between SAAST scores and symptom levels of *nonalcoholic spouses.* Furthermore, significant correlations were restricted only to the social-behavioral subscore of the SAAST. No comparable relationships could be established between physical consequences and treatment history subscores and the SCL–90 symptom level. A review of the actual computed correlation coefficients, as summarized in table 1.1, indicates how clear-cut these findings actually were.

An Interpretation of the Research Findings

The findings in this study suggest, in the first place, that if alcoholism has had a stressful impact on families, it is the nonalcoholic spouse alone who has experienced this stress and is aware of having developed overt psychiatric symptomatology. In the example of our earliest case history, we saw that though Noah did the drinking, it was his youngest son who suffered the consequences. And though Lot was the one who was plied with wine, it was his daughters who may have developed overt psychiatric disorders as a consequence of the alcohol-related incestuous incidents.

Second, and perhaps more important, the fact that we have been able

TABLE 1.1

Pearson Product-Moment Correlations Between History of Alcoholism (SAAST Subscores)
and Psychiatric Symptomatology (SCL–90 Scores)
in Thirty-one Alcoholic Spouses (AS) and Thirty-one Nonalcoholic Spouses (NAS)

SCL–90	Physical		Social-Behavioral		Treatment	
	AS	NAS	AS	NAS	AS	NAS
Somatization	−.01	.11	−.05	.28	−.24	.08
Obsessive-Compulsive	−.06	.23	.04	.48†	−.17	.23
Interpersonal Sensitivity	−.18	.12	.13	.49†	−.07	.18
Depression	−.03	.13	.02	.49†	.00	.28
Anxiety	.06	.17	.02	.58‡	.00	.31
Hostility	.04	.21	.19	.59‡	−.04	.29
Phobic Anxiety	.11	.23	.03	.38*	.00	.07
Paranoid Ideation	−.05	−.09	.11	.10	−.11	−.17
Psychoticism	.14	.10	−.07	.38*	−.01	.10

(SAAST SUBSCORES)

SOURCE: "The Impact of Alcoholism on the Family: Relationship between Degree of Alcoholism and Psychiatric Symptomatology" by P. Steinglass, 1981, *Journal of Studies on Alcohol,* 42, p. 296.
*$p < .05$
†$p < .01$
‡$p < .001$

to demonstrate significant correlations between SAAST and SCL–90 scores indicates that a considerable variation in degree of distress is experienced by the nonalcoholic spouses. Some spouses are not only highly symptomatic, but also report significant social-behavioral consequences (such as physical fights, lost friendships, drunk-driving arrests, job difficulties, and marital discord) as a consequence of the family's chronic struggle with alcoholism. The experience of other nonalcoholic spouses is clearly quite the opposite. For them, alcoholism has had little impact on their personal, family, social, and work lives, and they also experience little psychiatric symptomatology. Simply put, for some of these subjects, alcoholism has had devastating consequences, but for others, alcoholism appears to have had little impact.

We have emphasized that the level of distress seems totally unrelated to current level of drinking. That symptom levels appear unrelated to indexes of the "seriousness" of the alcoholic spouse's drinking behavior is further underscored by the fact that attempts to establish associational relationships between symptom levels and either physical consequences or treatment-history SAAST subscores (comparable to the significant correlations found for social-behavioral consequences) proved totally unrewarding. That is, the physical consequences subscores, which clearly reflect the extent of the alcoholic spouse's physiologically addicted and alcoholism-related physical illness (or the seriousness of the alcoholism), had no consistent relationship to levels of distress experienced by either the alcoholic or nonalcoholic spouse. And furthermore, the history of treatment context, yet another seemingly logical measure of the seriousness of alcoholism, also did not yield significant correlational findings.

Clearly then, these data indicate that seriousness of alcoholism, as measured either by the amount of alcohol consumed or by the magnitude of physical and treatment consequences of chronic drinking, does not provide the key to why some nonalcoholic subjects in our sample were highly symptomatic while others appeared relatively free of depression, anxiety, and other feelings. In fact, quite a different explanation appears likely. A third factor must be present that—depending on the shape it takes for each of the families studied—either acts as a protective agent against the stresses and strains attendant on chronic alcoholism or leaves the family and its members vulnerable to the condition's negative consequences.

Finally, the striking pattern of correlational findings reported between nonalcoholic spouse SAAST and alcoholic spouse SCL–90 scores was a pattern that held true primarily for a specific subset of families in our sample. These were the families in which the alcoholic spouse not only was currently drinking, but also had been actively doing so for a period of at least six months prior to the study. In subsequent chapters, we will be referring to this drinking pattern as a *stable wet* drinking pattern. This last set of data, summarized in table 1.2, indicates that for the ten stable wet families in the sample, the relationship between SAAST social-behavioral subscores and SCL–90 scores of nonalcoholic spouses was almost perfectly linear (the correlation coefficients here are unusually high for clinical studies of this type).

The analysis of our research study began with a seemingly straightforward question: how stressful is alcoholism for families that have to deal with it? The data generated by our study suggest, however, that the answer is far from simple or straightforward. At the very least, we are forced to conclude that the answer is, "It depends"—on at least two and possibly many more factors.

One factor that has been clearly identified in our sample study is the current pattern of drinking in the family. A second factor, however, has not been so clearly identified. This we will call a "vulnerability" factor. (It might reflect a single variable but can conceivably represent a complex of variables.) We believe that this vulnerability factor is multidimensional,

TABLE 1.2

Pearson Product-Moment Correlations Between Social-Behavioral Consequences
of Alcoholism (SAAST Subscore) and Psychiatric Symptomatology
(SCL–90 Scores) in Thirteen "Wet" and Ten "Stable Wet" Families[a]

SAAST Subscore × SCL–90 Subscores	Wet	Stable-Wet
Somatization	.54	.82†
Obsessive-Compulsive	.50	.80†
Interpersonal Sensitivity	.65*	.87‡
Depression	.55*	.85†
Anxiety	.71†	.87‡
Hostility	.69†	.83†
Phobic Anxiety	.57*	.86‡
Paranoid Ideation	.13	.48
Psychoticism	.43	.88‡

SOURCE: "The Impact of Alcoholism on the Family: Relationship Between Degree of Alcoholism and Psychiatric Symptomatology" by P. Steinglass, 1981, *Journal of Studies on Alcohol,* 42, p. 299.
[a]In wet families the identified alcoholic was drinking at the start of the study; in stable wet families the identified alcoholic drank throughout the six months of the study.
*p < .05
†p < .01
‡p < .001

but that a significant component of it lies within what is known as the family's internal environment. This is a set of behaviors, attitudes, values, and beliefs that help to determine how the family regulates its internal life and its relationships with the outside world. One of our main tasks in this book will be to explore further what the dimensions of this vulnerability factor are and how they influence the complex life history and, at times, seemingly unfathomable relationships that develop when chronic alcoholism exists in a family.

CHAPTER 2

Prevalence and Diagnosis: The Family Perspective

ALCOHOLISM is a protean condition, of interest to investigators and clinicians from many disciplines. Investigators have looked at an alcoholic and seen many different things—a person with a genetically transmitted disease; a culturally determined behavior pattern; ethanol molecules attacking liver cells and distorting central and peripheral nervous system functioning; someone in need of medically oriented treatment; someone in need of a fellowship of peers and a new sense of values to overcome a self-destructive addiction; a societal menace who endangers innocent people on the highways and undermines the country's economic strength.

In this book, this same individual is seen from yet another vantage point. For us, he or she is a person embedded in a family system, and it is that family as much as its alcoholic member that is our focus of interest. Two sets of questions immediately arise in regard to alcoholism and the family:

1. How common is the situation we are talking about? What about the old image of the alcoholic individual as a homeless, Skid Row resident (usually male) who has cut off all meaningful ties to immediate family? And for those families who do have alcoholic members still at home, what sorts of problems arise as a result of the alcoholism? These questions center, then, on the issue of *prevalence*—prevalence not only of alcoholism as a family based clinical condition, but also prevalence of associated physical, behavioral, and social complications relevant to family life.

2. If alcoholism is such a diverse condition, problems of *definition* (diagnosis) must be rampant. What diagnostic systems do we favor and how does one adapt individually based definitional systems of alcoholism to the family perspective? Diagnosis is a controversial issue in the alcoholism

field. We therefore need to place the alcoholic individuals (family members) studied into the context of the differing views about diagnosis of alcoholism.

These two sets of questions—dealing with prevalence and diagnosis, respectively—set the scene for what follows. The extensive clinical descriptions of families that we use to illustrate theoretical and therapeutic issues must be viewed in proper context. Are the situations we describe unusual or frequent? We also describe findings from a series of research studies that look at interactional behavior in families. How have we selected the families we studied? Have we used diagnostic procedures familiar to clinicians and researchers who think of alcoholism as a disease of the individual? Again the question is: Are our ideas and findings appropriate only for a highly restricted population of families, or are they broadly applicable?

In this chapter we provide answers to these questions. We argue that not only is alcoholism a highly prevalent condition, but that the most common environmental setting in which to find an alcoholic is not a Skid Row flophouse, a military barracks, or even a college dormitory, but rather a structurally intact, and by and large competently functioning, family. We also discuss the controversies that have arisen about diagnosis and detail the criteria that we have used for our studies. To anticipate this discussion, we have utilized only widely accepted diagnostic criteria, despite the fact that these criteria focus exclusively on the individual. However, a close examination of commonly used diagnostic criteria not only reveals some of the major problems that remain in defining alcoholism clearly, but also illustrates the tension that exists between individually based and family based approaches to alcoholism diagnosis and treatment.

The Prevalence of Alcoholism

In January 1981, an article in the *Washington Post* provided a "follow-up" to a news story that had gained wide coverage the preceding year. A man in his late sixties, who lived with his wife in a house in a Baltimore suburb, had "after a dozen years of harassment by teenagers and an evening of terror in which his home was repeatedly bombarded with snowballs, his screen door kicked in, and his life allegedly threatened—emerged from his row house and, pistol in hand, fatally shot" an eighteen-year-old boy and critically wounded his sixteen-year-old friend. The article documented, in moving language, the devastation wrought on the two families involved (the man who had done the shooting and his wife; the parents and siblings of the dead youth).

Buried among the details of the unsuccessful attempt of one family to grieve for their now dead member and of the other family's forced relocation because of neighborhood hostility, were two paragraphs about a visit the reporter made to the dead youth's "snow covered grave." Another of the boy's friends, who showed the reporter the grave site, was quoted as saying (as he stood in the cemetery looking at the grave), "At night, we always throw a beer over to Albert. . . . He loved to drink."

This brief reference to alcohol is the only one in the article. Nowhere else is there any intimation that it was a night of heavy drinking that had precipitated the behavioral excesses and neighborhood rampages that had ultimately provoked a seemingly stable man to come out of his house shooting. Yet one has the uncomfortable suspicion that such was the case.

But how likely is it that the outside world would focus on alcohol use as a critical component of this tragedy? The newspaper article gives no hint that either of the two families involved see alcohol as a cause of the events that so dramatically disrupted their lives. And what about us? What should we conclude? Is it reasonable to point to such a story as evidence of the devastating influence of heavy drinking on family life, or is the alcohol issue largely irrelevant, merely one of a number of factors indicating that the young man who was killed was prone to impulsive behavior, excessive aggressiveness, and poor social judgment? Clearly a difficult question to answer.

Take another example. In recent years, a strong association has been documented between alcohol use and family violence (Hindman, 1979). It has become popular to interpret these data as suggesting that alcoholism has a *causative* role in incidents of child abuse, incest, and wife battering (e.g., Browning and Boatman, 1977; Flanzer, 1981; Kempe and Helfer, 1972). The assumption is that it is the disinhibiting effect of alcohol that precipitates incidents that would not otherwise occur.

But this is not a uniformly held interpretation of these data. Gelles and Straus (1979), two family sociologists who have carried out perhaps the most thorough studies to date of violence and the family, argue that alcohol may well be a red herring—that family violence would occur even if total abstinence was somehow imposed on the family. The coexisting presence of alcohol helps to perpetuate the cycle of violence insofar as husband and wife believe that the violent act was the result of drinking (because of disinhibition, memory loss, and so on). But, argue Gelles and

Straus, this is probably a false belief (not to mention a dysfunctional one in that it diverts both spouses from the primary problem of spouse abuse).

These examples are but two of dozens that might be cited illustrating how difficult it has been to pin down what might seem at first glance a relatively straightforward question: How serious a problem alcoholism is for the family. Writings in the field suggest that the impact is considerable. A formidable list of behaviors, all of them unquestionably negative in their impact on the family, have been linked in one way or another to alcohol use. Among the more prominantly mentioned are spouse and child abuse (Hindman, 1979), significantly higher divorce rates (Schuckit and Morrissey, 1976), depression and suicide (Winokur 1974, 1979; Woodruff, Gruze, Clayton, and Carr, 1973), and occupational disruptions (Berry, Boland, Smart, and Kanak, 1977). As a consequence, there is a strong impression that alcoholism has a highly disruptive impact on family life.

Our own view is that the picture is a far more complex one. We are impressed first of all by the many examples, such as the two cited above, suggesting that although alcoholism often appears as a coincident condition and hence is correlated with such phenomena as family violence and suicide, there is little solid evidence that these factors are causally linked. Second, we have been impressed by how many families seem to be "making do" despite having an alcoholic member in their midst.

By "making do," we mean that a substantial group of families with alcoholic members seem to remain intact over their life span (no divorce; continue to live with the alcoholic member), are economically viable, avoid the more dramatic and devastating types of family violence, and suffer no higher levels of anxiety and depression than the general population. Presumably these families also lead compromised lives as a consequence of their exposure to alcoholism. But this impact, this constriction of family life, if it does occur, does so in ways far more subtle than is seen in those dramatic examples of family pathology represented by spouse abuse, incest, and the like.

How do we know this last statement is correct? In part, it can be inferred from a careful reading of survey data on drinking practices in the United States and their consequences. These data suggest that families with alcoholic members are often confused about how alcoholism specifically has compromised their lives. They seem to know that they are hurting, but it feels more like a dull ache than a sharp, localized pain.

For example, a 1982 Gallup Poll reported (with considerable fanfare) that 33 percent of respondents answered yes to the question, "Has drinking ever been a cause of trouble in your family?" This figure represented an 11 percent increase over the affirmative response rate from a survey taken only one year previously, and double the rate obtained in 1976. This would appear to be impressive evidence both of the prevalence of self-perceived alcohol-related family problems and of societal awareness of the "ache."

But when more specific questions are asked, as was done in 1979 in a major National Institute on Alcohol Abuse and Alcoholism (NIAAA) funded national survey of adult drinking practices (Clark and Midanik, 1982), respondents were hard-pressed to point to specific family-related adverse effects associated with excessive drinking, although again, the numbers of people reporting problem drinking were very high. Thus once again, the "ache" is there, but the attempt to localize the pain is unsuccessful.

We therefore contend that the clinical literature focusing on the more dramatic events associated with alcoholism gives a misleading picture of its impact on the family. In fact, when we look at large-scale survey data about U.S. drinking patterns and their consequences (we review the findings from these surveys later in this chapter), we get a very different picture from that in the clinical literature.

Instead, these data suggest that for many families the relationship between alcoholism and family life is more analogous to that of a virulent but symbiotic pathogen and its victim. Apparently, a substantial number of families are not "killed" by alcoholism, but instead evolve a long-term relationship that may entail significant restrictions of family life. Over time, alcoholism may sap the family's energy and resources, but, in the short run, it may not be perceived by the family as a significant threat to its survival.

Thus while the clinical literature has alerted us to the need to ask about spouse and child abuse and incest whenever there is a history of alcoholism (and vice versa), it also has diverted attention from other aspects of family life that may be affected by alcoholism.

These "other aspects" are often subtle, especially when compared to blockbuster events like violence or unemployment. Thus they can easily be overlooked, not only by the clinician but also by the family. Yet, as we illustrate in this book, it is the impact of alcoholism on the fundamental aspects of family life—daily routines, family rituals, family problem-solving strategies—that affects many families dealing with alcoholism so profoundly as to shape the entire course of their life history.

It is this second group of families that is the subject of this book. We are writing about alcoholism and the family, not about family violence, or incest, or vehicular homicide, or devastating medical complications of alcoholism. None of our studies has explicitly addressed any of these issues (although in the course of these studies we have worked clinically with families who had such problems). Instead, we have studied families that are structurally intact, usually economically viable, and even have reasonable occupational histories. And since one of our central themes is that, contrary to popular belief, many families dealing with alcoholism are in fact highly stable and predictable (albeit compromised) behavioral systems, large-scale survey data consistent with this view is worth a closer look at this point in our discussion.

Survey Studies of U.S. Drinking Practices

The best sources of data on the prevalence of alcohol abuse and alcoholism in the United States are (1) the extensive Drinking Practices surveys carried out by research teams at the Alcohol Research Group, University of California in Berkeley, and George Washington University (Cahalan, 1970; Cahalan and Room 1974; Cahalan et al., 1969); and (2) the NIMH-sponsored Environmental Catchment Area (ECA) study carried out by psychiatric epidemiologists from Washington University, Yale University, and the Johns Hopkins University (Myers et al., 1984; Robins et al., 1984).

Regarding the Drinking Practices studies, a total of six national surveys using probability sampling techniques were carried out in the 1960s and 1970s under the overall scientific leadership of Don Cahalan and Ira Cisin. The most recent survey, done in 1979, included details not only of quantity-frequency of drinking but also extensive data concerning problems associated with drinking and family-social consequences of problem drinking.

Regarding the ECA study, in the early 1980s NIMH funded a large collaborative study intended to provide accurate epidemiological data about the incidence and prevalence of major psychiatric disorders in the U.S. population. The study utilized a structured questionnaire, the NIMH Diagnostic Interview Schedule (Robins, Helzer, Croughen, and Radcliff, 1981) designed to provide the necessary data to make *DSM-III* diagnoses on respondents. More than twenty thousand individuals were interviewed from five environmental catchment areas in the United States (Baltimore, New Haven, St. Louis, Los Angeles, and rural North Carolina). Included in the interview schedule were questions related to *DSM-III* criteria for alcohol abuse and alcohol dependence (we discuss the *DSM-III* later in this chapter).

The picture that emerges from these two studies (Drinking Practices and ECA) is as follows:

Overall Prevalence. The prevalence of abusive drinking among the adult population in the United States is truly staggering. In the 1967 survey (see Cahalan, 1970; Cahalan et al., 1969), 13 percent of men and 2 percent of women questioned reported a drinking pattern characterized by the investigators as "heavy"; that is, they were people who "sometimes drink five or more drinks per occasion of at least two beverage types *and* who report that they drink on at least ten occasions per month" (Cahalan, 1982, p. 101). In the 1979 survey (see Clark and Midanik, 1982), results were almost exactly comparable (12 percent for men; 3 percent for women). Since most researchers feel survey data of these kinds tend, if anything, to represent an underreporting of the magnitude of drinking, the consistent findings of heavy drinking patterns in such a substantial percentage of the adult population means that in virtually any social, community, work, or clinical setting, one is bound to be exposed to substantial numbers of people whose drinking reaches the "heavy" end of the scale, as defined by the Cahalan-Cisin group.

These figures, of course, report only drinking patterns. The prevalence of problem drinking requires additional information about symptoms of physiological dependence, and/or evidence of negative social-behavioral consequences of drinking. In the 1979 survey, questions that would permit assessment of the above parameters were also asked. These data were used to construct three different scales reflecting problem drinking—an alcohol-dependence scale; a loss-of-control scale; and an adverse-social-consequences scale (the parameters of these scales are listed in table 2.1).

Using these scales as estimates of the prevalence of problem drinking, results indicated that more than 20 percent of all male drinkers and 10 percent of female drinkers reported having experienced some or many of the items on the alcohol-dependence and loss-of-control scales during the year immediately preceding the survey. Nine percent of male drinkers and 5 percent of female drinkers reported having experienced adverse social consequences (these findings are summarized in the last two columns of table 2.2).

The Drinking Practices surveys were intended to provide information about the magnitude of drinking and indexes of problem drinking, not to assess how prevalent alcoholism, as a psychiatric diagnosis, was. The ECA study, on the other hand, used a survey instrument that systematically assesses the presence or absence of the specific criteria used in the *DSM-III* to diagnose alcohol abuse and alcohol dependence (see table 2.3). Using these criteria, the investigators reported an overall lifetime prevalence rate of 13.6 percent for alcohol abuse or dependence (a figure comparable to

TABLE 2.1

Cahalan Social Consequences, Alcohol Dependence, and Loss of Control Scales

---

Social Consequences Scale
    In the past 12 months, *one* or more of the following events have occurred *due to drinking:*
    —Spouse, friend or relative threatened to break off relationship
    —Friends advised reduction in drinking
    —Police questioned person or gave warning about drinking
    —Arrested for drunkenness or drunken driving
    —Serious accident (auto or other) secondary to drinking
    —Work colleagues advised reduction in drinking
    —Failure to obtain job promotion or pay raise
    —Near or actual loss of job

Alcohol Dependence Scale
    In the past 12 months, *two* or more of the following have occurred:
    —Skipping meals when drinking
    —Sneaking drinks
    —Morning drinking
    —Drinking before a party to "get enough"
    —Blackouts
    —Gulping drinks
    —Hands shaking after drinks

Loss of Control Scale
    In the past 12 months, *one* or more of the following have occurred:
    —Fear that one was an alcoholic
    —Unable to cut down or quit drinking despite attempts to do so
    —Kept on drinking despite promising not to
    —Difficult to stop drinking before becoming completely intoxicated

---

SOURCE: "Epidemiology: Alcohol Use in American Society" by D. Cahalan, 1982, in E. L. Gomberg, H. Raskin White, and J. Carpenter (Eds.), *Alcohol, Science and Society Revisited.* Ann Arbor: University of Michigan Press, p. 104.

those of the Drinking Practices surveys) (Robins et al., 1984). Further, this prevalence rate was quite stable across ECA sites. Thus a prevalence figure of 10 to 14 percent of the adult population seems a reasonable one in estimating U.S. alcoholism rates.

Prevalence by Age Group. In addition to providing overall prevalence rates, both the Drinking Practices and the ECA studies analyzed their drinking data by subject age groupings. The analyses indicated that prevalence rates vary considerably by age, with the highest rates of heavy drinking occurring in men twenty-one to thirty and in women thirty-one to fifty. For example, the Drinking Practices figures indicate that 36 percent of men twenty-one to twenty-five and of men twenty-six to thirty surveyed in

1979 were heavy drinkers, and that 9–10 percent of the women thirty-one to fifty fell into this category (again summarized in table 2.2).

These figures become particularly telling when one stops to think about how drinking practices might be playing themselves out in the typical family context. For these two age ranges are, of course, the ages when most families are launched and children are raised. Thus for many families, the critical formative years—the years when children are being reared and when adolescents are first experimenting with alcohol—are also the years when adults in these families show the greatest prevalence of heavy drinking patterns.

TABLE 2.2

Drinking Patterns and Drinking Problems, by Age and Sex,
1979 National Probability Survey
(in Percent*)

Age	N	Abstainers	1–60 Drinks/ Month	60+ Drinks/ Month	Social Conse- quences	Loss of Control or Depen- dence†
Men						
18–20	37	5	79	17	15	37
21–25	82	10	54	36	13	28
26–30	87	20	50	29	10	32
31–40	154	25	55	19	8	21
41–50	107	27	52	21	2	11
51–60	130	32	51	17	3	8
61–70	91	38	53	8	5	11
70+	72	41	45	13	4	4
TOTAL MEN	762	25	54	21	7	20
Women						
18–20	52	31	64	5	5	24
21–25	130	15	78	6	6	16
26–30	125	30	65	5	3	10
31–40	208	27	65	9	5	12
41–50	137	43	46	10	4	9
51–60	143	50	46	4	1	8
61–70	102	61	38	1	0	0
70+	103	61	39	0	0	0
TOTAL WOMEN	1010	40	54	5	3	10
TOTALS	1772	33	54	13	5	15

SOURCE: "Alcohol Use and Alcohol Problems among U.S. Adults: Results of the 1979 Survey" by W. B. Clark and L. Midanik, 1982, in NIAAA, *Alcohol and Health Monograph No. 1, Alcohol Consumption and Related Problems.* Washington, D.C., U.S. Government Printing Office, p. 29. *Percentages are weighted and may not total 100 due to rounding, nonresponse, etc." †This column reflects percentages of drinkers only (abstainers not included).

Social Consequences.   If we take a closer look at the adverse-social-consequences part of the picture, we see that the most frequently mentioned problems involve difficulties at work (having lost or nearly lost a job because of drinking; feeling that drinking may have hurt chances for promotion; absenteeism because of drinking, etc.) and inappropriate behavior in social settings (especially increased belligerence). Remarkably few respondents indicated that problems with friends or spouses had arisen as a result of their drinking.

Thus if the figures for problem drinking are combined with the figures for specific spouse- or friend-related problems, it seems clear that many heavy drinkers who experience significant degrees of alcohol dependence, loss of control, and adverse social consequences *do not* report any overt threats on the part of the spouse to dissolve the marriage. This is not to say that these are trouble-free marriages. No questions were asked about verbal or physical fighting, sexual difficulties, or disturbances in children. But around the simple question of whether families can maintain structural stability in the face of "problem" drinking, the survey data suggest that in a majority of cases the answer is yes.

Implications of the Drinking Practices Data

The 1967 and 1979 Drinking Practices survey data strongly support our suspicion that alcoholism is a highly prevalent *family* condition. But they also illustrate that the social and behavioral consequences of alcoholism that are most important to the family are not those associated with violence and lack of impulse control. Even taking into account an underreporting of the incidence of these consequences, the rates emerging from these surveys are so low as to represent only a small fraction of the concerns expressed by families about the impact alcoholism is having on their lives.

These findings coincide with our own impressions gleaned from the families with whom we have worked. For these families, most of whom have alcoholic members who drink primarily in their homes, alcoholism is a very real presence, not only affecting their daily lives but also raising concerns about future generations (the transmission issue). Thus our decision to have focused attention in our studies on the day-to-day life of the family rather than on the more dramatic potential concomitants of alcoholism places us in the mainstream of the *family's* concerns.

Diagnostic Issues: The Family Perspective

Alcoholism has proven to be a difficult condition to define. Because attitudes toward alcohol consumption are largely a reflection of cultural, religious, and historical perspectives, it is not surprising that a wide range of views about drinking exist in American society. As a rough generalization, however, one can identify two fundamentally different perspectives—a moral-legal perspective that views alcoholism as a form of deviant moral behavior; and a medical perspective that views alcoholism as a syndrome of aberrant behaviors and physical symptoms.

The moral-legal perspective assumes that the individual is responsible for his or her deviant behavior and should be held up to community standards, judged against these standards by the legal system, and *sentenced* according to these standards. In contrast, the medical perspective sees the same individual as suffering from a disease, consequently qualifying for what medical sociologists have called a "sick role," and therefore being entitled to *treatment* within the medical system for that disease.

Over the past several decades, there has been a cyclical battle between representatives of these two perspectives, with first one side and then the other gaining prominence. One year alcoholic individuals might find themselves locked up in a "drunk tank" following a bout of public inebriation; the next year they might be in a residential treatment setting.

Most recently, the trend has been toward accommodating both views. For example, "driving while intoxicated" is seen as a moral-legal problem, and programs have been instituted to protect society from this deviant behavior. Absenteeism and industrial accidents resulting from drinking, on the other hand, have been relegated to the medical perspective, with the consequent institution of employee assistance programs designed to identify alcoholism and refer individuals for treatment. In this instance, the goal is to protect the individual from the consequences of medically defined deviant behavior.

Definitions of Alcoholism

Of the above two perspectives, the moral-legal perspective has more easily established definitions of what it considers alcoholic behavior. A person suspected of driving while intoxicated is asked to take a breathalyzer test, and if blood alcohol concentration is above a particular standard, the legal system cranks into motion.

The medical definition of alcoholism has proven more problematic. The difficulty is that alcoholism can be defined along three very different sets of dimensions—a cultural set, a behavioral set, and a physiological set. Culturally based definitions emphasize that alcoholism is a form of deviant behavior. That is, alcoholism is defined as drinking behavior that falls outside culturally acceptable limits. Therefore, alcoholic behavior in one society might well be normative (and hence nonalcoholic) behavior in another society. Behaviorally based definitions have focused on the distinction between *alcohol use, alcohol misuse,* and *alcohol abuse.* Alcohol misuse refers to occasional examples of adverse consequences related to alcohol use. Alcohol abuse, on the other hand, refers to a *chronic* pattern of excessive alcohol consumption in the face of recurrent adverse physical or behavioral-social consequences. Physiologically based definitions have focused on the concept of *addiction* (also called *alcohol habituation* or *alcohol dependence)* and utilize two major diagnostic criteria—tolerance and withdrawal symptoms. Tolerance implies that larger and larger amounts of alcohol must be ingested to achieve the same behavior effect; withdrawal symptoms refer to a syndrome of physiological responses that occur when blood alcohol levels initially return to zero.

The culturally based definitional approach is most clearly reflected in the World Health Organization (WHO) definition of alcoholism (Kramer and Cameron, 1975). WHO suggests that the term *alcohol-type drug dependence* be substituted for alcoholism. The definition of this term is as follows:

Drug dependence of the alcohol type may be said to exist when the consumption of alcohol by an individual exceeds the limits that are accepted by his culture, if he consumes alcohol at times that are deemed inappropriate within that culture, or his intake of alcohol becomes so great as to injure his health or impair his social relationships.

Although the WHO definition has its advocates, culturally based definitions of alcoholism have not garnered much support in the United States. Instead, medically oriented perspectives of alcoholism have relied on behaviorally based and physiologically based approaches to definition. Both these approaches were incorporated in the 1980 American Psychiatric Association (APA) definitions of psychiatric disorders, the *DSM-III,* and have been retained as well in the *DSM-III-R,* the 1987 revision of this diagnostic system.

In the *DSM-III*, an attempt was made to differentiate situations in which both behavioral and physiological concomitants of excessive alcohol use were present from those in which only behavioral consequences were present. Two separate diagnoses for alcoholism were listed—Alcohol Abuse (diagnostic code 305.0x); and Alcohol Dependence (diagnostic code 309.0x)—whose essential features were as follows:

Alcohol Abuse is a pattern of pathological use for at least a month that causes impairment in social or occupational functioning.

Alcohol Dependence is a pattern of pathological alcohol use or impairment in social or occupational functioning due to alcohol, and either tolerance or withdrawal.

The dichotomy was therefore one of psychological dependence (Alcohol Abuse) versus psychological *plus* physical dependence (Alcohol Dependence).

In the *DSM-III-R*, this sharp distinction is no longer made. Instead, a new term is introduced—psychoactive substance dependence—the essential feature of which is "a cluster of cognitive, behavioral, and physiological symptoms that indicate that the person has impaired control of psychoactive substance use and continues use of the substance despite adverse consequences." (p. 166) Although the terms Alcohol Dependence (*DSM-III-R* diagnostic code 303.00) and Alcohol Abuse (diagnostic code 305.00) are retained, the differentiating factor is now seen to be the intensity of symptoms and behaviors, not the presence or absence of physiological addiction. In the words of the *DSM-III-R*, "The symptoms of the dependence syndrome include, but are not limited to, the physiologic symptoms of tolerance and withdrawal (as in *DSM-III*)." (p. 166)

Diagnostic Criteria Sets

The *DSM-III* and *III-R* approaches to diagnosis have another important feature in addition to their reliance on behaviorally and physiologically based definitions of alcoholism—their reliance on objectively defined criteria sets as the basis for making diagnoses. The specific intent in devising the *DSM-III* was to bring a degree of rigor to psychiatric diagnoses not possible with prior approaches, which had emphasized dynamic aspects as well as objective criteria (an intent that is retained in the *DSM-III-R*).

By focusing on objectively observable symptom clusters and prespecified intensity and duration levels, the *DSM-III* allowed clinicians to substantially increase the reliability of their diagnoses. In adopting this approach to

TABLE 2.3

DMS-III Description of Alcohol Abuse and Alcohol Dependence

Diagnostic Criteria for Alcohol Abuse

A. Pattern of pathological alcohol use: need for daily use of alcohol for adequate functioning; inability to cut down or stop drinking; repeated efforts to control or reduce excess drinking by "going on the wagon" (periods of temporary abstinence) or restricting drinking to certain times of the day; binges (remain intoxicated throughout the day for at least two days); occasional consumption of a fifth of spirits (or its equivalent in wine or beer); amnesic periods for events occurring while intoxicated (blackouts); continuation of drinking despite a serious physical disorder that the individual knows is exacerbated by alcohol use; drinking of nonbeverage alcohol.

B. Impairment in social or occupational functioning due to alcohol use: e.g., violence while intoxicated, absence from work, loss of job, legal difficulties (e.g., arrest for intoxicated behavior, traffic accidents while intoxicated), arguments or difficulties with family or friends because of excessive alcohol use.

C. Duration of disturbance of at least one month.

Diagnostic Criteria for Alcohol Dependence

A. Either a pattern of pathological alcohol use or impairment in social or occupational functioning due to alcohol use:
Pattern of pathological alcohol use: need for daily use of alcohol for adequate functioning; inability to cut down or stop drinking; repeated efforts to control or reduce excess drinking by "going on the wagon" (periods of temporary abstinence) or restricting drinking to certain times of the day; binges (remaining intoxicated throughout the day for at least two days); occasional consumption of a fifth of spirits (or its equivalent in wine or beer); amnesic periods for events occurring while intoxicated (blackouts); continuation of drinking despite a serious physical disorder that the individual knows is exacerbated by alcohol use; drinking of nonbeverage alcohol.
Impairment in social or occupational functioning due to alcohol use: e.g., violence while intoxicated, absence from work, loss of job, legal difficulties (e.g., arrest for intoxicated behavior, traffic accidents while intoxicated), arguments or difficulties with family or friends because of excessive alcohol use.

B. Either tolerance or withdrawal:
Tolerance: need for markedly increased amounts of alcohol to achieve the desired effect, or markedly diminished effect with regular use of the same amount.
Withdrawal: development of Alcohol Withdrawal (e.g., morning "shakes" and malaise relieved by drinking) after cessation of or reduction in drinking.

SOURCE: *Diagnostic and Statistical Manual of Mental Disorders (third edition)* American Psychiatric Association, 1980, pp. 169–170.

diagnosis, the *DSM-III* modeled itself after two prior psychiatric diagnostic systems—the Feighner criteria (Feighner et al., 1972) and the Research Diagnostic Criteria (Spitzer, Endicott, and Robins, 1975). Both these systems had been used extensively in clinical research, where demands for greater reliability of psychiatric diagnoses had made them attractive.

Thus we find that both in the *DSM-III*, and *III-R*, diagnoses relevant to alcoholism were made by comparing the clinical assessment of the patient to a highly specific criteria set (see tables 2.3 and 2.4). If the patient's symptoms and behaviors met the minimal criteria listed, then the diagnosis was made; if the criteria were not met, then the patient did not *have* Alcohol Abuse or Dependence.

The 1987 revision of the *DSM-III* criteria for substance abuse and depen-

TABLE 2.4

DMS-III-R Criteria for Psychoactive Substance Use Disorders

Diagnostic Criteria for Psychoactive Substance Dependence

A. At least three of the following:

1. substance often taken in larger amounts or over a longer period than the person intended

2. persistent desire or one or more unsuccessful efforts to cut down or control substance use

3. a great deal of time spent in activities necessary to get the substance (e.g., theft), taking the substance (e.g., chain smoking), or recovering from its effects

4. frequent intoxication or withdrawal symptoms when expected to fulfill major role obligations at work, school, or home (e.g., does not go to work because hung over, goes to school or work "high," intoxicated while taking care of his or her children), or when substance use is physically hazardous (e.g., drives when intoxicated)

5. important social, occupational, or recreational activities given up or reduced because of substance use

6. continued substance use despite knowledge of having a persistent or recurrent social, psychological, or physical problem that is caused or exacerbated by the use of the substance (e.g., keeps using heroin despite family arguments about it, cocaine-induced depression, or having an ulcer made worse by drinking)

7. marked tolerance: need for markedly increased amounts of the substance (i.e., at least a 50% increase) in order to achieve intoxication or desired effect, or markedly diminished effect with continued use of the same amount

Note: The following items may not apply to cannabis, hallucinogens, or phencyclidine (PCP):

8. characteristic withdrawal symptoms (see specific withdrawal syndromes under Psychoactive Substance-induced Organic Mental Disorders)

9. substance often taken to relieve or avoid withdrawal symptoms

B. Some symptoms of the disturbance have persisted for at least one month, or have occurred repeatedly over a longer period of time.

Criteria for Severity of Psychoactive Substance Dependence:

Mild: Few, if any, symptoms in excess of those required to make the diagnosis, and the symptoms result in no more than mild impairment in occupational functioning or in usual social activities or relationships with others.

Moderate: Symptoms or functional impairment between "mild" and "severe."

Severe: Many symptoms in excess of those required to make the diagnosis, and the symptoms markedly interfere with occupational functioning or with usual social activities or relationships with others.

TABLE 2.4 *(Continued)*

In Partial Remission: During the past six months, some use of the substance and some symptoms of dependence.

In Full Remission: During the past six months, either no use of the substance, or use of the substance and no symptoms of dependence.

Diagnostic Criteria for Psychoactive Substance Abuse

A. A maladaptive pattern of psychoactive substance use indicated by at least one of the following:

1. continued use despite knowledge of having a persistent or recurrent social, occupational, psychological, or physical problem that is caused or exacerbated by use of the psychoactive substance

2. recurrent use in situations in which use is physically hazardous (e.g., driving while intoxicated)

B. Some symptoms of the disturbance have persisted for at least one month, or have occurred repeatedly over a longer period of time.

C. Never met the criteria for Psychoactive Substance Dependence for this substance.

SOURCE: *Diagnostic and Statistical Manual of Mental Disorders (third edition, revised)* American Psychiatric Association, 1987, pp. 167–169.

dence includes a number of major changes, changes that reflect concerns arising from five years of experience with the original criteria. An examination of these changes is instructive in several important respects. There was an implication inherent in the way the *DSM-III* criteria were structured that Alcohol Abuse was merely a less serious form of Alcohol Dependence. (In

TABLE 2.5

Symptoms and Duration of Heavy Drinking in Heavy Drinkers, Aged 45–64

Symptom	Percentage with this Symptom	Median Years of Heavy Drinking with this Symptom
DTs	7	30
Hospitalization for drinking problem	15	27
Lost job because of drinking	16	26
Drinking led to arrest	19	26
Trouble on job from drinking	21	25
Benders (more than 2 days without sobering up)	25	22
Trouble with wife over drink	28	22
Family objected to his drinking	38	21
Felt guilty about his drinking	41	20
Felt he drank too much	53	17

SOURCE: "The High Rate of Suicide in Older White Men: A Study Testing Ten Hypotheses" by L. N. Robins, P. A. West, and G. E. Murphy, 1977, *Social Psychiatry,* 12, p. 17.

fact, the *DSM-III* manual included the statement, "Alcohol Dependence has also been called Alcoholism," suggesting that Alcohol Abuse is not quite the real thing.) The implication, therefore, was that Alcohol Abuse and Alcohol Dependence were hierarchically ordered. Alcohol Abuse is bad, but Alcohol Dependence is worse.

Some support for that contention can be found in a study carried out by Lee Robins and her colleagues (Robins, West, and Murphy, 1977) to examine whether the symptoms typically used to diagnose alcoholism are scalable. In particular, they were interested in whether these symptoms conformed to a Gutman-type scale, that is, a hierarchical scale in which the rarer symptoms tended to occur only in subjects with longer drinking histories. The assumption here is that symptoms appear in consistent order as the natural history of alcoholism progresses.

The Robins study was able to demonstrate that, in fact, in a sample of male heavy drinkers, aged forty-five to sixty-four, the frequency of symptoms did arrange themselves hierarchically in a Gutman-type scale (see table 2.5). What is particularly interesting is the fact that symptoms of marital and family difficulties appear in the scale before symptoms of dependence on alcohol. This finding suggests that most men experiencing symptoms of probable dependence (e.g., hospitalization) have already experienced family and marital difficulties secondary to drinking. A comparable hierarchical ordering of symptoms versus duration of drinking was reported for a Veterans Administration population by Gomberg (1975).

However, despite evidence such as the Robins et al. data suggesting that behavioral and physiologic symptoms associated with alcoholism are hierarchically ordered, this distinction has not been a popular one among psychiatrists. The implication that physiologic addiction is a more serious condition than behavioral addiction simply has not correlated with the experiences of most clinicians. Hence the decision to retreat from this position in the *DSM-III-R*. Thus we see that the impact of alcohol use on "major role obligations at work, school, or home," or the giving up of "important social, occupational, or recreational activities . . . because of substance use" now count as much as physiologic tolerance or withdrawal symptoms as criteria for the diagnosis of Alcohol Dependence.

The other major change in the *DSM-III-R* criteria set, the grouping of all psychoactive substance dependence and abuse under a common criteria set, reflects the growing awareness of the phenomenon of polysubstance abuse in the U.S. However, it is also a reflection that the behavioral patterns set in motion by the persistant overuse of psychoactive substances (whether they be alcohol, opiates, hypnotics, anxiolytics, etc.) are highly comparable ones, a stance in relation to diagnostic criteria sets significantly more compatible with the position taken in this book vis-à-vis alcoholism and the family than that reflected in the *DSM-III*.

Goodwin Criteria

The Feighner criteria were first published in 1972 and the Research Diagnostic Criteria in 1975. Although both these sets included diagnostic criteria for alcoholism, a number of studies examining genetic factors in alcoholism antedated their publication (see Goodwin, 1971a, 1971b). These twin and adoption studies relied on a somewhat different criteria set for diagnostic determination (see table 2.6). This set has been called the Goodwin criteria, after the principle investigator who carried out these studies.

Although the Goodwin criteria proposes a four-tiered hierarchy of drinking categories—moderate drinker; heavy drinker; problem drinker; and alcoholic—the criteria used to make a determination of problem drinking are highly analogous to those used for the *DSM-III* diagnosis, Alcohol Abuse. Likewise, the criteria for alcoholic drinking are comparable to the Alcohol Dependence criteria in *DSM-III*. Although the way these criteria are organized differs somewhat from the *DSM-III* groupings, to meet crite-

TABLE 2.6

Goodwin Criteria for Drinking Categories

Moderate Drinker:	Neither a teetotaler nor heavy drinker
Heavy Drinker:	For at least 1 year, drank daily and had 6 or more drinks at least 2 or 3 times a month; or drank 6 or more drinks at least once a week for > 1 year, but reported no problems
Problem Drinker:	a. Meets criteria for heavy drinker b. Had problems from drinking but insufficient in number to meet alcoholism criteria
Alcoholic:	a. Meets criteria for heavy drinker b. Must have had alcohol problems in at least 3 of following 4 groups: Group 1: Social disapproval of drinking by friends, parents; marital problem from drinking Group 2: Job trouble from drinking, traffic arrests from drinking, other police trouble from drinking Group 3: Frequent blackouts, tremor, withdrawal, convulsions, delirium tremens Group 4: Loss of control, morning drinking

SOURCE: "Drinking Problems in Adopted and Non-adopted Sons of Alcoholics," by D. W. Goodwin, F. Schulsinger, N. Moller, L. Hermansen, G. Winokur, and S. B. Guze, 1974, *Archives of General Psychiatry,* 31, pp. 164–169.

ria for alcoholic drinking, a person must have shown evidence of alcohol-related problems in either Group 3 (withdrawal symptoms) and/or Group 4 (similar to, but not the same as, tolerance symptoms), plus some evidence of social or behavioral problems secondary to alcohol use.

As a research tool, the Goodwin criteria have all of the advantages already discussed in relation to the *DSM-III* and *III-R* criteria. They are highly objective, and can be rigorously applied. The categorical distinctions between heavy, problem, and alcoholic drinking are clear-cut. Thus inclusion criteria for research subjects can be specified and reliably adhered to. One can also safely assume that a subject who had met Goodwin criteria for problem or alcoholic drinking would also meet *DSM-III* criteria for Alcohol Abuse or Alcohol Dependence, and *DSM-III-R* criteria for Alcohol Dependence.

In selecting research subjects for the studies described in this book, we used the Goodwin criteria. Although they are individually based and our research subjects were families, not individuals, their use ensures that the subjects we studied were comparable to those studied by Goodwin and his colleagues in their genetically-oriented family studies. Further, by carefully examining the Goodwin criteria, the reader should be able to ascertain the clinical status of the identified alcoholic family members we will describe in later chapters.

Implications of DSM-III and Goodwin Criteria

Both the *DSM-III* and Goodwin criteria are systems for diagnosing alcoholism in individuals. Neither system purports to make diagnoses of family psychopathology. Further, both approaches are cross-sectional rather than longitudinal in their approach to diagnosis. They compile evidence about whether minimal criteria for a current diagnosis exists. They do not address prognosis, nor do they deal with the longitudinal (developmental) course of alcoholism. Thus they make no attempt to reconcile their criteria with such approaches as the "natural history" approach advocated by George Vaillant (1983). Their strength lies in the across-clinician reliability of the diagnostic procedure they achieve.

The original *DSM-III* (1980) and Goodwin approaches also reflect the view that sees alcoholism as hierarchically ordered, moving from social drinking through abusive drinking (drinking despite behavioral-social consequences), and finally to alcohol dependence (addiction). As previously noted, several studies have provided support for the hierarchical model of alcoholism diagnoses. Yet, despite such findings it is still not clear how useful a construct the notion of hierarchical ordering of abuse versus dependence is in the clinical setting. If one's concern is functional impairment, either behavioral or physical (as it is for most clinicians), then the distinction between abuse and dependence may be of little value (that is, unless the decision being made is whether hospitalization is necessary to accomplish detoxification).

On a case-by-case basis, it is entirely possible, for example, for someone to experience dire personal and family consequences directly attributable to chronic alcohol abuse, yet to show no evidence of physiological withdrawal from alcohol—no shakes, no D.T.'s, no craving—if he or she suddenly stops drinking. On the other hand, another individual may need a drink first thing in the morning to combat tremulousness, look forward to a four-martini lunch, have developed a clear-cut tolerance for alcohol, and may have experienced recurrent blackouts after parties, but continue to work in a steady and relatively competent fashion, "hold his liquor" well, maintain a complex social life, and impose little or no restrictions on his family as a result of his drinking. It is this view that won out when the *DSM-III-R* criteria for Alcohol Dependence and Abuse were developed. However, the back and forth history of reliance on behavioral versus physiologic criteria for identifying different subtypes of alcoholism suggest that diagnostic issues in this field are still far from reaching consensus.

Looking at definitional issues from a family perspective does not simplify the task. At first glance, it might seem that for the family, the areas of primary concern should be the social-behavioral consequences of alcoholism—occupational difficulties, disrupted social relationships, sexual dysfunction, marital violence, and so on. Therefore it might seem that a diagnostic scheme based solely on parameters of alcohol abuse would be the most relevant one. Physical dependence on alcohol, if it were present, would only be of import if it contributed to disturbances in interactional behavior. In other words, presence of physiological dependency would be of decidedly secondary interest to the family clinician-researcher. What we want to know instead is whether the presence of withdrawal symptoms, tolerance to alcohol, blackouts, and so on, have led to poor work performance, to marital violence, or to economic deprivation. If they have not, then one would think that such cases are best left to the biomedical researcher or gastroenterologist to study and treat.

But it turns out that in the family field as well, a definitional scheme that defines alcoholism solely in terms of disrupted behavioral functioning proves to be an oversimplification. In at least one area of critical importance to family life—the transmission of alcoholism across generations—a series of twin and adoption studies has not only suggested that alcoholism may have a genetic predisposition, but that the genetic factor is particularly relevant for those types of alcoholism associated with physical dependence (Goodwin, 1983). As word of these studies has found its way into the popular press, the public has become more aware of a possible genetic component to alcoholism. Genetic or not, it is not unlikely, therefore, that families with alcoholic members have developed increasing sensitivity to the transmission issue and are asking questions about the vulnerability of their children. (In chapter 9, for example, we describe a family that takes preemptive action to protect children from an alcoholism "virus" initially caught by the husband-father in the family, and now apparently affecting the oldest child in the family as well.)

It is still too early to tell whether different types of alcoholism have substantially different consequences for families. We mentioned the reported connection between the more severe types of alcoholism and genetically determined transmission across generations. But later on when we talk about the data generated by two of our major studies—the Transmission study and Heritage study—we show that even as regards transmission, family environmental factors play a major role in the transmission process regardless of the diagnostic classification of the alcoholic member. And we have already discussed (in chapter 1), a study indicating that the potential negative impact of alcoholism on family life (measured in terms of levels of psychiatric symptomatology of husband and wife) was not correlated to magnitude of alcoholism (as measured by quantity-frequency indexes, physical consequences of drinking, and so on).

Therefore, the bulk of the available evidence (albeit still far from complete) indicates that if our concern is the family perspective, a fine-tuned approach to the definition of alcoholism is probably not necessary. At the same time, we should not underestimate the erosive influence that definitional problems have had on research in this area. If one believes, for example, that alcoholism is present whenever an individual continues to drink in the face of clear-cut negative *or* psychosocial consequences, then a vast and broad-based series of clinical situations is being encompassed under the term alcoholism. If on the other hand, one feels that evidence of substance addiction (tolerance and withdrawal symptoms) is the sine qua non of alcoholism, then a far more restricted group of individuals will be diagnosed as alcoholic.

Because we are cognizant of such potential difficulties, we have applied relatively stringent, traditional criteria to all the research subjects included in our studies. In addition, the clinical case histories reported in the book are of families in which the alcoholic member has been diagnosed as alcohol dependent or an alcohol abuser using a medically (psychiatrically) oriented diagnostic scheme.

PART II

THE LIFE HISTORY MODEL OF THE ALCOHOLIC FAMILY

S CIENTIFIC MODELS serve a number of important functions, among them the ability to stimulate theory building and the ability to focus attention on interesting questions (hypothesis generation). In clinical work, they serve three additional functions of critical importance:

First, they organize the search for data. In the usual clinical situation the clinician-researcher is subjected to an information input of staggering proportions. These data must be prioritized and reduced in a way that allows the clinician to generate meaningful clinical hypotheses. A good clinical model not only suggests such a prioritization, but also suggests a perceptual stance for the clinician to take in order to maximize the quality of data available to him.

Second, a theoretical model, in order to be useful in a clinical setting, must include a conceptualization of pathology. Although norms and normal variability are of relevance and importance, clinician-researchers are successful or unsuccessful depending on their ability to distinguish maladjustment from adjustment. It is therefore critical that they have available to them a set of suggested criteria against which selectively filtered data can be matched and adjudged acceptable or unacceptable.

And lastly, any clinical model worth its salt will also provide a blueprint for intervention. This blueprint usually includes at least two parts—a model suggesting why and how behavioral change occurs; and a suggested role for the clinician in the process of change.

In chapters 3 and 4, we will provide a detailed description of the theoretical model that has guided the clinical and research data presented in this book. The model is firmly grounded in family systems theory. But because the model places unusually heavy emphasis on the unique *developmental* history of the Alcoholic Family, we call it the Family Life History (FLH) model.

Family Systems Theory and the Concept of the Alcoholic Family

In 1928, the Austrian biologist Ludwig von Bertalanffy initiated a discussion of a new approach to biological problems. The approach was intended to introduce into scientific discussion a fundamentally different view of the nature of biological events, a view that stressed an "organismic" rather than a "reductionistic" approach. In von Bertalanffy's view, traditional science, firmly based as it was in linear cause-and-effect explanatory models, had major limitations, limitations that could only be overcome through the development of a radically different approach to scientific explanation. By 1945 a set of integrated concepts for tackling holistic problems in science had been proposed and dubbed by von Bertalanffy General Systems Theory (Gray and Rizzo, 1969).

The essence of the systems approach is an attention to organization, that is, to the relationship between parts, to a concentration on patterned, rather than linear, relationships, and to a consideration of events in the context in which they are occurring rather than in isolation from their environment. The approach's attraction for family theorists and clinicians should therefore be self-evident, and it is hardly surprising that it has become the dominant theoretical model for family therapy (although it has been less successful as a research model).

The sine qua non of a system is the consistency of its organizational characteristics; elements should be related to each other in a consistently describable or predictable fashion. This consistency is brought about, systems theory tells us, through the interplay of three forces, forces we might think of as the core concepts of systems theory. They are: the concept of *organization;* the concept of *morphostasis* (or internal regulation); and the concept of *morphogenesis* (or controlled growth).

The concept of organization is at the heart of the organismic principles espoused by systems theory, whose single most important concept is that the organizational characteristics of the system produce a whole that is greater than the additive sums of each of the separate parts. That is, the fit between the elements of the system, the pattern with which the parts come together, produces something that cannot be predicted from a knowledge of the separate characteristics of each of the component parts. Just as we cannot predict the characteristics of a chemical compound from the properties of the separate elements that combine to form it, we cannot predict the behavioral properties of a family simply through a knowledge of the separate personalities of the husband, wife, and children. Conversely, we say that no system can be adequately understood or totally explained once it has been broken down into its component parts.

Furthermore, no single element or subgroup of elements within a system can be thought of as acting independently. Instead, an organized entity is proposed in which "the state of each unit is constrained by, conditioned by, or dependent on the state of other units" (Miller, 1965, p. 68). The behavior of family members, when they are in the context of their family, is shaped and constrained by the simultaneous behaviors of all other members of the family, singly and in combination.

The concept of organization is therefore a descriptive one. Systems theory also sees living systems as dynamic entities, responsive to the interplay of the other two major forces: a morphogenetic force associated with growth, change, development, and a tendency to become organizationally more complex over time; and a morphostatic force (often called *homeostasis*) usually conceptualized as a set of regulatory mechanisms useful in maintaining stability, order, and control of systems functioning. Although living systems such as families are thought to be responsive to both these forces, morphostatic mechanisms, insofar as they serve a regulatory function, tend to balance and shape the weight and direction of morphogenic characteristics.

In terms of the family, this means that there is always an interactive jockeying between a family's desire to maintain stability and its desire to change and grow. In some families, the need for stability seems to win out and change occurs only in response to tremendous pressures. Morphostatic mechanisms in such families exercise a tyrannizing effect, bottling up developmental aspirations until they can no longer be contained and explode, often in the form of a major family crisis. In other families, alterations and changes seem to be always occurring. Such families, often described as chaotic, appear disorganized, unregulated, and out of control. The "healthy" family is one that has developed an appropriate balance between morphogenesis and morphostasis, the key being a coherent fit of regulatory mechanisms and developmental themes.

In this book we focus on a particular type of family system—the Alcoholic Family. In using this term, we are suggesting that it is possible for an entire family to "have alcoholism." This does not mean that every member of the family is drinking. Rather it means that even if only one member of the family might be identified as alcoholic (by other family members and by the outside world), behaviors related to alcohol use have come to play a major role within both morphogenetic and morphostatic mechanisms of the family system. In this sense, these two important systemic forces within the family have, to a significant degree, become organized around, or distorted by, the presence of alcoholism. Morphostatic behaviors have been shaped by, or have incorporated, aspects of alcohol-related interactional behavior. The overall shape of family development (the family's life cycle) has been distorted by the superimposition of an alcohol life history on the customary family life cycle. In other words, these families have become *alcoholic systems.*

To anticipate our later discussions of developmental and regulatory distortions in the Alcoholic Family, the life history of these families is one in which distortions occur both in the importance given to alcohol-related tasks (and the corresponding demotion of nonalcohol-related developmental tasks), and in an alteration of the balance between morphogenetic and morphostatic forces within the family system. Ultimately, it is the reshaping process that has the more important developmental consequence for the family. Basically, this reshaping takes the form of inappropriately long and extended periods of phase-related behavior (dominated by morphostatic principles) and a corresponding tendency to ward off developmentally appropriate transitional behavior (the times when morphogenetic forces characteristically hold sway).

Another way to put this is that emphasis is placed on short-term stability of family life, to the detriment of all other issues. Thus challenges to this stability (that is, life within a developmental phase) are interpreted primarily as threats to the status quo; the possibilities for growth inherent in these challenges are ignored. As a consequence, movement into a developmental transition is thwarted, and the family's current developmental phase is extended far beyond its natural life. The clinical impression is that the family is frozen in time; the developmental implications are a flattening out of the customary life cycle.

This is not to say that transitions never occur in Alcoholic Families. But when they do, they are the result of extraordinary challenges to the status quo, and thus it is only when families are forced to deal with extraordinary stresses that transitions from one developmental stage to the next are successfully negotiated.

Paradoxically, much of our understanding of how developmental distortions occur in Alcoholic Families has come not so much from a focus on morphogenetic behaviors, but rather from our studies of family regulatory behaviors, those behaviors that are reflective of morphostatic principles at work in the family. It is the way the family controls and regulates its life that has been most useful to us in understanding why some families seem to proceed through the life cycle in an orderly fashion, while others become stuck or diverted from a healthy course.

For the Alcoholic Family, regulatory behaviors are important in two respects: First, they help shape overall patterns of family behavior, and these patterns are differentially receptive to the presence of chronic alcoholism. That is, certain family styles seem conducive to alcoholism flourishing within the family; other styles seem incompatible with chronic drinking. In the former situation, alcoholism has a greater likelihood of taking hold; in the latter situation, the likelihood is that nascent alcoholism will either be arrested or the alcoholic will be extruded from the family. This fit between family personality, as reflected in its regulatory behaviors, and drinking is, as we will see in later chapters, a highly specific one. Not only are certain regulatory patterns more conducive to the development of a chronic "Alcoholic Family," but there is even a fit between different patterns of alcoholism and different family regulatory styles.

Second, regulatory mechanisms can themselves be taken over by alcoholism and alcohol-related behaviors. In such instances, regulatory behaviors are not only co-opted by alcoholism, they are actually *altered* to make them more compatible with the maintenance of alcoholism. For example, family short-term problem-solving strategies—one of the regulatory behaviors we focus on—can over time actually come to rely on alcohol-related behaviors (e.g., increased affective expressiveness) as core components of problem-solving efforts. In such instances, alcoholism has in effect *invaded* a fundamental aspect of family life. Having once taken hold in such a fashion, alcoholism is actually *maintained* by the family's regulatory behaviors rather than being contained or eliminated from family life.

Our family systems model of the Alcoholic Family can therefore be thought of as having four basic tenets:

1. Alcoholic Families are behavioral systems in which alcoholism and alcohol-related behaviors have become *central organizing principles* around which family life is structured.
2. The introduction of alcoholism into family life has the potential to profoundly alter the balance that exists between growth and regulation within the family. This alteration most typically skews the family in the direction of an emphasis on short-term stability (regulation) at the expense of long-term growth.

3. The impact of alcoholism and alcohol-related behaviors on family systemic functioning is most clearly seen in the types of changes that occur in regulatory behaviors as the family gradually accommodates family life to the coexistent demands of alcoholism.

4. The types of alterations that occur in regulatory behaviors can in turn be seen to profoundly influence the overall shape of family growth and development—changes in the normative family life cycle that we have labeled "developmental distortions."

Our detailed description of the Family Life History model is therefore divided into two main parts: first, a description of the fundamental properties of morphostasis within the family system and an explanation of how regulation is typically altered when alcoholism enters the scene; and second, a focus on family growth and ways in which the more normative course of family development can be distorted when the family comes to organize its life around chronic alcoholism.

CHAPTER 3

Regulating Behavior in the Alcoholic Family

A BASIC ASSUMPTION of clinicians and researchers working with families is that family behavior is patterned, predictable, and stable. Yet the degree of regularity and stability of behavior evidenced by most families is truly remarkable. After all, the family is constantly being subjected to a potentially overwhelming series of challenges. It is challenged from without by economic forces, political decisions, and the demands of larger organizations within which it holds membership. It is also challenged from within. Its individual members have their own agendas, psychological needs, and physical requisites.

Aware of the existence of this multiplicity of internal and external stresses, the observer of family behavior cannot help but be impressed by the ability of the family to manage and control these challenges. Despite living in a constantly changing environment, and despite sudden and unpredictable encounters, the family is able to maintain a sense of balance, a coherence, a regularity to its life. It is quite an impressive performance. To account for it, it seems that there must be powerful "built in" mechanisms that regulate family life by providing organizational structure and by helping to determine the rules that govern sequential behavioral processes.

Family systems theorists have used the term *morphostasis* to describe this phenomenon. Another familiar term here is *family homeostasis*.

Family Homeostasis

The term *family homeostasis* was first coined by the family therapist Don Jackson (1957). It was his belief that the physiological concept of homeostasis (Cannon 1939) was an excellent metaphor for family regulatory processes as well. Jackson was impressed by the propensity of families to behave as though they have built-in mechanisms (behaviors) that are activated whenever family life is disrupted by internal and external forces, behaviors that seem, in turn, to return the family to its previous state of balance.

In the original physiological model, the organism's environmental constancy was thought to be maintained via a series of neurological and hormonal forces collectively called *homeostatic mechanisms.* Many of these processes have by now been described in intricate detail. The key elements are a series of peripheral *servomechanisms* that act as sensory devices appraising the current state of the environment and feeding this information to a central processing unit, the brain. Output (action) takes the form of an integrated series of responses that are constantly being adjusted or modified as revised information about the environment is fed back to the central processing unit by the peripheral sensors.

There are thus three essential features to the homeostasis model of physiological regulation: (1) the need to maintain the internal environment within a delimited range because optimal functioning is achieved within that range; (2) the existence of sensory devices to continually monitor important environmental parameters; and (3) the presence of coordinated input-output mechanisms arranged in a series of reverberating circular loops (what we call feedback loops). Jackson's unique contribution was his proposal that such a model was an apt descriptor of regulatory behavior in families as well.

The physiological model of homeostasis also suggests three ways in which homeostatic mechanisms might malfunction. The first would be a failure of peripheral sensors. The sensors might, for one reason or another, simply be exhausted and unable to function properly. Or, the change that is occurring in the environment might be one that the sensing mechanisms are simply not in a position to ascertain. For example, biological organisms have no built-in sensors to monitor environmental levels of radiation.

Second, response patterns might be ineffective or inappropriate. This might be due to a failure of the central processing unit to correctly interpret incoming data and to activate an appropriate response, or it might be due to a failure of the response system itself. For example, heart disease or peripheral vessel disease makes it impossible to adequately control blood pressure, no matter what signals are being sent out.

The third, and for our purposes perhaps the most interesting, type of "failure" occurs when environmental sensors are inappropriately calibrated. Let us use as an example the inappropriate calibration of a thermostat connected to a central heating system. Thermostats are preset to a specific range. When the thermostat "senses" that temperature in the home has exceeded this optimal range, a circuit is deactivated and the central furnace is turned off. When the temperature drops below the optimal range, the reverse occurs and the furnace again starts heating the home. If we set this on-off range at five degrees, many people will experience the temperature swing as uncomfortable. The home will be first too cold, then too hot. Sweaters will be put on, then taken off. The purpose of the thermostat has been defeated. It might be as easy for people to get up and turn a manual heating switch on and off as it would be to get up to get clothing or put it away. Suppose, on the other hand, the temperature range is set at 0.5 degrees. This now finely tuned thermostat will be sending signals to the central furnace that turn it on and off dozens of times in an hour. Room temperature might be kept at "perfect" levels, but the electrical motor operating this central heating system will have to be replaced in one year rather than in the ten-year operational period for which it was designed.

If we move back to families once again, we can envision failures in homeostasis arising from the same three sources. Some families simply cannot sense when their internal environment has moved an unacceptable distance from its optimal range. Other families are perfectly capable of sensing that something is wrong, but mobilize either inappropriate or ineffective behavioral programs in response to this information. Finally, some families have established inappropriately narrow or inappropriately wide environmental limits for the activation of corrective homeostatic mechanisms.

It is this last type of homeostatic failure that is most relevant for the Alcoholic Family. When, for example, we talk about a characteristic rigidity of regulatory mechanisms in the Alcoholic Family, we are referring specifically to the tendency of these families to set their internal thermostats at an inappropriately narrow range. Homeostatic mechanisms are too easily activated in these families. The slightest change in the environment calls for reactions that, in dictatorial fashion, maintain overall stability and predictability within the family's internal environment.

Time and again we will see this theme emerging in our research and clinical data. Families seemingly misinterpret normative developmental changes, assuming that they are unacceptable threats to overall homeostasis. Responses are rapid and seem geared toward maintaining the status quo. The family and its behavior seem organized around a primary objective of maintaining short-term stability. As a consequence, developmental challenges are misinterpreted and mismanaged. The family proves to have remarkable stability, if one measures stability solely in terms of predictability of behavior, but this stability is achieved at the expense of resiliency and adaptability.

The overall effect is one of increasing rigidity in the face of developmental or environmental demands. When these demands finally exceed the dictatorial powers of the family's homeostatic mechanisms, the result is usually explosive. The family disintegrates the way a totalitarian regime does when pressures for growth and change exceed the elaborate mechanisms of control established by the regime.*

Deep Regulatory Structures

Because the family behaves *as if* it is governed by underlying regulatory principles (homeostasis) that, in turn, generate a set of rules that establish guidelines for behavior and produce patterned rather than random sequences of behaviors, it is tempting to infer the existence of specific regulatory mechanisms that bring this all about. Yet if such regulatory mechanisms exist, where do we look for them, how do we measure them, and how do they exercise their functional capacity? As convinced as many people are that these mechanisms exist, they have been hard-pressed to bring them to the surface; they are elusive constructs, a set of presumed mechanisms incorporated into theoretical models of family functioning.

Although sometimes characterized as observable, surface level properties of families, regulatory mechanisms are best conceptualized as *deep*

---

*It has become common in clinical settings to apply the term *homeostasis* to any situation in which therapeutic change is being *resisted* by the family. Yet family homeostasis, if it is to closely follow the example of its physiological cousin, should be viewed as a largely positive and necessary component of family life that serves the purpose of keeping the family on an even keel. The mechanisms families mobilize to deal with environmental challenges are as important to the ongoing viability of the family system as, for example, temperature regulation is to the viability of the biological organism. Homeostasis is only a negative force when it continues to dominate family response patterns during times of normative developmental transitions, thereby inadvertently impeding family growth.

structures, metaphorical family properties that are located deep within the core of the family. These mechanisms can neither be directly observed, nor systematically measured. If there were such a thing as a family nucleus, a family command center, that is where these structures would reside, giving shape and form to those family behaviors and functions that give the family a coherence of organization, a recognizable structure and personality.

Unfortunately, too often the term *family regulatory mechanism* is used as if the properties or structures it describes actually exist—that family boundaries, for example, are concrete structures capable of being visualized, touched, felt. Insofar as these constructs are described in such terms, they are being misused. However, they are very valuable when viewed as metaphors representing, in a condensed and symbolically rich fashion, a complex set of observations about family behavior.

Two constructs that have proven particularly useful as descriptors of underlying regulatory mechanisms in the Alcoholic Family are the constructs of *family temperament* and *family identity.* Because these constructs suggest ways in which important differences between families can be identified and provide a series of dimensions along which to compare families, they advance our understanding of the unique processes of regulation of behavior in the Alcoholic Family.

Family Temperament

Temperament is a psychological construct that refers to a set of enduring behavioral response styles and activity patterns that have their origins in an individual's early life. Family temperament is an analogous construct. It refers to characteristic activity levels and response styles exhibited by families as they go about shaping their daily routines and solving problems. Although presumably an additive product of temperamental characteristics of individuals within the family, family temperament is also the product of the unique fit between individual temperaments. In this sense, it is truly a systemic property of families, one of those underlying, deep structures that guide the regulation of family life.

We are largely indebted to the work of Thomas, Chess, and their colleagues from the New York Longitudinal Study of temperamental characteristics of children for our understanding of temperament as a determinant of individual behavior (Thomas and Chess, 1979). This study has documented a "fact" long known to parents but previously ignored by developmental psychologists and pediatricians, namely that infants, as early as the first day of life, differ dramatically in their behavioral response patterns and activity levels. Thomas and Chess initially focused on differences in the behavior of newborns while still in the hospital nursery and identified nine different temperamental dimensions along which these differences occur. These are: activity level; rhythmicity; approach-withdrawal behavior; adaptability; threshold of responsiveness; intensity of reactions; quality of mood; distractibility; and, finally, attention span and persistence. Thomas and Chess have characterized these dimensions as reflecting the "how" rather than the "what" of behavior—for example, the difference between crying (a content or "what" judgment) versus persistent crying (a temperament or "how" judgment); or the difference between sleeping-awakeness ("what") versus rhythmicity of behavior ("how"), the latter being the temperamental characteristic.

What are the comparable dimensions of family temperament? *Family temperament is the product of three fundamental properties:* (1) the family's typical energy level; (2) the family's preferred interactional distance; and (3) the family's characteristic behavioral range. These three temperamental properties in turn exercise a regulatory function for the family by, in effect, establishing a set of acceptable guidelines within which family behavior tends to occur. The family's energy level establishes guidelines about behavioral activity; the family's preferred interactional distance establishes guidelines regarding boundary permeability (for both internal and external boundaries); and the family's behavioral range establishes guidelines about the degree of variability the family manifests in its patterns of interactional behavior. Once these guidelines are in place, the family develops a set of recognizable behavioral traits, traits that are the observable correlates of its underlying temperamental properties. It is at this point that we begin describing one family as a high-energy family, another as a low-energy family ("hot" vs. "cool" families); one family as flexible, another as rigid (high vs. low tolerance for novelty); one family as open to the outside world, another as protective and closed.

Just how stable family temperament is over the life cycle is, as yet, an unexplored question. Clinical experience and research findings concerning the stability of individual temperament suggest that family temperament also is a fundamental and relatively unchanging property. Clearly, as new members are added or lost, family temperament will undergo shifts to accommodate these changes. But in all likelihood the degree of these shifts will itself be consistent with properties of family temperament as they already exist. Families whose temperament allows them a greater range of behaviors, a greater tolerance for uncertainty, a greater flexibility in the patterning of behavior will probably accommodate new members in a more flexible fashion. Families at the other end of the spectrum will tend to impose the family's behavioral style on a new member in dictatorial fashion, often with unfortunate consequences.

The concept of temperament has proven particularly helpful in interpreting "interactive" data about changes in behavior that occur when individuals are placed in different environmental contexts. Why is it, for example, that the same child will exhibit very different patterns of behavior when placed in a closed versus an open classroom environment? One explanation offered is that the child's temperamental characteristics potentially "fit" with the environmental characteristics of one classroom, but "clash" with the other. For example, children with high motoric activity rates might

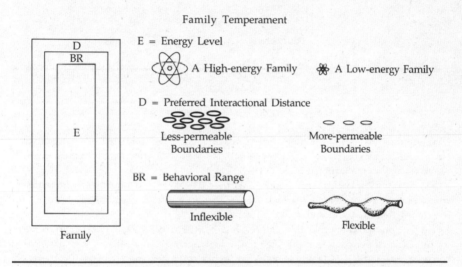

Family Temperament

E = Energy Level

A High-energy Family   A Low-energy Family

D = Preferred Interactional Distance

Less-permeable Boundaries   More-permeable Boundaries

BR = Behavioral Range

Inflexible   Flexible

FIGURE 3.1

The Three Dimensions of Family Temperament

In this graphic representation of the construct of family temperament, its dimensions are represented as layers in a three-dimensional space. At the core is the dimension of *typical energy level,* a "fuel source" that in turn drives (establishes guidelines for) behavioral activity within the family. A family with a "hot" fuel core would be expected to be a high movement, high interaction behavioral system; low energy family would be exactly the opposite.

At the outer layer is the dimension of *preferred interactional distance.* In our graphic representation, this dimension is depicted using the familiar metaphor of boundary permeability.

Finally, we have the dimension of characteristic behavioral range, represented as a tube of variable resiliency. In one family the tube might be made of a stiff, inflexible, rigid material that would only accommodate a highly restricted range (sizes and shapes) of behaviors; in another family the tube might be made of a highly pliable, rubbery, flexible material that could accommodate many different sizes and shapes of behavior without rupturing.

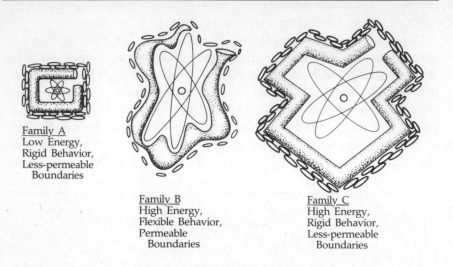

Family A
Low Energy,
Rigid Behavior,
Less-permeable
Boundaries

Family B
High Energy,
Flexible Behavior,
Permeable
Boundaries

Family C
High Energy,
Rigid Behavior,
Less-permeable
Boundaries

FIGURE 3.2

Three Different Family Temperaments

Different combinations of the three dimensions of energy level, preferred interactional distance, and behavioral range produce qualitatively vastly different family temperaments. Three examples are illustrated here.

In Family A, a low energy level combined with rigid behavior and impermeable boundaries would likely produce a family that, were we to observe it, would appear highly constricted, frightened, inhibited, and dull.

Family C, on the other hand, although also highly rigid in its behavioral range and its rules for interactional behavior, is at the same time a high energy family—that is, lots and lots of behavior, lots and lots of family energy, but highly structured and predictable patterns of behavior with little tolerance for deviance. Family C is not a family that would easily tolerate spontaneous behavior; yet at the same time it is a family where behavioral activity rates would be quite high.

Family B would likely manifest yet a third very different temperamental style. Here a high energy family is at the same time quite tolerant of a wide range of behaviors and is open to close internal and external contact in its behavioral style.

Keep in mind that the differences in family temperaments depicted here have no global (unidimensional) implications regarding functionality/dysfunctionality of family behavior. Rather, we would have to assume that each would have its own unique strengths and weaknesses, excelling in some tasks relative to other families, but coming out second-best in others.

experience difficulty concentrating in an unstructured classroom setting, but do better in a setting that limits their potential distractibility.

When we explore the relationship between family temperament and chronic alcoholism, we also focus our attention on behavior-environment "fits." But this time it is the "environment" that is sensitive to temperamental guidelines. The environment of interest is the family's internal environment, one that to a significant degree takes shape in response to temperamental imperatives—the family's activity level, variability of interaction, and so on. The "behavior" of interest this time around is alcoholism. The focus becomes the association between family temperament and patterns of alcohol use. The crucial question is whether certain temperamental styles and certain patterns of alcohol use tend to go together, whether they, in effect, reflect a *goodness-of-fit* that becomes mutually reinforcing. Such a process, were it to exist, would help us understand why in certain families chronic alcoholism and family behavior seem to form a stable, rather than a volatile, bond.

Studies of individual-environment fit or goodness-of-fit between dyads have suggested that when temperamental characteristics don't "fit," a number of potential solutions are available to deal with the resulting clash. First, one of the participants can change. For example, in mother-infant dyads, the mother typically adjusts to accommodate the temperamental style of the infant. If it is a question of individual-environment fit, the individual might alter his or her behavior to better fit the environmental context. Second, a process of mutual accommodation can be undertaken. Newly married couples invariably go through just such a process. Or third, one or both parties can decide to give up. If the clash is between the individual and his or her environmental context, then the "solution" might be to find a better suited environment rather than to try to change the environment.

The same three choices exist when the issue is alcoholism and the family. Alcoholic individuals are not all alike. Their behaviors, including their drinking patterns, vary widely and consequently place very different demands and constraints on the environments in which they are attempting to thrive. If we read "family" for "environment" in this equation, then different types of alcoholism will place different demands on families. In some instances, the family will find these demands intolerable and will either force the individual to stop drinking or to get out. In other families, however, an acceptable "fit" will be achieved. That is, in such instances, family temperament is fully compatible with the coexistence of the particular type (pattern) of alcoholism manifested by the alcoholic family member (daily drinking, binge drinking, etc).

Family Identity

Family identity is the family's subjective sense of its own continuity over time, its present situation, and its character. As such, family identity is an underlying cognitive structure, a set of fundamental beliefs, attitudes, and attributions the family shares about itself. It is the gestalt of qualities and attributes that make it a particular family and differentiate it from other families. This fundamental cognitive nature of family identity also helps to distinguish it from family temperament, a deep systemic regulatory structure that is primarily responsive to biological factors.

As a family-level construct, family identity is analogous to the individual-level construct of ego identity conceptualized by Erikson (1959). Like ego identity, it is subjective and reflexive; by definition, it must resonate within the family whose identity it is. In Erikson's formulation, there is a merging of the individual's core and the inner coherence of the group or groups with which he or she is identified: "The term identity expresses . . . a mutual relation in that it connotes both a persistent sameness within oneself and a persistent sharing of some kind of essential character with others" (p. 102).

Family identity is also characterized by subjectivity. However, our notion of family identity goes beyond the supposition that family is one determinant—albeit powerful—of individual identity. It is, instead, a group psychological phenomenon that has as its foundation a *shared system of beliefs.* Shared belief systems are the implicit assumptions about roles, relationships, and values that govern (regulate) interaction in families and other groups.

These shared belief systems have gone by many terms, for example, family paradigm (Reiss, 1981), family themes (Handel, 1967), family rules (Ford and Herrick, 1974; Jackson, 1965; Riskin, 1963), and family myths (Ferreira, 1966). Each of these terms connote a somewhat different, but also overlapping, segment of the universe of shared belief systems that families hold.

Family paradigm refers to "the family's shared view of its environment [a view that] may be partly a product—directly or indirectly—of the perceptual and cognitive response dispositions of its members and the influence of these dispositions on one another" (Reiss and Elstein, 1971, p. 121). These views, in turn, shape family behavior. A similar capability is postulated for underlying *family themes,* which are described as "pattern(s) of feeling, motives, fantasies and conventionalized understandings" that organizes the family's view of reality (Handel, 1967, p. 18). Themes are found in the family's implicit directions, its notions of "who we are" and

Family Identity

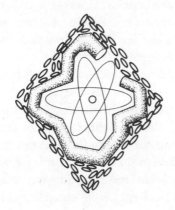 

FIGURE 3.3

The Diamonds versus the Squares

Depicted here are families with two very different identities despite having comparable temperaments. In one family, family identity is represented as a diamond—that is, the family sees itself as valuable, masterful, and so forth. The second family, the Squares, have a very different qualitative sense of themselves—nondescript, run-of-the-mill, and so forth.

Both families have high energy, impermeable boundaries, and inflexible behavioral range temperaments, but these same temperamental styles have been further shaped by shared cognitive processes within these families to produce family identities of very different character.

Although it is possible to imagine certain temperamental styles that would preclude the development of a particular family identity, we would contend that the deep regulatory structures of family temperament and family identity reflect two quite different domains—the first determined largely by biological factors; the second largely by cognitive factors.

"what we do about it." The term *family rules,* on the other hand, emphasizes the binding rather than the organizing nature of belief systems. Ford and Herrick (1974) posit that family rules are binding directives concerning the ways in which family members should relate to one another and to the outside world. "Smaller" rules help to regulate behavior, while "larger" rules "express a philosophy, contain a definition, and refer to a theoretical ideal or goal. They have character and style" (p. 62).

What attitudes and assumptions comprise this "system of shared beliefs"? What are the components of family identity? First, and most fundamental, family identity incorporates certain beliefs about family membership, that is, who belongs and who does not, both now and in the past. For example, in some families second cousins are members; in others they are not. And second, family identity is greatly influenced by its beliefs and recollections about past history. An elusive historical aspect shapes family identity and the extent to which the family understands its present condition as part of a continuum over time. For most families, the past motivates the family to preserve its identity from one generation to the next.

Although family identity is a cognitive construct—the product of a shared belief system—it is not always in the conscious awareness of all family members. Most of the time, one has only a diffuse sense of connectedness, a feeling of membership, not a clearly defined and explicable version of the shared belief systems that make up the unique identity of a particular family. In fact, family identity would cease to function as an effective regulatory structure if it were a surface phenomenon, clearly understood and in full view of the family. Regulatory structures, to be effective, must serve as guidelines for behavior, not as the driving forces for specific behaviors.

Yet there are times in the life of the family when these shared belief systems emerge in much more explicit forms. These times are during major developmental transitions—especially when children split off from their families of origin to form their own families. At such times, the family wants to impose its important values, rules, and belief systems on this new family. To do so, the core identity aspects must first be packaged in discernible form. Thus these components emerge from the shadows and are expressed in explicit form for all to see and, it is hoped, comprehend.

Thus family identity has two separate components—one implicit; the other explicit. Further, the two components have a dynamic relationship to each other. As the family goes through different development phases, the relationship between the implicit and explicit components changes. Major crises also alter this balance. Crises also are characteristically accompanied by an emergence of an explicit family identity as a prelude to the family's action.

Most people are part of and influenced by two family identities: that of the family in which they are reared, and that of the family they form through marriage and procreation. To the extent that elements of the origin family experience—attitudes, values, patterns of behavior—carry over into the nuclear family, we can say that this "new" family has or has not adopted that particular heritage. *Heritage* is the measure of continuity. At each generational transition, therefore, a family's identity faces one of three fundamentally different fates: (1) it might continue in unaltered form into the next generation; (2) it might blend with aspects of the identity of the other spouse's family of origin; or (3) it might disappear as the new family embarks on a course determined by the spouse's family or by a new and novel family identity.

Thus family identity plays a far more powerful role than family temperament in regulating the *transmission* of core systemic properties of families across generations. If one of the shared beliefs of the family is that alcoholism is a central organizing principle for family life—our definition of the Alcoholic Family—then the continuance versus discontinuity of this family identity will be a major determinant of whether alcoholism is also transmitted across generations. Whenever we focus attention on alcoholism issues at times of major family life transitions, family identity will be one of the central constructs in those discussions.

Family identity is thus a powerful explanatory construct whenever we are addressing continuity-discontinuity issues in the Alcoholic Family. At a two-generational level, the focus is on cross-generational transmission. At a multigenerational level, the ability of the family to maintain its core identity determines whether the family will take on *dynastic* qualities. As this term is most commonly used, it refers to the ability of the family to establish a set of traditions and shared beliefs that are powerful enough to demand full adherence by all family members across multiple generations. Individual identity, in such instances, is submerged and subjugated to an identity framed by membership in the family. Thus one is a Rockefeller, a Rothschild, or a Kennedy, and feels one's life shaped (and perhaps dominated) by this sense of the primacy of the family legacy.

We would contend that just as a family dynasty can be built around economic or political power, it can also be built around alcoholism. In this sense, alcoholism can have as powerful an impact on family members as community status in shaping their shared beliefs and sense of their role in life. Thus *alcoholic family identities* that have survived intact across multiple generations can produce alcoholic dynastic identities that demand the loyalty of each and every family member and, in interactive fashion, influence behavioral expectancies (e.g., that the next generation will, of course, include alcoholic members).

Observable Regulatory Behaviors

Family identity and family temperament are both theoretical constructs. Although we assume that they are powerful factors in the regulation of family life, we also recognize that they cannot be directly assessed and measured. However, in that family identity and family temperament, as regulatory structures, presumably determine the characteristics of surface-level family behaviors important in the overall continuity and regularity of family life, their underlying characteristics can be inferred from a careful examination of these surface behaviors.

As an analogy, think about how individual temperament is currently assessed. A series of highly specific, readily observable behaviors is systematically measured—motor activity, response to novel stimuli, regularity of sleep-wake cycles, and others—and the data obtained are then used as descriptors of the underlying temperamental dimensions of activity level, adaptability, and rhythmicity. Another analogy is the relationship between deoxyribonucleic acid (DNA) and protein metabolism. The observable products of the underlying regulatory structure (DNA) are the multitude of proteins produced by the organism. Although molecular genetics now has a technology for *directly* measuring the structure of DNA molecules, the DNA model was proposed long before this technology was available.

What then are the observable family behaviors that provide a window into the nature of underlying family regulatory processes? Three categories of behaviors prove particular useful as such windows: (1) daily routines; (2) family rituals; and (3) short-term problem-solving episodes. Each of these behaviors is a component of life in all families; can be directly assessed via interview and/or observational methods, and serves a specific function within the family's internal environment and in providing a sense of its own uniqueness.

FIGURE 3.4

Observable Regulatory Behaviors

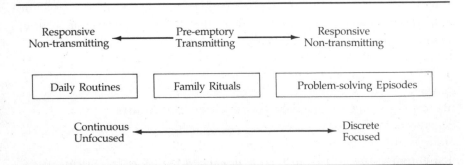

These three types of behaviors—daily routines, rituals, and problem-solving episodes—are also excellent tools for the family clinician-researcher because they can be systematically studied. Family daily routines can be directly observed and recorded by the researcher. Family rituals can be reconstructed via careful inquiry of family members. Family problem-solving strategies can be accurately gleaned from clinical material in therapy sessions or from performance at simulated tasks in laboratory settings. In fact, we have systematically studied each of these regulatory behaviors as they are manifested in Alcoholic Families and the findings from these studies are one of the major data sources used to describe life in the these families.

Family Daily Routines

The first category of regulatory behaviors is in many ways the most mundane. Routines are those background behaviors that provide structure and form to daily life. All families, no matter how chaotic, impose some order on the pace and patterning of their day-to-day lives. Sleep-wake cycles, meal preparation and eating, housekeeping, and shopping are obvious examples of activities that must be structured and reliable in order for family life to proceed. When one talks about constancy of the family's internal environment, the clearest observable concomitants of this internal stability are the routine behaviors the family carries out, day after day, in relatively unchanging fashion.

Although daily routines can be observed being carried out in many different settings, the most important of these settings is the family's home. The home is the most concrete representation of the family's internal environment. The way the family organizes its use of space in the home is, in effect, a projective representation of the structure of the family's internal environment. The use of time at home is a reflection of the degree of patterning (organization) in this environment. The family's use of space and time at home not only is clearly reflective of the qualitative characteristics of its internal environment but also serves as a window into the behavioral regulators of the constancy of this environment.

Daily routines are rarely flashy in nature. To the outside observer they may well seem repetitive and boring. Yet differences between families in the way they structure time and space are immense. It is this difference that bestows on daily routines a sense of the dramatic. For example, recall how dramatically different first impressions of a family's home can be. One home immediately conveys a sense of order, warmth, and distinctiveness;

another home appears totally chaotic and disheveled. We react to these differences as if we are viewing, via this brief glance around a home, the family's personality writ large—its self-esteem, internal sense of pride, values, and sense of order.

In the same way, daily routines provide for individual family members a sense of order and comfort. That is, they provide these feelings when the routines themselves have a recognizable pattern to them and are predictable. This is not to imply that order and predictability are synomymous with orderliness and stereotypy. A familiar sense of messiness can be as comforting to a family member as "everything in its place" is to the member of another family. What is comparable is the sense of familiarity that is evoked by these daily routines.

Our extensive observations of Alcoholic Families in home settings suggest that differences between these families in the way they carry out daily routines are probably as great as for the general population. The fact that no single pattern of daily routines can be detected for Alcoholic Families means that such routines in these families are the product of each family's personality, not the product of alcoholism per se.

Of the two underlying family regulatory structures we have previously described—family temperament and family identity—daily routines are more clearly reflective of temperamental properties of the family. That is, although daily routines are in part a product of a family's collective sense of itself, the way these routines are structured is more directly determined by such properties as the family's characteristic energy level, preferred interactional distance, and behavior range (the core properties of family temperament). Thus daily routines are convenient surface markers of families' underlying temperamental properties. Further, differences between the structure of families's daily routines can be best described by paying attention to such dimensions of behavior as interactional activity rates, physical mobility, and variability of behavior from day to day.

Thus in describing daily routines, we find ourselves focusing on such aspects of behavior as rhythmicity, intensity, variability of behavior, and the like. But when talking about daily routines in the Alcoholic Family, we find that routine behaviors are not the only aspect of life that has the above qualities. Alcoholism itself (or more explicitly drinking behavior) can be described using the same sorts of dimensions. That is, the drinking behavior of alcoholic individuals also has a characteristic rhythmicity (daily drinking, binge drinking, and so forth), a typical level of intensity (degree of intoxication), and a characteristic degree of predictability. Thus drinking patterns also can be thought of as reflecting temperamental properties—perhaps in this case the temperament of the alcoholic individual.

As you will recall, the construct of temperament has often been invoked when the subject at hand is an explication of the "goodness of fit" between individuals and their environments. For the Alcoholic Family, the issue is the goodness of fit between the family's personality and the drinking behavior of the alcoholic (e.g., drinking rhythmicity, intensity, and so forth). Hence daily routines are the regulatory behaviors that best help us understand why the alcoholism family environment fit "works" in some situations, but doesn't in others.

Family Rituals

In order to qualify as a ritual, a behavioral episode must have four critical characteristics: (1) the behavior must be *bounded* in time, with a clear-cut beginning and end, and have an uninterruptable quality; (2) the family must be *consciously aware* that special behavior is being carried out; (3) the behavior must be able to *preempt* any other behaviors occurring at that time, that is, it must have primacy whenever it is being enacted; and (4) the episode must have a strong *symbolic* component that invests the behaviors with importance beyond their objective value.

Family rituals have one more characteristic, one that is unique to this class of regulatory mechanism. Rituals are *transmitting.* That is, rituals have the capacity to transmit important aspects of family culture from one generation to the next. Rituals are, above all else, memorable. Though each nuclear family creates its own celebrations, traditions, and patterned routines, frequently they contain elements of rituals performed in previous generations. By the same token, the rituals of the present will persist in some form into the future.

Three categories of behaviors in family life have the capacity to become ritualized—family celebrations, family traditions, and patterned routines. Family celebrations are those religious holidays (Christmas, Passover), secular holidays (Thanksgiving, Fourth of July), and rites of passage (weddings, funerals, baptisms, bar mitzvahs) that call forth highly patterned, symbolically rich behaviors, behaviors often highly cherished by individual family members. Family traditions, although usually less culture-specific and more idiosyncratic, are also recurrent behaviors invested with specialness and meaning by the family. Here we include birthday traditions, family vacations, family reunions, and so on. Patterned routines, the least obvious family rituals, although comparable to daily routines, can be distinguished from this more general category because they are routines that also have been conciously imbued by family members with that sense of specialness that is a primary characteristic of ritualized behavior. Here we include such behaviors as bedtime and dinnertime rituals or leisure-time rituals.

Although all families practice such rituals, they differ dramatically in the importance rituals play in their lives, and in the extent to which celebrations versus traditions versus ritualized routines are practiced. Thus both *level of ritualization* and distribution of *areas of ritualization* differ from family to family.

Families also differ in the *degree of orthodoxy* with which they carry out their ritual behaviors. Orthodox or rigid families tolerate few if any deviations in their ritual practices. Role relationships in these families tend to be hierarchical, with parents in command, and expect all family members to follow the script scrupulously. In the least conventional families, by contrast, rituals are subject to modification or revision, even for inconsequential reasons. Role relationships tend to be egalitarian, and any member can make changes in the preparations for or the carrying out of a ritual; rituals deemed important in earlier years may be abandoned because of simple lack of interest. Finally, a third type of family has a more flexible stance towards its ritual life. In these families, the parental hierarchy is supported, but children gain power in the family as they mature. Rituals are valued, but variations on old themes are permitted, even encouraged, to the extent that they reflect or capitalize on changes in the family.

Thus comparisons of ritual behavior across families can be made along three dimensions: (1) the extent of ritual performance across family life (level of ritualization); (2) the rigidity of role performance and patterning of behavior during ritual enactment (ritual clarity); and (3) the conscious importance of the ritual to family members (intentionality).

Alcoholic Families, like families in general, evidence a broad range of ritual behaviors and quality of rituals. Hence they also show considerable variation in level of ritualization, clarity of ritual performance, and intentionality regarding ritual enactment. Thus these three dimensions are effective descriptors of differences between Alcoholic Families regarding ritual performance.

However, it is the dimension of intentionality that is particularly important for the Alcoholic Family. Alcoholism can easily disrupt the carrying out of family rituals. Holiday times, vacations, and similar times are susceptible to being undermined by the intrusion of alcoholic behavior or the need to accommodate an alcoholic member. Hence the family often has to work at preserving its rituals in order not to have them disrupted or taken over by alcoholism issues. *Intentionality* is another term for the family's resolve and persistence in preserving its rituals in the face of chronic alcoholism.

Short-Term Problem-Solving

The third category of observable regulatory behaviors is, of the three, the one that is most closely linked to family homeostasis. The core concept of family homeostasis is that families, as living systems, are able to preserve the constancy of their internal environments in the face of a highly inconstant external environment. How is this constancy actually maintained? One proposal is that the family activates complex behaviors whenever challenges to internal stability arise, behaviors that bring the family back into line. For example, two spouses initiate a period of intense sexual involvement following an extramarital affair on the part of one spouse—an affair supposedly carried out without the other's knowledge. As a second example, a husband increases his vigilance over his children following his wife's acknowledgement that she has been too restrictive with the children (an acknowledgement that her husband's prior criticism of her overprotectiveness is correct).

Many such behaviors can be imagined that have this self-correcting quality in reestablishing the stability of the family's internal environment. In fact, it has been postulated that a number of the striking aspects of family behavior vis-à-vis alcoholism have this goal at their core (Ewing and Fox, 1968). For example, a wife hosts her first large party following her husband's discharge from a residential alcoholism treatment program. At the party, alcohol is freely served ("our friends wouldn't understand if drinks weren't served; we can't ask them to stop drinking as well"). During the party, the husband tests his ability to have "just one drink," but by the evening's end is again quite drunk.

Many family therapists would see in the preceding sequence of behaviors an attempt to return the family to an alcoholic state—that the move toward sobriety, while welcomed, was also experienced as a destablilzing turn of events for the family. One way of conceptualizing such seemingly paradoxical family behavior is to think of it as an effort at problem-solving. That is, the threat to family stability is a "problem," and the reactive family behaviors in response to the challenge are the family's attempt at problem-solving. It is just such a situation we refer to when we talk about "short-term problem-solving strategies" as a form of regulatory behavior on the part of the family.

Because many problem-solving episodes occur in response to specific challenges to family stability, they are behaviors that are triggered only when challenges first occur. Thus problem-solving surfaces as a discrete set of behaviors; once stability has been restored, the behaviors again recede into the background. Thus two important behavioral characteristics of short-term problem-solving episodes are that they (1) are highly discrete, and (2) are focused, that is, they arise in response to a specific challenge.

However, family problem-solving strategies are not invented de novo each time a new challenge arises. Rather, the family, over time, develops a characteristic style of problem-solving, a style that is distinctive enough as to be recognizable by an outside observer—a kind of family trademark. If we attempted to describe this trademarked problem-solving style, we would find that three dimensions of family behavior are particularly useful descriptors of the stylistic differences to be found between families.

The first dimension is the degree of *stereotypy* of problem-solving behaviors. That is, how predictable is the family's response to destabilizing events? Are all such events lumped together, with the family always responding in a particular way, irrespective of the type of challenge? Or does the family employ different strategies for different types of problems? And once employed, how automatic is the sequencing of the behaviors that the family carries out in response to the problem? Do these behaviors unfold in a preprogrammed way, or are they modified in response to the parameters of the problem at hand?

The second dimension is the *affective expressiveness* associated with short-term problem-solving. For some families, heightened affect is used to alert the family that problem-solving behaviors must be activated; for example, intense verbal battles may be used as a prelude to getting down to business. Other families get very quiet whenever a serious problem is close at hand. In addition to activation of behavior, families also differ dramatically in the range and type of affective expressiveness that is tolerated while problem-solving is actually in progress.

The third dimension is the degree of *intrafamily cohesiveness* that occurs during problem-solving. In some families, all problems must be tackled by the family as a group. Each family member has a defined role, and the process unfolds in a highly coordinated fashion. A single view of the problem is achieved, and the family reacts as a single unit. In other families, members seem to approach the problem as individuals. Little attempt is made to work in a coordinated fashion. Rarely is there a conjoint discussion that might review family options for coping with the problem. Although in such situations the behavior of each family member might be highly predictable (e.g., father emotes, mother gets advice from friends, children become involved with schoolwork and seemingly ignore the problem), the family rarely works as a cohesive unit in the service of problem-solving.

The problem-solving styles of Alcoholic Families can be compared along the same three dimensions. That is, some Alcoholic Families are highly stereotypic in their response to problems; others vary their responses depending on the type of challenge they are facing. Some Alcoholic Families explode whenever a destabilizing event occurs; others become affectively flat and expressionless. Thus there is no single response style that is typical of Alcoholic Families.

However, two aspects of problem-solving in Alcoholic Families are distinctive and important to note. The first is the inordinate sensitivity to destabilization in these families. We have already noted that Alcoholic Families have "homeostats" that are inappropriately narrow in their settings. By this we mean that these families respond vigorously to any challenge to the status quo. Any event that destabilizes the family's internal environment provokes a strong response regardless of the event's real threat to the family. Thus one characteristic of problem-solving in the Alcoholic Family is that it is easily activated and often is disproportionately aggressive in relation to the magnitude of the problem at hand. This is one way in which a regulatory style leads to the behavioral rigidity typical of the Alcoholic Family.

The second aspect of problem-solving in Alcoholic Families is not only distinctive, it is truly unique to alcoholism. We noted above that all families have special behaviors that are activated as part of the problem-solving

FIGURE 3.5

Family Regulation of Behavior: A Summary

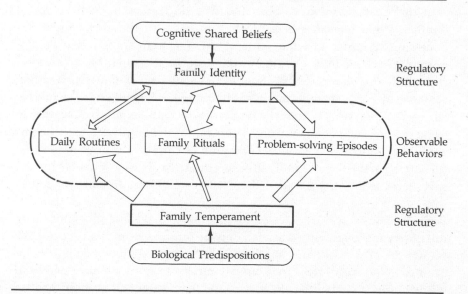

69

process. In many Alcoholic Families we find that a subset of these behaviors are only activated *in the presence of alcohol.* That is, they occur only when active drinking is also going on; they don't occur during sobriety. For example, the family's affective expressiveness increases dramatically when a member is in an intoxicated state and only at such a time. Thus if heightened affect is an important component of family problem-solving (as a mobilizer of other behaviors used by the family for this type of regulatory behavior), family problem-solving in such a family becomes inexorably linked to intoxication. That is, a unique feature of alcoholism is incorporated into family problem-solving strategies.

We call this aspect of behavior in the Alcoholic Family the *sobriety-intoxication cycle.* It is such an important aspect of life in the Alcoholic Family that we devote the whole of chapter 6 to it.

The Impact of Alcoholism on Regulatory Behaviors

Alcoholism has many profoundly negative consequences for families. Lost income, spouse and child abuse, public sanctions, deterioration of physical health, all immediately come to mind. But of even greater consequence is the impact of alcoholism on the two most fundamental systemic properties of families—regulatory processes, and family growth and development.

In this chapter, we have been focusing on regulation of behavior in families. What relevance does alcoholism have for these processes? We have already hinted at what some of these consequences might be. For example, we have indicated that alcoholism has the capacity to become a central identity issue for the family and that once families assume an alcoholic identity, alcoholism can easily become an organizing principle for all sorts of behaviors within the family. We have also pointed out that in some families temperamental characteristics of the family are highly compatible with the behavioral concomitants of chronic alcoholism and that these two parameters of family life merge together in a closely knit pattern that serves to encourage, rather than attenuate, the continuance of drinking.

Once again, however, we need to underscore that these phenomena are not observable ones, but rather can only be inferred from clinical data. We cannot directly assess the impact of alcoholism on family identity, for example. Nor, since we cannot directly measure family temperament, can we determine exactly how alcoholism and temperamental properties relate to each other. But we can assess regulatory behaviors. So our efforts at understanding how alcoholism affects regulatory processes in families should be directed at a close examination of the impact of alcoholism on observable regulatory behaviors. Thus although we cannot "see" how an alcoholic family identity develops, we can directly assess how family rituals are altered in the face of alcoholic behavior. In like fashion, demonstration of strong associative links between patterns of daily routines and patterns of drinking behavior helps us to understand the underlying phenomenon of alcoholism-temperament fit.

The key to an understanding of the impact of alcoholism on family regulatory processes is the concept of *invasion,* which can be explained as follows: Regulatory behaviors, although quite robust structures, can be shaped and altered by a large number of factors. For example, daily routines are strongly influenced by the work and school schedules of family members. Routines are also shaped by such factors as home architecture, family size, and neighborhood configurations. But if our construct of family temperament as a major determinant of daily routines is correct, the family will, to whatever extent possible, select jobs, homes, and neighborhoods that allow routines compatible with temperamental predispositions. If incompatibilities exist, unless the external factor is critical to the family, it will be given up or changed in favor of preserving patterns of daily routines. But if the family does not have a choice in the matter, the resulting clash of external factors and internal routines (and the necessity to alter routines) will create considerable internal family distress.

As a relatively straightforward example, imagine a family that has to contend with a work schedule that includes irregular daytime and nighttime shifts (e.g., that of an airline worker or a repairman for a utility company). For some families, such an alternating and irregular schedule is relatively innocuous, but for others, it creates such havoc with family routines and emotional stability that it leads to a showdown—"Either the job goes or I go!" Yet it is also possible that the family will substantially alter its routines to accommodate the demands of a job schedule. In such an instance, we say that the outside job has *invaded* this type of family regulatory behavior.

The relationship between alcoholism and family regulatory behaviors is quite comparable to the work-schedule example cited above. Alcoholism is also a powerful condition. The behaviors associated with drinking are often preemptive in that they overwhelm and push aside behaviors characteristic of the sober, nonalcoholic state. Faced with the very real demands of these behaviors, most families have the same three options noted in the above example. In option one, the specific vagaries caused by alcoholism faced by that particular family are by and large compatible with the patterns the family has already developed for regulating family life. Thus, at most, only minor changes are required and alcoholism does not pose a threat to regulatory processes. In option two, a fundamental incompatibility exists and the family asserts the primacy of its already established regulatory structures. In such instances, alcoholic behavior is directly challenged and regulatory behaviors are protected from the intrusive influence of alcoholism.

In the third option, however, the family's response is one of accommodation. Here regulatory behaviors are adjusted, altered, or completely restructured to prevent a showdown. Unsure of what the consequences of such a showdown might be, the family reactively adjusts its behaviors enough to reestablish internal stability. Although these adjustments might be quite subtle, over time the cumulative effect is that major alterations in regulatory behaviors have occurred. It is at this point that we can look back and say that alcoholism has *invaded* this most important aspect of family life. This is the situation that occurs in the Alcoholic Family. In fact, if we were to point to the one construct that most clearly encapsulates the notion of the Alcoholic Family (a family organized around alcoholism), it would be this construct of invasion of family regulatory behaviors by alcoholism.

The evidence that invasion of regulatory behaviors by alcoholism has occurred is somewhat different for each type of behavior. The most dramatic example is that of short-term problem-solving. Here the family actually compartmentalizes key aspects of problem-solving behaviors. Some aspects come to be associated with alcoholism to such an extent that they occur only when drinking is occurring. An example might be confrontational behavior that is an important component of the family's ability to protect itself from manipulation by outsiders.

This complex process, in which some behaviors are sobriety-linked and other intoxication-linked, is one of the most unusual concomitants of life in Alcoholic Families. Thus compartmentalization of behaviors tied to sobriety-intoxication cycling is the clearest evidence that alcoholism has invaded problem-solving behavior. (See chapter 6 for a complete discussion of this phenomenon.)

Invasion of daily routines takes on a somewhat different form. Here what seems to happen is that there is an amplification of those aspects of daily routines that are most compatible with the specific drinking pattern of the alcoholic member of the family. That is, routines are not necessarily invented out of whole cloth to accommodate alcoholism, but rather existing routines are skewed and adapted to fit more closely with drinking patterns and the consequences of alcoholism.

It is rare for the alcoholic member to change his or her drinking behavior to better mesh with family routines—but the reverse is quite common. Thus such behaviors as food preparation and mealtimes, social activities in the home, housekeeping, and the like are often arranged to minimize the likelihood of interference from alcoholism (or to minimally interfere with drinking behavior). (Chapter 7 reports the results of a study of home behavior in Alcoholic Families and amplifies on the above points.)

Finally, we have the invasion process in family rituals, a process that can lead to the effective disruption of these practices. Most commonly in this process, ritual behavior is altered to ensure that the alcoholic member can remain a full participant in the ritual. For example, the time and site of a Thanksgiving dinner may be changed from a relative's house to the family's own home so an intoxicated alcoholic family member can be brought downstairs to the dining room table for at least part of the dinner. Or a vacation plan may be altered so that travel is not too strenuous for the alcoholic member. The problem with such alterations in ritual behavior (which may at first glance seem minor) is that they may significantly diminish the important symbolic meaning of the ritual for the family. Alcoholic behavior has in this case taken precedence over the performance of the ritual. This disruption of an existing family ritual furthers the reinforcement of an Alcoholic Family identity. (Chapter 8 is devoted to a discussion of rituals in the Alcoholic Family.)

Thus for each type of regulatory behavior, invasion by alcohol takes a somewhat different form. But in each case, the regulatory behavior has been modified. And the direction of this modification is one that makes it more, rather than less, likely that alcoholism will continue to thrive. Hence the family system has been modified in a direction supportive of chronic alcoholism, and is now a system organized to maintain the constancy of its internal environment in the face of what was previously a destabilizing force—chronic alcoholism.

CHAPTER 4

Growth and Development in the Alcoholic Family

IN THIS CHAPTER we address *morphogenesis,* the second major component in our systems model. When family systems theorists talk about morphogenesis, they usually quickly move to a discussion of what has been called the *family life cycle.* However, most models of the family life cycle are in fact framed by the developmental history of individual members of the family. For example, attention is often paid to compositional factors (numbers and ages of children) in defining the different stages of the life cycle.

We attempt a very different approach. Instead of tying family development to the life cycle of individual family members, we propose a family life cycle built around the notion of systemic maturation. That is, we pay particular attention to those observable growth patterns that derive from the unique properties of families as behavioral systems. In effect, this approach creates a developmental model of *family-unit growth* (as opposed to a model that ties family growth and development solely to changes precipitated by individuals within the family).

In applying such a model of family growth and development to the Alcoholic Family, the most important question to ask is: In what ways is systemic maturation of families *altered* by the presence within the family of chronic alcoholism? Thus, we pay particular attention to those changes in the customary family life cycle (or *developmental distortions* as we term them) that typically occur when families organize their lives around chronic alcoholism as a core family identity issue. We therefore have two main tasks in this chapter: one, to lay out the fundamental principles of family growth; and two, to describe how alcoholism affects this growth process.

74

But first, we should perhaps ask an even more fundamental question: Is it correct to say that families "grow"? Individual growth and development is relatively easy to conceptualize and track. People are born, go through a clearly perceivable process of physical maturation followed by an equally definable period of aging, and finally die. Similarly, individual cognitive development can be traced through a series of stages (the Piagetian model), and aging here too has recognizable characteristics that are widely accepted. Models have also been proposed for describing the growth and development of morality, of ego functioning, and the like. Each of these models has led to the development of methods of systematically assessing properties associated with different stages of growth (e.g., performance tasks that measure whether cognitive stages have been reached), and the data generated by these procedures have buttressed the validity of the claims made by these models.

But how does one apply such standards to the family when one can't even clearly define when the family begins and ends. In fact, terms like *birth* and *death* make little sense when applied to families. If anything, family development is circular. That is, families are multigenerational systems. Continuity is ensured by the fact that individuals are simultaneously children in their families or origin and "founders" of their own families of procreation. Marriage—the typical "starting point" for the family—is merely a starting point of convenience, a punctuation mark that artificially separates one generation from another.

Take, for example, the important growth issue of the transmission of family identity issues across generations. The "newly formed" family struggles to define its unique identity as a family. But against what standard? Usually against the legacies handed down by its two families of origin. And what of these families of origin? Aren't they at the same time struggling with what they wish to transmit, as a legacy, to future generations? Is transmission an internal process, or is it one that occurs across the synapse dividing the old family from the new? This is hard to say, since at least some of the actors in the drama are members of both systems. Is the transmission of alcoholism, for example, more correctly viewed as a late-phase developmental phenomenon in the life of Family 1, or as an early-phase phenomenon in the life of Family 2? Obviously neither answer is by itself correct.

Why underscore these points? Because although discussions of family development borrow heavily from constructs and models used to describe individual development—especially the construct of the life cycle—one must keep in mind that the resulting models of family development arise from *observer-imposed punctuations* of what is in fact a continuous and circular process. Since this book is divided into three sections intended to focus on three developmental phases in the life cycle of the Alcoholic Family, we are clearly guilty as well of using this artificial punctuation method. But as long as the reader keeps in mind, for example, that families described as struggling with early-phase issues (the focus of chapter 5) could as easily be discussed as dealing with late-phase issues (and hence, relegated to chapters 9 and 10) by simply altering the perspective to that of the older generation, then the risk of misreading our intent should be minimized.

Change versus Growth

Concepts about family development can be roughly divided into two groups: those that focus on *change,* and those that focus on *growth.* Although often used interchangeably, the terms change and growth in fact address two different aspects of development.

Change is a term that can be used to describe *any* alteration in the systemic organization of the family. Most often it is thought of as a systemic response to an event or process that temporarily disrupts family homeostasis. That is, it is a response to a challenge of sufficient magnitude to disrupt internal family stability. The challenge might be an externally generated crisis (a job loss, an accidental death, a school closing, an unanticipated job opportunity requiring relocation); or an event generated by a process internal to the family (a physical illness, an extramarital affair, psychiatric symptomatology in a child, a breakdown in role functioning). Irrespective of its source, however, the crisis evokes a characteristic family response aimed at restabilization of the family's internal environment.

For many families, such crises lead to changes that yield major benefits for the family. The ability to successfully tackle the crisis increases the family's cohesiveness and self-confidence. But not all families resolve crises successfully. Many times, solutions are nothing more than compromises between family pressures to stay the same versus the need to change. Alcoholic Families often handle crises in just such a fashion, and the compromises they arrive at result in compromised lives. It is also possible for crises to overwhelm family resources and functional capacities. Many a family has failed to survive an alcoholic crisis, a crisis that has effectively led to a disintegration of the family. (For a thorough discussion of the relationship between crisis, regression, and family change, see Reiss, 1981.)

Another term we might use to describe these destabilization-restabilization cycles is *oscillations* (as in swings of an electrical current).* This is the term we prefer for designating such developmental events in family life. *Change* is thus a general term applicable whenever oscillations in the status quo occur at such a frequency or magnitude as to force on the family a fundamental systemic reorganization (as opposed to a minor correction that merely restabilizes and returns the family to its previous position).

Growth, on the other hand, is a term that should be reserved for a *predictable* type of change. It is a pattern of change that has a recognizable framework, a characteristic sequential order, a typical time course. Further, such predictable sequential changes in family organizational and behavioral characteristics happen because families, as living systems, are subject to certain built-in developmental pressures. Most fundamental among these development pressures is the need to either "grow or die."

That is, because of the biological constraints of its members, families must either periodically expand (add new members) or fade into memory. Thus family development can be seen to be divided into alternating cycles of systemic expansions interspersed by periods of systemic consolidation, perhaps best represented as a sine curve alternating between phases of expansion and phases of consolidation.

Further, this scheme also suggests that family development is shaped by the sequential cycling between periods of high systemic oscillation (expansion phases) and extended periods of low systemic oscillation (consolidation phases). Although individual variation in this cycling may be considerable, a normative pattern can be identified and aberrant growth patterns therefore clearly spotted when they are occurring. As already noted, in discussing family development (growth), this recognizable framework has been called the *family life cycle.*

The Structure of the Family Life Cycle

The concept of the family life cycle was first suggested by sociologists Evelyn Duvall and Reuben Hill in the late 1940s. They attempted to apply to families the then novel "psychosocial" developmental model being

---

*Breunlin (in press) has proposed that oscillation theory is so rich a model that it can be used as the primary framework for understanding family development.

proposed by Erik Erikson (1950) for individuals. Eriksonian concepts of development remain central to all subsequent versions of the family life cycle as well (including the Family Life History [FLH] version of the family life cycle). Five concepts have been particularly pertinent: (1) an epigenetic orientation; (2) sequential developmental staging; (3) specific developmental tasks associated with each stage; (4) characteristic transitional periods initiated by expectable developmental crises; and (5) the concept of regression as a universal behavioral phenomenon during times of developmental transition.

All family systems theorists are also in agreement about one further aspect of family development. Family growth occurs in fits and starts. That is, the shape of the developmental curve is one of briefer periods of intense activity and change interspersed by longer periods of normalization and stability. But agreement stops there. Beyond this one small area of confluence lies a panoply of life cycle models based on very different views of the forces that drive family development.

The FLH model takes a clear-cut position with regard to the structure of the family life cycle. Its basic premise is that a life cycle model should be constructed around those *systemic properties* that are common to development in all families. What are these common properties? Family development is always at its core a continuous process in which periods of systemic expansion are interspersed by less-turbulent periods of systemic consolidation. New families are formed, mature, and in turn participate in the creation of yet another generation of new families (unless systemic expansion fails to occur and the family line dies out).

Expansion-consolidation cycles come in two very different forms. In one form, the expansion is explosive, as an entirely new family unit is created and splits off from existing units. Marriage is the clearest example here. In the second form, the expansion is more modest in scope, is internal to a single family unit, and does not lead to the creation of an additional family unit. Birth of children is an example of this second type of expansion. We will subsequently be referring to these two types of cycles as *phases* versus *stages* of family growth.

Authors of many family life cycle schema have constructed their models of family development solely around stages of family growth. Births of children, developmental level of oldest children, and the like are invoked as core stimuli, and family life cycle stages are built around such events. The original life cycle scheme proposed by Hill and Duvall (see Hill and Rodgers, 1964) was based entirely on such criteria in delineating stages of development. Subsequent schema proposed by family clinicians (e.g.,

Carter and McGoldrick, 1980; Haley, 1973) are also heavily dependent on such individually based criteria. But more often than not, these parameters prove to be highly idiosyncratic from family to family and others of only limited applicability.

The FLH version of the family life cycle, in contrast, sees family growth as responsive to (shaped by) two very different types of changes. The first are changes that are stimulated by systemic properties of the *family as a unit.* The second are changes that are stimulated by properties attributable to *individual family members.*

An example of a family-unit change is the need for the family to differentiate itself from the families of origin that spawned it. It is only if this task is successfully negotiated that the new family is able to present itself as a distinctive system (rather than a simple extension of an already existing system). Without having undertaken the task of defining itself in this way (a sort of bounding of itself in space), the new family simply doesn't exist as a distinct entity. This task is therefore an essential one if the family is to be perceived (and to perceive itself) as a unit with its own identity and functional integrity.

By way of contrast, an example of an individual-unit change is the alteration in family priorities and role distributions that occurs in families as children move into adolescence. Since this change is dependent on the family having adolescent members, it is one that some families will experience, and others will not.

Developmental tasks tied to family-unit change are, we would argue, universal ones. That is, because these tasks emanate from changes induced by properties of the family as a system, they are axiomatically challenges experienced by all family systems. It should therefore be possible to describe a family life cycle common to all families that is centered on the sequential (epigenetic) emergence of these family-unit developmental tasks. In fact, this is exactly the approach we take. In our model, this family-level developmental time line is called the *systemic maturation* time line.

Developmental tasks tied to individual-unit changes, by way of contrast, are far from universal. These tasks clearly vary greatly from family to family depending on (1) the age and composition of individual family members, and (2) the unique properties and experiences that these individuals bring to the family. That age and composition of family members would dictate a different series of developmental tasks should be self-evident. This premise is, in fact, the basis on which traditional versions of the family life cycle are constructed (e.g., Hill and Rodgers, 1964). That unique properties and experiences of individual family members also lead to wide variation in developmental tasks may not be quite as self-evident, but on reflection should also be easy to grasp.

For example, consider a family in which a child early on demonstrates a unique athletic talent in swimming. If such a family decides to subsidize this talent, a series of tasks inevitably arise having to do with allocation of time and financial resources, establishment of shared values regarding the primacy of supporting this child's athletic aspirations, and so on. Or take a family in which a serious chronic illness emerges and the family decides to reorganize itself in order to provide the best possible rehabilitative care for this chronically ill member. Or, to bring it closer to home, what about the family that has a chronic alcoholic member. Here too, the unique demands of this chronic behavioral disorder force upon the family a set of tasks and decisions that are simply not comparable to those arising out of family-unit developmental changes.

Thus the major difference between family-unit and individual-unit developmental changes is that in the latter, the family change that occurs is in response to pressures generated by individual family members, not from pressures emanating from the process of systemic maturation. Thus these family changes, even though they surely occur, are not changes instigated by the family. Rather, they are *reactive* changes that occur because the family is undergoing a process of accommodation and reorganization in the face of challenges presented to it by its individual members. This is an issue we will be returning to at a later point in this chapter.

Family-Unit Developmental Tasks

Although each family has many unique features that color and shape its course of development, all families must deal with three fundamental issues:

1. All families must define their external and internal boundaries. Every family must delimit where the natural borders of the family end and how the internal structure of the family is to be constructed. This issue is basically one of family membership—these are the people who are in our family; those other people are not in our family. Defining external boundaries includes both differentiating nuclear from extended family and drawing the outer boundaries around the extended family. Defining internal boundaries includes adding and losing core members (children, spouses,

siblings, grandparents) and altering the relationships between family sub-systems as the cast of characters and ages of family members change.

2. All families must choose a limited number of major developmental themes. These themes are the priority areas to which the family is committed. No family can encompass the full range of options available to it; some selection process has to occur. These developmental themes, in turn, become organizers for behavior within the family. Not only are internal and external relationships shaped by these major life themes; so too are family decisions about allocations of important family resources—money, time, space, and so on. Not all families develop consistent life themes that continue over decades. Instead, many families jump from one issue to another as they move along in their life history. When families behave in this manner, however, their life histories have a peripatetic quality that itself tells us much about what life must be like within them. Of particular importance to us here is the recognition that alcoholism can become one of the major developmental themes for the family. In fact, it is the organization of family life around alcoholism as a major developmental life theme that is one of the cardinal features of the Alcoholic Family.

3. Finally, all families must eventually develop a set of shared values and views, values and views not only about the world in which they live, but also about what kind of family they are. This shared sense of the family is a characteristic we have previously called *family identity* (see chapter 3). Although we defined family identity as one of the deep regulatory structures in the family system, it has a developmental component as well. Not only is family identity itself constantly evolving as the family grows, but it also plays a role at times of developmental transitions, a role that we will be spelling out in detail below.

Although all families must take on the three major developmental tasks outlined above—definition of boundaries, selection of major developmental themes, and evolution of shared values and views of the world—families are not always tackling all three issues with equal vigor. Rather, each of these developmental issues has its own natural history (see table 4.1). There are periods of time when a particular issue is predominant and absorbing of the bulk of family time and effort. At a later point in development, the same issue might have receded into the background. It is not that the issue is no longer relevant, but merely that another issue is the dominant one at that particular phase of development.

For example, the issue of boundary definition is predominant at the earliest stage of family development. A newly formed family has broken off from two (or more) separate families of origin. Previously, members of these two families of origin had free access to the one spouse who was also

TABLE 4.1

Changing Importance of Family Tasks at Different Phases

Family Tasks	Developmental Phases		
	Early	Middle	Late
Emphasis on Boundary Definition	+++++	++	+++
Thematic Specialization	+	+++++	++
Clarification of Shared Beliefs	+++	+	+++++

a member of that particular family. Now that degree of access has to be redefined. Does one have to make an appointment to visit the new home, or is it okay to drop in at any time. Is the new family intending to develop its own ways of celebrating holidays and planning vacations, or will it be attempting to accomodate the rules and regulations of both families of origin.

Each of these decisions helps define the structure and permeability of this newly formed family's external boundaries. This process, this natural evolution of a family, is part and parcel of its systemic properties. For the family to establish itself as a separate entity, it must first tackle the developmental tasks associated with boundary definition. Until its boundaries are firmly established, it will be constantly susceptible to a re-merging process with one or both families of origin. It simply will neither treat itself or be treated by others as a separate entity.

Although these new boundaries may continue to be tested for some time by both families of origin, once it is clear that the new family has taken firm charge of delimiting its boundaries, this developmental issue loses much of its punch and immediacy. Thus, although a milder version of boundary testing may always be present, and boundaries will continue to be redrawn as the cast of characters changes, for the maturing family a different set of issues moves to the fore.

Instead of focusing primary attention on boundary definition, the maturing family now takes on a more sophisticated form as it turns its attention to selecting a limited number of life themes as it begins to specialize as a behavioral system. If this delimiting process does not now occur, the family will remain at its current organizational level. It will not move ahead to a more complex organizational state, a more highly differentiated state. In systems terms, morphogenesis will flatten out at that point.

Let us step back and focus for a moment on the two-step process outlined above. Three key points have already been made about family development: First, there is a logical and invariate sequencing pattern in which an emphasis on boundary definition must preceed an emphasis on areas of developmental specialization as the family moves along its developmental time line. Second, the nature of the tasks involved are universal and must be tackled by all families regardless of their compositional characteristics, cultural backgrounds, and so on. And third, the relative emphasis placed on each of the three major groups of developmental tasks also changes in predictable fashion as the family proceeds down its developmental path (see table 4.1).

This last factor, when combined with the other two, suggests that the overall shape of the family life cycle can be best perceived if one tracks the natural ebbs and flows of the family's differential attention to the three categories of developmental issues outlined above. The shape or "time line" that emerges has all the characteristics associated with the classical Eriksonian model of development. Not only are a series of critical developmental tasks identified, but these tasks are of differential importance at different points in development. Further, one can discern a series of developmental stages—each characterized by the unique blend of tasks that occur at this phase of development—that build one atop another in an invariate sequential order (an epigenetic order).

What is most important about this time line, however, is that it addresses developmental properties of the family as a system. It is for this reason that it is a *universal* developmental time line. And hence it is also the most fundamental and important time line in family development. Because this time line takes its shape from the unfolding emergence of tasks associated with systemic properties of the family, we will be calling it the "systemic maturation" time line.

The Systemic Maturation (Family-Unit) Time Line

Systemic maturation is a process that takes its shape from the evolving and changing nature of interpersonal relationships within the family. Although systemic maturation is a continuous process, it can be conveniently demarcated into three separate phases.

In the *earliest phase* of development (an expansion phase), boundaries are established in response to the rules set down for the way various family members are to relate to each other and to their families of origin. Later on, during a *middle phase* (a consolidation phase), the thematic options selected by the family are highly responsive to the types of relationships that have by now been established among its members. In one family, spouses might have an egalitarian relationship in which a dual set of careers naturally evolves. In another family, the primacy of parental behaviors might be confluent with the emergence of child rearing as a major developmental theme. Finally, in its fully mature *late phase* (also an expansion phase), the family becomes future-oriented. Attention changes from a focus on selection of thematic options, an establishing of developmental priorities, to a focus on the family's "place in history."

Family relationships thus move through an aging process highly analogous to biological aging in individuals. Roughly speaking, the maturational phases in this relational aging process are (1) an attachment phase; (2) a stabilization phase; and (3) a loss phase. The analogous biological phases are that of rapid growth, adult maturation, and senescence. The crucial difference in families, however, is that intergenerational relationships overlap. That is, most individuals are at least at one time in their lives simultaneously members of two overlapping families. It is this factor that introduces a unique dynamic to the course of family development.

It is also for this reason that the phases of systemic maturation are best described not only in biological terms (aging), but also in psychological (cognitive) terms. Thus the early phase of systemic maturation should be thought of not only as an attachment phase, but also as one dominated by the establishment of a unique family identity. The middle phase is not only a phase of stabilization; it is also a phase of relational commitment. Finally, the late phase is a phase of identity clarification and transmission as well as one of major losses.

There is a close analogy between this systemic maturation model of family development, and our earlier model of systemic regulation in families. The latter postulated the existence of two deep regulatory structures (family temperament and family identity) that together serve as "homeostats" establishing guidelines for the regulation of family life. Family temperament was conceived of as a biological construct; family identity was conceived of as a cognitive construct. The second major postulate was that these regulatory guidelines were most clearly perceived (and in turn reinforced) by three categories of observable regulatory behaviors (daily routines, family rituals, and short-term problem-solving styles).

The model of systemic maturation postulates that family development also is shaped by underlying dynamic forces—forces associated with the natural evolutionary process of relational aging in the family. And here as well, these fundamental processes are conceptualized as existing in two different domains—one primarily biological; the other primarily cognitive. Further, these processes are best observed by tracking the family's attention to three surface-level developmental issues (boundary definition; developmental themes; evolution of shared beliefs).

Systemic maturation is a process that unfolds in the same invariate sequential order for all families (albeit at often highly variable rates). That is, whatever the ages of the participants, the family they create follows the same systemic maturation time line. When two people in their fifties get married, the family they create is just as "young" a family as one formed by two twenty-year-olds. The wisdom these middle-aged spouses bring to their relationship may help them to tackle developmental issues associated with the earliest phase of systemic maturation in a more efficient fashion, but the issues will be the same ones for both marriages. Whether fifty or twenty, the need for boundary definition will take primacy over all other issues. The boundaries for the fifty-year-olds may have to be drawn between the new marriage and their ex-spouses (rather than between newlyweds and parents), but the tasks are essentially comparable.

Growth and development in families entails ever-increasing degrees of organizational complexity. Looked at from the other direction, this means that in order for families to mature as systems, they must have the necessary degree of complexity (functional capacity, communicational sophistication, and so on) to sustain this growth. Since systemic maturation is, at its core, most highly dependent on the nature of evolving relationships within the family, the more complex and sophisticated the nature of these relationships, the greater the capacity of the system to sustain a high degree of specialization. The more primitive and basic the types of relationships established within the family, the more basic and undifferentiated the family is likely to be developmentally.

Since alcoholism is a highly complex condition, a family that organizes itself around alcoholism as a major life theme is likely to have established a sophisticated set of internal and external relationships to support this life theme. Thus within this view of family development, the Alcoholic Family is one that has reached a high level of systemic complexity—it is surely not a primitive way for family development to proceed.

The Three Phases of Systemic Maturation

The Early Phase: Establishing Boundaries and Identity Formation

Normative Families. The early phase of family development is in many ways the most dynamic and exciting phase in a family's life. Not only is there the feeling of starting off fresh, but it is a time of intense activity and rapid change. Most families begin this phase with a sense of optimism about the future and their ability to tackle whatever will come their way. No matter whether it is a family of young newlyweds, a blended family, or a second marriage of aging spouses, at no other time in family development does day-to-day life bring with it so many new questions to be answered and so many new perspectives. For this is the time when the family must work to establish the limits of its systemic boundaries and the nature of its shared rules and belief systems.

Irrespective of family type, the critical developmental issues for all early-phase families is the need to establish a structure and identity as an independent, freestanding system. No matter what the compositional characteristics of this new family might be, its members will have come from at least two different families of origin, families that have their own ideas about how life should be lived. It is this fundamental dynamic—the tensions and exchanges occurring between multiple and overlapping family systems—that makes this phase of development so exciting and vibrant. At no other time in the life cycle are internal systemic oscillations so intense; at no other time do the stakes seem so high. For the issue at hand is nothing less than the ability of the new family to survive as a fully independent unit, distinct from its families of origin. Juxtaposed against this developmental imperative, is the desire of both families of origin to keep the new family closely bound and loyal to the old family identity.

Although much effort is being expended during this phase in the service of establishing basic rules for family functioning (distribution of tasks, allocation of space, rules for sexual behavior, rules regarding external friendships) the crucial issue is what to do about the two families of origin. Each member of an early-phase family has recently been a major participant in a family of origin that had its own rules for behavior and its own set of developmental themes and priorities. The sense of loyalty to this prior family varies widely among individuals. One person might feel a great sense of affection and loyalty toward his or her origin family. This sense of loyalty might take the form of a desire to continue, in the newly formed family, important characteristics of the origin family. Another person might hold very different sentiments. She or he might decide to establish a new family that is as different from the origin family as can be imagined.

The excitement of the early phase comes in part from the inventive ways families devise to play out the struggle over their emerging identities. In some families, the issue might be dramatically enacted around "visitation rules." For young newlyweds, this term translates into a set of rules about how often and with what advance notice visits by parents are to be permitted. For a blended family, the struggle might occur over custody arrangements.

In other families, distribution of space in the home and decorating of the house might be the metaphorical issues that stir up the most intense battles. Should the wedding gift from a favorite aunt be given a prominent place in the living room, or should it be relegated to the closet because it simply "isn't our taste"? Is it important that each child in a blended family gets his or her own room, or should they double up? And if they are to be mixed up, what rules should be used to determine the combinations— should full siblings be kept together to reflect the primacy of the old family identity over the new, or should they be separated to instill in them, right from the start, the idea that this new family will have its own ways of doing things?

As these examples immediately convey, the all too familiar struggles of the early-phase family are, at bottom, struggles to establish boundaries. Many of the struggles involve the structuring of internal boundaries— relationships between children in a blended family; spousal relationships of young newlyweds. But even when the focus is on the internal organization of the family, the underlying issue is the establishing of boundaries between the new family and families of origin. In each case, the question is, what aspects of one or the other family of origin will be replicated in the newly formed family. The rules governing spousal relationships is as convenient a vehicle for addressing this issue as is the subject of visits by parents. That is, one way of ensuring the continuance of the shared beliefs of a particular origin family is to establish in the new family the same type of marriage as the one one's parents have had.

Often the behavior of family members at this time seems contradictory. One might find, for example, that a young couple blows up when parents suggest a visit, but this same couple is lovingly reproducing dinnertime rituals that they associate with these same parents and assigning work within the home in just the same way as their parents did. Yet, these seemingly paradoxical behaviors are, in fact, not at all incompatible. The couple is merely choosing certain behaviors as vehicles for establishing delimited boundaries around the young marriage (parental visits), while at the same time allowing continuity of identity issues from families of origin to be expressed via other behaviors (dinnertime rituals). Both goals are important ones for the early-phase family; hence both must be addressed if the family is to successfully negotiate this phase of development.

Alcoholic Families. What about the early phase of development in the Alcoholic Family? Do these families face a different set of developmental issues? Does alcoholism impose a unique set of developmental demands on them? The answer is no. The developmental tasks of the early phase of family systemic maturation are universal ones. However, the introduction of alcoholism carries with it important implications for the process of identity formation during the early phase. These factors may also considerably heighten the tensions existing between families of origin and the new family, tensions that are played out around boundary formation during the early phase.

Whenever alcoholism surfaces in a family, one of the crucial decisions the family must make is whether to challenge this behavior or to accommodate to it. Although it is not necessary that this decision be a conscious one on the family's part, if the family chooses the accommodation route, it is highly likely, as mentioned earlier, that alcoholism will ultimately become a central organizing principle for family life. That is, that alcohol will be incorporated into the family's emerging identity.

The struggles that go on in early-phase families around alcohol often have well antedated the actual formation of the new family. Many children growing up in Alcoholic Families come to their own marriages with firm ideas about whether or not alcoholism will be tolerated in them. A major factor in mate selection may well be whether or not there is evidence of alcoholism in the intended spouse (alcoholism here may mean either active drinking on the spouse's part or a history of alcoholism in the spouse's family of origin). On the other hand, many children of alcoholics seem totally obtuse regarding early signs of alcoholism in an intended spouse.

Since alcoholism is a familial condition with a likely genetic predisposition, the seeds of a future alcoholic identity were often being sown in a family of origin that is itself an Alcoholic Family. How important a child from such a family considers establishment of a nonalcoholic identity in his or her own family is likely to be a major factor both in the mate-selection process and in the way identity issues are approached during the early phase.

The Middle Phase: Commitment And Stability

Normative Families. The middle phase of family development is a time of orderly consolidation. It is characterized by the emergence of three features. The first is the commitment to a finite number of central organizational themes for family life. After a process of delicate and often torturous early-phase negotiations between individual members of the family, each of whom has been an advocate for differing developmental priorities, a commitment is made to a finite number of options that collectively represent the family's emergent sense of direction. Of equal importance, the family has specifically ruled out alternative options that, however enticing, are not to be part of its life. The central themes of family life are now in place. Although alterations can always be made and some options even discarded in the future if they prove dissatisfying, for the time being the family has made a commitment. The time of exploration of options has been replaced by a sense of purpose, of organizational behavior, of regularity to life.

The second characteristic of the middle phase of development is the commitment to a set of stable and consistent rules regarding role behavior and relationships within the family. Consistency here does not necessarily mean rigidity. The family may decide that flexible role performance regarding work, child rearing, responsibility for social relationships, and so forth, is preferable to stereotyped and inflexible role assignments. But the key, once again, is that a commitment has been made; the family has made a choice.

The third feature of the middle phase is the emergence of a set of repetitive and highly structured behavioral programs for organizing the family's daily routines, special events (holidays, vacations, and the like), and strategies for solving the myriad problems of daily living that come up in family life. These behavioral programs provide structure and coherence to family life. But they also serve another critical function—they reinforce and conserve (through repetitive performance) the underlying commitments and rules the family has established as part of its movement into the middle phase of development. In this sense, these behaviors also serve a regulatory function for the family.

Although the middle phase of family development varies a great deal from family to family—for one family it will be a phase of tremendous richness, accomplishment, and exciting new adventures; for another it will represent the dashing of fondly held dreams, or a period characterized by boredom and the tyranny of daily routines—the middle phase of family development only occurs once a family has made its commitment to a finite set of options. The family that still feels adrift in its physical environment; that feels that a decision about whether or not to have children is "premature at this time"; that feels that no lasting occupational commitments have been made; that continues to fight with families of origin over holiday arrangements; frequency and formality/informality of contacts; that still takes a "wait and see" attitude about whether the marriage is working out—this is a family still in its early phase of development.

The middle phase of development is characteristically the longest phase in the family life cycle. During this time, the overall pace of change slows. In contrast to the high-oscillation quality of the expansionist early phase, the middle phase is dominated by regulatory, rather than growth, forces. Hence it is during this phase that observable regulatory behaviors—daily routines, family rituals, short-term problem-solving strategies—are most prominent. In some families, they dominate life to such a degree as to effectively freeze the development of relationships within the family. In other families, although still preeminent, they may nevertheless be flexibly exercised, thereby allowing ample room for the continuation of orderly growth within the family.

Alcoholic Families.   The key to an understanding of middle-phase development in the Alcoholic Family is what happens to family regulatory behaviors in these families. As has been previously discussed in chapter 3, one of the major impacts chronic alcoholism has on family life is its capacity to *invade* family regulatory behaviors. The most dramatic example here is what happens when behaviors associated with intoxication become incorporated in family short-term problem-solving strategies. However, the willingness of families to alter ritual behavior to accommodate an alcoholic family member is an equally clear-cut example of this invasion process. Similarly, the insidious organization of daily routines around the temporal characteristics of a drinking pattern shows that routines can also be invaded by alcoholism.

Thus the powerful impact of alcoholism on middle-phase regulatory behaviors can be seen in each of the types of behaviors we have highlighted in the FLH model. Further, in each instance, the invasion process leads to a fundamental alteration of these behaviors in the direction of an amplification of alcoholism-compatible aspects of the behaviors, and a comparable downplaying of alcoholism-incompatible features. The likely outcome of this skewing of regulatory behaviors is a *reinforcement* of alcoholic behaviors.

This is not to say that the middle-phase Alcoholic Family consciously intends to reinforce the drinking behavior of its alcoholic member. Most probably the family would vigorously deny such an intent, were it asked about it directly. But because the invasion process occurs slowly, with the family making its accommodations to alcoholism one small increment at a time, it is only after substantial changes have already occurred and are firmly in place that the distance the family has traveled is readily apparent. However, the cumulative effect is nevertheless a powerful one—family regulatory behaviors now actually play a major role in *maintaining* chronic alcoholic behavior.

As this invasion of regulatory behaviors takes hold, the middle-phase Alcoholic Family also becomes developmentally more rigid. The family is now organized to blunt the destabilizing impact of alcoholism, but it also acts to blunt *any* potentially destabilizing event in family life. Included here are the normative developmental oscillations associated with individual-unit change that we have already said are part and parcel of middle-phase family life.

Thus, in the Alcoholic Family, such normative developmental issues as individual growth (say the movement into adolescence, or career changes) get very short shrift. More often than not, they are simply ignored as a family-level issue, leaving family members to fend for themselves. Hence the reports of the overwhelming sense of ennui and emotional distance reported by individuals growing up in such families. And even when attended to, these normative developmental pressures are actively *combated* and stifled, rather than being perceived as healthy challenges to growth.

The Late Phase: Clarification and Legacy

Normative Family Development. The late phase of family development can be best characterized as one in which the family's focus gradually shifts from the present to the future. During the middle phase, day-to-day decision making, daily routines, holidays, and vacations dominate family life. The major markers of shifts in family organization are stimulated by those micro-expansions generated by the addition of new family members, relocations to new homes, shifts in work settings, and attendant routines associated with new jobs. These micro-oscillations in family life are in turn followed by periods of restabilization, and the family then moves on at this new organizational level. Sometimes the family experiences life during the middle phase as tumultuous, but more often than not life seems quite stable and predictable. Although the family organizes its life around a series of major life themes, these themes are often background phenomena. Identity issues are more implicit than explicit during this phase.

Toward the end of the middle phase, two challenges characteristically arise that serve to disrupt the customary coherence and stability of middle-phase life. The first challenge is the confluence of an uncharacteristically large number of losses experienced by the family. These losses include not only the physical loss of important family members—grandparents dying; parents becoming fragile; children leaving the family to start new families of their own—but also changes such as retirement or decrement of productivity at work that represent losses for the people involved. The second challenge comes not from losses suffered by the family, but from a series of new gains. At the same time that the family is struggling with losses, it is also being challenged by the pressure of new members and new ideas. For example, children's new friends and romantic involvements bring with them different perspectives and values. Family members are often lobbying intensely to have these new ideas incorporated into family customs, values, and developmental priorities.

As these pressures begin to mount, they increasingly strain the ability of family regulatory behaviors to maintain stability. The family's internal environment begins to show cracks and family boundaries start to leak at the edges. Faced with these mounting pressures, the family tends to fight back, most commonly by reinforcing existing behaviors. This is a behavioral response that strategic family therapists have called "more of the same." This response style, a sort of bullying of family members to get everyone to toe the line and relinquish their desires for changes in family behavior, often works quite effectively. When this is the case, the family is able to restabilize at its old organizational level, and the middle phase of development then proceeds apace. But this response style comes with a large price tag appended; the more successful the family is in neutralizing the developmental pressures generated by the above losses and additions, the more likely a developmental rigidity will set in and effectively freeze the family in time.

A second, more adaptive response to these developmental pressures is a gradual movement onto a new developmental level, a level we are calling the late phase of development. The most telling characteristic of this movement into late phase is the family's increasing focus on what we will call its "place in history." For it is at this point in its life cycle that the family must either expand and multiply or face the very real possibility that it will fade into oblivion. Once again a concern with a redefinition of family boundaries becomes a high-priority developmental issue. But an even more compelling issue is the renewed interest in family identity.

Family identity was also a very important issue during the early phase of development. But at that time, the central issue was the need to define those ways in which the newly formed family was *different* from its two families of origin. Now, as the family moves into the late phase of development, the focus is on *commonality* rather than uniqueness. The primary goal is to cull out of all the rules, values, and so on that make up the family's shared perception of its identity, those aspects that are most central, most clearly representative of the *essence* of the family as a group.

Why is this process so important at this phase of development? It is because the central developmental issue facing the family is the preservation of its identity. If the family system is to survive this next macroexpansion phase, it must clone on to the next generation an accurate representation of itself and its values. It must be able, after the next family generation has been split off, to see itself clearly reflected in this new family. A good metaphor for this process is the notion of a *family legacy,* a sort of time capsule into which the family places those items that, *in condensed form,* most clearly convey to future generations the essence of the present family.

A two-step process is involved. As a first step, the family must identify what it wants to convey. As a second step, it must somehow transmit this condensed package of themes, values, and rules to the next generation. The first step is therefore one of *distillation* and *clarification* of core aspects of family identity. The second step is the *transmission* of this condensed version of the family's identity to the next generation.

The process of identity clarification requires that during the late phase, what had previously been implicit in family life, now become explicit. What had previously gone unspoken, is now shouted out to any and all who will listen. Behaviors that previously had been carried out in relatively automatic fashion, are now talked about and defined in great detail before being carried out. For example, a holiday ritual that during the middle phase could be enacted "with our eyes closed," must now be made very explicit. Family members now talk openly about the aspects of the ritual that must be preserved or else "it just won't be Christmas." Previously all family members trusted each other to be on the same wavelength and to therefore know exactly what to do.

One might analogize the process to that of making out a will. When one first makes a will, the primary interest is the preservation of a legacy, a legacy that surely includes financial assets, but also includes instructions about important symbolic possessions, and about how the next-generation family should be constructed (who gets the money is often a statement about how the legacy is to be used to preserve important family characteristics).

Anyone who has gone through the process knows that the first version of a will is often a relatively rough and undifferentiated version of how to distribute assets. Subsequent versions have to be drafted to reflect the increasingly sophisticated sense of legacy that evolves over the years. In like fashion, the emergence of a family will is a process that may extend over many years. It may go through multiple revisions as the clarification process unfolds. An initial try at drafting such a will might occur when the oldest child in the family first leaves home, but subsequent events might convince the family that it doesn't yet have it "exactly right." So additional work has to be done to refine and further clarify those aspects of family identity that are to go into the will. Thus, as with other phases of systemic maturation, the late phase is not a static one.

Alcoholic Families. How are late-phase developmental issues played out in the Alcoholic Family? The first issue—that of identity clarification and *distillation*—in the Alcoholic Family becomes the question of whether the family's alcoholic identity is to be one of the items put in the time capsule; whether an alcoholic identity is to be a part of the family's legacy to future generations. Throughout the middle phase, the family has been repeatedly tested regarding the strength of its commitment to alcoholism as an organizing principle for family life. There have most likely been medical crises, job-related crises, and the like, crises that force upon the family a decision about whether to work toward sobriety or whether to allow these other problems to fester in the service of maintaining an alcoholic life. (Remember, these decisions are not necessarily conscious ones.) From time to time, children and extended family members have also been attempting to pressure the family to move toward sobriety. But these pressures, these oscillations during middle phase, simply don't have the same weight as the pressures that arise as the family begins to face the losses and new additions that initiate the shift into late phase.

Now the family must clarify its position regarding alcoholism, and package this clarified position in highly condensed form. What happens vis-à-vis the alcoholism issue is exactly analogous to what is happening with other identity issues. Those alcoholism-related behaviors that had previously been implicit, now become explicit. A renewed battle ensues about whether the family will accommodate rituals and routines to the needs of the alcoholic member. The use of alcohol-related behaviors as part of short-term problem-solving strategies is again challenged by individual family members.

Faced with this mounting pressure to take a stance about its alcoholic identity, the family is forced to make an explicit statement about alcoholism. The nature of this statement in turn determines which of a number of possible options the family will follow as it moves into late phase. For example, the family can respond by converting from a wet to a dry state at this point in development and attempt to put alcoholism behind it. Here we would say that the family has relinquished its alcoholic identity entirely. We might therefore label such an option the "stable dry nonalcoholic family" option. On the other hand, the family might respond by both reiterating its unwillingness to stop drinking and by continuing to accommodate regulatory behaviors to the needs of its alcoholic member. In such an instance, we would say that the family has opted for a "stable wet alcoholic family" identity, and it is this very different type of identity that will shape the direction of development during late phase for this second family.

Two factors make the movement into late phase unusually traumatic for the Alcoholic Family. The first factor is the extreme rigidity of regulatory behaviors characteristic of the middle-phase Alcoholic Family. This rigidity means that the family will be unusually resistant to the types of changes that will be necessary if the family is to successfully negotiate the transition into late phase. As noted above, these families are prone to interpret developmental challenges not as opportunities for reevaluation and growth but rather as threats to family homeostasis. The "overkill" reactions that these families evidence whenever overall stability is challenged make it difficult to engage in the evolving process of identity clarification during late phase.

The second factor that compromises late-phase development for these families is the potential impact of loss of alcohol on the course of development. Alcohol is so important a developmental issue for these families that loss of alcohol (engendered by a precipitous cessation of drinking secondary to some alcohol-related crisis such as hospitalization for gastrointestinal bleeding) whenever it occurs, is often the stimulus for conversion from middle to late phase of development. Although it is certainly possible that loss of alcohol could be the product of a natural evolution within the family, the fact that it can also be stimulated by nondevelopmentally related factors means that the overall course of development is to some extent hostage to external events. The possibility of significant distortion of development at this time is therefore greatly heightened.

Individual-Unit Developmental Time Lines

Systemic maturation, although the most fundamental developmental process in families, is not the only process capable of shaping the course of family development. In addition to this most fundamental process, the family life cycle is also responsive to developmental pressures emanating from individual family members. These pressures are of two different types. The first of these is the developmental pattern (growth) of individual members within the family. The second is the emergence of unique individually based identity issues, issues that, because of their preemptive and intrusive nature, take on major developmental significance for the whole family as well as for the individual member. Alcoholism is one such issue.

Individual Growth and Family Development

At the same time that the family is maturing as a system, its individual members are also proceeding along developmental pathways of their own. These pathways are the products of the unique biological and psychological histories of these individuals. Although individual growth and development is also responsive to surrounding environmental factors (including family factors), it clearly has a life independent of where the family might be as a system. For example, biological growth (infancy, childhood, adolescence) has its own internal clock.

Since families are comprised of individuals who have these independent clocks ticking away inside themselves, it stands to reason that family growth will also be shaped by the ages and developmental stages of its individual members. When families add new members, these infants bring with them their own developmental needs, and family behavior must be altered and adjusted to accomodate these needs if the infant is to grow and develop in a healthy fashion. Similarly, families must adjust their lives whenever they are challenged by such individually based developmental needs as the shift into adolescence, career demands during middle age, and the need to care for aging parents.

However, families are highly idiosyncratic in the pacing and sequential ordering of the developmental challenges imposed by the needs of individual members. In one family, children are added during the early phase of systemic maturation; in another family, they aren't added until the family is well into its middle phase. In one family, the cast of characters might include stepchildren as well as new children; in another family all three generations might be living together in a tightly bound situation.

The number of possible combinations—both in terms of family composition and sequential ordering of developmental events—is virtually endless. Hence the difficulty family clinicians have had in constructing widely applicable family life cycle models based on such individually grounded developmental events. (The FLH model of development is in clear-cut contradistinction to those life cycle models, such as the Hill-Duvall model, that base their staging concepts on compositional and individual-age criteria.)

Nevertheless, we are also aware that many families themselves identify their developmental stages as closely tied to the ages and stages of individual members. For example, couples about to have their first child find they can relate to other couples they meet in childbirth classes. Their life issues often seem quite comparable; that is, their lives are very much dominated by this single powerful event, an event that is also a developmental event for an individual member of the family. Similarly, families in which the oldest child is moving into adolescence, or about to leave home for college or work, also find themselves in familiar company when they talk with other families at this same stage of development. Thus it stands to reason that the overall shape of family development will also be strongly influenced by such events.

Therefore, the overall shape of a particular family's life cycle is influenced not only by systemic maturation, but also by the unique combination of the developmental patterns of individual family members. This second factor we call the "individual growth" time line.

Unique Individual Properties

Finally, we have one last factor to contend with. Family development can also be highly responsive to unique conditions or characteristics of individuals within the family. These individual properties, when they persist over long periods of time, are so intrusive, compelling, and invasive of family life as to evolve into family-level, as well as individual-level, developmental themes. As family behavior and priorities become increasingly influenced by these factors (usually few in number), *family* identity issues and developmental decisions begin to be shaped by the reorganization of the family around this "individual" issue.

A few examples would help clarify what we mean here. Suppose a family becomes organized around individual-level work and career issues.

In such a family, not only might routines and rituals be organized to accommodate work schedules and deadlines, but the family's shared view of itself might come to center around values of productivity and the work ethic; with goal-directed behaviors taking primacy over sharing of feelings, and so on. In another family, the central identity issue might be child rearing. That is, the family's main product would be its children—it feels it will make its mark on society through the accomplishments of its children. Family resources and behaviors must therefore be geared toward maximizing the likelihood that children will realize their full potentials.

For our purposes, the issue of the potential influence of individual-unit properties on family development is a particularly important one. For as has already been repeatedly emphasized, chronic alcoholism (basically a property of the alcoholic member of the family) has the capacity to become one such central identity issue for families. In fact, the whole concept of the Alcoholic Family is built around this premise. What might start out as an individually based behavioral problem can easily come to absorb more and more of a family's time, more and more family energy. Thus in Alcoholic Families, not only is alcohol a core identity issue, not only are family regulatory behaviors powerfully influenced by the invasion of alcoholism, but the shape of family growth and development may to a significant degree be responsive to the unique demands that alcoholism and alcohol-related behaviors place on the family.

Developmental Coherence versus Developmental Distortion

As we have gradually added to the list of factors that can influence and shape the course of family growth and development, the true complexity of the family life cycle has begun to emerge. But this complexity does not defy rhyme and reason; though the course of each family's growth and development is unique, this uniqueness can be thought of as the fine-tuning of what is still a universal phenomenon of family development—its fundamental responsiveness to the core systemic properties of families as living systems. That is, all families must go through a maturational process that either produces cyclical phases of systemic expansion and systemic consolidation, or leads to the death of the family as a unit. This is the essence of the systemic maturation time line.

Nevertheless, family development is responsive to the unique developmental needs and demands of individual family members (including such unique characteristics as alcoholism). The overall shape of family development, then, is an integrative product of the confluence of individual member issues with the basic pattern of systemic maturation.

This point cannot be emphasized too strongly. As much as families are responsive to the needs of their members and to their important identity issues, "healthy" family development is dependent on the ability of the family to integrate these individual member needs with the imperative that the family respond to systemic maturational factors as the basic template upon which all developmental issues will ultimately be placed. For systemic maturation to proceed in orderly and timely fashion, a fundamental *coherence* must exist between the two types of time lines outlined above (the individual-unit and family-unit time lines). That is, the pacing of the growth of individual family members stimulated by their unique developmental needs must be effectively integrated with the phasing of systemic maturation for family growth and development to take on a coherent and responsible direction.

As an important corollary, when such an integration of the different time lines does not occur, family development loses this sense of coherence and overall systemic maturation is disrupted. We have been using the term *developmental distortion* to describe this process. Within our model, therefore, developmental distortions arise whenever the confluent developmental pressures of individual-unit and family-unit time lines are incompatible. In such a situation, systemic maturation cannot proceed in a coherent fashion. Instead, some alteration in this maturational process ensues and that alteration derails the course of family development.

For our purposes, the most significant of these distortions are the ones that occur when incompatibilities arise between alcoholism-related developmental issues and systemic maturation. In fact, this issue is so central to our understanding of the life history of the Alcoholic Family as to suggest that the single most important factor of life in these families is the way in which chronic alcoholism distorts their customary growth and development.

The impact of a complex condition like alcoholism on systemic maturation is bound to vary widely from family to family. Not only does the age of onset of alcoholic drinking behavior vary, but so too does the context of drinking, the degree of physical and verbal abuse associated with drinking, the degree of economic deprivation caused by drinking, and the degree of disruption of family and social relationships. Whether drinking occurs primarily in the home or with drinking buddies outside the home is just one of many contextual variables associated with alcoholism that have a powerful effect on family life. The cultural attitude toward alcohol is another powerful such factor.

In attempting to obtain a better understanding of the impact of alcoholism on family development, how can we deal constructively with its many different combinations and permutations? Although it is true that Alcoholic Families come in many different varieties, the best way to organize a discussion of the impact of alcoholism on family development is to focus explicitly on the characteristic interrelationships between alcoholic behavior and systemic maturation in these families.

Although the role of ordinary individual-member growth and development issues is not to be minimized, for the Alcoholic Family, the most profound effects of an individual-unit factor on family development occur as a result of incongruities between alcoholism-related events on the one hand, and systemic maturation on the other. Some of these consequences are the direct outgrowth of family efforts to cope with alcoholism; others result from factors inherent in chronic alcoholism that arise totally independent of the course of family development.

An example of the first type would be the hypertrophy of family regulatory behaviors characteristic of middle-phase development in Alcoholic Families—a tipping of the family system toward morphostasis and away from morphogenesis that is largely independent of other systemic needs coming up at that phase of development. An example of the second type of consequence is the sudden cessation of drinking that might occur as the result of a medical crisis, a change in alcohol status that presents the family with a dramatically changed set of circumstances at a time when it is organized systemically to ensure internal family stability (and hence is poorly equipped to deal with sudden and dramatic change).

If we were to attempt a categorization of the different types of developmental distortions that typically occur in Alcoholic Families, we would have to say that they come in three varieties. The first are distortions that occur because the family is inappropriately rigid and narrow in its definition of acceptable developmental themes. These types of distortions we will call *thematic overspecialization*. The second type of distortions occur because the family remains in a developmental phase too long. An appropriate term for this type of distortion is *developmental arrest*. The third type of distortions occur because the family is forced to take on a major developmental task too early. This last type of distortion we will be calling *premature developmental closure*.

Although these three types of developmental distortions can occur at any of the three phases of systemic maturation, there are also characteristic times in development when they are most likely to arise. Thematic overspecialization is a characteristic distortion of the early phase of Alcoholic Family development. Developmental arrest, on the other hand, most frequently occurs during middle phase. Finally, premature developmental closure is the most important distortion of the late phase of development.

The types of distortions that are likely to occur at each phase result from the different developmental issues existing at that phase of systemic maturation. During the early phase, when the crucial issues are boundary and identity formation, a skewed approach to these issues is most likely to result in thematic overspecialization as the consequent distortion. On the other hand, during middle phase, when commitment and stability are the central issues, a family that has developed unusually rigid regulatory behaviors as a result of co-option by alcoholism is likely to resist movement out of that phase. The resulting plateauing of development is a distortion directly attributable to the extended stay in the middle phase. Lastly, because loss of alcohol can be a precipitant forcing the family prematurely into late-phase developmental issues, premature developmental closure occurs most frequently during the late phase of development.

In some of the examples we describe in later chapters, the process of distortion is a dramatic one. But more often than not, the influence of alcoholism on family development is a subtle one, recognized only in retrospect, as one looks back on a family life cycle that has become skewed by the repetitive, seemingly minor choices the family has consciously or unconsciously made to accommodate to the special needs of its alcoholic member.

Another way to describe this phenomenon is to point out that as alco-

TABLE 4.2

Developmental Distortions in the Alcoholic Family

Developmental Phase	Developmental Challenges	Typical Developmental Distortions
Early phase	Family identity formation	Thematic overspecialization
Middle phase	Orderly growth around areas of specialization	Developmental arrest
Late phase	Clarifying and transmitting family identity	Premature developmental closure

holism takes hold in the family, an interactive process occurs in which on the one hand, family behavior undergoes changes to accommodate alcoholic behavior (a reactive response), while at the same time, alcoholism is becoming an organizing principle for family life (an active response). Thus, even as these families try to co-opt alcoholism by adjusting interactional behavior to minimize the impact of the condition on family life, they are also finding alcoholism insidiously becoming a way of life.

It is this second aspect of the formula that contains the more serious consequence for the family. For the family not only acclimates itself to living with alcoholism, it also actually comes to count on certain types of alcohol-related behaviors for assistance in the overall regulation of its life. And as the family increasingly builds its daily life around alcohol-related behaviors and issues, it no longer suffices to think of it as a family with an alcoholic member. Instead, the term *Alcoholic Family* is now the appropriate one.

PART III

THE EARLY PHASE
OF DEVELOPMENT

I N THIS SECTION dealing with the first of the developmental phases in the family's life history, we focus attention on those developmental issues that each family must successfully negotiate as it moves to establish itself as a distinct entity. As discussed in chapter 4, the early phase is one of systemic expansion. A new family is being formed, but its members are at the same time also members of other family systems—the families of origin. Loyalties are divided, and the fledgling family can easily find itself overwhelmed by powerful and domineering influences imposed on it by one or more of these families of origin. If the new family is to establish its own systemic integrity, two major tasks must be successfully completed: (1) the family must clearly delineate its external and internal boundaries; and (2) the family must work to develop a set of shared beliefs, values, and rules of behavior to which its members can ascribe.

Families differ tremendously in the style and pacing they bring to these two fundamental tasks. For some families this is an explosive time, in which boundaries and shared beliefs only emerge after considerable conflict and trial and error. Other families find it quite comfortable to continue past traditions and to establish permeable boundaries that include extended family members without compromising the integrity of the new family. Still other families find these tasks overwhelming and change their boundaries and ideas so often during early phase that they leave both themselves and their families of origin hopelessly confused.

Yet whatever the course these tasks take for a particular family, the outcome of the process is the gradual emergence of a *family identity* that subsequently serves as one of the major regulatory principles for family life. It is the development of this family identity that can therefore be looked upon as the primary goal of early phase. Thus, of the many constructs we might choose as vehicles for tracking the key developmental issues in the early-phase family, the one we have chosen is that of family identity because it is this construct that seems most fundamental to the challenges faced by this group of families.*

Alcoholism can affect this process of identity formation in one of two fundamentally different ways. The first occurs when the family enters early phase with an already established alcoholism problem (either in a family of origin or in a member of the newly formed family). In such a circumstance, alcoholism is an already-present issue, and the challenge for the newly formed family is whether or not to adjust to this "fact of life." The second way alcoholism affects the process of identity formation occurs when this condition arises de novo at the same time that the family is working out its identity issues. Here the family is subjected to a new experience.

However, whatever its type of presentation, alcoholism always challenges the early-phase family with the same fundamental dilemma—whether to adjust and accommodate itself to the demands of this potentially destabilizing condition, or to effectively exclude it from all important aspects of family life. When a family takes the first of these courses, the likelihood is that alcoholism will, over time, become part and parcel of the family's emerging identity—that is, the family will adopt an Alcoholic Family identity.

In the next chapter, we follow this course of identity formation in the early-phase family, paying particular attention to those factors that influence the emergence of alcoholic versus nonalcoholic family identities.

---

*Not all family clinicians would necessarily concur in this judgment. For example, Don Jackson (1965) proposed that particular attention be paid to the development of "family rules" during this phase of development. Jackson suggested that what is going on in the young family is a process of rule formation that frequently takes form of a "quid pro quo," a sort of negotiation between competing needs of individuals within the family.

CHAPTER 5

Developing an Alcoholic Family Identity

I had long before made the discovery that I lacked the parents and ancestors I needed.
—John Fowles, *The Magus*

RICHARD AND BARBARA Cowden had been married five months when they sought a consultation because of what was described as increasingly poor communication, aggravated by Mrs. Cowden's weekly explosive outbursts and tirades against her husband. Both spouses were in their thirties, and both were marital veterans (this was his fourth marriage, her second).

Although the couple had been only recently married, they had known each other for five years. They met at a time when her first marriage was deteriorating and he had recently separated from his third wife. With both feeling insecure and troubled, they gravitated toward each other and cemented a relationship around their mutual distress and need for support and reassurance. The relationship that was established took on a strong teacher-student cast; apparently Richard felt that, having gone through three divorces, he could counsel Barbara about how to reach a decision regarding her first marriage and put her life together again.

Sometime after Barbara and her first husband had separated, she and Richard decided to live together, along with her five-year-old son. The relationship proved stormy. Barbara accused Richard of being unavailable and unloving, or, alternatingly, of being self-assured and domineering. He found her baffling and unpredictable. On two occasions he engineered a consultation for her with a therapist and insisted that she remain in therapy as a precondition to his continuing to live with her. She found the therapy of little use, but went along with his demands.

Following one of Barbara's outbursts, in which she accused him of being the cause of all her problems, Richard decided that it was best that he leave. This precipitated a major emotional crisis for Barbara, which she described as the most dysfunctional period in her life. She was profoundly depressed, unable to manage her daily affairs, and concerned about her ability to care for her child. Nevertheless, she ultimately confronted these issues, and began to bring some order to her life. She obtained a full-time job and for the first time in her life was economically self-sufficient (she had been living on support money from her first husband). The couple continued to see one another, although they were no longer living together. At that point, ostensibly because of Barbara's significant improvement in functioning, the couple decided to get married.

The young marriage was almost immediately challenged by a major crisis. Richard, a university professor, accepted a sabbatical position in another city, precipitating the family's geographical relocation. Barbara was forced to relinquish her newly won job and move to a city away from any immediately available new job opportunities *and* from her relatives, from whom she had received a great deal of support during prior crises. Although the couple had supposedly discussed together the ramifications of his acceptance of this position, we can only assume that these discussions were patterned after others we had heard about—in which it appeared that the decision antedated the formal discussion and reflected the apparent discrepancy in power distribution between the couple. The seeds of a potential crisis were therefore sown, and were reaped shortly after the couple relocated.

In this new locale, Barbara felt depressed, isolated, and devalued. Her perception of the importance of the loss of her job to her lack of self-esteem only increased as she found herself subject to alternating fits of depression and rage. These emotional swings were occurring in an atmosphere not only of isolation and loneliness, but also one pervaded by alcohol. Her husband, who had always been a heavy drinker, seemed to increase his alcohol intake, perhaps as a result of the stress of his new job.

Although his increased drinking was imperceptible to Richard, it was a source of constant concern to his wife. Barbara's own family background was one of at most light social drinking, and she described herself as "totally out of my depth" in the heavy drinking environment Richard was establishing within their home. Barbara's concern was only further heightened when she attempted to talk to her husband about the alcohol issue. For, what she identified as the profoundly disturbing patterning of the couple's social life around alcohol-focused activities (cocktail parties, social gatherings in bars, relaxed evenings in which large amounts of alcohol were ultimately consumed), Richard saw only as a customary and reasonable way of life.

Within this atmosphere, a striking pattern began to emerge. On an approximately once-a-week basis, Barbara found herself deliberately drinking a full bottle of wine, starting around supper time and ending in late evening. She would usually finish the bottle an hour or two after her husband had gone to sleep. In the middle of the night, she would explode, wake him up, and "rant and rave" at him, hurling a series of invectives and accusations that she knew (even while she was saying them) made little sense.

For his part, Richard came to anticipate these explosive episodes, knowing in the back of his mind when seeing her drinking heavily in the evening, that this would be one of the nights he would be awakened. His initial stance, always one of extreme rationality and understanding, only infuriated her further, escalating the explosive interaction pattern between them. It was against this background of alcohol-associated behaviors that they came in for the consultation.

It should be emphasized that this case, an example of identity formation in an early-phase family, is in fact one that describes the behavior of two marital veterans. Yet, despite their past experience, these two people find themselves struggling, in the first months of their marriage, with what we have clearly identified as early-phase developmental issues. Thus the first tenet illustrated by the case is the universality of the systemic maturational issues faced by *all* early-phase families.

For the Cowdens, however, early phase developmental tasks are being worked out within a context framed by alcoholism. Barbara, a novice to heavy alcohol use, is being drawn to episodic bouts of intoxication and is terrified of the long-range implications of her behavior. She is particularly articulate in voicing her fears that her growing number of alcohol-induced emotional explosions is locking her into a behavioral reliance on alcohol use that will be increasingly difficult to overcome.

Barbara's fear that she might become dependent on alcohol seems related to her belief that her explosive alcohol-associated behaviors are not purely random, but instead are quite purposeful. In particular, they seem to be serving two purposes—first, to discharge the sense of anger, helplessness, and frustration that she feels about having been forced to acquiesce in her husband's decision regarding his sabbatical; and second, to challenge, in dramatic fashion, a nascent *alcoholic identity* that she fears is developing in their marriage.

In using alcohol-related behaviors to address an unresolved problem in their relationship, Barbara is embarking on a path not dissimilar from that taken by Lot's two daughters in the Sodom and Gommorah story (chapter 1). That is, Barbara's alcohol-related behaviors are being used for problem-solving. This "young" couple is sharply divided as to how their individual needs are to be jointly accommodated. Thus far, all major decisions have been dictated by *his* occupational needs, to the detriment of hers. The resulting imbalance has created severe strains in their relationship, and this still-fragile marriage is surely in jeopardy. Enter here Barbara's episodic bouts of intoxication, her way of obtaining temporary relief from the almost unbearable tensions in the relationship and of expressing anger that she fears might otherwise destroy the marriage.

The likely outcome, were this to continue, is that alcohol would increasingly come to have adaptive (Davis, Berenson, Steinglass, and Davis, 1974) as well as nonadaptive consequences for the marriage (discharge of angry affect, allowing Barbara to remain in the sabbatical location despite its affects on her self-esteem). Over time, it is just such a process that causes alcoholism to become an integral part of family regulatory mechanisms, one of the crucial steps down the road to becoming an Alcoholic Family.

On the other hand, the "outrageous" form her drinking behavior takes is being used to challenge this growing reliance on alcohol that she fears will engulf their marriage. So in this sense, her drinking is a direct challenge to the formation of an Alcoholic Family identity. That is, a struggle is going on about which of two very different attitudes toward alcohol and drinking practices are to be adopted by this young couple. Barbara talks about her experiences at home as if she had moved to a foreign country and was experiencing culture shock. What she is talking about, however, is the pattern of daily drinking (six to eight beers on an average night, spiced with wine for dinner) that she finds herself immersed in and totally baffled by. For Richard's part, his wife's concern about the amount of alcohol he is consuming is just as foreign an experience to him.

Is Richard's view (and his past family experience) to prevail or will Barbara's attitudes to alcohol ("inherited" from her family of origin) be adopted by the couple? They both agree it is a critical decision. Barbara seems to be suggesting that if her husband's rules are adopted, she is headed for a serious bout of alcoholism. He seems to be suggesting that acceding to her "emotional needs" (that is, her psychopathological needs) for an alcohol-free family environment would be asking an unfair price of him, and he would probably quietly walk away from the marriage as a consequence. The two sides are therefore clearly drawn, the process is in motion, and a decision about the ability of the couple to survive early phase awaits their resolution of this issue—the issue of whether or not to challenge the emergence of a budding Alcoholic Family identity.

To summarize, the Cowden case highlights three very important issues relevant to the early-phase family:

First, we can clearly see that when alcohol abuse emerges in early phase, it has preemptive power as a developmental issue. That is, it proves such a powerful and compelling force in family life that all other issues tend to be recast in "alcohol terms." Struggles about values become struggles about whether or not alcohol abuse is to be tolerated. Struggles about rules governing interpersonal relationships within the family are most forcefully engaged when rules for interpreting and managing intoxicated behavior must be worked out. Delineation of external boundaries often centers around who is to be let in on the alcoholism issue and how they are to be "briefed."

Second, we also see that members of early-phase families are (quite naturally) powerfully influenced by the families they have been (and may still be) members of. Most important of these are their families of origin. If one or more of these families of origin are Alcoholic Families, then one of the very important challenges faced by the early-phase family becomes what to do about this alcoholic heritage. Should it be treated as relatively innocuous and therefore something that can be by and large ignored? Or should it be perceived as a fundamental threat to the future integrity of the new family? Obviously, the family's shared perceptions of this alcoholic heritage will dictate very different response patterns depending on which side of the issue the family is on. But it may also be the case that during early phase, considerable tension exists between family members about how to view alcoholism in the previous generation (or a prior marriage). This is the tension we see between the Cowdens as they debated the alcoholism issue in terms of his versus her past family experiences with alcohol.

Third, early-phase families have many options available to them as they respond to the alcohol-based challenges that arise during this juncture in their development. With the Cowdens, we were able to see only a brief cross-sectional slice of this developmental history. Hence we don't know what they finally decided to do. But our brief look into their history makes it clear that they were surely positioned to go either way on the issue of whether or not to organize their lives around alcoholism as a central identity issue. Further, they had many choices available regarding how to model their rules of interaction and what shared beliefs to adopt at this stage in their lives. For example, they not only had two very different models in their respective families of origin, but they also had tried out different types of family organization in their prior marriages. And if one of these models seemed still not quite the right one, they always had available the option of designing a new type of family identity that either would be built up from scratch or that incorporated aspects of prior family experiences they valued.

Family Identity Options

Family identity, the set of shared impressions the family holds about itself and the external world, typically represents, in part, values and behaviors inherited from earlier generations and, in part, innovations distinctive to the couple. It is through the construct of family identity formation, therefore, that we can most clearly track the struggles the early-phase family must go through to successfully disengage itself (split off) from its families of origin yet still maintain appropriate ties to extended family. It is a process entirely analogous to the developmental tasks of the transition from late adolescence to early adulthood, so graphically described by Erik Erikson (1959), whose description also relied on the concept of "identity" as the core construct.

As we saw with the Cowdens, when alcoholism is a component in this process, it poses special challenges. Yet there are many versions these challenges can take. Imagine, for example, a couple married for eighteen months; the husband regularly drinks to excess with his buddies from work. His wife is often privy to these heavy drinking sessions, and she's worried that he's becoming physically dependent on the alcohol. She's particularly alarmed when on Mondays he takes a drink in the morning before going back to work. They are expecting their first child, and she is beginning to think about the prospect of raising the child with an alcoholic father. But she's never encountered alcoholism before, either in her family or among friends she had before her marriage. Now she feels that the drinking is progressively taking over and becoming a core part of the interaction between her and her husband. Their arguments and lovemaking revolve around it. The husband, on the other hand, discounts his wife's concerns by criticizing her naïveté about drinking and argues that it is a normal part of adult life. She just has to accept it and get used to it, he says. How can this couple stem a certain tide toward an Alcoholic Family identity?

In another case, the husband of a recently remarried couple had previously been married to an alcoholic. His children, though living with them, continue to see their still-drinking mother. His new wife does not approve of heavy drinking, and the two of them have decided that neither would drink because of all the pain caused by his ex-wife's drinking. His new wife doesn't mind because she's never been much of a drinker anyway. Even so, two questions keep nagging them: (1) how will they keep his first wife's drinking at bay and limit its influence on the children, and (2) are they going too far in the opposite extreme by not having alcohol in their home, thereby creating a less-than-healthy drinking model for the children? Is this couple headed for a nonalcoholic family identity or are they simply substituting a dry alcoholic identity as a response to the experience in the husband's first marriage?

Finally, consider the couple who enters marriage with the explicit agreement that they will keep their drinking under control. Both husband and wife had grown up in families with alcoholic parents, and neither wishes to repeat the past. Prior to their marriage, the husband had done a lot of partying in college with his fraternity brothers. Eyeing his drinking with great alarm, his then-fiancée laid down the law. Either he slow down substantially, or he could forget the marriage. He acquiesced. However, immediately after the wedding vows were given, the husband proceeded to become intoxicated during the reception, as did his father and her father. The honeymoon got off to a rocky start, with the husband nursing a hangover and the wife fuming and petulant. What is our prognosis for this couple? Will they go on to establish an alcoholic or nonalcoholic family identity, or will they complete early phase with an unresolved family identity regarding the role of alcohol in their lives?

In this chapter, we propose that the process of family-identity formation—the core regulatory principle of first phase—has a tremendous influence on the eventual outcome (as far as alcohol is concerned) for the couple's family. Keeping in mind that all couples must deal with establishing a family identity of their own early in marriage, regardless of whether or not alcohol is an issue, we focus our attention on the alcohol-related aspects of this regulatory principle. Furthermore, we place considerable stress on the experience of those families in which there is a history of alcohol-related problems either in the couple's generation or in previous generations. In a society exhibiting as much ambivalence about alcohol use and alcoholism as ours and having as high a prevalence rate of alcoholism, we are talking about a widespread phenomenon even when we restrict our discussion to families that have alcohol issues in their pasts. While familial alcoholism transmission is a continuous process over the family life cycle,

113

what transpires during first phase is especially critical. On the one hand, couples can turn things around, clean up their family's act, and embark upon a nonalcoholic course. Or they can perpetuate the Alcoholic Family identity with consequences for the current and future generations.

Thus we now narrow our focus to those early-phase families in which at least one family of origin has a chronic alcoholic member. As such a family struggles with the developmental tasks of early phase, the alcoholism issue in the prior generation is likely to be one of the most prominent issues. For example, as the new family works on delineating its boundaries, are these structural properties to be determined by a desire to exclude the Alcoholic Family of origin from a meaningful role in the early-phase family's life? Or is contact with this origin family to be extensive and in no way distinguishable from contact with a nonalcoholic origin family (if one spouse comes from an Alcoholic Family and the other does not)?

Similarly, in developing its shared values, beliefs, and rules of behavior, are these to be *deliberately* modeled after the nonalcoholic origin family (or if none exist, developed de novo as shared beliefs unique to the new family)? Or will the early-phase family indiscriminately model itself after an alcoholic origin family without regard to the alcoholism factor and its implication for identity formation in the new family?

Clearly the choices the early-phase family makes in regard to the critical developmental tasks of boundary definition and establishment of shared beliefs dictate very different outcomes regarding emergence of the identity of the family as early phase progresses. Although these outcomes are in many ways unique, for our purposes the critical question is whether or not an Alcoholic Family identity emerges as a result of this process.

Thus, of the possible options a family with an alcoholic legacy can take regarding identity formation, our attention will be focused on three: (1) a nonalcoholic family identity; (2) an unresolved Alcoholic Family identity; and (3) a wet Alcoholic Family identity. The best way to describe each of these family-identity options is to present a detailed case example. The three cases that follow were subject families in a study explicitly designed to explore the role of family rituals in Alcoholic Family identity formation. The study—the "Heritage study"—is reviewed in greater detail later in the chapter.

A Nonalcoholic Family Identity: Brian and Jennie

Couples forging a nonalcoholic family identity ordinarily exhibit a purposefulness in other aspects of their life. Brian and Jennie Clark both came from Alcoholic Families, but were headed on a nonalcoholic family identity course. In their early twenties they had been married a little more than two years and had an infant daughter. Brian's father had become progressively addicted to alcohol during Brian's adolescent years, but had "gone straight" in the past two years. Both of Jennie's parents were alcoholics. Although they still drank, they sometimes abstained during important family get-togethers. As the son of an alcoholic, Brian was at particular risk for alcoholism himself (Cotton, 1979).

However, from an early age, Brian was able to separate the image of his respected, highly intelligent father from his obnoxious, pathetic, alcoholic father: "We were the proudest family when he wasn't drinking." Brian carefully studied his father's erratic behavior and determined that in his own life he would take far better responsibility for himself and for his family. He looked to his mother for the stability and security that she provided the children when his father did not and found her a much more appealing role model. Furthermore, because the family included eight children—Brian was the sixth—the siblings were able to give much-needed solace to each other during the most trying and unpleasant times. Thus, by the time he married, Brian had some pretty clear ideas for how it was possible to improve upon his father's role in the family.

Although Brian and Jennie had been married a relatively short period of time, they had known each other since junior high school. He looked her over long and hard before asking her to marry him. It was essential that she meet his standards for the life he intended to carve out. She did. According to Jennie, "I spoil him, and I am a bit old-fashioned." Brian had told Jennie from the start that he wanted someone to take care of him and give him what he wanted. Jennie agreed. He is the "boss" in the home, and they both liked it this way. In getting married, he saw himself "putting life in order."

Putting life in order in this couple's case encompassed the details of daily living and grander special occasions. Both Brian and Jennie were very hard workers, holding down full-time jobs and taking care of their baby and home. He planned to finish college and was enrolled part-time. They had big plans, and in taking explicit direction of their lives and establishing priorities, they viewed themselves as quite different from either set of parents. From the organization of family roles to the celebration of their holidays, they have a clear plan for what they want to do and how they plan to do it. Thus far, they have been following through on that plan, though that often required a great deal of effort. Although Brian tended to decide most things for the family—including how much money to spend on food and furniture, where to buy things, and which holidays to celebrate—they discussed these decisions in advance and both voiced their opinions. Even though the main control for selecting from among the possible routines and rituals available from their origin families was taken by Brian, they were in full agreement, at least at this point in their marriage, that that is right and proper. They were a highly deliberate couple.

Similarly, they had drawn some careful boundaries between themselves and their extended families. In their case, this had not been done at the expense of closeness. They retained a moderate amount of contact with both sets of parents and looked to their families for social and emotional ties. However, they had not overdone it. Rather than emphasizing the similarities, they mostly saw differences between the way they led their lives and how each of the origin families continued to live theirs. They did look to Brian's parents for some practical advice from time to time, but with his father especially, they did this in a highly selective way. Both realized that his father could offer brilliant analyses one moment and useless pontifications, the next. Looking back on his childhood, Brian recollected a close-knit family that in some ways he tried to emulate. He placed a high priority on closeness in his own home. However, he did not rely too heavily on their parents to realize that closeness. The nuclear family was of primary importance. Jennie connected Brian's determination to develop such a strong and circumscribed family identity of their own to his mother's influence: "She has a lot of push and lot of drive for Brian, and he is very responsible and reliable as a result."

When it came to their own rituals, Brian held extremely strong ideas about the observation of dinnertimes. He made no attempt to emulate his origin family and their noisy and boisterous dinners; instead he aimed for quiet and calm. Brian preferred to remain silent while eating, waiting until after the meal to talk. Based upon what she had heard and what she had observed in his parents' home, Jennie saw a vast difference between their dinnertime and how it was for him as a child. "It is really important for him to take it easy. When he was younger, I am sure it was hard for him. . . . it wasn't peaceful. You know, when you have eight kids and you have eight kids' friends, you know how it would be. His family was always on the go. I can see now why he likes it peaceful." And so it goes in his family. Brian made his wishes and intentions clear to Jennie. He had married a woman who would organize his life and demote some of her own desires in order to meet his expectations and to make him happy. Thus they had dinners that followed his prescription, one that was diametrically opposed to that of his own childhood.

This couple did not abstain from alcohol, but drinking was not an important part of their lives, and they rarely drank during the week or attended parties where drinking was the main attraction. Brian observed: "I like sitting around talking, but just cannot stand parties where everybody's out to get ripped." Jennie thought that that is another reason that they get along so well. "If we went to parties and everybody was just sitting around with their eyes rolling around, we'd leave." They were in firm agreement about such matters. Jennie, under most circumstances, drank almost nothing, especially since the birth of their child. Brian drank beer on weekends, on the average finishing less than a six-pack. As with many aspects of their lives, enough is enough. Brian thought that "overabuse is wrong." Basically they had a take-it-or-leave-it attitude about alcohol. It was not one of those things they talked about much, and not one of those things that they went out of their way to avoid. In other words, they were not preoccupied either with drinking or with the avoidance of drinking. They accepted their own parents' drinking problems as part of their pasts. Brian and Jennie had moved on to other concerns.

Although it is really too early to know for sure that this couple will not develop an alcoholic family identity, at this crucial period of their family-identity formation, they seem to be setting clear priorities and following through on them. While we might wonder whether the imbalance between the two spouses in decision-making power will be good for the marriage in the long run, thus far they both seem to be happy with the status quo.

An Unresolved Alcoholic Family Identity: Karen and Ted

Because of its progressive and chronic nature, alcoholism often presents a very confusing dilemma for the spouses of budding alcoholics, let alone for the alcoholics themselves. Coming from an Alcoholic Family can frequently make it even more difficult to deal with. What often happens in such situations is that the early-phase couple goes through a long period when their family identity remains unresolved as far as becoming alcoholic or nonalcoholic is concerned. Even the most well-meaning spouse faces serious odds in attempting to set a course to a nonalcoholic identity. While the spouse may have a very clear plan about how she or he would like the family identity to develop, these plans may get waylaid by the ambivalent behavior of the heavy-drinking spouse.

The extent to which the couple organizes its social life around alcoholic contexts often becomes a major concern of such spouses. When they cannot decide as a couple the course to take in the role of alcohol in their ties with other people—family, friends, co-workers—there is probably an unresolved alcoholic-nonalcoholic family-identity issue. Differences in viewpoint about alcohol use can easily become fuel for the fire in lasting antagonisms between spouses around the development and maintenance of social boundaries.

Karen and Ted Roberts, with their three-year-old daughter, traveled in two divergent social circles. Hers was nonalcoholic; his alcoholic. Karen came from a family with an alcoholic mother and knew all too well the tragedy of alcoholism in the family. While Ted's drinking had not consistently reached alarming levels, his inclination to associate with friends who drink and to go his own way were worse than unsettling for Karen. He did not like being tied down at home, and she did not approve of his wanderlust.

This was a couple that could not agree on how to set its course and had not been able to deliberately select from among their heritage options in establishing daily routines and special rituals. Karen did have some clear ideas of what to do and what not to do, but she could not get Ted's cooperation. Thus, her desire to be deliberate was frustrated.

The contrast in their social preferences could not be much sharper. Karen's friends were Mormons who never drank, while Ted's were sports and work buddies who drank whenever they got a chance. Both spouses avoided each other's friends. Furthermore, Ted's work environment constantly exposed him to drinking. His respected position in a government agency entailed considerable travel and drinking with his superiors and peers. They drank at lunch, after work, and while traveling. To Ted, this seemed perfectly normal and, in fact, a necessary part of his job.

To Karen, though, Ted's "extracurricular" activities were simply a symptom of his irresponsibility to his family. She saw his enthusiasm for sports—soccer, hockey, racketball—as "overdosing." They argued (in the research interview) over just how many evenings a week he played sports. While he preferred not to spend his evenings at home, Ted often invited Karen to attend the games. But, as he pointed out, Karen is "pure" and is "not interested in hanging out with his kind of folks." They had reached a stalemate.

Karen, having grown up in a home dominated by the exigencies of an alcoholic mother, naturally had her own reasons for being wary of organizing her and her husband's lives around alcohol-laden events. Thus, although her parents lived less than one mile away, Karen had increasingly segregated her own family from her origin family—and her mother's all-too-frequent bouts—since marrying Ted and especially since her daughter was born. When Karen's mother came to visit, Karen took control of the liquor and made sure her drinking was limited. She could not exercise quite as much control when visiting her parents' home, so after some really ugly scenes at Thanksgiving a couple years earlier, Karen and Ted had switched to celebrating most of their holidays in their own home. They invited her parents, but also controlled the flow of alcohol. That made it bearable, even though tensions remained over how her mother would comport herself. As this indicates, they did maintain contact with her alcoholic origin family, but it was to a moderate degree, and painstakingly controlled.

Such demonstrated skill at isolating Karen's mother's alcoholic influence did not carry over to the couple's own family. Though she tried, Karen could not develop a nonalcoholic family identity on her own. At least she could not as long as Ted held his current attitudes about alcohol and maintained his current life-style. He would not cooperate. While he totally agreed about taking charge of Karen's mother's drinking, he would not permit Karen to dictate rules about his social life and drinking. They had no significant shared social domains when it came to this issue. While Karen had her daughter to focus her emotional and social energy on, Ted kept his distance there also. In short, while they did not maintain a high degree of contact with alcoholic family legacy, they had not succeeded in developing a nonalcoholic identity thus far.

As a further contribution to this difficult and ambivalent situation, Ted was not one to cherish family rituals. Dinnertime was often the focus of confusion and argument. Regularly, Ted said he would come home at a certain time, but ended up drinking with his friends and not showing up until much later. Karen's best intentions as to how to develop this family ritual were thwarted again and again.

There is no doubt that Ted was a heavy drinker. He drank considerable amounts of alcohol, but thus far had experienced relatively limited consequences aside from his wife's displeasure. He had not as yet encountered problems at work, with the law, or with his friends. No one in the extended family had called attention to the amount he drank or to his drinking-connected behavior. Only Karen seemed to notice. At least she was the only one to comment. However, Ted's tolerance to alcohol was on the decline, by his own admission, and he was getting more and more frequent hangovers and experiencing serious bouts of depression that they both thought were alcohol-related. Surrounding himself with drinking colleagues and friends only exacerbated his inclination to drink abusively. While Ted wanted very much to maintain his existing life-style, he saw the writing on the wall in such a way that worried even him. He did not know if he could physically continue to drink at the same rate and frequency without dire consequences to his health. That mattered much more to him than any worries about his family.

The future of this couple's family identity remains cloudy. We are left wondering what comes next. It does seem clear that they will not be able to continue on the same course without considerable ramifications. Something has to give somewhere. Karen's already limited willingness to accept Ted's frequent absence from his family and his detachment from their rituals is likely to give out. Yet Ted, with his firm commitment to personal independence, is probably going to continue resisting Karen's interference in his recreational life. Karen is fighting the encroachment of alcohol on their own family identity. Through his passive but persistent resistance, Ted is encouraging the development of an Alcoholic Family identity. So far, it remains unresolved.

An Alcoholic Family Identity: Jeff And Peggy

In their mid-twenties, Jeff and Peggy Snyder had been married a few years and had a six-month-old son, Henry. They had known each other since their early grade school years. Both Jeff and Peggy had fathers who were recovering from alcoholism. Earlier in their marriage, Peggy had been a problem drinker, but was now drinking moderately. Jeff was recovering from alcoholism after an automobile accident.

Alcohol problems had invaded both family backgrounds. In addition to these alcohol-loaded family legacies, Jeff and Peggy were involved in a very heavy drinking peer group when they were in high school. This aspect of their social life continued well into their marriage and was halted only after Jeff's drinking became so severe that he almost killed himself. Following treatment for his injury, Jeff stopped drinking. Over these early years, however, they had developed an Alcoholic Family identity. What the future holds for them is not yet determined.

Neither Jeff nor Peggy were very deliberate in selecting a family heritage early in their marriage. To the extent that they opted for a particular family heritage, it was one modeled implicitly on Peggy's alcoholic family background. They inadvertently followed many of the ritual and day-to-day patterns of her family, and were clearly moving in the direction of developing a family-ritual heritage like the one she had grown up with. But they were doing this with virtually no intentional planning on the part of either one of them. It was just happening.

Following the wedding, both sets of parents lived in the same town as Jeff and Peggy and continued to influence their lives substantially. At the time, Peggy's father was still drinking alcoholically, and the couple was pulled into traumatic alcohol-related conflicts within the family. Meanwhile, Jeff's drinking accelerated. In an attempt to get out of the draft—an attempt that worked—Jeff went on a bender: "It took me about a year, but

I convinced them finally that I was crazy. I simmered down a little bit after that, but. . . ." After "simmering down," he got arrested several times for driving while intoxicated (DWI), drove without a license for long periods, and his marriage went sour.

This couple's life changed suddenly. As Jeff's drinking got more and more out of control and his behavior became increasingly erratic, Peggy left him and went "home." She found that she could no longer tolerate his driving his car at breakneck speeds. Shortly thereafter, he was almost killed in an automobile accident. While recuperating in the hospital, Jeff contemplated his future and his marriage seriously for the first time. The couple started to talk. At that point, they realized that they had never developed any boundaries between themselves and their origin families and adolescent friends and that they had never begun to form a clear sense of their own family identity. Peggy had retained a very dependent and enmeshed relationship with her own family, and whenever she had any disagreement with Jeff, she would go "running to her folks." Similarly, Jeff went running back to his familiar friends, who were always drinking. Before the accident, they had never leaned on each other or worked out their own solutions to their problems.

At the start of their marriage, neither Jeff nor Peggy had thought out their expectations for their future together. Instead, they were locked into their pasts. Peggy took it for granted that they would replicate her own family. Jeff did not agree. He was really uncomfortable with the frantic rush and clamor of life in Peggy's large family. But instead of addressing this difference openly and squarely, Jeff retreated more and more from Peggy and her family and had increasingly associated with his drinking buddies.

As he lay in bed at the hospital, Jeff came up with a short-term solution to their marital crisis. They would leave the community, where they were so strongly tied to their alcoholic pasts, and move far away for a year. This would permit them to break away from both the overpowering influence of Peggy's family and Jeff's peer group. When faced with this option, Peggy agreed, a little reluctantly at first. Her parents were very pleased and supportive. While part of the problem themselves, they could at least see that it was not good for Peggy to be so dependent on them and to run home to them every time problems erupted. And, in fact, a year away did seem to provide the distance necessary for Jeff and Peggy to begin their own family anew and to set a course toward a possible new and nonalcoholic family identity.

Whatever the eventual outcome of their family identity as they enter middle phase, it is clear that during early phase, Jeff and Peggy developed an Alcoholic Family identity. This identity was associated with a low degree of deliberateness in selecting from among various family-heritage options and a high amount of contact with an alcoholic family background. As a result, their lives continued to revolve around alcohol.

Factors Influencing Alcoholic Identity Formation

The three case histories we have just reviewed were selected to illustrate the three different options early-phase families have in forming an Alcoholic Family identity. We chose to focus on families in which one or both families of origin had alcoholic members because the issues are more sharply delineated in such situations.

When alcoholism arises de novo in an early-phase family, it is presumably a novel experience for all family members, and the responses that evolve tend to be highly idiosyncratic. When one or more members of the early-phase family have alcoholism in their backgrounds, however, it is a very different story. Here alcoholism (and it potential impact on family life) is an already known quantity. The response patterns of the offspring from such families, as they move on to form their own families, can therefore be more effectively categorized. Further, the consequences of these response patterns can be systematically studied in the service of understanding better the factors that increase or decrease the likelihood that an Alcoholic Family identity will emerge in the new early-phase family.

We have said that the early-phase family is dealing with two major developmental tasks—the delineation of its internal and external boundaries; and the working out of a shared set of beliefs, values, and rules that will guide family behavior. As the work on these two tasks progresses, the structures and shared beliefs that emerge are incorporated into the family's evolving collective sense of itself (its identity). But how are we to adequately track this processes as it unfolds?

In the case histories, the way we approached this task was to pay particular attention to the relationships between the early-phase family and its two families of origin. Since we were primarily interested in the different patterns associated with the development of alcoholic versus nonalcoholic family identities, much of the clinical detail centered on the decisions the new family was making about its relationships with its alcoholic family of origin. For example, how much contact did the early-phase family have with the members of this family. We also talked about the degree of deliberateness the new family evidenced in its intention not to mimic and repeat the behavioral patterns (rituals) it associated with the alcoholic family of origin.

These particular clinical details were included in the case histories because they are unusually clear-cut indexes of the family's progress and strategies in tackling the two major developmental tasks of early phase. That is, the family's decisions regarding boundary definition can be quite clearly tracked by observing the degree of contact it has with members of the two families of origin. (A similar case could be made for the importance of tracking the degree of contact between the family and the premarriage social networks of the two spouses, or the prior families if this is a blended early-phase family. However, the clearest example of how boundaries are being drawn vis-à-vis alcoholism is how the new family is interacting with an alcoholic family of origin.)

Similarly, the extent to which alcoholism is being included in the emerging belief system of the early-phase family can be sensitively tracked by paying attention to the decisions regarding continuation of ritual patterns from the prior-generation families. The decision to perpetuate rituals from a family of origin that itself has an Alcoholic Family identity is likely to lead to a very different outcome than a decision to break with such traditions.

Since we are primarily interested here in the factors that contribute to the formation of an Alcoholic Family identity, it would seem logical that our efforts should be directed toward the identification of factors that increase the likelihood that such an identity will emerge in early phase. For example, we might propose that a family's decision to model itself on a family of origin that is itself an Alcoholic Family is, de facto, a decision that will increase the likelihood that this new family will itself emerge from early phase with an Alcoholic Family identity. Thus, if an early-phase family comes from one alcoholic and one nonalcoholic family of origin, and it decides to select rituals from the Alcoholic Family as the model for its own ritual practices, such a family should have an increased chance of developing an Alcoholic Family identity.

In fact, our efforts at systematic study of this question were quite explicitly driven by such a strategy. However, the findings from our most ambitious study of this question to date (to be reviewed shortly) suggested instead that it is easier to identify factors that decrease the likelihood of Alcoholic Family identity than the reverse. That is, when we ask early-phase families to discuss how they have handled an Alcoholic Family heritage, it seems easier for those families who have opted for a nonalcoholic identity to articulate what they have done to proactively *block* the perpetuation of such a heritage in their own families, than it is for those families who have opted for continuation of the Alcoholic Family heritage to describe what they have done to encourage a perpetuation of an alcoholic identity.

In the latter case, therefore, the development of an alcoholic identity is most probably a result of the confluence of multiple proactive and reactive decisions that have the combined effect of increasingly organizing the family around alcoholism. Because of their complexity, they are difficult for both the family and the researcher to reconstruct. Thus as we move ahead in the chapter, our discussion is increasingly focused on those factors that appear to protect the early-phase family that would otherwise be at risk of developing an alcoholic identity.

Focusing on protective factors also makes sense from a clinical perspective. Even though we are interested in this book in following the Alcoholic Family through all three phases of its life cycle, factors that short-circuit this process, and thereby attenuate the effects of alcoholism on the family, are of obvious clinical relevance and importance. Hence although we deal (in later chapters) with families who haven't been able to mobilize the protective factors we are about to highlight, for the moment, a discussion of those factors seems very much in order.

Family of Heritage

As we looked at the process of identity formation in the early-phase family, we approached this issue from the perspective of the major developmental tasks of this phase of systemic maturation. The basic argument has been as follows:

The two most fundamental tasks of the early phase of systemic maturation are the delination of family boundaries and the establishment of a set of shared beliefs and rules that guide subsequent family behavior. As these two tasks are undertaken, family efforts in these two arenas are gradually incorporated into the family's emerging definition of itself—its family identity. Because this process is both a highly complex and a subtle one, it is best tracked by focusing attention on a more delimited series of behaviors that encompass and reflect the more complex underlying process of identity formation that is going on at this phase of development. Thus, judgments about the mechanisms and factors that influence identity formation are inferred from a systematic study of these more delimited behaviors.

We have proposed that the most parsimonious way to track identity formation is to pay careful attention to the relationships the early-phase family has with its various families of origin. In particular, we have used the metaphor of *family heritage* as the vehicle for guiding us here. That is, the early-phase family must make some decisions about what behaviors and values from the past it wants to incorporate into its own early-phase identity. In other words, it must decide what aspects of its past experiences it wants to perpetuate in this new family. Nowhere is the process more clearly etched than in the negotiations the early-phase family is carrying out with its various families of origin. Thus by asking the family to carefully delineate where its newly implemented rules, beliefs, and values, come from (do they mimic some past experiences or have they been made up de novo), we can trace not only the sources of family-identity components, but also better identity what those components actually are.

In applying this argument to early-phase families with Alcoholic Families of origin, we have said that in such situations alcoholism is usually so powerful an issue as to preempt all others and to force a recasting of customary developmental issues in "alcohol terms." Thus, boundary delineation becomes focused around whether or not alcoholism is to be included within the family's internal environment. Shared beliefs and values about alcohol take on paramount importance. And identity formation is, at its most fundamental level, a question of whether or not the family is to perpetuate an Alcoholic Family identity.

Let us therefore take a closer look at how the relationship between the early-phase family and its families of origin influences the differential outcome of alcoholic versus nonalcoholic family-identity formation.

Boundary Definition: Level of Contact with Origin Families

In order to establish a family identity, all early-phase families must separate from each family of origin and negotiate a distinct relationship of their own. This entails a shift in loyalties. In addition to the differentiation of the couple as a unit from prior familial relations, new ties to friends are worked out, and substantial changes are made in those connections. It is this series of decisions—about who to include as critical members of the family's kinship and social networks, and what kind of access these people are to have to the inner circle of family life—that make up the process of boundary definition for the early-phase family.

Thus, encompassed within boundary definition are considerations about *composition* or the selection of those individuals who are accepted into the inner sanctum and within the broader social realm of the family; the *permeability* of the family's social boundaries; and the extent of social *contact* with this "cast of characters." While some families greatly restrict their circle of close family and friends, perhaps not ranging much beyond the immediate nuclear family for meaningful social ties, others are much more inclusive, including a variety of extended family members, friends, and neighbors within their social world.

In Alcoholic Families, a critical consideration in boundary definition is the presence of alcohol problems among other family members and among close friends. Current attitudes and behaviors around drinking refer back to the experiences both spouses had as they are growing up and possibly in earlier marriages. If they come into the marriage with a legacy of alcohol problems, this will flavor the extent and quality of contact with other family members. And when husband and wife have differing views on what constitutes acceptable drinking practices in their own lives, they often have different opinions about making friends. One spouse may wish to separate from friends or family members who drink heavily, while the other spouse may not. Disagreement over these issues can prevent resolution of boundary conflicts (as in the case of the Cowdens).

Knowledge about a couple's alcoholism legacy and their contact with family and friends who have an alcoholic identity is paramount in understanding the hows and whys of their experience with alcohol during early phase. When the relationship between husband and wife is enmeshed with other relationships that are affected by alcoholism, their chances of developing or maintaining alcohol problems of their own are increased (as in the case of Jeff and Peggy Snyder).

Thus the *degree of contact* the family has with an alcoholic family of origin, with alcoholic friends, or with alcohol-centered social activities becomes an excellent behavioral index of the types of boundaries the early-phase family is drawing vis-à-vis alcoholism. If the family has had no prior significant experiences with alcoholism, then a decision to include an alcoholic friend as part of the family's "inner circle" may be of little consequence. Similarly, contact with a social environment in which heavy alcohol use is the norm may also have little long-term impact on family-identity formation. But if one or more family members already have experienced difficulties with alcohol, or if a family of origin contains an alcoholic member, then the drawing of family boundaries to "include alcohol" is bound to also increase the likelihood that the family will move toward developing an alcoholic identity.

The clearest example of this process at work occurs when one or more families of origin contain alcoholic members. In such a situation we can say that the early-phase family's level of contact with this alcoholic family of origin is an ideal behavioral marker of the extent to which alcoholism is being incorporated into the emerging family identity. The logic of this model suggests that low levels of contact (especially when combined with high levels of contact with a nonalcoholic family of origin) would predict the emergence of a nonalcoholic family identity. High levels of contact would increase the likelihood that an alcoholic identity will emerge.

Shared Beliefs: Family Ritual Selection

Many aspects of life in the early-phase family contribute to the complex process of development of shared beliefs, values, and rules for behavior. The process is, in fact, so complex, and often so subtle, as to make it almost impossible to follow as it unfolds. Therefore it is necessary to isolate more discrete behaviors reflective of this process and to track these behaviors instead. We have argued (in chapter 3) that the best window into this process is family-ritual behavior. These symbolically rich practices are, in effect, highly condensed units of behavior that have encompassed in them prepackaged versions of the very shared beliefs and values we are interested in.

Although family rituals can be created out of whole cloth, most early-phase families look to past experiences for models of the rituals that they want to perpetuate in their own families. The rituals that emerge are often an amalgam of the contributions of several family members. Each person, looking back on his or her own experiences in a family of origin (or a prior marriage), identifies aspects of ritual life that they cherish enough to want to continue in the new family. In this sense, rituals are part of the legacy this family member brings with him or her into the new family.

If we focus for the moment on a traditional family situation in which a couple in a first marriage is engaged in establishing its shared beliefs and rules of behavior, the legacy here is one that is handed down from two different families of origin. The choices available in such a situation are for the early-phase family to (1) mimic the husband's family of origin; (2) mimic the wife's family of origin; (3) blend the "best" aspects of both families; or (4) develop novel beliefs and rules of behavior not previously experienced in either family of origin.

Although all families perpetuate some cherished rituals from their previous families, it is usual for one family of origin to be mimicked more than the other, or for the early-phase family to reject both their families and embark on a path intended to be distinctively its own. When the first type of situation occurs, we say that the family of origin that is most significantly represented in the new family's ritual behavior is the *family of heritage* for that early-phase family. When both prior families are "rejected," we think of the new family as having moved to develop a *unique* family identity.

When one of the families of origin is an Alcoholic Family, a decision on the early-phase family's part to continue rituals originally learned from it would surely reflect an identification with that family of origin. If the Alcoholic Family is also the family of heritage for the new early-phase family, we would assume that in such a situation the likelihood that the new family would eventually develop an alcoholic family identity of its own would be substantially increased. Similarly, a decision to select rituals from a nonalcoholic family of origin should decrease the likelihood that a family will become an Alcoholic Family (that is, it should act as a protective factor vis-à-vis alcoholic family-identity formation).

Thus the process of *ritual selection* (which family of origin is to be mimicked) becomes an excellent marker of the influence of past families in the development of shared beliefs by the early-phase family. When alcoholism is present in the prior generation, it also should be useful as a marker of alcoholic family-identity formation.

But there is yet another dimension of critical importance here. The process of ritual selection is one that in some families is handled with considerable forcefulness and conviction. In other families, the same process unfolds in a seemingly uncaring and almost casual fashion. Thus for some families, the decision to continue (or discontinue) ritual behavior from the previous family generation is a conscious and highly deliberate one, while in other families, hardly any attention is paid to these behaviors as they begin to take shape.

We have labeled the dimension just described, the dimension of *deliberateness*. Deliberateness is best thought of as a holistic concept that is characterized by the extent to which a couple desires to, and can, shape its future. As we now move on to describe a study that was designed to systematically track the process of alcoholic identity formation in early-phase families, the dimension of deliberateness should be kept clearly in mind, as it proved to be a critical factor in the prediction of whether or not an Alcoholic Family identity emerges during the early phase of development.

The Family Heritage Study

The Family Heritage study was designed to answer many of the questions we have asked about Alcoholic Family identity formation in the early-phase family. Its core design feature was the use of systematic assessments of family-ritual selection as a vehicle for tracking early-phase identity issues in families formed by adult children of alcoholic parents.

The decision to design the study around an examination of ritual behavior was based on the success of an earlier study that had used rituals to track issues related to intergenerational transmission of alcoholism. This earlier study (which is described in chapter 10) had demonstrated that a careful reconstruction of family-ritual behavior during periods of heaviest drinking proved a useful method for tracking the process of alcoholism transmission. By paying particular attention to whether family rituals were altered to accommodate the family's alcoholic member, we were able to predict the likelihood of cross-generational transmission of alcoholism.

The Heritage study approached the issues related to early-phase identity development by focusing attention on what factors might account for differential development of alcoholism in children of alcoholic parents. In such a model, all the offspring presumably have comparable genetic predispositions to develop alcoholism, and differential outcomes might reasonably be attributed to family environmental variables. In particular, we were interested in why it is that some early-phase families who have one or more alcoholic families of origin seem not to develop alcoholic identities, while other families with quite comparable heritages carry the alcoholic tradition into the next generation.

The Study Design

The study we designed attempted to explore the above question by comparing the family identities of sibling families where the siblings had a shared alcoholic family of origin. The study had two key design features: the type of family being studied, and the focus on ritual behavior as the vehicle for tracking identity formation in the subject sample of families.

Type of Family. The type of family being studied was a two-generational one composed of a parental generation in which at least one parent was alcoholic, and a child generation in which at least two siblings had grown to adulthood and were already married. A representative subject family can therefore be diagramed as shown in figure 5.1.

However, in this modal family, the "subjects" who were recruited and interviewed were the siblings and in-marrying spouses. The parental generation was not directly queried by the research staff, but data about this generation were obtained from the child generation. That is, each adult

FIGURE 5.1

A Representative Subject Family

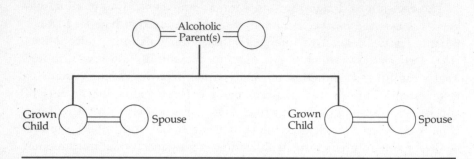

child and his or her spouse took part, first, in an individual interview regarding family life when he or she was a child ("origin family interview") and second, in a couple session focusing on their present family ("nuclear family interview") (Bennett and McAvity, 1985). A semistructured format was used for both sessions. Parallel questions were asked in the origin family and nuclear family interviews regarding the individual and shared experience of husband and wife. We inquired about six areas of family life: family demography; nuclear family relations; extended family relations; alcohol history for three generations; dinnertime; holidays; and family structure.

The key advantage for us in the type of family studied is that the alcoholism status of the two "sibling families" can be quite variable. That is, these families could both be alcoholic (meaning either sibling or marry-in spouse is alcoholic), could both be nonalcoholic, or, in the most interesting variant, could include a combination of alcoholic and nonalcoholic families. A design utilizing this type of extended family thus allows the researcher to ask the question—what factors might differentially increase or decrease the likelihood of a second-generation alcoholic identity developing.

What we have in the modal family being studied are two siblings who have grown up in a family that contains an alcoholic parent. Both these siblings are therefore presumably exposed to the same genetic *and* family environmental factors. These siblings now reach adulthood and marry. At this point they are exposed to a second family culture, that of the spouse's family of origin. By the time we recruit the two siblings and their spouses for our study, they have had time to evolve their own family identities, and we find that although for some sibling pairs both new families have alcoholic identities, for a larger number only one of the two sibling marriages is contending with alcoholism in this next generation. This subject sample then allows us to explore further the factors *in the early-phase family* that appear to have attenuated the development of alcoholism in some of these "next generation" families, but not in others.

Ritual Behavior. The second important design aspect of the study was its focus on ritual behavior. As we have repeatedly emphasized, no other family regulatory behavior is so clearly reflective of underlying identity issues as is family ritual behavior. In that these behaviors represent, in highly condensed and neatly packaged form, key aspects of the family's shared belief system, they can be assumed to be the closest approximation, at the level of surface behavioral manifestations, of family identity. Further, because they are so condensed in form and richly symbolic, they can be reconstructed via careful interview techniques. And, finally, it may even be the case that rituals are a mechanism for the conveying of important components of family identity to new family members. Thus rituals might even be a vehicle for the transmission of important shared beliefs and values (including those surrounding alcohol use and alcohol-related behavior) to the next generation.

In chapter 8 we discuss at some length the method we use to ascertain the important details of a family's ritual behavior. Suffice it to say at this point that the method utilizes conjoint interviewing to reconstruct the nature of ritual practice in such areas of family life as holidays, vacations, and dinnertimes. Because the method is intended to generate data about family members' shared perceptions of ritual behavior (it does not claim to be producing verifiably accurate data about *actual* ritual behavior), the method is as appropriate for the reconstruction of past ritual practices as it is for current ritual behavior.

In this study, we were particularly interested in comparing the ritual behavior in the child generation family with that of the families of origin. Thus the interview included detailed probes about current ritual practices in two family areas (holidays and dinnertimes) *and* about the same two ritual area practices as carried out by the two families of origin when the spouses were children. A comparison of ritual practices in the current family with those of the two families of origin is then used in the study to ascertain whether the family is differentially selecting one family of origin over the other as a model for its own ritual practices. Specific questions about the *deliberateness* of such a selection process are also included in the interview.

It is this data base that then becomes the vehicle for ascertaining heritage continuity in these families. That is, after the interviews are completed, they are transcribed and given to coders whose primary task is to determine heritage continuity based on which family of origin has been the principal contributor to the pattern of rituals in the current generation. This determination was carried out as a two-part process:

First, coders decided whether the couple resembled each origin family on four separate characteristics (dinnertime and holiday rituals, family structure, and the general quality of relationships). Two final variables—heritage choice and level of heritage—resulted. Second, the degree of deliberateness evident in final heritage selection is determined for each couple.

These two sets of variables, derived from the detailed coding of the ritual interviews, then become the primary vehicles for tracking the process of identity formation in these families. Insofar as a family is willfully attempting to break with an alcoholic past (as reflected in the above measures), the study would predict that that family would be less likely to itself develop an Alcoholic Family identity.

Thus the Heritage study is essentially a two-generation, sociocultural study exploring the question of sibling differences with respect to variable cross-generational transmission of alcoholism. Further, by using family rituals to examine the cumulative family experience of now-adult children of alcoholics, we are able to account for three presumably independent aspects of family development. First, we are able to consider the *origin family history*, especially with respect to the impact of parental alcoholism upon already established family rituals. Second, we are able to examine the influence of family ritual and alcoholism backgrounds of *spouses' families of origin.* And third, we are able to reconstruct the process of *heritage selection* in the current generation as this new family goes about the business of developing its own family identity.

From the vantage point of the son or daughter of an alcoholic parent, each step unfolds chronologically. In the first step—origin family ritual experience—children of alcoholic parents participate in family rituals that depending upon the extent of alcoholism intrusion, contribute to the increased likelihood of subsequent transmission. The selection of a spouse—the second step—then adds an intermediate connection; it takes into account the in-law family's ritual heritage and alcoholism background. Spouse selection is seen as promoting or inhibiting the transmission outcome for each child. The final step considered in this study is the couple's establishment of its own family-ritual heritage and the amount of contact the couple maintains with the alcoholic origin family.

Thus the study incorporates the key factors dealing with alcoholic identity formation discussed in the previous section. In this study, we are now asking whether these factors systematically and significantly differentiate those couples who wind up continuing an Alcoholic Family legacy from those couples who do not.

The Analytic Strategy and Findings

The overall strategy of the Heritage study was a relatively straightforward one. We had recruited and interviewed at least two grown married siblings and their spouses from a total of thirty families in which at least one parent was alcoholic. In all, sixty-eight couples from these thirty families participated in the study. However, these couples, although all had at least one Alcoholic Family of origin, were quite variable as regards their own alcohol status. All together, twenty-seven couples included at least one problem drinker or alcoholic following marriage (alcohol status determined by the Goodwin criteria described in chapter 2). That meant that forty-one of the sixty-eight couples evidenced no problems with alcohol. Further, of the twenty-seven couples with alcohol problems, in twenty-one cases it was the husband who was the identified drinker, while in three instances the alcoholic was the wife, and in three couples both spouses were alcoholic.*

The central goal of the study was to identify those factors (predictor variables) that seemed most strongly associated with this variability of alcoholism status (criterion variable) in the sixty-eight couples. The statistical model used was multiple regression. Because of the ability to gather detailed information from the couples both about their families of origin and about their decisions regarding selection of rituals and contact with origin families, the study was able to generate a rich data base not only about life in the current generation family, but also about factors in the prior generation families that might have contributed to variability of alcoholism outcomes.

Predictor Variables. The regression model we used was designed to allow us to explore the independent contributions of three major sets of variables

---

*Although no controls were built into the study to ensure comparability of the alcoholic and nonalcoholic family subgroups noted above, a series of preliminary t tests were performed comparing the two groups along a wide-ranging series of demographic, structural, and compositional variables, and no statistically significant findings emerged (we used a p value of .10 as our confidence level). We also performed an extensive series of analyses of severity of alcoholism in the parental generation to ensure that differences here might not introduce a confound for subsequent analyses, and here as well, all t tests proved statistically nonsignificant.

to the variance in the alcoholism status variable. First of all, there is the contribution attributable to family membership. If, for example, there was a very high sibling concordance rate for alcoholism versus nonalcoholism status, then family membership itself might be a stronger predictor of alcoholism status than any other variable. Thus this variable must be examined as a predictor of outcome. (However, it should be added parenthetically that had this finding been the one to emerge from our regression analyses, it would have been a disappointing one in that the emphasis in our study was on the potential import of family-identity formation on alcoholism status, not on family membership per se.)

The second and third sets of predictor variables were: those having to do with characteristics of the two families of origin, and those having to do with characteristics of the nuclear family (child generation marriages). The second set (origin family contributions) included demographic characteristics of purported importance in the development of alcoholism (e.g., birth order), aspects of the alcoholism status of origin family members, and ritual behavior evidenced by the child and spouses families of origin when the children were still living at home. The third set (nuclear family contributions) included nuclear family behaviors reflective of heritage family choices being made during the early phase of development. These behaviors focused especially on degree of contact with the two families of origin and on ritual selection (both described earlier). The complete list of the two sets of variables examined are summarized in table 5.1.

Multiple Regression Analyses. The multiple regression analyses we performed were designed to answer two central questions about the relation-

TABLE 5.1

The Independent Variables in the Model

Origin Family Contributions	Nuclear Family Contributions
Level of ritualization of child's* origin family dinners	Heritage choice
Level of ritualization for child's origin family holidays	Extent of heritage
Level of ritualization of spouse's† origin family dinners	Deliberateness evident in final heritage choice
Level of ritualization of spouse's origin family holidays	
Disruption by alcoholic behavior of child's origin family dinners	Novelty in family identity
Disruption by alcoholic behavior of child's origin family holidays	
Birth position of child	Extent of contact with child's family
Sex of alcoholic parent and sex of child	
Alcohol status of spouse's parents	

*"Child" refers to the adult child of the family with the alcoholic parent.
†"Spouse" refers to the spouse of the adult child.

134

ships between the predictor variables cited in the table and the alcoholism status of the child generation families:

First, we wanted to know about the independent contributions of the three sets of predictor variables (family membership, origin family characteristics, nuclear family characteristics) as groups, to the alcoholism status variance. This question is a global one in that it addresses the issue of whether, for example, the sum total of nuclear family characteristics is systematically associated with alcoholism status outcome. A set-wise, hierarchical regression analysis was therefore performed to answer this question.*

Second, we wanted to know about the contribution of each of the predictor variables, independent of its type, to the outcome variance. Here we were interested in which of the fourteen origin family and nuclear family predictor variables were the most powerful predictors of alcoholism status. A standard regression analysis was therefore performed to answer this question.

The set-wise regression analysis was carried out as follows: As the first step in the analysis, we tested for the relationship between joint origin family membership among siblings and alcoholism transmission in the couple. Modeled on a nested analysis of variance approach, each of the thirty origin families was treated as a separate dummy variable. For example, in Family 1, all sibling couples were rated "yes" and all couples from families 2–30 as "no." This process was repeated for all families until the number $n - 1$th family was reached. The $n - 1$ family membership variables were then entered as a set into a hierarchical, multiple regression analysis.

In the second step, we entered the independent variables as two sets reflecting the two-generation model of alcoholism transmission (e.g., the nine origin family variables and the five nuclear family variables). We then assessed whether the increment in variance accounted for by these variables above and beyond the variance due to shared family membership exceeded chance levels.

The principal findings of this analysis are summarized in table 5.2. If we look first at the importance of family membership as a predictor of outcome, we find that when all thirty families are placed into the multiple regression, 46.7 percent of the variance of transmission outcome for the couple is accounted for (R^2 of .467 for "shared family membership" predictable variable set). This R^2 represents the amount of variance in alco-

---

*For those readers interested in the use of set-wise and hierarchical regression techniques, a thorough discussion of these statistical procedures can be found in Cohen and Cohen (1983).

holic status attributable to unknown (i.e., unmeasured) properties of the families to which the couples belong.

In the second step, we placed the group of nine origin family variables—reflecting the first generation's contribution to transmission to the couples—in the regression equation. The total variance accounted for now jumps up to 68.6 percent (R^2 of .686), an incremental R^2 increase (of .219) that proved to be statistically significant at a < .05 level. What this means is that origin family predictor variables, when treated as a single group, contribute substantially to the overall explanation of couple alcoholism outcome.

Finally, when we add the last remaining set of predictors—the five nuclear family variables—we find the R^2 has now jumped up to .802 (total variance explained = 80.2 percent). An assessment of the statistical significance of this final increment in predictive power indicated that it was significant at a confidence level of p < .01.

These analyses thus confirm that even though family membership clearly accounts for a substantial amount of the variance in alcoholism status (as one might expect), the independent contributions of origin family and nuclear family characteristics (characteristics that focus on ritual behavior and the heritage-selection process) are substantial. Most crucial to our understanding of how alcoholic identities develop in early-phase families is the finding that even the most conservative strategy of data

TABLE 5.2

Hierarchical Set-wise Multiple Regression Analysis: Incremental Increases in Transmission Outcome due to Predictor Variable Groups

(n = 68)

Predictor Variables	R	Increment over Family membership	Incremental F	Probability of Increment
Shared Family Membership	.467	—	—	—
Family Membership +9 Origin Family Variables	.686	.219	2.21	< .05
Family Membership +9 Origin Family +5 Nuclear Family Variables	.802	.335	2.91	< .01

SOURCE: "Couples at Risk for Alcoholism Recurrence: Protective Influences," by L. A. Bennett et al., 1987, *Family Process,* 26, p. 125.

analysis (entering the family membership and origin family predictor sets into the regression equation first) still leaves a very substantial role for nuclear family variables as predictors of couple alcoholism status. Thus a model of identity formation that focuses attention on the quality of early-phase family behavior vis-à-vis its origin families is surely consistent with the data emerging from the Heritage study.

While the primary goal of our data analytic strategy was to test the two-generation model of alcoholic identity formation by examining the independent effect of the origin and nuclear family variables as groups, it is also useful to consider the contribution of individual variables to the transmission outcome. Therefore, in a second multiple regression analysis (this time a standard, stepwise regression), each of the fourteen origin and nuclear family variables was entered in order of its contribution to the explained variance in couple alcoholism status.

Most important for our purpose is that this type of multiple regression procedure enters predictor variables based on their *unique* contribution to outcome variance (that is, the contribution of that particular variable when all other variables are held constant). These unique contributions, expressed as partial-order correlation coefficients, can also be subjected to standard procedures for establishing confidence levels (*p*-values), levels that are accurate reflections of the power of the contribution of each variable to the overall prediction of outcome variance.

The results of these procedures are summarized in table 5.3. The *F* ratios reported are for the partial-order correlation coefficients of each variable. The direction this contribution takes (either as a risk factor or as a protective factor) was determined by examining the direction of the partial-order correlations (these correlations are not reported in the table).

The findings summarized in table 5.3 indicate that five of the nine origin family variables (three from the child's side and two from the spouse's side) and two of the five nuclear family variables contribute the most to the outcome of transmission. Of these seven variables, two clearly contribute most substantially. When the child in the couple is a son of an alcoholic father, the couple is at significantly greater risk for transmission. On the other hand, those couples that were most *deliberate* in the choice of a family heritage are most protected from transmission. Three other variables—all representing the origin family experiences of the child and spouse—are moderate contributors to the outcome. When the spouse comes from a family where dinner was highly ritualized, the couple is relatively more protected from transmission. Similarly, when the child's origin family dinners remained distinctive under the influence of the alcohol abuse

TABLE 5.3

Specific Independent Variables Contributing Most Significantly
To Transmission Outcome
(n = 68)

Independent Variable	Direction	F	Probability of F	Category
Child is son of an alcoholic father	Risk	10.63	< .002	Origin Family: Child
High level of deliberateness in family heritage	Protective	8.66	< .006	Nuclear Family
Spouse's family dinner ritual level high	Protective	5.30	< .02	Origin Family: Spouse
Child's family dinner kept distinctive	Protective	4.09	< .05	Origin Family: Child
Spouse's family has an alcoholic parent	Risk	3.17	< .08	Origin Family: Spouse
Contact with child's origin family	Risk	2.62	< .115	Nuclear Family
Child is second born	Protective	2.56	< .12	Origin Family: Child

SOURCE: "Couples at Risk for Alcoholism Recurrence: Protective Influences," by L. A. Bennett et al., 1987, *Family Process,* 26, p. 125.

behavior of the parent, the couple is less likely to be alcoholic. However, when the spouse also comes from an Alcoholic Family, the couple is at increased risk for alcoholism.

Two "borderline" contributors to outcome include an origin family and a nuclear family variable. Those couples that maintain a high degree of contact with the child's origin family evidence more transmission. However, when the child in the couple is second born in his or her family, the couple is relatively more protected against being alcoholic.

Conclusion

The study presented in this chapter speaks to influences on transmission across the entire family life cycle. Two dimensions, however, are especially pertinent to early phase. Deliberateness in family-ritual development, and extent of contact with the alcoholic origin family not only set the tone for family-identity formation; they also, according to the results of our study, are linked to whether or not the couple perpetuates the alcoholism from the previous generation.

The key finding was that early-phase couples clearly have a choice about whether to actively break with an alcoholic past or to passively accept it. This is the meaning of the finding that those couples who are highly deliberate in their selection of family rituals and who do *not* maintain a high degree of contact with the alcoholic side of the family are relatively more protected from recurrence of alcoholism than those couples who are very undeliberate and *do* maintain a great deal of contact.

These data seem to be tapping an inclination on the part of some couples to successfully take control of their lives. They may choose to emulate part—or even a good deal—of the previous generation's rituals. The critical point is that they *choose* a certain path and are able to follow through on that choice. Similarly, couples do not necessarily need to shut off their social ties with the previous generation; it is only those who maintain a *high* amount of contact with alcoholic parents who are at greater risk for alcoholism recurrence. Setting their boundaries in such a way that the alcoholic members do not *predominate* in their social activities seems adequate enough protection from an alcoholic past.

In comparison with later phases of the family life cycle, early phase offers a special opportunity to modify injurious family legacies from the past and to develop a healthier family identity than was evident in the previous generation. It is also a highly vulnerable time for the new couple, because they must set the tone of their family identity, which then becomes increasingly difficult to change as they move into middle and late phase.

It is for this reason that we argue that early phase is an ideal time for couples to face issues of family-identity formation, as well as concerns over repeating an Alcoholic Family legacy. As increasing numbers of people are becoming aware of the significant possibilities of familial alcoholism transmission, they are similarly more receptive to the idea of early intervention in a troublesome marital situation. Early phase is by far the best time to redirect family-identity formation away from tendencies to repeat alcoholism. Not only is alcoholism more likely to be avoided, but if couples have already embarked on an alcoholic path and are "prevented" before they move into middle phase, we observe that they are less likely to develop a dry Alcoholic Family identity.

Thus the early-phase decision about identity formation is a critical choice point for families with alcoholism heritages. Many such families seem to clearly recognize what is at stake, and move with considerable deliberateness to effect a separation from this alcoholism-laden past. Al-though this is not the last time families will have the opportunity to challenge an alcoholic identity, it surely is the best time to do so.

Yet it is also the case that many early-phase families either fail to recognize what is at stake as they evolve identities that incorporate impor-tant features from their alcoholic legacies, or are simply so passive in approaching these early-phase developmental tasks that they allow an Alcoholic Family identity to emerge. Although we have no good estimates of what percentage of families with alcoholic heritages choose each of the identity options, the very high familial incidence of alcoholism suggests that a very large proportion of these families emerge from early phase with fully developed Alcoholic Family identities. It is this group of families we will now follow as they move into the second phase of systemic matura-tion—the middle phase.

PART IV

THE MIDDLE
PHASE OF
DEVELOPMENT

T HE MIDDLE PHASE of development is a time of specialization. The family must begin to focus on a finite set of options, to state its priorities, to bypass other opportunities. Emphasis changes from the establishment of a distinctive identity, the primary theme of the early phase, to maintenance of a stable and predictable family environment. Families that can't make these shifts remain fixated at the early phase of development.

For the Alcoholic Family, the maintenance activities of the middle phase are built around alcohol-related behaviors as a central core. A balance is struck between stabilizing family life, and disrupting as little as possible the needs of the alcoholic family member. In this way, alcoholism increasingly plays a central role, not only in the family's sense of itself, but also in the very behaviors it uses to regulate and control its life.

For most families, the middle phase of development is one not only of specialization, but also of orderly growth. The family moves ahead in stepwise fashion to manage a series of normative and anticipated developmental tasks. For the Alcoholic Family, however, the emphasis during the middle phase is on a set of rigidly maintained homeostatic mechanisms that produce not only an inflexible commitment to the status quo but also a plateau effect that profoundly alters the customary slope of family development. Investment in short-term stability becomes paramount, often at the expense of orderly long-term growth. The key step in this process is the intricate relationship that develops between alcoholic behavior and family regulatory mechanisms.

Thus, an understanding of the developmental implications of alcoholism for the middle-phase family is best achieved by focusing on those regulatory behaviors that play such a critical role in the management of the family's internal and external environments. How does alcoholism affect these regulatory behaviors and what are the consequent implications for the family? Three aspects of family behavior—short-term problem-solving, daily home routines, and family rituals—are the tools we use to explore this question.

Regulation of stability of the family's environment can be looked at within two different time frames—a microscopic time frame in which we look for behaviors that, on a day-to-day basis, serve to correct what might be seen as potential destabilizing forces within the family; and a macroscopic time frame in which we look for patterned behaviors that, over periods of months to years, provide consistency and form to family behavior.

Within the microscopic time frame, we are thus interested in the way the family manages short-term problems, those day-to-day challenges that arise to upset the family applecart. The style the family uses in handling short-term problem-solving has profound implications for the pattern of growth it manifests during the middle phase. Many perfectly normal, healthy developmental changes initially can be perceived by the family as problems. They are shifts from the status quo; they create tension and anxiety. They are often new and unfamiliar experiences for the family. The family with an intolerance for uncertainty can easily overreact to such challenges and prematurely close off opportunities for growth. Alcoholic Families by and large behave in this fashion.

But what is the mechanism that brings this about? It turns out that the key link is the relationship between the often-dramatic shifts in family behavior that occur when the alcoholic member moves from sobriety to intoxication, and family strategies for short-term problem-solving. We discuss this issue in chapter 6, using as the core data base contrasting clinical observations that we have made of Alcoholic Families during states of both sobriety and intoxication.

Within the macroscopic time frame, we focus on two aspects of family behavior that appear critical to the conservation of family stability and family identity over long periods of time—daily routines and family rituals.

As discussed previously, daily routines are those patterned but largely unconscious behaviors that provide structure to daily living. They are largely background phenomena, are occurring continuously, and both reflect but also reinforce the underlying regulatory principles the family follows in maintaining the constancy of its internal environment. The best place to study daily routines is the home. We therefore, in chapter 7, describe a research project in which home observations of Alcoholic Families were carried out using a highly structured behavioral coding system that concentrated on measurements of the family's patterns of time and space use in the home; this is one way of contrasting important differences between the ways families organize their daily routines. Chapter 7 provides details about both the project and the unique relationships that exist between patterns of home behavior and patterns of drinking behavior in the Alcoholic Family.

Family rituals, in contrast to daily routines, are discrete, conscious, and symbolically rich behaviors that can be thought of as the surface expression of a family's sense of itself, that is, its unique identity. The way the family celebrates holidays, the way it plans and carries out vacations, the way it ritualizes mealtime behavior, all reflect this translation of family identity into specific patterns of behavior.

The establishment of a family identity was the main developmental task of the early phase. In the middle phase, this now-established identity serves to define the family's continuing sense of itself. How does it do this? One way is through the performance of family rituals, those highly structured, repetitive, symbolically rich sequences of behaviors associated with holidays, major family events, mealtimes and child-rearing practices. The critical issue, just as for short-term problem-solving, is the extent to which this aspect of family life is protected from involvement with alcoholic behavior. Although the developmental consequences of the relationship between alcoholism and family rituals are most profoundly felt during the late phase of development (around the issue of transmission of alcoholism to future generations), the seeds of this process are being sown during the middle phase. We describe this process in chapter 8, using data from a study that carefully reconstructed, via semistructured conjoint interviews of family members, the middle-phase ritual behavior of a group of Alcoholic Families.

CHAPTER 6

The Sobriety-Intoxication Cycle: Family Problem-Solving and Alcoholic Behavior

WE HAVE SEEN in chapter 5, how alcoholism can take hold in early-phase families and become incorporated in what we have called an Alcoholic Family identity. The task in relation to middle-phase families is to describe how a potentially destabilizing chronic condition becomes instead an organizing principle around which a number of critically important aspects of family behavior take shape. In particular, we want to focus on those aspects of behavior that seem tied to underlying regulatory mechanisms used by the family to shape and stabilize its life during middle phase.

In this chapter, we focus on the first of three such behavioral aspects: short-term problem-solving. In many ways this is the most fascinating aspect of middle-phase Alcoholic Family behavior because it directs attention to what is the most unique part of the alcoholism syndrome and the trademark of chronic alcoholism—the repetitive cycling between states of intoxication and of sobriety.

Perhaps the most baffling and intriguing question about chronic alcoholism and the family is why alcoholism has such a tenacious hold on most Alcoholic Families? Why is it that so many of these families tolerate the drinking behavior of their alcoholic member? Surely living with someone who is repeatedly intoxicated is a most unpleasant experience. Why then would upwards of 15 percent of our adult population, not to mention children, continue to live compromised lives, replete with economic deprivations, legal complications, serious medical illnesses, periodic violence, and the like, when they are not even the ones consuming the alcohol. Why not, to paraphrase the song lyrics, just "kick the blaggard out"?

In this chapter we discuss one possible explanation for this seeming paradox. It turns out that family behavior, during times of intoxication, is hardly chaotic. In fact, it is just as predictable and patterned as behavior during times of sobriety. And furthermore, specific behaviors the family expresses only when its alcoholic member is drinking, actually assist in providing short-term solutions to specific problems that have arisen for the family. In other words, family behavior associated with intoxication is *not*, as has often been suggested, almost purely defensive. In certain important circumstances, it helps the family deal in the short run with problems that are perceived as potential threats to family stability, albeit at a very high price. Let us see how this might be so.

The Intoxicated Interactional State

A thirty-five-year-old woman (we will call her Alice Clarion), recalling her adolescent years growing up in an Alcoholic Family, shared a particularly vivid memory. Week after week she would return home from school late on Friday afternoon and notice a half-empty liquor bottle on the dining room table. Her response, she related with some bitterness, was to "go on automatic pilot" for the rest of the weekend. Looking back, she realized that the open bottle, the physical evidence that her father had started his regular weekend drinking binge, provided all the stimulus she needed to set in motion a preprogrammed set of behaviors, behaviors that would presumably run an inevitable course until her father's drinking, also predictably, came to a halt as the next workweek approached.

What were these behaviors? She remembered that *all* family members systematically avoided one another; that meal patterns changed from communal family breakfasts and dinners to a haphazard pattern of catch-as-catch-can meals taken whenever someone was hungry. Although a "meal" might still be prepared, each family member would eat at a different time, often in a different room. She recalled spending long blocks of time isolated in her room engaged in busywork and taking great pains to make sure that her friends did not visit.

She also remembered that, occasionally, intense and bitter arguments would break out. However, despite these arguments, Alice could not recall feeling frightened or in physical danger. She recalled actively participating in these arguments *despite* her conscious conviction that they were both inconsequential and incapable of meaningful resolution. However, it was also true that during these exchanges, she would direct verbal barbs not only at her father, but also at her mother and brother. And she could recall a vague and somewhat troubling sense of satisfaction accompanying these confrontations, even though she was sure they would be of no lasting consequences.

As we examine these recollections more closely, a surprising finding is suggested. Alice Clarion's behavior is strikingly similar in form and content to the behavior we would have expected of *her father.* In fact, except for the actual consumption of alcohol, as she recalls it, each and every member of this family displayed remarkably similar behaviors. All family members were avoiding one another. All family members stopped eating regular family meals and instead were on a haphazard, hunger-activated schedule typical of the alcoholic person during a drinking binge. Each member of the family walled him or herself off from neighbors, friends, and relatives. Just as an alcoholic individual might isolate himself from society by retreating to a Skid Row, each nonalcoholic member of this family had established rigid and impermeable rules about entry of outsiders into the home. Finally, everyone in the Clarion family was actively engaged in the types of explosive, vitriolic, and abusive arguments that are such a familiar consequence whenever people have been drinking too much. However, only one of them had actually been drinking.

Although Alice could not explain why the family kept participating in these fruitless arguments, the fact remains that they continued to do so, albeit almost despite themselves. A characteristic family-level series of interactions was predictably occurring in this family every time Mr. Clarion started drinking. Hence, the sensation of "going on automatic pilot." Also, Alice Clarion had emphasized that these behaviors occurred *only* in association with her father's intoxication. Sober behavior in this family was quite different.

Let us look at another example of the contrast between "sober" family behavior and behavior when an alcoholic member is intoxicated. We asked the Pridgett family to participate in a unique series of interviews. Carl Pridgett, the identified alcoholic in the family, was, at the time of the interview, a research volunteer in a study that included a two-week period of "experimentally-induced intoxication."* He had been recruited from a residential alcoholism treatment center where he had gone (for the fourth time) for detoxification. The center is one that catered primarily to homeless alcoholic men who can opt for participation in a treatment program or can use the facility as a temporary residence. Because Carl had made it clear to the staff at the center that he had every intention of returning to drinking when he left the facility, he had been provided an opportunity to volunteer for a research study designed to explore biochemical correlates of chronic drinking. In contrast to most of his covolunteers for this research program, however, he was married, the father of three children, and lived at home with his family between stints at the rehabilitation center.

During the first interview, he joined his wife, Sophie, and two of his children, a twenty-year-old daughter and a thirteen-year-old son, to talk with a family psychiatrist about their experiences in living with alcoholism. The format was a relatively nonintrusive assessment of the family using an open-ended conjoint interview format. The interview setting also provided Carl an opportunity for a reunion with his family, who had not seen him for the previous six weeks.

During the first interview, Carl predictably found himself isolated as Sophie Pridgett, in coalition with her two children, mounted a highly successful attack against him, placing on the table a seemingly inexhaustible list of accusations, all of which were uniformly supported by her children. A powerful, invisible barrier seemed to exist between Carl and his family and he reacted with increasing withdrawal, looking for all the world like a whipped and defeated child. The only thing he seemed to share with the rest of his family was a sense of depression and despair, which hung over the interview like an emotional blanket.

The second interview, which occurred a week later, had a unique aspect to it. Thirty minutes prior to the interview, Carl Pridgett was asked to consume six ounces of 100-proof alcohol. He was given an additional six ounces to take with him into the interview and was told he could drink it as he wished during the course of the interview. Of course, the ground rules for this "intoxicated family interview" had been carefully explained to all members of the family and they had agreed to participate in a venture that had been described to them as research, not therapy.

What did we observe during this second interview? A number of our

---

*The study for which this man volunteered was one of a series carried out at the Laboratory of Alcohol Research of the National Institute of Alcohol Abuse and Alcoholism during the late 1960s and early 1970s under the direction of Drs. Jack H. Mendelson and Nancy K. Mello. Summaries of these studies can be found in Mello's (1972) chapter, "Behavioral Studies of Alcoholism," published in *The Biology of Alcoholism,* edited by B. Kissin and H. Begleiter.

observations coincided with popular stereotypes of intoxicated behavior. For example, Carl proved to be far more animated in this second interview. His depression seemed to have lifted; he was assertive and confrontational in his dealings with other family members. What came as a surprise to us, however, were the reactions of the rest of the family. Much to our amazement, they demonstrated the same dramatic increase in animation that we noticed in our intoxicated subject.

In the first interview, each family member sat rigidly in his or her seat, facing the interviewer. They rarely made eye contact with one another and surely made no effort to turn toward one another to make postural or verbal contact. In his second interview, however, they were behaving quite differently. Husband and wife, although seated side by side on the same couch, were now facing at 45-degree angles *toward* one another. He had his arm extended across the top of the couch, reaching out toward her and this time she seemed receptive to his overtures. Mr. Pridgett and his children now repeatedly leaned toward one another as they were talking and with the exception of the thirteen-year-old son, Kenneth, all family members now made direct eye contact one with another when they were talking. (Although Kenneth refused to look at his father, he engaged in several long, albeit combative, exchanges with his father during this second interview; during the first interview there was virtually no verbal contact between them.)

Even more striking was the affective tone of this second meeting. The first meeting was characterized by a sense of depression and defeat. During this second interview, the family seemed suddenly to have awakened. Everyone seemed attentive, ready for interaction, eager to do combat. If we were merely to count the number of verbal interactions between family members, we would find that they had almost doubled. And most surprising of all, the family was *laughing*. Granted, Carl's combative, accusatory tone often led him to escalate subject matter to the point of absurdity, lending a comic note to his assertions and pleadings. But this was a family that had supposedly suffered greatly from his chronic love affair with alcohol. Many of his speeches even referred back to a number of his more ludicrous escapades. So why were they laughing? The interviewer, struck by the apparent incongruity of content, context, and affect, pointed this out to the family. What was the family's response? Even more laughter.

One week after this second interview, the family was asked to come back for a "debriefing" session. As part of this session, they were shown several preselected segments from the videotapes of both the sober and intoxicated interviews. A striking thing happened. As the four members of the family watched the videotapes, they reproduced in almost perfect parallel fashion their behavior during the interviews themselves. As they watched the sober interview, they once again appeared depressed, withdrawn, quiet, slumped in their chairs, staring at the screen without looking at one another. As they watched the intoxicated interview, however, they again became animated, physically attentive, began to shoot glances at each other, point fingers at the screen to make sure other family members had caught a particular exchange, and once again the room was filled with laughter.

How are we to understand this behavior? In part we might attribute it to the usual differences that occur between initial and second interviews. Families are often apprehensive and on guard in what is for them a strange experience. When they return a second time, they no longer have to contend with a novel environment and are often more open and relaxed. Surely, however, this simple explanation does not adequately account for the extraordinary differences we have described. After all, the bottom line remains that in the second interview the family was being directly challenged by Carl regarding his alcoholism. In drinking to a state of intoxication, he was signaling his commitment to continue his alcoholic behavior despite the profound financial and emotional consequences it has had for family life. (We will detail some of these consequences; suffice it to say at this point that the family was dealing with real problems, including major financial difficulties, directly attributable to Carl's alcoholism.)

These two vignettes—the "automatic pilot" incident, and our interviews with the Pridgett family—highlight three important issues regarding the sobriety-intoxication cycle, issues that, in turn, help us to understand the relationship between this cycle and short-term problem-solving in alcoholic families:

First, we are privy to two examples of families, *as whole groups,* evidencing clear-cut changes in their behavior seemingly dependent upon whether their alcoholic member is, at that moment, sober or intoxicated. As we listened to Alice Clarion's recollections, we were struck by how similarly family members behaved. Emotional distance is one example. There was no evidence that the nonalcoholic members of the Clarion family were brought closer together in a coalition against the "identified patient." They were not attempting to provide solace for each other; nor did they seem capable of sustaining the customary "sober" patterns of daily life.

Second, the introduction of alcohol, whether during a typical weekend drinking binge (the Clarions) or during an "intoxicated interview" (the Pridgetts) profoundly but *predictably* altered the behavior of the family as a group. By predictably, we mean that the changes associated with the introduction of alcohol occur repeatedly, and in a patterned fashion. In the

Clarion family, Alice recalled not one, but a composite of numerous, repeated episodes that seemed always to play themselves out in the same way. For the Pridgetts, the family's reactions to the videotapes was strong evidence of a repeated pattern.

The third important issue highlighted by these two vignettes is that the exact behavior manifested by the family during the period of intoxication could not have been predicted from our knowledge of the family during sobriety alone. This issue is particularly well illustrated in our experience with the Pridgetts. The interviewer, despite his credentials as an experienced family therapist and alcoholism researcher, was initially dumbfounded by the family's behavior during the intoxicated interview, especially their persistent laughter. Familiarity with this family's customary behavior during sobriety seemed of little help in predicting what would happen when alcohol was introduced into the family system.

These three issues, when combined, suggest that although it is almost impossible for an outsider to predict how a family will behave when its alcoholic member switches from sobriety to intoxication, once "intoxicated" family behavior is observed, it can be expected to follow a repetitive (and therefore predictable) course from one drinking episode to the next.

What about the behaviors themselves? Do these two families behave in similar fashion when alcohol is introduced? Here the answer seems to be, no. In the Clarion family, alcohol was associated with increased interactional distance, decreased affect, and disruption of group activities. The Pridgett family, on the other hand, moved in the direction of increased animation, closer interactional distance, greater physical contact, and even a sense of excitement during the intoxicated interview.

This is not to say that were we to have more data available and examine these two families in greater detail we might not be able to identify important parallels in their styles of behavior. But we are surely left with the impression that the introduction of alcohol does not in and of itself lead to a characteristic set of behaviors in each and every family. The cases of the Clarion and the Pridgett families also draw attention to at least three dimensions of behavior that seem particularly sensitive to this sober-intoxicated alternation. The first of these dimensions is the alteration in *interactional activity rate* as the family moves from "sobriety" to "intoxication." The second dimension is reflected in the *interactional distance* among family members. The third is reflected in the quantity and the quality of *affect* displayed by family members.

For example, if we contrast the Clarions and the Pridgetts along the interactional distance dimension, we are effectively contrasting a family that moves toward a "distant" position to a family that moves toward a "huddling" position when alcohol enters the scene. In the Clarion family, interactional space expands and emotionally the family cools off. Although Alice Clarion had described occasional bitter arguments breaking out during the intoxicated interactional phase, her description of these arguments suggests that they had the effect of pushing family members away from one another even as they were occurring; in this sense, they were quite different in flavor and outcome from the arguments we witnessed in the Pridgett family during the intoxicated interview. These arguments seemed to heighten the sense of engagement of family members to each other.

To summarize, then, the Clarions and Pridgetts illustrate a phenomenon that appears unique to the Alcoholic Family, a characteristic cycling between two interactional states that occurs in these families—one associated with sobriety and one associated with intoxication. Each family has its own characteristic pattern of behavior during the intoxicated interaction state, so we can't say that all Alcoholic Families look alike during periods of intoxication. But we can say that the critical element here is this curious parceling out of types of behaviors with some in the "sober" pile and others in the "intoxicated" pile. This is the critical element because it means that in Alcoholic Families, we will *only* be seeing certain patterns of interactional behavior during periods of intoxication. In fact, in the Clarion and Pridgett families, this separation of sober and intoxicated behavioral styles along the dimensions we highlighted in our clinical descriptions—interactional activity rates; interactional distance; and quality of affect—was so dramatic as to make one feel that these dimensions are "state-dependent" properties in these families. That is, their characteristics are dependent upon whether the family is at that moment in an alcohol-on or an alcohol-off state, perhaps analogous to the notion of state-dependent learning.*

Lastly, the phenomenon of sober-intoxicated behavioral cycling is an aspect of the Alcoholic Family that is present irrespective of the type of drinking pattern evidenced by the family's alcoholic member. Mr. Clarion, a weekend drinker, had developed a drinking pattern that was sustained in unchanging fashion over years. Mr. Pridgett, on the other hand, had a labile, binge drinking pattern in which he alternated between periods of heavy drinking and periods of dryness. Hence his track record of having

---

*The concept of state-dependent learning has been invoked by a number of investigators as a partial explanation for the characteristic memory deficits experienced in chronic alcoholism. In particular, the phenomenon of alcoholic blackouts is thought to be related to state-dependent learning. The chronic alcoholic can only recover memories of events and places "learned" during a drinking episode by again becoming intoxicated. When sober, he or she has a total "blackout" of recall for those events. Although we are not proposing a neurological basis for the changes in interactional distance and affect display associated with sober-intoxicated cycling, as a psychological phenomenon the analogy seems useful.

been admitted on multiple occasions to alcoholism rehabilitation centers. But in both families the same dual-state pattern of behavior could be seen.

So, the intoxicated state is a widespread if not universal, aspect of life in the middle-phase Alcoholic Family. Now we need to explore its functional implications for these families.

The Intoxicated Interactional State and Short-Term Problem-Solving

The question still remains, why does alcohol have such a tenacious hold on these families; why does it occupy such a central position, a position that had led us to label them Alcoholic Families? The answer lies in a perception on the part of the family that the unique (for the family) behaviors it carries out during the intoxicated interactional state are not merely alcohol-related, but are actually alcohol-induced. In other words, the perception (not necessarily conscious) that these behaviors occur not merely when alcohol is present, but *because* alcohol is present.

This perception, namely that alcohol facilitates behaviors that cannot be performed during sobriety, is a view shared not only by family members, but by many behavioral scientists as well. Some of these behavioral scientists invoke the physiological effect of alcohol as an explanation for the behavioral changes associated with alcohol use. Others claim that psychological or cognitive perceptions are the critical factors. Still others invoke cultural norms and societal expectations.

For our purposes, we need not take sides in this issue. What is more important to us is what the family members themselves think. And for them, regardless of why it's happening, they are convinced that they have one life when alcohol is around and another when it is not. Therefore, they associate alcohol use with the availability of critical behaviors used to regulate family life. Unless the family is willing or helped (via outside intervention) to perform these behaviors in the absence of alcohol, alcohol becomes a necessary component for the overall maintenance of family stability.

What then, from the family systems point of view, are the critical aspects of alcohol-related behavior to which the family has become so addicted? One aspect we have already mentioned. Alcohol-related behavior is predictable. An observer, having watched the family several times in its intoxicated interactional state, knows just what will happen the next time around. For rigid families, families that have a low tolerance for uncertainty (and Alcoholic Families are often just such families), predictable behavior has an obvious attraction. "Even if it is a hell of a way to live, at least we know exactly what is coming, at least we are never caught by surprise. We know exactly what the dimensions of our heartaches will be. And that is better than never knowing when the roof will cave in."

But predictability alone cannot be the whole story. The key to this issue lies in the fact that these alcohol-related behaviors actually serve a useful purpose. What might this purpose be? *It turns out that these behaviors have become critical components of strategies used by middle-phase alcoholic families in short-term problem-solving.* Through the vehicle of regulation of interactional and emotional distance, these behaviors have come to play a crucial role in helping the family deal, in the short-run, with the myriad problems that arise in day-to-day living. Many of these problems are internal to the family—sexual difficulties between spouses, the need to control explosive feelings, role conflicts, and so on. Others have to do with the relationship between the family and its community—conflicts with neighbors, demands at work, needs for more assertive behavior, and so on. In other words, important problems. And therefore, insofar as the family believes that the behaviors it uses to deal with these problems are *only* possible when alcohol is present, that is, are only possible during the intoxicated interactional state, the family's commitment to alcoholism becomes less baffling to us.

Two clinical vignettes will help illustrate these points. The first comes from a family therapy session; the second from a follow-up interview with one of our research subject families.

The first family, the Leighners, had sought help in dealing with a late-developmental-phase alcoholism issue (we return to this aspect and discuss the Leighners more fully in chapter 11). Three of the four children in the family, ranging in age from eighteen to twenty-eight, had banded together to seek help with the chronic drinking problems of both their parents, two professionals in their late fifties who had been married for thirty years and had experienced alcoholism problems throughout their marriage. (A twenty-five-year-old daughter was living abroad. According to her siblings, she had two years previously vowed "never to set foot in the same room with my parents again.")

Although the three children who participated in therapy were convinced that their parents were alcoholics, both parents challenged this diagnosis. Nevertheless, there was general agreement that both husband and wife behaved quite differently when they were drinking. Joan Leighner seemed susceptible to even small amounts of alcohol, becoming dysarthric, confused, and quite combative, especially with outsiders. Henry Leighner, a systems analyst, usually drank larger amounts of alcohol than his wife, but showed few behavioral signs of intoxication. People sensed that he was drunk when he got nasty and sarcastic. Outsiders would therefore know that Mrs. Leighner, an accountant, was a "drunk," but would be surprised to hear that her husband also had an alcohol problem.

The incident we are interested in occurred in the tenth family therapy session. In this session, Joan told a story that dramatically illustrated how alcohol-related behaviors can be incorporated by the family into their problem-solving strategies. A massive epidemic of absenteeism (which had been a problem all along) had resulted in the absence of three family members, leaving only Joan and her middle son, Michael. The therapist, feeling a growing sense of despair about his potential usefulness to the family, and finding Joan sober on this particular occasion (she would frequently arrive at sessions intoxicated), reviewed the pattern of alcohol-on, alcohol-off therapy sessions that had contributed to his sense of frustration. He confronted both of them, perhaps more vigorously than was his custom, suggesting that the family might not be serious about wanting to tackle the alcoholism issues that ostensibly had brought them into treatment. Joan and Michael were evasive in their responses, and the session appeared to be at a stalemate.

As the therapist warmed to his subject and increased the pressure he was putting on the two to respond to his challenging query about whether they were serious or not, Joan suddenly began narrating a story. The introduction of this anecdote was so abrupt as to appear, at first glance, to be the product of a thought disorder. But the punch line left no doubt about why she was telling the story.

Pointing to her son sitting beside her, she told the therapist that when Michael was six years old he developed a particularly severe, febrile illness. Joan, concerned that Michael was seriously ill, called her pediatrician in the early evening to ask for advice. The pediatrician, apparently failing to sense her concern, or perhaps not trusting Joan as an accurate informant, responded with the customary advice to bring the child's temperature down with aspirin and to come to the office in the morning. Aspirin, followed by cold baths and alcohol rubs, brought Michael's temperature down somewhat, but Joan continued to "feel in her bones" that her child was desperately ill.

As her sense of apprehension mounted, she tried to talk the problem over with her husband. She seemed unable, however, to convince him that a crisis might be at hand. He was unwilling to challenge the pediatrician's telephone opinion, and insisted that the doctor's response meant the child's illness must be routine.

Joan was becoming quite animated at this point in the session as she got into her story, describing with zest her argument with her husband and his lack of support. The therapist almost wondered if she had somehow lost track of the point of the whole story, when she suddenly told him that it was at this point that she retreated to her bedroom and started drinking. A half-hour later she picked up the telephone and called the pediatrician back. It was now close to midnight. When the pediatrician answered the phone, he found a very different person on the other end of the line. Rather than the apprehensive but meek and perhaps somewhat confused woman he had spoken to several hours before, he now found himself talking to a loud, aggressive, cursing, bundle of fury. He was accused of incompetence, insensitivity, and challenged to respond. His response, Joan told us, was to advise her this time to bring the child into the hospital emergency room, and to assure her that he would meet them there.

When they arrived at the hospital, Michael was examined, found to have all the signs and symptoms of an acute surgical abdomen, and soon underwent emergency surgery. The surgeons found that he had suffered a burst appendix, which is considered a potentially life-threatening condition, and they performed an operation to correct the condition.

Joan then delivered the punch line. Putting her hand on her son's shoulder, she turned to the therapist and said, "And that, Doctor, is why I drink!" The message seemed abundantly clear. "Had I not gotten drunk that night," she seemed to be telling the therapist, "my son would not be alive today."

This story, of course, had all of the properties of a family myth. It is a tale about the past that had taken on symbolic meaning. It had probably been repeatedly told, and it had a moral attached to it. Whether or not the incident occurred exactly as Joan related it is not important. What matters is that it illustrates, in dramatic fashion, the importance that this woman had placed on alcoholism as a critical element in family *problem-solving*.

In fact, Joan even went on to tell the therapist, immediately after finishing her story, that she knew that he is well-intentioned, but that perhaps he would be better advised to leave well enough alone. That is, he should not persist in attempting to take away from the family a mechanism that had been critical in their approach to dealing with crisis. Without alcohol, Mrs. Leighner was contending, the family would be unable to mobilize outside help in times of need. Their internal resources—Joan's ability to communicate with the pediatrician and the ability of the marital couple to bolster each other in their effort to obtain outside help—were inadequate to the task. It is only with the introduction of alcohol-related (or in the mind of Mrs. Leighner alcohol-induced) behaviors, that the crisis could be managed.

This example of the use of alcohol (via intoxicated behavior) as a critical step in dealing with a crisis-induced problem surely highlights our basic thesis in dramatic detail. However, though we were alerted to the relationship between alcohol use and problem-solving via such dramatic incidents, the customary relationship between these two factors is usually a less dramatic and more subtle one. It often goes on at a level outside the conscious awareness of family members. In fact, it is most frequently the family's perception that alcoholism is their major problem, not, as we have been suggesting, a perceived necessary vehicle or component of solutions to everyday problems.

However, what appears to the family to be a hindrance to problem-solving, often on reexamination can be seen to serve a functional purpose. Our second clinical vignette illustrates this more subtle relationship between alcohol use and problem-solving. It comes from a conjoint interview with one of the married couples who participated in the home observation study described in greater detail in the next chapter.

In the interview, the couple, Sam and Sheila Herbertson, described the steps that led to their decision to send her daughter (his stepdaughter) to a boarding school. Danielle, the daughter, had a long history of dyslexia and behavioral disorders. She had been in and out of therapy situations and had been subjected to considerable verbal, if not physical, abuse at the hands of her mother and stepfather. (We had been witness to the intensity of this verbal abuse during multiple home visits with her family.) Her father and mother had originally separated when she was three, and her father had "dropped off the face of the earth," not to see his daughter again until several months before this interview took place. Sheila had at that time contacted her first husband to "inform him" that it was time for him to once again take up his responsibilities as a father. This was one of several major steps that were taken as a result of a feeling that the conflict between the couple and their daughter had reached the breaking point.

Yet despite the potentially explosive forces at play within the Herbertson family, the couple, looking back on the steps they had taken in attempting to find a solution to the problem they were having with Danielle, were pleased with the resolution they had worked out. They were able to identify a sequence of events that led to Danielle's moving out of the house (most likely an appropriate step, given the circumstances) and also permitted her to do so in a way that seemed beneficial to her educational needs and to have the positive consequences of reuniting her with her natural father and her father's new family.

In summing up the family's response to this crisis, Sam Herbertson emphasized that despite all the turmoil, family members seemed able to remain "fairly sensitive to each other's needs. . . . the major thing was that we did have Danielle's best interests at heart. This was the major thing. Somehow we managed to do something that seemed best for her but also something that relieved the terrible tension. We did not want to put her into a situation that was bad for her, but it was also clear that she had to be out of that house, or we weren't going to last much longer."

The role of alcohol in this problem-solving process proved to be of critical importance. At first glance this did not seem to be the case. For example, everyone (the Herbertsons and members of our research team who visited their home) agreed that abusive verbal behavior always seemed to occur when Sheila had been drinking heavily. From a family systems perspective, however, a review of the ultimate effect of the drinking suggested a different conclusion, namely, that the alcohol-related behavior *helped* facilitate the successful resolution of the problem with Danielle.

We can follow this shift as the conjoint interview unfolds. In reviewing this episode with the couple, the interviewer first asked the couple to think about aspects of their customary style of dealing with problems that they feel hinder resolution of problems. Sam picked up on this theme by talking about his explosive temper and its relationship to the abusive behavior we have noted above. His wife agreed that his temper was a problem for them, and that he was easily set off, but she added that her own temper, although initially more restrained, tended to get vicious when set off, leading to the explosive arguments and verbal abuse witnessed by our behavioral observers. But how do these arguments get started? "I drink and then I retreat," Sheila told us, "and that really seems to get to him." Asked if she thinks her drinking tends to make the intensity of the arguments much worse, she replied, "Well it certainly doesn't help. It just seems to *delay* [note this word] everything. We can't make up our minds about anything once I start drinking. I will drink and just push it all away."

"And then I see that happening," Sam added, "and I get ticked off at her for the drinking. I see her drinking and I find that's all I can think about—sort of a feeling that here we go again and she's backing away again. That she just won't confront anything; she just seems to retreat into the bottle."

At first glance, therefore, the situation seems clear-cut. A problem has arisen with an adolescent girl, and her mother and stepfather seem incapable of handling it. She retreats into her alcoholism and he rants and raves in hopeless and futile frustration. In the end, they just throw up their hands and send her away. However, it is not quite that simple. It turned out that Danielle was doing very well at the boarding school, that she enjoyed her new relationship with her biological father, and that Sam and

Sheila, far from acting impulsively in this matter, had actually spent the better part of a year investigating various schools, seeking advice from friends and work acquaintances who also had children in boarding schools, reallocating family finances, and engaging in a protracted set of negotiations with Danielle's father and stepmother. These things take time. This family supposedly had a low frustration tolerance. How had they been able to effectively manage the situation? The interviewer put it to them this way:

"When you described it before, in a funny way it almost sounded as if the drinking, by allowing you to step out of the situation for the time being, might have temporarily relieved some of the pressure. That perhaps whenever you were on the verge of moving toward a precipitous solution, the drinking would start, everybody would explode, and nothing would get decided. If that solution you were about to make was being made in large part out of frustration, it was probably good in the end that you got diverted by the drinking and never went through with it."

At this point in the interview, both Sam and Sheila started smiling, as if the interviewer had tapped into a private piece of knowledge shared by the two of them. The discussion of this issue then concluded with the following exchange:

SHEILA: Well, I'm sure I would have acted more impulsively had not . . .

SAM: . . . this is an excellent point. . . . In fact it's very pertinent to this problem. In fact, my wife would even sometimes make a similar point to me—you know, that the drinking was maybe relieving the pressure—but I would always tell her that it was a bunch of crap, just an excuse to keep drinking, that she was really just aggravating the situation even more by doing this [drinking]. But it sure is true that I couldn't get a decision out of her once the drinking had started and we got into another one of those knock-down-drag-outs.

INTERVIEWER: [turning to Sheila] So you would raise the same idea. That the drinking is just a way of blowing off steam and relieving the pressure temporarily, like a valve on a pressure cooker?

SHEILA: Oh yes . . . naturally [note the use of this word].

INTERVIEWER: [turning to Sam] And you thought that it was just a lot of crap. . . . You felt it was just an excuse for the drinking?

SAM: Well I understood what she was saying, at least I thought I did. But I still thought that it was just aggravating the situation. Of course I've never faced a problem relative to alcohol in my family. Nor in anybody, really. We come from two pretty diverse backgrounds on that score.

INTERVIEWER: [to Sam] So you meant that you didn't understand all of the ramifications of the drinking?

SAM: I still don't.

SHEILA: He doesn't understand drinking. . . . I'm not making excuses for drinking. But the fact is that I come from a family of alcoholics. . . . It's just a way of life with us. The first thing you do to handle a problem—any problem—is find a bottle.

INTERVIEWER: Umm-hmm.

So here we have a family prone to explosive, impulsive actions attempting to deal with an extremely critical issue, a crisis with a sixteen-year-old daughter. We can readily appreciate the forces at play and the weaknesses in family structure and function that would contribute to premature closure of the issue. The likely outcome, were that to happen, would be a scapegoating of this troubled young woman and a withdrawal of family support, rationalized in all likelihood by a statement about the hopelessness of the situation. The alternative view that emerged during the interview was that alcohol, rather than provoking or facilitating an impulsive decision, by acting as a temporary divergence, caused the family to step back from the brink and to review their options once again. This family, seemingly chaotic and highly destructive on the surface, proved in the end capable of engaging in a coordinated series of steps to arrive at an acceptable solution.

The Leighner and Herbertson family vignettes serve as examples of the puzzling connection that seems to exist in some families between alcohol use and problem-solving behavior. Joan Leighner was quite explicit in pointing out this connection to us. She remained convinced that her ability, while intoxicated, to act in a forceful and assertive manner very much at variance with her customary behavior, had life-saving implications for her daughter. For the Herbertsons, the modulating effect of Sheila's periodic alcohol-induced withdrawals on their ultimate decision about her daughter's schooling was not a conscious, deliberate strategy. However, our clinical perceptions suggested that our conclusion was an appropriate one, and Sam and Sheila seemed easily persuaded that our point-of-view was correct. Sam, a man of action, would clearly have urged a rapid, and in retrospect, premature closure of the issue. His wife, a woman with strong predilections to push aside unwelcome and disturbing issues, was, by herself, helpless to address this difficult problem. Either one, attempting to deal with the issue alone, would have moved toward a "solution" fraught with difficulties. They dealt with the problem successfully only by managing to coordinate their efforts, thereby creating a balance between the extremes of impulsiveness and procrastination. In other words, their alcohol-induced behaviors—both Sheila's alcohol-induced withdrawal and her husband's expressions of exasperation—became inexorably entwined with the actual decision-making process.

However, we have also seen in these two vignettes, an explicit assumption that seems to exist in these families, that at times of crisis they will be forced to turn to alcohol in order to deal with the problem. Were we to ask them about this issue directly, their explanation of why this is so would probably vary. Joan Leighner would probably tell us that her needing to resort to alcohol-induced behaviors is necessitated by her husband's appalling lack of decisiveness and his poor judgment, coupled with his nasty and vindictive nature. Sam Herbertson, on the other hand, would probably explain the couple's problem-solving style as a reaction to having to adjust the decision-making process to his wife's uncontrollable need for alcohol.

One person reading these cases might therefore propose that drinking is reactive to the presence of pathology in the family, while another might state the reverse; that family behavior is reactive to the presence of a pathologically addicted family member. For our purposes, however, whether alcohol-induced behavior (the family's intoxicated interactional state) is cause or effect is by and large irrelevant. The crucial issue for the middle-phase Alcoholic Family is that an association has been established between alcohol-induced behavior, on the one hand, and family problem-solving, on the other. The critical issue is that time and again, the family will find that as it attempts to deal with crises, the intoxicated interactional state becomes part of the crisis-management strategy.

Our appreciation of the associative links between alcohol-induced behavior and family problem-solving provides a framework, a suggestive pathway, for understanding the puzzling tenaciousness of alcoholism in these families. We have asked why these families would continue to tolerate, nay, even subsidize, the drinking behavior of their alcoholic members; why so many of these families seem to experience such difficulty in distancing themselves from the alcoholic individual; how chronic alcoholism manages to survive within the context of family life; why it is not extruded. Here we see, for the first time, a possible "benefit" of alcoholism for certain families.

Our previous discussions of the forces leading to an alcoholism-centered family identity and our descriptions of regulatory processes in Alcoholic Families were useful in providing a functional description of some of the processes at work. However, all that we could conclude from these discussions was that they helped us understand the relationship between alcoholism and family life. In our discussion of family problem-solving, a different aspect has emerged for the first time. This time we suggest that, by focusing our attention on short-term crisis-management issues, we are able to see that from this limited perspective, alcoholism might serve a *functional* role for many of these families.

The Sobriety-Intoxication Cycle

We are, of course, at the same time aware that this perception of alcoholism as functional for family life (that is, via the specific role of alcohol-induced behaviors in problem-solving strategies) is valid only insofar as we view the family within the narrow framework of short-term crisis management. It is our assumption that any benefits the family might receive in this regard are benefits obtained at a very high price. We have alluded to this price in our earlier assertion that these families appear intent on trading long-term growth for short-term stability. But for the moment, we take up this more narrow focus on crisis management alone. To provide an overview of this issue, we turn at this point to some clinical data collected as part of an unusual study in which alcoholic couples were cojointly hospitalized for a ten-day period and their behavior while drinking systematically observed.

The Conjoint Hospitalization Study

The Conjoint Hospitalization study, carried out in the 1970s at the Laboratory for Alcohol Research of the National Institute on Alcohol Abuse and Alcoholism, was a study centering on the evaluation of an experimental treatment program for married couples with alcoholism problems.* Couples were admitted to a six-week program that relied heavily on multiple couples group therapy and included, as its most unique aspect, a ten-day period of conjoint hospitalization during which clinical and research staff had an opportunity to directly observe the couple's interactional behavior.

But the research protocol included yet one more unprecedented feature. During this period of conjoint hospitalization, alcohol was made freely available to the couple and they were instructed that this drinking experience was specifically intended to help the therapist gain a better understanding of the role that alcohol consumption was playing in their lives.† Toward that end, the research ward had been designed to replicate, as much as possible, a home environment. Each couple was provided with a two-room suite and given the option of designing their own sleeping arrangements, and a large living/dining room area was comfortably furnished to simulate middle-class living quarters. Couples were asked to shop for and prepare all their own meals, arrange for recreational activities,

*Two of our colleagues, Drs. David Berenson and Donald Davis, provided invaluable assistance in the conceptualization, implementation, and analytic phases of this study.

†Already published reports of this study (Steinglass, Davis and Berensen, 1977; Steinglass, 1979) have detailed the medical monitoring procedures that were used to ensure that subjects were not at physical risk as a result of consuming large quantities of alcohol. There were no cases in which a subject had to be discharged from the study for medical reasons.

and schedule ancillary treatment opportunities. Therefore, although the artificial nature of the hospital ward was acknowledged, the simulated environment was appropriate to the instructions given to each couple to reproduce as closely as possible their usual interactional behavior and drinking patterns. Here, then, was an opportunity to observe firsthand the sobriety-intoxication cycle in a group of alcoholic couples.

The clinical observations made during this study were entirely consistent with the major themes of this chapter as we have discussed them up to this point. For example, without exception, behaviors exhibited during the intoxicated interactional state were, first, exaggerated or amplified in comparison with interactional behavior already observed during sobriety, and second, significantly more stereotyped. And, as was the experience of the family interviewer in dealing with the Pridgett family, neither the research nor the clinical staff was able to accurately predict, using their intimate knowledge of the couple's sober interactional behavior as a base, the precise pattern of interactional behavior the couple would exhibit once drinking had started. However, having once seen the couple "in action," predictions of what would happen when drinking resumed in a day or two improved dramatically. In other words, these couples were behaving not only in an exaggerated and stereotypic fashion, but also in a highly predictable fashion, once drinking had begun.

This research study, involving as it did the conjoint hospitalization of the couple, probably induced a distortion of behavior along the lines customarily seen whenever families are placed in treatment settings (including traditional outpatient family therapy sessions). The basic element in this distortion process is a condensation of behavior, as the family attempts to adjust to the more restricted time frame of the treatment setting. Thus for these couples, asked as they were to reproduce their "typical behavior patterns" in relation to drinking but given only ten days to do so, we can assume that the *periodicity* of sober-intoxicated cycling we observed was a condensed version of the way they behave in their homes. It is possible that the more exaggerated aspects of behavior witnessed in this setting were also a product of this condensation process. If one were to observe these couples at home, it is probable that events would unfold at a more leisurely pace, diminishing the dramatic nature of many of the observations we made during this conjoint hospitalization study.

However, this condensation process, although introducing some distortion in the behaviors observed, also afforded the research team the unique opportunity to directly observe, within a relatively brief time frame, multiple sober-intoxicated-sober-intoxicated cycles. As a consequence, not only was the contrast in behavior during these two stages highlighted, it was also possible to explore our contention that aspects of behavior associated with the intoxicated interactional stage served a functional role as part of short-term problem-solving strategies employed by these couples.

In our earlier discussion of the intoxicated interactional state, emphasis was placed on three dimensions of behavior as particularly useful descriptions of the changes that occur when the family moves from the sober to the intoxicated interactional state. First was activity level (e.g., the Pridgetts, whose verbal interactive rate increased dramatically during the "drinking interview"). Second was the preferred interactional distance (e.g., again the Pridgetts, in whom we noted marked changes in posture, in eye contact, and in instances of physical contact after Carl Pridgett had been drinking). Finally was the level of affect. (In the Pridgetts, a depressed and moribund family seemed to "wake up" when alcohol was introduced. This disengaged and emotionally distant family became animated and involved during the drinking interview, and again when watching this interview on videotape playback.)

When we moved on to discuss the role of the intoxicated interactional state in family problem-solving, the case descriptions treated the problems themselves in more narrative fashion. The Leighners had to deal with an inattentive physician. The Herbertsons had to defuse a potentially explosive intergenerational conflict in a blended family situation. But were we to have looked more closely, we would have seen that the behavioral changes manifested by the Leighners and the Herbertsons also were occurring along the same three dimensions noted above. The families were more energized during the intoxicated interactional state, were more affectively expressive, and altered their interactional distance (albeit in different directions).

As we describe two case histories of couples who participated in the Conjoint Hospitalization study, note again that the changes in behavior reported in association with the onset of drinking occurred along the same three dimensions. At the same time, the "problems" being faced by the two couples we describe were quite different. In other words, alcohol-associated behaviors seem to produce characteristic changes in interactional behavior, but these behaviors are then combined in complex patterns unique to each couple, and by extension, are applied to the short-term solution of problems also unique to the particular couple.

The Bartletts. Don and Sue Bartlett, an upper-middle-class couple in their middle forties, had experienced a marked deterioration of their marriage in the months following the death of Sue's last remaining aunt. They had been heavy drinkers for many years, but their alcohol consumption increased markedly at this time. Within a year, their marital relationship had degenerated into an increasingly frequent and violent series of verbal fights, diminishing social life and social activities, and infrequent sexual contact.

During the period of hospitalization, it became clear that their fights only occurred when both husband and wife had been drinking heavily. At such times, they would hurl increasingly angry and destructive barbs back and forth. There would be a gradual escalation in tension until, at a critical point, Sue would "crack," exhibiting paranoia, massive projection, and severe agitation. Don would then become quiet and would assent to attempts by staff or other subjects to physically isolate her in her room.

One of these fights occurred during a multiple couples group therapy session. Behaviorally, the fight followed recognizable lines. Sue tended to be wildly abusive and ostensibly paranoid in her wide-ranging accusations of her husband; Don acted disgusted and intolerant of his wife's behavior (although, of course, it was merely another of hundreds of such fights they had had over the past several years). The content of Sue's accusations, however, centered around her husband's emotional coldness and distance since her aunt's death, and her labile affect included sobbing as well as shouting. The therapist took note of these content issues and treated them seriously rather than interpreting them as the incoherent ramblings of an intoxicated woman. In the next therapy session, he explored in some depth the issue of the relationship of both husband and wife to the aunt who had died and uncovered evidence that Don was equally attached to this warm, maternal woman. In short order, the discussion of her death had evoked first tears and then sobbing in *both* husband and wife.

It became obvious that here was a couple who had attempted to avoid expressing their mutual depression following the death of a critical maternal figure. Increased alcohol consumption during this time had been associated with the establishment of a pattern of intoxicated interaction that served to temporarily isolate what was viewed as an intolerable and potentially overwhelming mutual depression. Of course, this goal was served only at a very high cost. Both their individual growth and their marital relationship had become frozen around a patterned interaction reminiscent of the one Strindberg called a "Dance of Death." As we witnessed it during the period of conjoint hospitalization, isolation of depression was achieved in the following manner: As a result of her intoxicated behavior, Don was able to view his wife as crazy rather than depressed; as a result of his behavior, Sue was able to see her husband as sadistic and tormenting. Because these views were unacceptable, yet at the same time, relatively fixed, neither was able to focus on his or her own depression nor appreciate the intensity of the other spouse's depression.

The Gardners. Joe and Sally Gardner were a middle-class couple also in their mid-forties, but this time only one spouse, Joe, had an alcoholism problem. Joe and Sally were one of those couples often described in the literature—an overfunctioning, if sub–clinically depressed, woman married to an underfunctioning, chronic alcoholic man. Sally, a computer analyst, had achieved a position with significant supervisory responsibility. Joe, a salesman, had been out of work for the past year and had assumed most of the housekeeping duties for the family. (Since the Gardners had established a quite stable marital relationship over the fifteen-year history of Joe's alcohol abuse, we might wonder why they had volunteered for the experimental treatment program. The answer seemed to lie in a disruption of their previously homeostatic relationship caused by their daughter's move back into their home with her young daughter following the hospitalization of her alcoholic husband. Joe's drinking symptoms moved to center stage when his wife increasingly blamed his drinking for their inability to deal effectively with their daughter's difficulties.)

For this couple the sobriety-intoxication cycle was as follows: When sober, Joe talked only when spoken to and then only to support a position taken by the other "labeled alcoholics" in the multiple couples therapy group. Sally tended to be more assertive and offered organized, supportive, critical statements about problems raised by other couples in the group. Her style was quite businesslike and to the point. Both husband and wife were reluctant to allow their relationship to become a focal point for group discussions. When Joe started drinking, however, there was a marked increase in his affective display. He became more assertive, angry, and demanding, frequently expressing his desire for greater closeness and warmth with his wife. Sally, for her part, was able to express anger at him for his drinking, and welcomed the opportunity to have group discussion center on the difficulties she was experiencing. The couple was also able to discuss their sexual difficulties more openly. Joe verbalized his anger at his wife's obesity and her apparent unwillingness to make herself more sexually attractive. Sally expressed, with tearful affect, her sense of depreciation because her husband, for many years, would only approach her sexually when intoxicated.

This was a couple, therefore, who, with alcohol, seemed better able to demonstrate a wide range of behaviors, more capable and comfortable directly engaging one another, more attentive to each other's feelings and needs, and appreciably more animated. However, at the same time, these behaviors and feelings seemed capable of being expressed only because the couple has conceptually demarcated intoxicated interactional behavior from behavior during periods of sobriety. Affect and behavior expressed during intoxication held no applicability or validity for them during the sober state.

Their sexual behavior epitomized this cycle. Alcohol consumption both allowed for increased sexual expression by Joe and represented the basis for sexual rejection of his wife by him and of him by his wife. The outcome was increased interaction but the same sexual stalemate. Their joint concerns about body image problems (her obesity and his physical impotence) were effectively neutralized by drawing alcohol into their sexual interactions. With alcohol in the picture, Joe could become flirtatious and feel sexually potent, knowing that he would not have to follow through on his sexual advances. Sally, by feeling victimized and degraded, was able to avoid her feelings of contributing to her husband's impotence through her controlling and forceful role behavior and her physical unattractiveness.

Thus we have two examples of couples using interactional behaviors that they exhibit *only* when drinking, to effect a temporary solution to a problem in their relationship. The problems were different for the two couples, as were the specific patterns of behavior that they employed during the intoxicated interactional state. But once again, these were behaviors that were, first, substantively different from their style of interaction during sobriety; second, stereotyped, that is, highly patterned and perhaps even ritualistic; and third, predictable from one episode of drinking to the next, that is, they had been played out again and again in the same form hundreds of times over the years. And once again, we are describing a cyclical process—two couples who move repetitively back and forth between these two different interactional states.

Were we to diagram this process (as we have done in figure 6.1), we would use a feedback loop because we have been describing a sequence in which behaviors present only during the intoxicated interactional state are being used by the family to manage a potential challenge to family stability. That is, the family experiences the various problems mentioned in our clinical examples—physical illness in a child; overwhelming affect associated with loss of maternal figure; sexual inhibition; and so on—*as potential challenges to family homeostasis.* It is this challenge that must be neutralized in the service of maintaining constancy of the family's internal environment (the definition of homeostasis). And in functional terms, the relationship between the two interactional states is such that behaviors activated and associated with intoxication provide the necessary resources to temporarily solve, blunt, or neutralize (all these terms are applicable) perceived challenges to family homeostasis.

Figure 6.1 indicates that problems at any one of the three structural levels of family systems—individual, intrafamily, and family-environment—can be the precipitating challenge leading to perceived instability in the family system. But the critical functional concept is that behavior activated by the family only during the intoxicated interactional state is incorporated into the family's short-term problem-solving strategies that provide a temporary solution to this challenge and return the family to its prechallenged state. Hence the depiction of this process as a feedback loop.

All the clinical illustrations in this chapter emphasize this connection between intoxicated behavior and short term problem-solving. That is not to say, however, that alcohol ingestion and the intoxicated interactional state arise *only* when the family has a problem to solve. Clearly, alcoholic individuals establish relatively fixed patterns of drinking independent of the pace and status of family life. Although they will often contend that it is the family or their spouse that drives them to drink, implying that they are "set off" by conflicts within the family, this factor most likely accounts for only a small part of the problem.

For most individuals, drinking behavior becomes increasingly patterned, increasingly ritualistic over time. Daily drinkers do so in a relatively repetitive fashion day after day. For some this means the four-cocktail lunch plus an extended postwork "happy hour." For others it means steady-state drinking from the time they get up until they stagger into bed. Others are

FIGURE 6.1

Family Systems Model of Alcoholism Maintenance

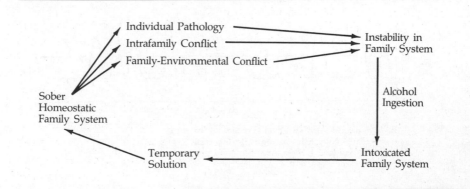

clearly weekend drinkers, people who start drinking on the way home from work Friday afternoon and drink steadily until Sunday evening and then try to get themselves into shape for Monday. The joke about avoiding buying a car that's been assembled on a Monday or Friday (because of postbinge hangover and anticipatory nervousness) reflects the shared recognition of the regularity of these drinking patterns. Then we have the binge drinkers—people who spend long periods of time "on the wagon"

FIGURE 6.2

Patterns of Alcohol Consumption in Alcoholic Families

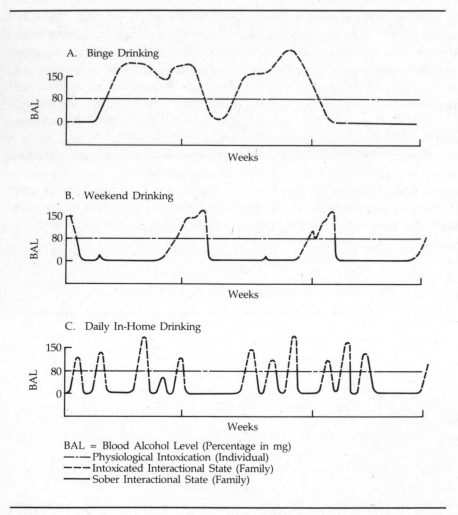

BAL = Blood Alcohol Level (Percentage in mg)
—·— Physiological Intoxication (Individual)
——— Intoxicated Interactional State (Family)
——— Sober Interactional State (Family)

only to precipitously initiate a drinking binge that might entail continuous intoxification for days to weeks.

These different drinking patterns therefore clearly have a life of their own. (It is foolish to contend that drinking starts only when there is a problem that needs a rapid solution. But we *are* contending that in some percentage of cases this is clearly what is going on. That is, the need to deal with potentially destabilizing challenges to family homeostasis does, in some instances, precipitate the onset of drinking. But even if the linkage is not so direct, in most instances, the cycling process is short-term enough that intoxicated interactional behaviors are available to the family and are used in the way illustrated in figure 6.1 well before the family has the time or inclination to deal with the problem in an innovative fashion (or even to decide in a more leisurely way whether a threat to family stability actually exists). If we were to diagram the cycling process for each of the three most common patterns of alcoholic drinking (daily, weekend, binge), as we have done in figure 6.2, in each instance we would depict the family as repetitively cycling back and forth between these two different interactional states.

One last point. As can be seen in figure 6.2, the intoxicated interactional state is diagramed as beginning *before* the level of physiological intoxication is reached. Although this is a hypothesized rather than systematically investigated phenomenon, it is our impression that for many families the mere presence of alcohol can initiate this shift. Remember, for example, Alice Clarion telling us that for her family, the mere presence of an open bottle on a dining room table seemed to set the process off. In other words, what might in its early stages be closely tied to actual physiological effects, over time becomes a pattern that is activated in anticipatory fashion, in the same way that classical conditioning experiments can shape and mold behavior.

Conclusion

In this chapter, we have been described a curious and unique phenomenon of behavior in the middle-phase Alcoholic Family—the intoxicated interactional state. In association with the drinking behavior of the family's alcoholic member, a complex but predictable series of interactions between family members is activated, patterns of behavior that get repeated time and again. The origins of these behavior patterns may well have been reactive—that is, the family's defensive efforts to minimize the impact of repeated episodes of intoxication on its life. One can easily imagine how families would be drawn toward accommodation rather than confrontation and gradually, step-by-step, develop a characteristic response, a set of behaviors that occurs whenever alcohol is present. And in this way, by the time the families we have been describing in this chapter reach this developmental phase, the repetitive cycling between two fundamentally different interactional states, one associated with sobriety and one with intoxication, has become part of their day-to-day living.

Although it seems reasonable to assume that the development of the intoxicated interactional state is primarily the product of a reactive process on the part of the family, our case illustrations have pointed to a surprising finding. Many family behaviors that we think of as healthy and potentially adaptive—interactive engagement, affective expressiveness, assertive pursuit of family interests with outsiders, protection of the stability of the family's internal environment, sexual expressiveness—are *more* likely to occur in the families we have been describing when the family is in the *intoxicated* interactional state. And because of the demarcation process noted previously, if it is during the intoxicated state that they occur, we will see them only during this state.

Life in the middle phase of a family's development, even if stable and rule-governed, contains an extraordinary variety of processes and interaction patterns. The middle phase of development also includes characteristic developmental challenges, as well as numerous minor and major disruptions that intrude on the stability of daily life. To be met successfully, these challenges and intrusions often require shifts in family behavior. In the healthy family, these behavioral shifts can be quickly activated in response to moment-by-moment needs. Overall, therefore, we can talk about a range of behaviors available to the family, behaviors capable of being activated as immediate needs dictate.

In the Alcoholic Family, however, a very different set of circumstances exist. The middle-phase Alcoholic Family takes the same range of behavioral functions and divides them up. Some are "sorted" into the sober interactional state; some into the intoxicated interactional state. As we have seen, families differ in how they accomplish this, but in every case illustrated in this chapter the sorting has been almost mutually exclusive, that is, functions and processes that are activated in the intoxicated state are almost never activated in the sober state and vice versa.

We have tackled this "sorting" process from two different prospectives. First, we have identified three dimensions of behavior—activity level; affective expressiveness; interactional distance—useful as descriptors of the differences that occur in family behavior as the family moves back and forth from sober → intoxicated → sober → intoxicated interactional states. We have pointed out that alcohol does not necessarily produce the same changes in interactional behavior in every family, but that each family has a characteristic pattern of change that is predictable for that family. Although for most of the families we have described, the intoxicated interactional state is associated with higher activity levels, greater affective expressiveness, and closer interactional distance, this is not uniformly the case. We have also observed families who tend to disengage when drinking starts, to become less animated, and even occasionally more flattened in their affective expressiveness. But for each of these families, what they do once, they will do every time they move into the intoxicated interactional state.

These observations, therefore, have led us to several conclusions about the intoxicated interactional state:

First, behaviors exhibited during this state are exaggerated or amplified compared to sober interactional behavior. That is, when alcohol is present, family behavior tends to move toward one or the other extreme along each of the three dimensions mentioned above. As one example, a family becomes either highly engaged or highly disengaged; moderation falls by the wayside.

Second, behavior during the intoxicated interactional state is stereotyped. Alice Clarion called it "going on automatic pilot." Another way of saying the same thing is that these are behavior patterns that are more repetitive, more highly patterned, more reliable (i.e., the family can count on their occurrence whenever drinking starts). This is not to say that these are behaviors that are any less complex or restricted than sober behavior. But it does mean that the pattern these behaviors take occurs with almost unfailing consistency. Because intoxicated behavior has characteristically been thought of as unpredictable, if not chaotic, this characterization of intoxicated interactional behavior as stereotyped and as even more patterned than sober interactional behavior represents a radical departure from popular conceptions.

Third, we underscored the failure of outside observers to accurately predict, based on data gleaned from sober behavior alone, how the family will behave during the intoxicated state. But after you have seen a family even once during the intoxicated interactional state, your chances of correctly predicting future behavior, of course, improved dramatically.

Then we moved on to a discussion of the relationship between the intoxicated interactional state and short-term problem-solving in these families. The extension is a reasonable one. If these families are in fact going through a "sorting" process that assigns certain behaviors exclusively to the intoxicated state, and if these behaviors happen to be vital in dealing with challenges and/or disruptions faced by the family, then it stands to reason that the family will have to activate the intoxicated interactional state in order to call forth these behaviors. Since, as we have pointed out above, many of the behaviors that are associated with intoxicated behavior in these families are the very ones we tend to think of as associated with adaptation and problem-solving, the link between intoxicated behavior and problem-solving now becomes a logical one.

The families described in this chapter have used alcohol-related behaviors to deal with a wide range of problems. Some of these have been internal to the family, for example, the neutralization of stress created by sexual difficulties, as illustrated in the Gardner couple (basically, a marital-level problem), or the restructuring of a blended family (the Herbertsons). Others have been problems in the relationship between the family and its outside world. The Leighners are the most clear-cut example here. Most frequently, however, the problems seem to exist at the level of the marital couple and could be characterized as efforts to neutralize a potentially destabilizing challenge to the status quo established by them.

This is an extremely important point because it underscores yet another characteristic of middle-phase Alcoholic Families that has been repeatedly alluded to in the book, namely, a remarkable intolerance for uncertainty. Perhaps it is this intolerance that motivates these families to adopt the curious "sorting" of behaviors noted above. Or perhaps their intolerance for uncertainty is merely an understandable reaction to the chronic stress associated with alcoholism. Whatever its antecedent causes, the final product is a family that can be characterized as unusually rigid, unusually quick to respond to any challenges to the status quo, unusually inflexible in its response pattern.

The end result is a skew toward morphostasis; an emphasis on day-to-day stability that precludes the normal growth changes characteristic of the middle phase of development (see chapter 3). In the adaptive family, normative developmental challenges are met with by an initial curiosity, a willingness to delay a definitive response until the family has ample time to decide whether the challenge truly threatens homeostasis or simply represents an interesting opportunity to experience something new in its life. In the Alcoholic Family, the same challenge is rapidly and prematurely neutralized by the onset of the behavioral programs associated with alcohol use.

Over time, there is a remarkable circularity to this process. Again and again the family cycles between these two interactional states, but there seems to be little overall progress. We look at the family over a period of months or years and feel that they are developmentally stagnant. Problems seem to be emerging, and solutions appear to be attempted, but viewed from a longitudinal perspective, growth appears to have leveled off. In system terms, morphostasis and morphogenesis are no longer in dynamic interaction with one another. Homeostatic priorities dominate family life. It is as if interactional behavior has been transformed into a series of stereotyped behavioral sequences that are being repeated over and over again. We see a lack of variability of interactional behavior over time, coupled with an apparent absence of innovative or unusual solutions to problems that are repetitively presenting themselves, a predictability of behavior that in turn ensures that any substantive problem that calls for family reorganization and growth will never be satisfactorily handled, only temporarily eased.

Initially, there is a close link between presenting problems, the onset of drinking, the induction of the intoxicated interactional state, and the availability of behaviors that are used to achieve a temporary solution. Surely, that is how the process started in the Bartlett family. For the Leighner family, a physician needed to be persuaded that their son was having a medical crisis and Joan Leighner was convinced that she could only carry this off when she was drunk.

Over time, however, as the cycling process between the sober and the intoxicated interactional states repeats itself again and again, it begins to take on a life of its own. To some extent it is a natural process, a ritualization of behavior carried out by families prone to rigid, rather than flexible, behavior patterns. To some extent it represents a preemptive managing of anticipated difficulties, tensions, problems, affects, that never reach a level where they cause problems because the intoxicated interactional state periodically defuses the situation.

Alcoholism and family problem-solving, linked together in such a marriage, mutually reinforce one another. Although the family's underlying assumption—that intoxicated interactional behavior is made possible because alcohol is present—may be an erroneous one, its hold on the family is fierce and brutal. That it is an erroneous assumption offers room for therapeutic optimism. But it is a force that should never be underestimated.

CHAPTER 7

Daily Routines as Regulators of Home Life

Nobody who has not been in the interior of a family can say
what the difficulties of any individual of that family may be.
—Jane Austen, *Emma*

WE NOW TURN to a different set of regulatory behaviors, daily routines. Our task is to demonstrate that the pattern of drinking of the family's alcoholic member, and the pattern of daily routines that makes up the fabric of the family's home (internal) environment, are, for the middle-phase Alcoholic Family, two behavioral patterns that have become intricately intertwined.

Daily routines are another of those categories of family behaviors that, in our theoretical model, serve an important role as vehicles for the expression of underlying regulatory principles (the others being short-term problem-solving behaviors and family rituals). These behaviors, once established, serve to reinforce (conserve) such principles, thereby providing the constancy and structural definition that allows us to distinguish one family from another. Thus daily routines both reflect underlying family identity and temperamental characteristics, and at the same time, in reciprocal fashion, help to refine and reinforce these aspects of family personality.

Daily routines are unique among regulatory behaviors, however, in that they are continuous behavioral phenomena. By contrast, both short-term problem-solving behaviors and family rituals are discrete behaviors, called into play only when the appropriate circumstances arise. Daily routines are also unique in that they tend to be relatively unfocused and unconscious phenomena. Few families are aware of their routines while they are being carried out; nor are they deliberate about the exact details of such routines, though some families are, as we saw when we were discussing the role of family rituals in the early-phase family.

Yet, despite this "background" status, the disruption of daily routines can have as profound an impact on families as the disruption of rituals or the undermining of problem-solving behaviors. In fact, a number of prominent family stress researchers have postulated that a credible definition of the stress potential inherent in any life event is its ability to disrupt family routines (Olson, et al., 1983). The importance of daily hassles as a potential source of stress is another index of how central a role daily routines probably play in protecting people from the negative consequences of stressful events (Lazarus and Folkman, 1984).

Daily routines include behaviors related to home, work, school, and local community environments. But of these different settings, the most important one for the family is obviously its home. Nowhere else is the nature of the family's internal environment so clearly represented. Thus, when we went about designing a study to explore the role of daily routines in the Alcoholic Family, we naturally turned our attention toward the home environment.

For the Alcoholic Family at middle phase, the home setting is a critically important one. In the majority of cases, the alcoholic member is doing his or her drinking at home—sometimes privately, but often in full view of the rest of the family. Home-based events, such as meals and family entertainment, frequently occur at times when the alcoholic member is intoxicated. The family must also decide how friends and strangers are to be treated when active drinking is going on. Are they to be welcomed into the home, or kept at bay until the storm has passed? How is the day to be planned? How are household chores to be carried out when one is presumably never confident about what state one's alcoholic spouse or parent will be in at any particular moment?

As we have described the process, it is most likely an interactive one in which the family both accommodates itself to the needs of its alcoholic member—a reactive process—but also comes to use and actively organizes its life around alcohol-related behaviors—a proactive process. The end result is far from the highly unstable and chaotic family life envisioned by the average person, but instead is a family environment of remarkable stability. Of course, this day-to-day stability comes at a considerable price; it is most likely the product of a highly rigid life-style that places primary value on the reduction of uncertainty and thereby contributes heavily to the developmental distortion, the flattening of the family's growth curve, characteristic of the middle-phase Alcoholic Family.

This is not to imply that the home environments of all Alcoholic Families are similar. Just as individual drinking styles differ dramatically, so too are the daily routines of Alcoholic Families quite different. But for each family (as a unit of one), the theme is consistency. That is, each Alcoholic Family has developed a pattern of daily routines that remains remarkably consistent over long periods of time, although its own particular pattern might be quite different from that of another Alcoholic Family.

But the sine qua non that makes it an Alcoholic Family in the first place is that daily routines—just as was true for patterns of short-term problem-solving—are to a significant degree organized around alcoholism as a central developmental theme. For daily routines, this means that home environment and drinking patterns are clearly related—that a "goodness-of-fit" exists between the family's structuring of its home environment and the drinking behavior of the family's alcoholic member.

For example, imagine how different it would be to live in a family that had to contend with a binge drinker and one contending with a daily or weekly drinker. In the first situation, long periods of sobriety alternate with periods of rapid deterioration and return to drinking. Although the periodicity of drinking is at times predictable, often it is not. This is very different from the situation in which excessive drinking occurs every evening, or every weekend, or at every social function. And different from both these situations is that of families with a member who drank for years, but has now stopped. The atmosphere in this third type of situation is surely different from the often-extended periods of sobriety experienced by the family with a binge drinker. Suppose a family was intent on maintaining a stable family structure in the face of these different drinking patterns. Surely, different daily routines would be required to bring this about.

In the study we describe at length in this chapter, we were able to demonstrate just that. Home behavior of a sample of Alcoholic Families was studied and when these families were subdivided, with groupings based on the drinking pattern of the alcoholic member of the family, it was found that each subgroup of families had a quite distinctive pattern of home behavior. That is, a corelationship was found to exist between pattern of drinking and pattern of home routines (what we called above a "goodness-of-fit" between the family's organization of its internal environment and the demands placed on the family by the unique parameters of the drinking style of the alcoholic member).

The home observation instrument developed for the study focused exclusively on basic components of family behavior related to the family's use of time and space within its home, for example, the patterns of contact family members have with one another, how often they spend time in the same room together, the physical distance at which they carry out interactions, how often they engage in decision making, verbal exchanges, and so on. What is therefore remarkable is how distinctive the types of Alcoholic Families were one from another along these basic behavioral dimensions. And, that clinically relevant relationships could be shown to exist between patterns of alcoholism and family daily routines is the clearest illustration, at the level of home behavior, of how family life comes to be organized around alcoholism in the Alcoholic Family.

The bulk of this chapter is devoted to a discussion of our home observation study and the data it generated. But the emphasis in discussing the study, which was to our knowledge the first study to look systematically at home behavior of Alcoholic Families, is on daily routines as yet another set of regulatory behaviors helping to shape and stabilize life in the middle-phase Alcoholic Family.

The Alcoholic Family at Home: An Observational Study

Most systematic family research has fallen into one of four broad categories—studies of family behavior in clinical settings; studies of family behavior in the laboratory; studies of retrospective or current family behavior through interviews; and analyses of questionnaire data provided by one or more family members. Studies of families at home, on the other hand, have been rarely undertaken.

Nevertheless, the potential richness of in-home research has been amply demonstrated by a small, but profitable number of studies—primarily carried out by anthropologists, sociologists, psychiatrists, and developmental psychologists using participant observation and/or behavioral coding techniques (e.g., Gans, 1962; Hansen, 1981; Henry, 1967; Howell, 1972; Patterson, 1982; Kantor and Lehr, 1975; Lewis, 1959; Stack, 1974). Still, remarkably few studies of families at home have addressed family behavior in coping with psychopathological or physical illness. Instead the focus of most of this work has been on kinship (Firth, Hubert, and Forge, 1970; Young and Willmott, 1957) child-rearing patterns (Baumrind, 1971; Clarke-Stewart, 1973; Fischer and Fischer, 1966), and marital relationships (Bott, 1971; Scheflen, 1971).

The field of family and alcoholism is no different. Our work is among the first to attempt to study Alcoholic Families at home. A very small number of anthropologists and psychiatrists have entered this realm over the past decade (e.g., Ablon, 1980, 1985; Ames, 1977, 1982, 1985). Further-more, these few studies are interconnected, since they have drawn heavily upon each other's ideas (Ablon, 1984). Thus, although novelists and play-wrights have long provided us with rich (often autobiographical) views of the interior of the Alcoholic Family, it appears that clinician-researchers had until recently been dissuaded by real or imagined obstacles from attempting such a study. Having crossed the imaginary barrier between family researchers and the home environment, our research team designed a study that brought the observation team back to each family's home on nine separate occasions over a six-month period. Each visit was a four-hour one. Thus the basic data base for the study was a total of over thirty-five hours of observations for each family studied.

During each observation session, two behavioral observers made sys-tematic precoded notations about specific aspects of interactional behavior, using an instrument specifically designed for this study, the Home Obser-vation Assessment Method (HOAM). These observational data represent a body of information about family home behavior rivaled only by an-thropologically oriented studies in which participant-observers have "lived" with families for extended periods of time and accumulated pro-cess notes about the family's behavior. This time, however, the focus was on measurable aspects of behavior that could subsequently be submitted to formal statistical analyses.

However, in examining these data, we are interested not so much in a detailed analysis of minute-by-minute interaction between family mem-bers as in the way the family organizes its use of space and patterns its interactions. These latter parameters emerge only after analyzing data from hours of observations. In this sense, our study is quite different from other, perhaps familiar, home observation studies that have focused on child-rearing practices or specific aspects of parental disciplinary techniques. (Lytton's [1971] review article, although dated, is nevertheless a helpful reference here.) In these studies, detailed analyses of each behavioral act are utilized and observers are often exhausted after twenty minutes of applying the complicated coding systems developed in conjunction with this research.

So for us, both the design of the coding system used and the data analytic strategy employed was directed at pulling out of the mass of interactional data potentially available to an observer, those parameters that seemed the best *descriptors* of the broad patterns exercised by families in organizing life at home. It was assumed that such a coding system, applied to Alcoholic Families, would provide an accurate and useful pic-ture of the differences in the ways these families behave at home. With such descriptors then available to us (in the form of dimensions of interactional behavior), a variety of analyses could be performed to explore relationships between daily home routines and patterns of alcohol consumption.

Thus the study is best described as a within-group design. That is, analytic strategies are directed at uncovering meaningful differences between *subgroups of Alcoholic Families*. No attempt is being made to ascertain whether Alcoholic Families as a generic group are substantively different in their home routines from, say, families with schizophrenic members, or families contending with chronic physical illnesses, or even from families free of significant chronic pathology. Instead the focus is entirely on the corelationships between types of alcoholism and the different styles families evidence in structuring daily routines.

So basically, our discussion of the study has three components:

1. What are the different patterns of drinking behavior we are interested in, and why should they place unique demands on the way the Alcoholic Family organizes its home behavior?
2. How did we go about measuring home behavior and what are the dimensions of home behavior that were generated by the observational method we used?
3. What relationships emerged when patterns of drinking behavior were compared to patterns of daily routines at home?

Patterns of Drinking Behavior

In chapter 6, when we dealt with hypothesized links between short-term problem-solving and the intoxicated interactional state, the focus was on the day-to-day, or perhaps even hour-to-hour shifts in family behavior as the Alcoholic Family member starts drinking, becomes intoxicated, sobers up, returns to drinking, and so on. Yet this is not the only cycling process occurring in the Alcoholic Family. Drinking behavior also has a more macroscopic cyclic pattern. We refer here to the extended periods of time that demarcate phases of active drinking from those in which active drinking has stopped altogether. In the popular lexicon, these extended time periods are referred to as "wet" periods versus "dry" periods; as time of being "on the wagon" versus "off the wagon."

When we say that alcoholic individuals are in the middle of a "wet" phase, we don't mean that they are at that very moment physiologically intoxicated. Or even that they are drinking right then. But we do mean that if they are daily drinkers, they have had something to drink during that day; or if they are weekend drinkers, they were drinking heavily during the previous weekend; or if they are binge drinkers, they are either in the middle of one such binge or psychologically anticipating another binge at some time in the future. On the other hand, if such individuals are in the middle of a "dry" phase, we mean that they and their families are, with some degree of confidence, predicting that sobriety is to be the state of affairs for some time to come (or maybe even permanently).

FIGURE 7.1

Chronological Drinking Record—Subject 262

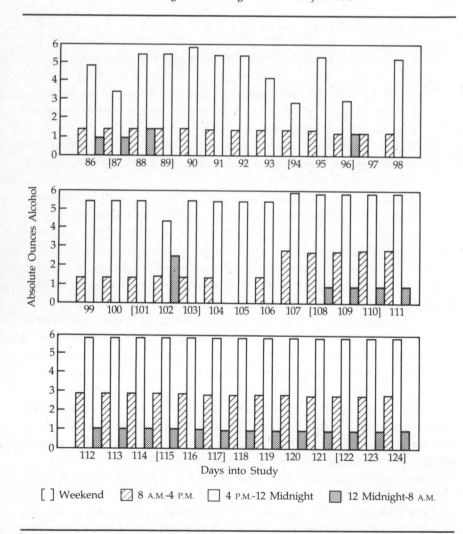

In this chapter, we focus on three such macroscopic patterns of drinking behavior. The first pattern—which we will call the *stable wet* pattern—is the one in which drinking occurs on a regular and predictable basis from day to day or weekend to weekend. That is, it is a pattern that encompasses both the daily and weekend drinker; but its hallmark is that the family can anticipate that its week-to-week schedule of daily routines will have to incorporate periods of time when the alcoholic member is actively drinking.

Behavioral logs, translated into histograms and reproduced in figures 7.1 and 7.2, illustrate the drinking patterns of the alcoholic members of two of the subject families in our home observation study that we will be labeling "stable wet" families. As part of the data collection for the study, a research assistant complied a behavioral log of alcohol consumption based on reports of daily drinking by subjects. In the histograms, alcohol consumption is reported for each of three eight-hour time blocks—the 8:00 A.M.–4:00 P.M. *daytime* block; the 4:00 P.M.–12:00 P.M. *evening* block, and the 12:00 P.M.–8:00 A.M. *nighttime* block. (Keep in mind that the ordinate reports alcohol consumption as ounces of *absolute* alcohol. Thus if a subject reported a four-ounce consumption, this means he or she consumed eight ounces of 100-proof whiskey, or eight bottles of beer, or a full quart of wine.)

Figure 7.1 illustrates how remarkably consistent the stable wet pattern can at times be. The woman in this case was, with absolute regularity, consuming ten to eighteen ounces of vodka every late afternoon and evening. (The accuracy of her reports of her behavior was confirmed by our behavioral observers, who were in her home while she was drinking.) Think for a moment about how predictable her behavior is, as viewed by her family. This is behavior the family can clearly "count on."

Figure 7.2 illustrates a somewhat different pattern, but one that is also predictable, from the point of view of the family involved. Here we have a weekend drinker who reports little alcohol consumption during the intervening weekdays. Yet after looking at this histogram, one can surely understand why (to paraphrase Alice Clarion's recollections reported in chapter 6) a member of such a family would be able to anticipate the weekend's events as soon as the first evidence of drinking appeared on a Friday afternoon. Hence, in the study, *both* subjects 262 and 421 belong to families who were classified as "stable wet" families.

The second drinking pattern we focus on—to be called the *alternator* pattern—is the one commonly described as binge drinking. In this pattern, the drinker typically alternates between periods of several weeks to months when active drinking is occurring (wet periods) and periods of

FIGURE 7.2

Chronological Drinking Record—Subject 421

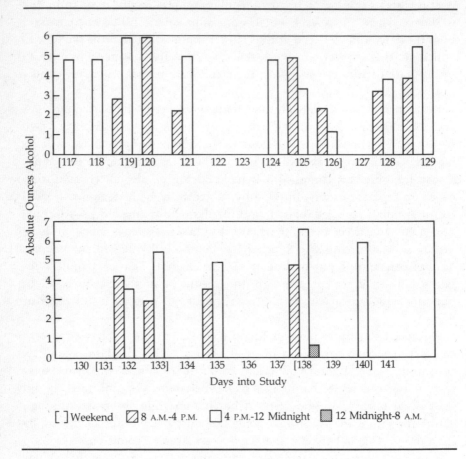

[ ] Weekend   ⧄ 8 A.M.-4 P.M.   ☐ 4 P.M.-12 Midnight   ▦ 12 Midnight-8 A.M.

weeks to months when no drinking is occurring (dry periods). But the sine qua non of this pattern is that the alternating between wet and dry periods has occurred multiple times during the life history of the family.

In contrast to the stable wet pattern, the alternator pattern is an unpredictable one. That is, it is extremely difficult for the family to know, with any sense of conviction, when drinking is either going to *start* or when it is going to stop. As Sophie Pridgett reported (during the family interview described in chapter 6):

We never knew when you were going to come home looped. Everything could be going fine; you could have a good job and all; you could leave happy in the morning; but then there you'd be in the afternoon—looped again. And then God only knows when you'd get it into your head that everything was okay again for old Carl, and then suddenly it was all promises and guarantees you were through with it *for good!*

Although the family (including Carl Pridgett) struggled mightily to try to come up with good predictors of when the alternating cycles would happen, they were, and would continue to be, unsuccessful. That is, each family member had a set of hypotheses about what would "set him off," but none had stood the test of time. So they were left instead in a constant state of bewilderment about it all.

Many alternator families are dealing with family members who leave the family for their periodic episodes of binge drinking. Carl Pridgett, at the time that we met him, was in a residential setting for detoxification following a binge lasting several months, during which time he had been living on a local Skid Row. But for each of the alternator families who were subjects in our home observation study, drinking, when it occurred, took place largely at home. None of the alcoholic subjects left the family (even overnight) when drinking was occurring. So family routines connected with the on-again, off-again pattern of drinking characteristic of the alternator pattern included the alcoholic member of the family.

The exact criteria used in our study to label a particular subject an "alternator" were, by necessity, somewhat arbitrary. For the purposes of the study, we decided to classify a subject an alternator if he or she either entered the six-month study dry (hadn't been drinking for the previous six months) and converted to wet status by the end of the six months of home observations or converted from wet to dry status during the course of the study. However, we were also able to verify that in every instance, the past drinking history of alternator subjects was one of multiple switches back and forth between wet and dry states.

The third drinking pattern focused on in the chapter is one we call the *stable dry* pattern. In these families, not only has drinking ceased, but family members are convinced that this is to be a relatively permanent state of affairs. Even if occasional "slips" occur, they will be aberrant periods in an overall pattern in which sobriety is the stable and fundamental alcohol state of the family. But for each of the stable dry families in the study, the past had included a period of at least five years during which the family had been in the stable wet pattern. So these families were all alcoholism veterans, but veterans who had reached a resolution regarding their alcoholic identity. In chapter 9, where we discuss this issue further, we identify the families as having opted for a "stable dry alcoholic family" pathway.

In the discussion of the home behavior of the families we studied, we, therefore, contrast the behavior of three basic subgroups of families—stable wet, alternator, and stable dry families. Although these labels were originally based solely on the drinking pattern of the family's alcoholic member, insofar as the study was able to demonstrate that each subgroup of families had a distinctive pattern of organization of home behavior, we now see these subgroupings as descriptive of fundamentally different types of Alcoholic Families. Hence the use of the terms "stable wet families," "alternator families," and so on to describe the kinds of families we studied.

The Subject Sample

In all, the research sample for this particular study consisted of thirty-one families divided as follows: ten were stable wet families; seven were alternator families; fourteen were stable dry families. Each family in the study had one spouse with a history of at least five years of active alcoholism as measured by the Goodwin et al. criteria set, and a positive score on a commonly used alcoholism screening test—the SAAST (Swenson and Morse, 1973). This latter instrument asks a series of questions about physical, treatment, and social-behavioral consequences experienced by the identified alcoholic member of the family during his or her period of heaviest drinking.

However, beyond meeting the above inclusion criteria, families varied considerably in their alcoholism histories, treatment histories, and demographic characteristics. For example, regarding treatment histories, a number of families had found AA and Al Anon helpful, yet many had little or no experience with self-help treatment programs but had experienced some success with psychologically or medically oriented treatment programs. Still others had tried multiple treatment approaches without success, or had systematically avoided treatment of any kind.

Alcoholism histories also varied considerably. In twenty-three families it was the husband who was the alcoholic spouse; but in eight families, the alcoholic spouse was the wife.* Some alcoholic subjects had struggled with symptoms of physical addiction to alcohol; others had shown little or no evidence of tolerance or withdrawal symptoms. The distinction here is between those who would have been called alcohol dependent versus

*Extensive analyses comparing male-alcoholic and female-alcoholic families were performed after observational data had been collected. Virtually no significant differences were found between these two subgroups of families. For those who are interested in these analyses, they can be found in an unpublished paper by Tislenko and Steinglass which is available upon request.

those who would have been called alcohol abusers had the *DSM-III* criteria set been available at the time the study was initiated (see chapter 2).

The sample consisted primarily of middle-class whites, but there was considerable variation in family size, years of marriage, age of the spouses, and size of the house (important because the study included measures of interactional distance, rates of movement about the house, and the like). However, the variation in these demographic characteristics proved to be comparable for the subgroups of stable wet, alternator, and stable dry families, as summarized in table 7.1. On the other hand, alcoholism and treatment histories were, not surprisingly, quite different for the different groups, a factor that will play an important role in the discussion below of the relationships between drinking pattern and home behavior pattern.

Although a few of the families were referred directly to the study by treatment programs or community service agencies, the vast majority volunteered for the study in response to newspaper, radio, or television advertisements that asked families that had a self-defined "problem with alcohol" to volunteer for a study designed to develop a better understanding of family factors and alcoholism. For some families, the study was perceived as "pseudo-therapy," an opportunity to learn more about themselves and receive some help without having to deal directly with their alcoholic member around the issue of formal treatment. These families made it clear that they were volunteering for research, not treatment. Other families found that it was the family aspect itself that appealed to them. They were concerned about a lack of cohesiveness in their families,

TABLE 7.1

*Comparison of Stable Wet, Stable Dry, and Alternator Families
Along Selected Demographic Variables*

	Means			
Demographic Variables	Stable Wet $n = 10$	Stable Dry $n = 14$	Alternator $n = 7$	F Ratios*
Husband's Age, yrs	42.00	43.21	43.86	.087
Wife's Age, yrs	39.30	40.07	42.86	.254
Years Married	13.00	17.50	15.86	.585
House Size, *sq. ft*	1742.40	1979.79	1611.29	.572
Social Class	2.10	1.86	2.29	Not calculated †

Source: The Alcoholic Family at Home: Patterns of Interaction in Dry, Wet and Transitional Stages of Alcoholism. by Steinglass, P., 1981, *Archives of General Psychiatry,* 38, p. 581.
*F (2,28) ratio for $p < .05$ is 3.34. All ratios nonsignificant.
†Social class is categorical data and sample size was too small for X^2 test.

a paucity of family-level activities. They saw the study as a way of participating, as a family, in a joint activity. Also included in the sample were families that were motivated by a felt obligation to help in the accumulation of knowledge about alcoholism.

Our main point in reviewing the characteristics of these families is that although they were not recruited via a probability sampling technique, they were sufficiently heterogeneous in their demographic and clinical characteristics to suggest that no obvious biasing had occurred in the selection of the sample. Since this was a study of only Alcoholic Families— no contrast or control groups were used for purposes of comparison—the strategy of the study, to look for meaningful distinctions *among* Alcoholic Families, was dependent on obtaining a variable rather than a uniform sample of families. This was clearly achieved. However, it is also the case that the method of recruitment probably eliminated that group of families that, because they were unusually withdrawn or antisocial, would have been unlikely to have found participation in our study attractive.

Assessing Home Behavior

Initial Home Visits. When we first became interested in daily home routines as part of studying the way Alcoholic Families structure their internal environments, we sent a research team to the homes of prospective subject families to discuss the possibility of the families volunteering to be studied in their homes. Although we were not sure what to expect when visiting these families at home, we anticipated that we would be able to identify common parameters that these families shared with one another. That is, we expected that these families would have developed similar patterns of behavior as a result of having attempted to cope for a period of many years with chronic alcoholism.

The reports we received from our research staff, however, were quite the opposite. In one home, the research team might feel relaxed, welcomed, and willing to share personal information with the family as part of their introduction to the members of the family. In another family, the team felt continually on guard—wary that they were somehow violating an as yet unarticulated and invisible rule of family life. Perhaps they were sitting in the wrong chair or asking the wrong questions. Perhaps, without realizing it, they had conveyed some negative reaction to the family about its home.

In retrospect, we believe that these impressions were often created by the *physical* arrangement of the home environment itself. Placement of furniture was important. Some living rooms simply could not accommodate a comfortable interaction between family members and strangers unless furniture was physically moved around the room. Both extremes could contribute to this difficulty. It was as difficult to feel comfortable with a family that seated you in the middle of a three-pillow couch with a family member on each side, as it was to have all three couch seats left for research staff who then were faced by the family in an inquisitorial manner. Similarly, a circular seating arrangement with a four-foot diameter was as disquieting as one with a fifteen-foot diameter. In the former arrangement one felt smothered and engulfed by the family; in the latter, one felt distant and unable to make contact with family members. In other words, the family's use of its physical space was an important factor in determining our differential impressions of them. (Keep this in mind when you read about the interesting relationships in these families between drinking behavior and use of space as reflected in the HOAM measure of family mobility and distance regulation in the home.)

Instructions to the visitors about rules of behavior in the home also were important in shaping our initial impressions. "Take-charge" directives from the family about which room to meet in and where to sit left one impression. A question from the family about where we would like to meet and confusion about where to sit left a very different impression.

Intimacy, both verbal and physical, was also important. In some families, individuals simply did not make eye contact, nor did they talk with one another more than was absolutely necessary to keep the home visit moving. Their questions left the impression that we were interviewing separate individuals who had no prior relationship or sense of a coordinated and organized approach to the task. In other families, questions by one family member would be picked up, extended, and perhaps clarified by a question from a second family member. Parents would help clarify children's questions and ensure that the answers were accurately understood.

Once again, however, it was behavior at either end of the spectrum that left the research team with a feeling of discomfort; the moderate position was the most comfortable one. Thus the overcontrolled family left one with a sense of regimentation and lack of spontaneity that was as unsettling as was a sense of emotional distance and an absence of cohesiveness in another type of family.

In reviewing these initial impressions of our prospective subject families, three conclusions about how this group of Alcoholic Families were managing their home environments stood out.

First, these were families who had established a highly heterogeneous range of home environments. Variety rather than uniformity was the striking feature.

Second, these were families who had used a range of styles to "manage" the observers during the initial contact. Although responding to the same stimulus—the welcoming into their home of the research team—the families had orchestrated this visit in very different ways. Since the visit had been described in a similar manner to all families, one has to assume that the family's differential management of the visit reflected their own very different definition of its purpose. These varying definitions—in effect, a set of hypotheses about the research project and its meaning for the family—were being translated into a set of behaviors that also varied considerably from family to family. Some of these families viewed the research team with curiosity and interest. Others, even though they were also volunteers for the study, viewed us with suspicion and apprehension. In other words, these were families with very different *personalities.*

Third, these families had major qualitative differences in the nature of the boundaries they constructed vis-à-vis their outside world. The way the family welcomed a group of strangers into its home was an effective representation of the way that they permitted strangers to move from the family's external environment, across its boundary, and into its internal environment. In our contact with some families, this had been a smooth process, leaving the strangers (the research team) with the subjective feeling of comfort about returning for the actual observation sessions. In other families, the process had been attenuated. At one extreme we had been kept at such a distance from the family that we, in effect, felt that the boundary had never been crossed. At the other extreme we had felt engulfed and encapsulated by the family, like a foreign body within the family's internal environment, a feeling that left us as effectively prevented from meaningful interchange with the family as if we were still outside the home.

So our initial impressions had already alerted us to major differences in these families regarding their management of their internal environments, their views of their external environments, and the types of boundaries they set up to regulate the flow of traffic between their internal and external worlds. But it remained for us to use a systematic method of recording these observations before the relationship between alcoholism and these family behaviors could move into clearer focus.

Nevertheless, one can already see, even in these subjective initial impressions of the home environment, why it was that in designing a systematic home observation study, we felt that it was necessary to build into our observation coding system, as important and relevant measures, indexes of the way the family utilized space, indexes reflecting the quality of internal and external family boundaries, and indexes of variation in patterns of interaction.

The Home Observation Assessment Method (HOAM). Studying families at home is a challenging (some would say insoluble) research problem. The technical problems of designing a valid and reliable home observation method are often cited as the major obstacle to this type of research, although one also suspects that the researchers' reluctance to go into families' homes may stem as well from the discomfort of leaving the familiar and cozy confines of their own laboratory.

Nevertheless, the technical problems associated with home observations are formidable. Suppose you were given the task of designing a reliable and valid method of measuring clinically relevant aspects of family home behavior. What aspects of behavior would you choose? And how would you instruct observers to collect the data? Investigators have answered these questions in very different ways, presumably depending on the research objectives and theoretical biases of the studies involved.

For example, in an often-cited home observation study, Clark-Stewart (1973) utilized observer ratings, interaction frequencies, and narrative notes as well as behavioral and attitudinal checklists to examine relationships between child-development characteristics and aspects of maternal care. Observation sessions began with observers first writing a paragraph describing the setting and the infant's state and appearance. Parent-infant interactions, coded in intervals of ten seconds (observers received timed ten-second signals via an earphone) were recorded using a categorical coding system. After each half hour of coding, observers stopped and wrote down what had happened in their own words. They then filled out a checklist that was a summary of the infant's language development, its play materials, and its attachment to the mother. After the session, a written assessment was made of the child's and mother's behavior.

In contrast, there is the coding system used by Bradley and Caldwell (1976), the Home Observation for Measurement of the Environment (HOME), devised to study the contribution of a child's early environment to changes in mental test performance. The HOME is an on-line coding system designed to focus on the quality of stimulation found in the child's early environment. Aspects of behavior not related to this theme are ignored.

Then there is the most ambitious on-line coding system developed to date for recording, in exhaustive detail, the components of parent-child or spouse-spouse interaction, the Behavioral Coding System (BCS), developed by Patterson and his colleagues (Patterson, 1982). The BCS divides interactional behavior into a series of stimulus behaviors and their elicited consequences. A series of twenty-one behaviors are operationally defined and are felt to provide a rough but comprehensive list of the important social behaviors included in family interaction. Behavioral categories are divided into verbal and nonverbal and first-order and second-order groups (the latter distinction a priority rating to focus the observer's attention preferentially on certain categories). Observations are recorded on a coding sheet that is divided into a series of lines, each line representing a thirty-second interval, and recording then moves to the next line. Each observer codes one family member at a time and during a particular coding session codes each member of the family for a continuous interval of five to ten minutes. These coding intervals are interspersed with breaks or rest periods. Coding, using this system, is tiring, and observation sessions therefore rarely exceed fifty minutes.

The BCS has proven particularly useful when the theoretical assumptions of the study are based on a stimulus-response model. For example, Patterson and Reid (1969), relying heavily on a version of social exchange theory, proposed the notions of reciprocity and coercion as two forms of behavior-consequence interactions that might be used to meaningfully distinguish types of family interaction. On the other hand, the types of variables we have been alluding to in our theoretical discussions as most reflective of family regulatory mechanism in the home—the unique features of the home, the traffic patterns of family members, interaction in relation to use of space, and so on—are by and large ignored as meaningful variables in this coding system.

The instrument we devised, the Home Observation Assessment Method (HOAM), is specifically designed to collect accurate data on interactional behavior in the home as it unfolds in a *real-time framework*. Three considerations were paramount in its design; first, it had to minimize the intrusiveness of the behavioral observers; second, the coding system had to be nonjudgmental, objective, and amenable to on-line coding; and third, because it was intended for use over extended time periods, it had to be a method capable of avoiding fatigue in both observers and family members.

In the HOAM system, two behavioral observers, each one assigned to one of the spouses in the family, follow that person about the house and accurately record seven aspects of that person's behavior: their physical location in the home; the identity of other people in the room with them; the physical distance between the subject and others in the home when they were talking to each other; the subject's basic interaction rates (both verbal and physical) with others in the home; the content of selected verbal exchanges that involved decision making; the affective level of the selected verbal exchanges coded; and the outcome of the verbal exchanges coded. (Details regarding coding instructions, training of behavioral observers, and the mechanics and reliability of coding are available from the authors.)

The form shown in figure 7.3 is used by behavioral observers to record the behavior of the subject they are observing. During each observation session, two behavioral observers join the family for a period of time ranging from two to four hours. Observers are assigned to one spouse or the other and are responsible for recording all relevant behavior of that spouse. The observation period is subdivided into time segments when active observation and coding is occurring (typically forty-minute periods), interspersed with fifteen-minute rest periods.

Within each coding period, time segments are further subdivided into two-minute time blocks. These blocks are indicated by heavy lines on the coding sheet. Within each time block, the coder records detailed information about the first verbal interaction engaged in by his or her subject (on the top line), including its content, affective level, and outcome (columns 76–80). In addition, continual recording is made of the subject's physical location in the home, who is in the room with him or her, and data relevant to interaction rates and interactional distances.

These data can then be entered directly into a computer file, using preassigned numbers for each type of code.

Thus the HOAM coding categories are clearly weighted in the direction of structural components of behavior, especially interaction patterns and use of space. Each of these aspects of behavior can be recorded by the observers with a high degree of reliability and, because of their nature, are much less prone to distortion than more content-laden aspects of behavior. For example, a subject might consciously attempt to censor what he is talking about when being observed, but is much less likely to alter significantly his basic rate of talking or who he is interacting with.

The behavioral observer is conceptualized as a "participant-observer" who will be "living with" a particular family for the time period of the observation (usually two to four hours). The "participant-observer" model seems an appropriate one to employ because it must be assumed that the coders, once they enter the family's home, have a specific, although undetermined, influence on the behavior that subsequently occurs. The behavioral observers are trained to assume a passive and quiet role in the interactional field, allowing the family to mold them into its interactional pattern, rather than the observers imposing their own set on the family.

FIGURE 7.3

Home Observation Assessment Method Coding Sheet

DATE _1_ / _ / _6_   SESSION TYPE _7_   FAM/SUBJ. # _8_ _ _11_   CODER _12_   SHEET # _

TIME 13-17	ALC. 18-19	20-21	22-23	24-25	26-27	28-29	30-31	32-33	34-35	36-37	38-39	40-41	42-43	PERSONS IN FIELD 44-53	PHYSICAL DISTANCE/ WHO TO WHOM 54-71	BEHAVIORAL CHARACTERISTICS 72-75	T 76-77	A 78-79	O 80

LOCATION (columns 26-43)

Row blocks repeated:

CS CO
CM
V NV

PERSONS IN FIELD:
H W 1 2 3
C O

PHYSICAL DISTANCE/WHO TO WHOM:
H___, W___

BEHAVIORAL CHARACTERISTICS:
P A E M S
C O W T U
N   X

However, whenever a method like the HOAM is used, critics question whether the observer is witnessing the *actual* behavior of families at home, or instead just another example of the family's "public" behavior, the image it wishes to project to the outside world. These critics are confident that the family, immediately upon closing the door behind the behavioral observers, at the close of the observation session, releases all the behaviors, emotions, arguments, and the physical demonstrativeness, that they had been holding in check for the previous several hours.

This criticism is, of course, based on an assumption of its own, namely, that home behavior is richly sprinkled with emotional mini-dramas—domestic soap operas and situation comedies played out night after night (albeit, more like reruns than original scripts). Family clinicians often fall into this trap. Accustomed to the intense emotional exchanges, revelations, and confrontations of the family therapy interview, they come to believe that family behavior in the consultation room is a reasonable approximation of family behavior at home. The research laboratory also encourages condensation of behavior. Families are customarily asked to deal with structured research tasks (such as an instruction to spend fifteen minutes discussing the plans for a family vacation). Hence problem-solving, family style, seems to be a delineated, tight affair, neatly packaged.

If behavior in the therapy session or research laboratory is an accurate reflection of home behavior, then one might expect to see, during the course of even a single evening's observation, a similar series of mini-dramas and problem-solving ventures. Even the accounts of family life drawn from participant observation studies leave a similar impression. Reports tend to emphasize those dramatic events in family life that make families stand out in bold relief.

Yet, the actual characteristics of family life at home suggest a very different picture. Dramatic events, if and when they do occur, are played out against a background of day-to-day living in which the preoccupation with routine events far outweighs attention to dramatic details. Reflection on one's own family life makes this point clear. Surely large segments of the day are occupied with what might best be described as "maintenance activities"—cooking, eating, sleeping, housekeeping, work activities both inside and outside the home. Sleep time aside, many families spend at most three to five hours during weekdays together in their homes. This is hardly enough time to engage, on a daily basis, in the types of dramatic episodes that seem to be the bread and butter of clinical situations—that is, if the food is to be put on the table and the beds made.

The issue is succinctly summarized in a soliloquy delivered by the protagonist of one of Philip Roth's novels *(The Professor of Desire)* as he reflects on the reasons for the disintegration of his marriage. "What do we struggle over mostly?" asks David Tarnapol.

In the beginning—as anyone will have guessed who, after three years of procrastination, has thrown himself headlong and half convinced into the matrimonial flames—in the beginning we struggle over the toast. Why, I wonder, cannot the toast go in while the eggs are cooking, rather than before? This way we can get to eat our bread warm rather than cold. "I don't believe I am having this discussion," she says. "Life is not toast!" she finally screams. "It is!" I hear myself maintaining. "When you sit down to eat toast, life is toast. And when you take out the garbage, life is garbage. You cannot leave the garbage halfway down the stairs, Helen. It belongs in the can in the yard. Covered." "I forgot it." "How can you forget it when it is already in your hand?" "Perhaps, dear, because it is garbage—and what difference does it make anyway! . . ."*

In the clinical setting, we tend to concentrate on dramatic events, often ignoring the background against which these events are played out. Observations of families in their homes, carried out during an average weekday evening, tend to highlight instead the background itself, the routines of daily living, those maintenance activities that are obviously essential to the ongoing life of the family. Although often far less dramatic and therefore easily overlooked, the family's pattern of organizing its daily life proves an excellent measure of how the family regulates its own environment.

HOAM Behavioral Indexes.   One advantage of utilizing a coding system like the HOAM to study the family's home environment is that the data collected can be subjected to statistical analysis. The initial step in this process is the creation of a series of behavioral indexes that accurately reflect those aspects of interactional behavior thought to be important descriptors of home routines.

For example, family mobility (use of space) has been discussed as one such parameter. In terms of HOAM data, this parameter can be represented by creating an index called "location shifts," calculated by counting the number of times a subject moved from one room to another during the observation session. Since interaction rates are thought to be important, we create an interaction rate index by calculating how often, out of the total number of two-minute segments in the observation session (the HOAM system divides coding into such segments) the subject was in the same room with another family member, say, the spouse. This, then, is an interaction ratio index of the percentage of *actual* physi-

*From *The Professor of Desire* (pp. 68–69) by Phillip Roth, 1977. New York: Farrar, Straus and Giroux.

cal contact to *potential* physical contact. Similar ratios can be calculated for verbal contact.

Since husband and wife have been separately observed, initially all indexes are separately calculated for each spouse. But it is then possible to combine the husband and wife score and calculate a couple-mean score for each index. Since the data for husband and wife also includes their interaction patterns with their children (if they have any), these couple-means will be referred to as *family-level* indexes in our discussion.

Once a range of behavioral indexes adequate to reflect the parameters of the home routines we are interested in has been defined and calculated, the next step is to examine the pattern of relationships between the various indexes (we utilized a total of twenty-five) via factor analysis. This step is performed with the goal of identifying a more limited number of dimensions (factors) that concisely define the critical dimensions along which one family can be statistically compared to another in its manner of regulating its internal (home) environment.

The twenty-five behavioral indexes created from the HOAM data were calculated by asking two types of questions about the seven aspects of behavior coded: first, how much of this behavior is occurring (that is, what is its level of activity); and second, how different is the behavior from observation session to observation session (its variability). For example, if we take the first of the seven aspects of behavior coded in the HOAM system—physical location in the home—an activity index is created by measuring the number of location shifts per hour (movements from room to room in the house). The variability index is then created by calculating the coefficient of variation (standard deviation/mean) for the means of the nine separate observation sessions. Thus a low "location-shifts variability" score for a particular family indicates that its motility rate is quite similar (stable) from session to session. Another family with a high variability index might be quite active one evening, sluggish another.

Differences Among Families in HOAM-Measured Behaviors.   Table 7.2 summarizes the overall means and ranges of the thirty-one families studied for the twenty-five HOAM variables we are interested in. The names of the variables suggest how the types of behavior relevant to home routines have been translated into statistical indexes. For instance, contact patterns between family members are reflected not only in the calculation of interaction ratios (which measure contact as a percentage of possible interactions with all people in the house at the time the observation is taking place), but also by separately calculating the amount of time each spouse spends alone (at one end of an isolation-engagement spectrum), and the percentage of time spent with extrafamily members (with or without other family members also present). This measure reflects how open the household is to outsiders during the time the observation takes place—a concrete measure of family boundary permeability, the dimension mentioned as so important a characteristic in determining the differential impressions of research staff toward families during the initial home visits.

Table 7.2 also provides important data about the distributional characteristics of the HOAM variables. We have been alluding, at several points in the discussion, to clinical impressions suggesting a marked heterogeneity of home behavior patterns in Alcoholic Families. The ranges and standard deviations of HOAM variables summarized in this table now provide statistical documentation to buttress these clinical impressions.

Although some of the heterogeneity reflected in these data should probably be attributed to measurement errors by the behavioral observers (coder reliability was solid but is never perfect when using a method like the HOAM), the magnitude of differences is an impressive statement about home behavior heterogeneity in these families.

For example, the family motility rates as reflected by the HOAM variable, "location shifts per hour," an index that measures each physical move made by a subject from one room to another in the home, ranged from eleven to fifty-four. At the high end of the scale, observers were noting that spouses left the room they were in and moved to a new location approximately once every minute they were being observed. And this was one move per minute not only for an entire four-hour evening time block, but for each of the *nine* separate occasions on which the family was observed. Although the image that might come to mind is of a Keystone Cops comedy played out in the confines of the family's home night after night, unfortunately the more accurate image (as reported by the observers) was of caged animals constantly prowling about their "house," unable to relax even for a moment despite the familiar surroundings.

At the low end of the scale, on the other hand, is a family as remarkable for its sedentary temperament. This family, with a mean rate of eleven location shifts per hour is moving, on average, once every six minutes. This may not be striking at first glance, but when one realizes that during mealtime preparation, movement is occurring at a much higher rate, it becomes obvious that this is a family in which members characteristically stay put for periods of thirty to forty-five minutes at a time. This is obviously a very different pattern from the high motility, fifty-four shifts per hour family.

An examination of the ranges for other variables indicates similar marked differences in the high and low ends of the family means. The

TABLE 7.2

HOAM Variables: Means and Ranges

Variable	Scale	Range	Mean/SD
Physical Location in Home			
Location Shifts/hr	No. of shifts/hr	11.1–54.10	28.55/10.55
Location Shifts/hr, corrected for Room Size	No. of shifts/hr × average room size	1,463–6,994	3,516.44/ 1,350.50
Location Shifts/hr, % to kitchen	0–1.0	.10–.36	.21/.06
Location Shifts/hr, variability	V*	.12–.71	.41/.12
People in Room with Subject			
% Time Alone	0–1.0	.09–.66	.32/.16
% Time with Family and/or Extrafamily Members	0–1.0	.00–.44	.07/.10
Interactional Distance			
Mean Dist., All Interactions	Actual feet	4.30–9.27	6.83/1.99
Mean Dist., Interactions When Alcohol Not Visible	Actual feet	4.10–12.00	7.15/1.46
Mean Dist., Vy** Across Sessions	V	.07–.44	.23/.08
Mean Dist., Vy Within Sessions	V	.50–1.14	.81/.17
Interaction Ratios			
% Interaction with Coder	0–1.0	.02–.51	.16/.11
% Interactions with Coder: Husband/Wife Skew	−1.0–+1.0	−.88–+.75	−.16/.40
Physical: Potential Contacts	0–1.0	.22–.77	.45/.11
Verbal: Potential Contacts	0–1.0	.19–.60	.36/.10
Verbal: Physical Contacts	0–1.0	.57–1.23	.81/.14
Physical: Potential Contacts, Vy	V	.15–.74	.31/.13
Verbal: Potential Contacts, Variability	V	.16–.61	.32/.11
Verbal: Physical Contacts, Variability	V	.07 .39	18/.08
Type of Verbal Exchange			
% Decision-making Exchanges of All Interactions Coded	0–1.0	.01–.17	.07/.04
% Decision-making Exchanges when Alcohol Not Visible	0–1.0	.01–.19	.07/.04
% Decision-making Exchanges, Vy	V	.29–2.06	.84/.41
Affective Level of Verbal Exchange			
Mean Affect	−3.0–+3.0	+.45–+1.21	.86/.20
Mean Affect, Variability	V	.07–.47	.25/.13
Outcome of Verbal Exchanges			
% Negative and Uncertain Outcomes	0–1.0	.01–.15	.05/.04
% Negative and Uncertain Outcomes, Variability	V	.44–2.00	.97/.43

SOURCE: The Alcoholic Family at Home: Patterns of Interaction in Dry, Wet and Transitional Stages of Alcoholism. by Steinglass, P., 1981, *Archives of General Psychiatry*, 38, p. 580.
*V indicates coefficient of variation (standard deviation divided by the mean).
**Vy-Variability

FIGURE 7.4

*A Midrange Family: Movement of Husband and Wife
During an Evening In—Home Observation Session*

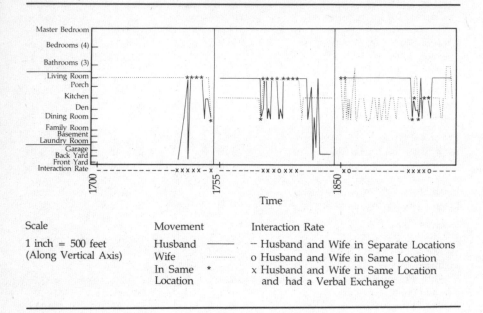

Scale	Movement	Interaction Rate
1 inch = 500 feet (Along Vertical Axis)	Husband —— Wife ············ In Same * Location	-- Husband and Wife in Separate Locations o Husband and Wife in Same Location x Husband and Wife in Same Location and had a Verbal Exchange

standard deviations (listed in the column on the far right) further support the contention that there is considerable variance in this sample of families along each and every interactional index being reported.

Differences in Physical and Verbal Interaction Rates   The variance in behavior can also be illustrated by taking one of the aspects recorded, the subject's physical location in the home, and charting it for a representative four-hour observation session. The HOAM coding system records each subject's physical location sequentially as he or she moves from room to room. It is therefore possible to reproduce the pattern of use of space during the observation session and, if husband and wife are charted on the same graph, the pattern of their interaction is clearly illustrated. Because we also know when they are talking to one another, we can chart their verbal interaction patterns as well.

Figures 7.4 to 7.6 are graphs illustrating the physical and verbal interaction patterns of three families in the sample, chosen to point out how starkly different these patterns can be. The first, a "mid-range" couple, illustrates a variable pattern of interaction in which blocks of time with

FIGURE 7.5

*A Huddling Couple: Movement of Husband and Wife
During a Weekend In—Home Observation Session*

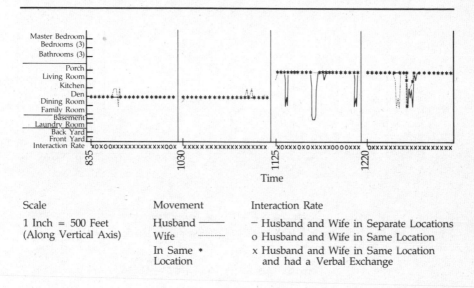

Scale	Movement	Interaction Rate
1 Inch = 500 Feet (Along Vertical Axis)	Husband ——— Wife ············· In Same * Location	− Husband and Wife in Separate Locations o Husband and Wife in Same Location x Husband and Wife in Same Location and had a Verbal Exchange

consistent physical and verbal contact are interspersed with blocks of time in which each spouse was in a different part of the house.

In contrast, the second family, one we might call a "huddling" family, seems never to leave each other's sight. It might be said that they simply enjoy each other's company. But it is our view that this is not the behavior of two people who want to spend time talking with each other, but rather the forced intimacy of a couple who remain tightly fused and mutually defensive in the presence of outsiders. The image that comes to mind is of apprehensive pioneers who have surrounded themselves with their wagons at night for protection against an unknown, but potentially hostile, outside environment.

In the third family, which we call a "distant" couple, the husband and wife are like ships passing in the night. During the observation session being charted, they spent virtually all their time in separate rooms. It was not that they were totally stationary. They moved, but seemed never to come together in the same place in the house. To manage this over a four-hour period is a truly remarkable feat, the product, we would argue, of a powerful rule of behavior reflecting an important aspect of the family's mechanisms for regulating space at home.

FIGURE 7.6

*A Distant Couple: Movement of Husband and Wife
During a Weekend In—Home Observation Session*

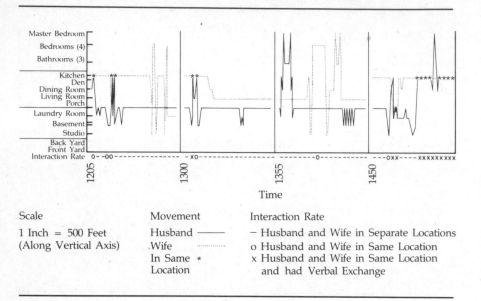

Scale	Movement	Interaction Rate
1 Inch = 500 Feet	Husband ———	— Husband and Wife in Separate Locations
(Along Vertical Axis)	Wife ··········	o Husband and Wife in Same Location
	In Same *	x Husband and Wife in Same Location
	Location	and had Verbal Exchange

Identifying Regulatory Dimensions. As we have demonstrated, even the raw HOAM data illustrate interesting differences between our group of Alcoholic Families. But for our purposes, the more important value of these data is that they can be combined in ways that allow us to identify underlying patterns of behavior. What emerges from such a process is a series of dimensions that reflect, in more parsimonious fashion, the critical aspects of the family's organization of its home routines. By extension, therefore, these dimensions reflect ways in which this regulatory behavior (daily routines) can be compared and contrasted across families. Factor analysis was the procedure used to identify these dimensions (see figure 7.7).

The factor analysis of HOAM behavioral indexes indicated the differences between the thirty-one families studied could be meaningfully described along five dimensions (factors).*

The first dimension was the extent to which family members were in

*Statistically the five factors identified are independent (orthogonal) dimensions of behavior. The five-factor solution was selected because a principal components analysis indicated the first five factors accounted for 67.4 percent of the variance in the thirty-one-family sample, with the sixth factor only accounting for an additional 5.7 percent. A five-factor VARIMAX rotation was therefore performed.

FIGURE 7.7

HOAM Factor Analysis

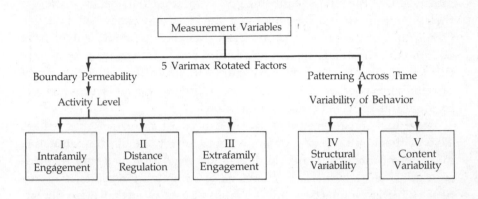

physical and verbal contact with each other. There was a greater than fourfold difference between the most active and least active family on this score. This measure, clearly a direct reflection of interaction rates within the family, is a measure of a family-level activity rate. We have therefore called it *intrafamily engagement.*

Second, families also differed in their patterns of interaction. In some families, everyone seemed to disperse to the four corners of the home, coming together only when they had something to say to each other. In such a family, it would be unusual to find two people sitting together in the same room, comfortably engaged in individual activities like reading or handiwork. If they were together, they were talking, not because they seemed to enjoy each other's company, but because that was the reason they had sought each other out. Even when in the same room, and talking with one another, they tended to do so at a distance, rarely coming within six feet of each other.

At the other extreme, some families seemed so coordinated in their movements as to never leave each other's sight, their interactional style a huddling one. They operated close to each other, in the process tending to wall themselves off from the behavioral observers. Family members in these families rarely spent time alone in a room. This does not mean that all the family members would always be together; they might be clustered in subgroups of twos or threes, but solitary activity rarely occurred. We have called this stylistic dimension of interaction *distance regulation,* because it so clearly reflects the family's use of space in the home.

A third dimension was the family's interaction rate with nonfamily members. Some families were wide open, with neighbors, friends, and relatives showing up frequently during observation sessions. Although informed that the family was being observed, these outsiders were nevertheless welcomed into the home and business was conducted as usual. Other families never had visitors. Even though two families might have children of comparable ages, in one family children's friends were always there, in another family friends never appeared. We have called this aspect of family behavior *extrafamily engagement,* a dimension that is a counterpart to the intrafamily engagement dimension.

These first three dimensions are all aspects of *activity rates* in families. Two of them, intra- and extrafamily engagement, are direct quantitative measures of interaction; the third, distance regulation, is a stylistic measure. All three, however, are reflections of a family's temperamental propensity toward interaction. But it should also be clear that these dimensions directly measure how the family organizes its internal and external boundaries. Extrafamily engagement, for example, reflects the permeability of the family's boundary vis-à-vis outsiders. The easier it is for outsiders to move across this boundary, the higher will be the family's extrafamily engagement factor score. Intrafamily engagement and distance regulation reflect the nature of the family's internal boundaries. Intrafamily contact patterns, for example, can be thought of as determined by the rules linking family members in various coalitions, subsystems, and so on as described by structural family theorists like Salvador Minuchin (1974). And the regulatory mechanism that translates these rules into behavioral patterns is best described using the metaphor of internal boundary permeability.

So the first three dimensions are descriptors of how family home behavior is patterned *spatially.* Because such patterning is governed by the placement and permeability of the family's internal and external boundaries, what is being regulated here is the amount of behavior that is to occur. Hence what we measure are behavioral activity rates. These three factors, then, are the behavioral manifestations of the first organizing principle mentioned in chapter 3 as determining the shape of daily routines—patterning in space.

The fourth and fifth factors, on the other hand, are reflections not of patterning in space but of the second organizing principle of daily routines—patterning across time. The fourth factor centers on the predictability of structural components of interaction. Some families proved remarkably constrained in this regard. Their verbal and physical interaction rates did not seem to change; traffic patterns in the home hardly varied. Life was highly structured; activities carried out in the same way and at the same time night after night. Clearly, all families demonstrate these properties to some degree. But in contrast to the highly structured family described earlier, others were far less predictable and seemed able to tolerate differences in these structural components of their lives. This property of family behavior has therefore been called *structural variability*.

Structural variability deals primarily with physical aspects of behavior. Interactional behavior, however, obviously also includes content-related variables. Three such variables are coded in the HOAM method: what people are talking about (in broad terms); the affect associated with verbal interactions; and the characteristic outcomes of such exchanges. As was the case for physical aspects of behavior, families also differed dramatically in the predictability of the content, affect, and outcome of their verbal exchanges. Some families never raised issues that called for decisions. When they talked to one another, they seemed always to be sharing information, nothing more. Perhaps because of this bland content, affective ranges were also highly restricted, that is, bland or neutral. Neither positive nor negative affect accompanied these verbal exchanges. Finally, most exchanges were simple and straightforward questions and answers. On those rare occasions when decisions were called for, they were also rapidly supplied. These families showed remarkably little tolerance for unresolved decision making, tending to bring everything to rapid (and often premature) closure. At the opposite end of this dimension were families who demonstrated a full range of affective responses, a range of content issues in their verbal exchanges, and a willingness to raise problems without demanding immediate solutions. We have called this final HOAM dimension, *content variability*.

Thus both the fourth and fifth factors deal with the way family home behavior is patterned across time. One factor addresses patterning of physical attributes of behavior; the other addresses content of behavior. But for both factors, the issue is that in some families behavior is highly predictable across time while for others a wider range of behavioral patterns is acceptable. In this sense, we can conclude that families demonstrating high structural and content variability have a higher tolerance for uncertainty, and therefore have less need for a rule imposing consistency of behavior on daily routines.

These then are the five dimensions of family daily routines identified via factor analysis of the HOAM data. These dimensions—three related to behavioral activity levels; two related to variability of behavior—are, in effect, a series of descriptors of the way each family manages its home environment. The family's factor score for each dimension is therefore a statistical reflection of its properties for that dimension relative to the other Alcoholic Families in the research sample (e.g., how high or low it is regarding intrafamily engagement).

We know, from an examination of the frequency distributions of the different variables that were used for the factor analysis, that this particular group of thirty-one Alcoholic Families varied widely in their home behavior. Families differed one from another by two, three, and even fourfold magnitudes on virtually every variable we used (summarized in table 7.2). We could not find a single aspect of behavior measured by the HOAM that proved uniform for the Alcoholic Families we studied.

The most interesting findings concerning the relationship between these HOAM dimensions of behavior and chronic alcoholism only emerged after the families had been subgrouped according to the specific drinking pattern of the family's alcoholic member (the stable wet, alternator, stable dry distinction discussed earlier in the chapter). Surprisingly, other aspects of alcoholism that one might think would be associated with differential patterns of family behavior, for example, evidence of physical addiction, AA and Al-Anon contacts, and total years of drinking, were not correlated to patterns of home behavior.

Drinking Patterns and Interaction in the Home Environment

As was noted earlier, the Alcoholic Families observed in this home observation study could be categorized as falling into one of three basic drinking patterns: a stable wet pattern, an alternator pattern, or a stable dry pattern.

As was detailed earlier in the chapter, of the thirty-one families studied, ten were in the stable wet category, seven were in the alternator category, and fourteen were in the stable dry category; and analyses of the demographic characteristics of families in these three groups indicated that they were comparable regarding age of the spouses, years of marriage, house size (important when one is examining differences in home behavior), and social class. The groups therefore differed only in terms of their alcoholism histories.

These families were therefore ideally suited for a study of how aspects of regulatory dimensions of the family's internal environment are related to important aspects of alcoholism at middle phase. Clearly, the current drinking status of the identified alcoholic and the characteristic alcoholism history of the family during middle phase is the most important such alcoholism-related variable. Some of these families (the stable dry group), despite an extended struggle with active alcoholism, appeared to have successfully challenged the problem at a critical point during middle phase.* Other families (the alternators) seemed to move back and forth in a seesaw pattern—first on the wagon, then off the wagon. Yet other families (the stable wet group) had been either unwilling or unable to challenge the active drinking of their identified alcoholic member. The question was whether the patterns of home behavior in these three groups of families were different.

Data analyses directed at answering this question were designed as a two-step process. First, the three groups of Alcoholic Families were compared regarding each of the five HOAM dimensions of behavior. The statistical procedure used was one-way analysis of variance (ANOVA). A probability statistic, the *F*-ratio, was calculated to indicate at what confidence level we could conclude that the three groups of families were significantly different in their behavior. To presage the results of these analyses, three of the dimensions—intrafamily engagement, extrafamily engagement, and structural variability—were virtually identical for the three alcoholism groups. Two dimensions, however—distance regulation and content variability—were significantly different.

In the second data analytic step, a multivariate procedure called discriminant function analysis (DFA) was used. In this procedure, information from all five HOAM dimensions was combined to produce a linear function that maximally discriminated the Alcoholic Family subgroups from each other. The procedure also indicates how accurately one can predict the drinking type (stable wet, etc.) of each family in the sample based solely on a knowledge of the family's home behavior patterns (HOAM data). As it turned out, the DFA produced a clear-cut differentiation of the three subgroups of families.

Step 1: The Analyses of Variance

In table 7.3, we have summarized the results of the separate ANOVA's performed not only for the drinking pattern subgroupings but also for two additional subdivisions of the sample of thirty-one families. The families were divided into three subgroups based first on the number of years the spouses had been married, and second on the size of the family.

These two additional ways of subdividing the families utilized traditional developmental parameters (years of marriage and family size) as contrast variables to the variable of central interest in the study—family

---

*However these families still seemed to perceive themselves as "having a problem with alcohol," as the advertisement used during the recruitment campaign asked families to contact our research center if they thought that alcohol was a problem in their family.

TABLE 7.3

Univariate ANOVA* Summary Table:
Three Family Developmental Scheme

| | Group Means for HOAM† Factors | | | | |
Groups	Intrafamily Engage-ment	Distance Regulation	Extrafamily Engage-ment	Structural Variability	Content Variability
Family Drinking Pattern					
Stable Wet	.18	.67	−.20	.55	−.25
Stable Dry	−.09	−.11	.34	−.39	.47
Alternator	−.08	−.74	−.39	−.00	−.58
F-Ratios‡	.22	5.48§	1.57	2.92	3.58||
Years Married					
0–6	1.19	−.02	−.07	.01	−.49
7–20	.02	−.16	.18	−.12	.28
>21	−.82	.31	−.27	.20	−.17
F-Ratios	13.09§	.62	.59	.27	1.51
No. of Children					
0	.24	.58	.10	.74	−.59
1	.12	−.07	−.45	−.10	.13
>1	−.16	−.29	.08	−.36	.28
F-Ratios	.49	2.46	.60	4.36	2.51

SOURCE: The Alcoholic Family at Home: Patterns of Interaction in Dry, Wet and Transitional Stages of Alcoholism. by Steinglass, P., 1981, *Archives of General Psychiatry,* 38, p. 581
*ANOVA indicates analysis of variation.
†HOAM indicates Home Observation Assessment Method.
‡Univariate F ratio with 2 and 28 degrees of freedom.
§If value significant at $p < .01$.
\|\| If value significant at $p < .05$.

drinking pattern. They help sharpen interpretation of findings in two ways—first by helping to verify that alcoholism-related findings are not merely a confound created by the relationship between more basic family developmental variables and home behavior; and second, by providing interesting evidence of the specificity of the relationship between family drinking pattern and HOAM dimensions.

An examination of table 7.3 indicates that the three alcohol subgroups are significantly different along two of the five HOAM dimensions: distance regulation ($p < .01$) and content variability ($p < .05$). In addition, these two HOAM dimensions are *not* significantly different when the thirty-one families are subdivided according to either years of marriage or size of the family. Thus it appears that the association between family drinking pattern and the HOAM dimensions distance regulation and content variability is a relatively unique one.

Just how specific a relationship it is is hard to determine from this one study alone. We have not explored every possible alternative explanation for the findings and the results have not yet been replicated. In addition, the study only examines home behavior in Alcoholic Families. It does not compare these families to either a control group of "normal" families, or to a potentially interesting contrast group—for example, a group of families with a chronically ill member. (We will discuss a number of these issues in greater detail in a moment.)

But with this cautionary note in mind, the results of these initial ANOVA's suggest not only that the patterns of home behavior are significantly different for stable wet, alternator, and stable dry families, but that these differences express themselves along two "alcohol-sensitive" HOAM dimensions—distance regulation and content variable. That there is specificity in the relationship between drinking type and the HOAM dimensions of distance regulation and content variability is borne out in the findings regarding the relationships between the two comparison developmental variables—years of marriage and family size—and the five HOAM dimensions. For example, if one wants to describe the differences in home behavior as longevity of marriage increases, distance regulation is not a meaningful descriptor. Instead it is intrafamily engagement that proves to be the "longevity-sensitive" HOAM dimension. (The cynics among us will probably take pleasure in the evidence of dramatic *decreases* in intrafamily engagement as years of marriage increase.)

Let us therefore look more closely at these two "alcohol sensitive" HOAM dimensions:

Distance Regulation. The ten stable wet families were, as a group, high distance regulators. That is, they used the dispersal pattern for regulating space and interactional contact within the home. The seven alternator families were, as a group, at the other end of the spectrum. They were huddler families. In the middle were the stable dry families, evidencing a behavioral pattern that combined contact with dispersion; periods of time when the family sought out each other's physical presence alternated with periods when family members dispersed in the home to work separately on individual activities.

What is most surprising is the sharp distinction between the stable wet and alternator family subgroups. Both the stable wet and the alternator families were being observed during periods of active drinking (though the alternator families were not in a wet phase during all observation sessions). Yet these two groups of families manifested two dramatically different styles of home behavior.

Furthermore, because of the nature of the variables making up the distance regulation factor (a factor reflecting style of interaction), families scoring at either end of the range of factor scores manifested a highly consistent pattern of behavior. Whether it was the dispersal or the huddling pattern, it was relatively rigid and consistently adhered to by the family.

Most striking in this regard was the behavior of the alternator families. A series of secondary analyses that separately compared mean scores of HOAM variables loading on the distance regulation factor for "wet" observation sessions versus "dry" observation sessions yielded results that were statistically nonsignificant. A reasonable interpretation, therefore, is that the alternator distance regulation pattern is a consistent one, regardless of whether the Alcoholic Family member is actively drinking or not. In other words, it is a home behavior pattern associated with the drinking pattern *type,* but not with the current *phase* of drinking. (We are talking here about macroscopic drinking phases, i.e., wet versus dry phases. Presumably, these families are at the same time manifesting the changes in behavior associated with the intoxicated versus sober interactional states noted in chapter 6. But these changes are not being measured by the HOAM, which focuses on the more concrete aspects of daily routines, rather than on the fine details of short-term problem-solving.)

Therefore, it would appear that it is not drinking per se that is associated with specific styles of distance regulation, but rather the family's definition of itself as one of three fundamentally different alcoholic types. Furthermore, this is a phenomenon that is occurring at a family level. The high distance regulation group, the stable wet families, are, as families, dispersing in the home. It is not merely an attempt on the part of family members to avoid the identified alcoholic; all family members are avoiding each other. And similarly, the low distance regulation pattern of the alternator families is a pattern produced by the participation of all family members in this behavioral style.

It is also tempting, given the description of the distance regulation factor, to ascribe clinical properties to the various scores along the dimension. It seems at first glance that we are dealing here with a dimension of enmeshment-disengagement as described by structural family therapists (Minuchin, 1974) or with the "family closeness" dimension in the Beavers-Timberlawn scheme (Lewis, Beavers, Gossett, and Phillips, 1976). That is, it would appear to be as dysfunctional a response for a family to be huddling together in their home (as if needing each other's presence for emotional reassurance), as it would be for them to disperse to the four corners of the home. This is particularly true because it is the stable dry group (presumably the most successful of the families in our sample) who are scoring in the mid-range on the distance regulation dimension. But for now, the most important issue is that a clear-cut association has been established between an important descriptor of family home behavior and the drinking pattern of the family's alcoholic member.

Content Variability. Content variability, the second "alcohol-sensitive" HOAM dimension moves from a low extreme in which the variability in the topics of verbal exchanges, the range of affect associated with the exchanges, and the tolerance for extended decision-making processes are all low, suggesting a rigid pattern of behavior, to a high extreme with a full range of content, affect, and outcomes expressed. The lower the score, therefore, the less adaptive, the more rigid (and presumably the more pathological), the family interaction pattern.

Comparing the three alcohol groups, once again, the stable dry group was in the more flexible range of the spectrum. Their content variability was high. In contrast to distance regulation, however, this time both stable wet and alternator groups overlapped, both falling at the lower end of the content variability spectrum. Expressed statistically, the stable dry group was significantly different from *both* the stable wet and alternator groups, whereas these two groups were not significantly different one from another.*

Thus once again we see a statistical relationship between family drinking pattern and HOAM-coded behavior. And although this relationship is just as speculative as was that for distance regulation, the specific relationships for the three types of families regarding level of content variability make clinical sense.

The point is often made that families dealing with chronic illnesses such as alcoholism tend to develop rigid patterns of behavior, and that this inflexibility perpetuates the chronic illness behavior and makes them unreceptive to or unavailable for interventions and change strategies. If distance regulation and content variability are the key variables for Alcoholic Families, as they clearly seem to be, then we have substantial evidence for the rigidity of patterns of interactional behavior when, during the middle-

---

*The statistical procedure used to make these comparisons was the Tukey (A) multiple comparison procedure.

phase, the family has an actively drinking alcoholic member. The low end of the content variability dimension is clearly the rigid end. Both stable wet and alternator families are at this end. For distance regulation, both the high and the low ends of the dimensions are rigid extremes. It is only in the normative mid-range that families combine different patterns of behavior. Whether a family is rigidly dispersing or rigidly huddling in the home, the pattern of behavior is rigidly adhered to.

Analyses of the HOAM data thus demonstrate a clear-cut relationship between an important alcoholism variable, the family alcohol phase, and two dimensions of regulatory behavior (i.e., daily routines) in the home environment. Alcoholism and regulatory mechanisms have become inexorably intertwined in these families. When we say, therefore, that in the middle phase, family life has become organized around alcoholism (the sine qua non of our definition of the Alcoholic Family), we are able to point to concrete behavioral examples of this relationship. The concept of the Alcoholic Family thus has behavioral as well as metaphorical meaning.

Step 2: The Discriminant Function Analysis

The relationship between family drinking pattern and the HOAM dimensions of distance regulation and content variability illustrates the important connections in these families between the chronic disease process and central regulatory mechanisms of family life. But the statistical procedure that most clearly demonstrates the differences between stable wet, alternator, and stable dry families is a multivariate procedure called *discriminant function analysis*. This technique uses the maximal amount of information provided by the variance in HOAM data to develop profiles (discriminant functions) that best differentiate the three groups of families from one another.

Because three groups of families are being compared, the statistical procedure permits two different combinations to be developed. First a "best case" discriminant function is calculated that combines the five HOAM dimensions in proportions that maximally discriminate the three groups. Using our data, this first function produced a discrimination with a probability value of $p = .004$. A second best case combination is then calculated. This second discriminant function, for our data, was able to discriminate the groups from each other at a probability level of $p = .04$.

As a second step, the procedure then assigns each family a score for the two discriminant functions and uses these scores to plot the family on a two-axis graph. The discriminant function plot for our sample of thirty-one families is reproduced in figure 7.8. The first discriminant function scores are plotted on the horizontal axis; the second discriminant function scores are plotted on the vertical axis. Circles drawn around the groupings for the three family types demonstrate how clear-cut the discrimination between stable wet, alternator, and stable dry families actually is.

The discriminant function plot illustrates a second point. The three family types have three quite distinct patterns of home behavior. The first discriminant function (the horizontal axis) sharply differentiates stable wet from stable dry families. Alternator families are in the middle, overlapping

FIGURE 7.8

Discriminant Analysis of In-Home Interactional Behavior:
Comparison of Stable Wet, Stable Dry, and Alternator Families

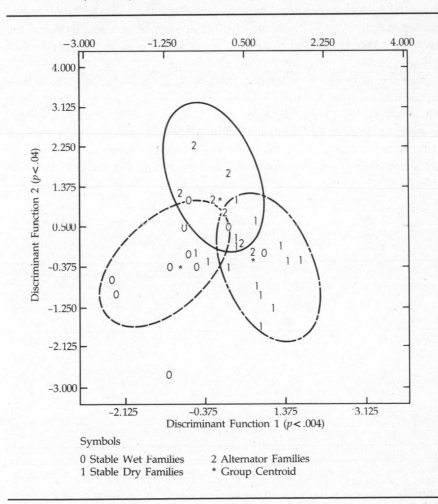

Symbols

0 Stable Wet Families	2 Alternator Families
1 Stable Dry Families	* Group Centroid

the territories of both the groups. The second discriminant function, however, differentiates the alternator families from *both* stable wet and stable dry families. The discriminant function plot strongly reinforces the finding already noted that active drinking alone is not the critical element determining home behavior, since both stable wet and alternator families contained actively drinking alcoholic members. These are clearly three different patterns of home behavior, each one characteristically associated with one of the three drinking pattern subgroups studied.

The second part of the standard discriminant function analysis involves a classification procedure using the discriminant functions described above. Each family in the sample is "classified" into one of the three family subgroups solely on the basis on its scores for the two discriminant functions (the same information used to plot the family on the graph reproduced in figure 7.8). The results of this classification process (summarized in table 7.4) indicate that three of every four families were correctly classified.

Another way of characterizing these findings is as follows: If we now come upon a new sample of Alcoholic Families and all we know about them is what their home behavior is like (as measured by the HOAM), and we want to predict whether each family in this new sample is a stable wet, alternator, or stable dry family, we will be able to do so with 75 percent accuracy—surely an impressive illustration of the relationship between family drinking pattern and patterns of daily routines discussed earlier.

TABLE 7.4

Discriminant Analysis Classification of Families

Actual Group	No. of Cases	Predicted Group Membership, No. (%)		
		Group 1, SW*	Group 2, SD	Group 3, Alt
Group 1, SW†	10	7 (70.0)	1 (10.0)	2 (20.0)
Group 2, SD	14	2 (14.3)	11 (78.6)	1 (7.1)
Group 3, ALT	7	0 (0.0)	2 (28.6)	5 (71.4)

SOURCE: The Alcoholic Family at Home: Patterns of Interaction in Dry, Wet and Transitional Stages of Alcoholism. by Steinglass, P., 1981, *Archives of General Psychiatry,* 38, p. 583.
*Percent of grouped cases correctly classified is 74.19.
†SW indicates stable wet families; SD, stable dry families; ALT, alternator families.

Conclusion

The home observation study described in this chapter is highly complex. Although it entails a relatively straightforward comparison of an alcohol-related independent variable (drinking patterns), and a family-behavior dependent variable (home routines), the strategies used to operationalize the independent and dependent variables are far from straightforward. In particular, this is so for the HOAM, a method designed to systematically assess the family's daily living routines. The basic finding of our study was that the family's patterns of behavior in carrying out these routines are, in two important areas—the regulation of spacial distance between family members, and the regulation of verbal and affective expressiveness by family members—significantly different from family to family, dependent solely upon a typing of the family based on the drinking pattern of the identified alcoholic member (what we have called the "family drinking pattern").

We have asked the reader to closely follow the description of the complex process of HOAM data reduction because it is our belief that the final products—the dimensions of intrafamily engagement, distance regulation, and the like—are among the most explicit examples available of what we have been calling *underlying dimensions of regulatory behavior.* To be more specific, the HOAM factors are the clearest examples we can point to of underlying *temperamental* properties of the family. When we proposed "family temperament" as one of the underlying deep regulatory structures responsible for overall maintenance of environmental constancy in the family, we posited that differences between families' temperamental characteristics could be described along three different dimensions: their typical energy level; their preferred interactional distance, and their behavioral range. The HOAM factor structure supports this view, in that the groupings of indexes of home behavior parallel these same three dimensions (see figure 7.7).

Thus the comparison of drinking patterns and HOAM-observed behaviors is in effect a comparison of an important aspect of alcoholism against a measure of family temperamental characteristics. The important finding that these two aspects of behavior are closely correlated therefore establishes a strong link between patterns of drinking behavior exhibited by the family's alcoholic member, and patterns of daily routines as measured by the HOAM.

At the same time, it is important to keep in mind the limitations of the study. No contrast groups were included in the study design. For example, because we did not also study nonalcoholic families, we are not in a position to ascertain whether the home behavior of Alcoholic Families as a group is significantly different from that of nonalcoholic families. Similarly, because we were not able to study these families prior to the onset of alcoholism, we do not know if their HOAM-measured behaviors (which we are positing reflects their fundamental temperamental properties) in fact antedated the emergence of alcoholism.

An alternative hypothesis is that the home behavior we observed was the reactive product of the family's having to cope with the exigencies of chronic alcoholism. For example, it might well be argued that the pattern of behavior exhibited by the alternator families was the product of years of on-again, off-again drinking by the alcoholic member in the family. This repetitive battering of the family, it might be argued, had taken its toll. The resultant pattern of home behavior was the product of a shared sense of defeat and hopelessness.

Another plausible hypothesis is that the differences in family behavior are the by-product of differential exposure of families to alcoholism treatment programs. That is, the behavior is being shaped by external forces, in this case the intervention of therapists who are actively attempting to alter family behavior.

This second hypothesis received at least superficial support from one of the many secondary analyses we performed on our HOAM data. This particular analysis compared the family's home behavior with its scores on the SAAST (Swenson and Morse, 1973), a self-administered screening questionnaire that ascertains levels of physical, psychological, and treatment consequences secondary to alcoholism (see chapter 1 for discussion of another study using the SAAST).

Although no relationships could be established between either physical or psychological consequences and home behavior, a strong relationship did exist between SAAST treatment consequences scores and one of the HOAM factors previously found to be "alcohol-sensitive" (distance regulation). A comparably strong association was found to exist between the treatment consequences score and the three drinking type subgroups (stable wet, and so on). The highest treatment consequences score was attained by the alternator group; the lowest by the stable dry group.

We could therefore conclude that the family's treatment history is a confounding event and that these different treatment experiences have, in turn, "produced" the specific interactional styles that we see reflected in HOAM-measured patterns of behavior. There is frankly no way to support or refute this hypothesis. But, on balance, it seems unlikely. The families in the study, insofar as they had treatment experiences, were not in uniform programs. If their treatment contexts were representative of alcoholism treatment in the United States, it is unlikely that these programs even had a family orientation, much less were sensitive to the kinds of concrete aspects of interactional behavior measured by the HOAM. The only quasi-uniform experience our families might have had that might differentiate them along treatment lines is AA affiliation. Yet when we divided the families according to whether they had ever been affiliated with AA or Al-Anon, we found only minor differences in home behavior between them.

A facile conclusion might be that we are dealing with a variable that reflects seriousness of alcoholism, and that one group of families is responding to having been repeatedly and systematically battered by this condition, while another has escaped relatively unharmed. This experience with alcoholism is then reflected in the pattern of behavior at home, including the important and interesting dimension of distance regulation.

However, there is a great deal of evidence, including the SAAST scores, suggesting that this is simply not the case. You will recall that there are two other subscores for SAAST data—a physical consequence subscore and a social consequence subscore. This last subscore, which measures the impact of alcoholism on social, work, and family relationships, is not correlated with any of the HOAM dimensions. Thus, even though low distance regulation families have high treatment consequences subscores, they show no differences in their social consequences subscores from those of high distance regulation families.

Furthermore, other potential measures of "seriousness" of alcoholism are also uniform for the groupings of families as we have divided them. For example, there are no differences in years of drinking for the three alcohol life history family groups, nor is there a difference in the age or sex of the family's alcoholic member. Finally, and perhaps most telling of all, there is no difference in the reported psychiatric symptom level of the members of the different groups of families. Alternator families may have dramatically different patterns of distance regulation that are even more sharply differentiated if families are grouped based on treatment consequences subscores, but there is absolutely no difference in the levels of anxiety or depression experienced by either alcoholic or nonalcoholic spouses in these families. This is not to say that there is not considerable variance in symptom levels from one subject to another, but group means for, say, stable wet versus alternator versus stable dry, or high versus medium versus low treatment consequences families are not significant.

Thus, the combined evidence points to a conclusion that there is indeed a relationship between the alcoholism-related characteristic of these families and their patterns of home interactional behavior, but these relationships are not reflected in (and presumably, therefore, are not stimulated by) differential disruption of family life precipitated by alcoholic behavior. In other words, the families are, group by group, relatively equal in their level of behavioral stability, their level of experienced symptomatology, and their level of dysfunctional behavior.

Therefore, although alternative hypotheses such as the ones discussed earlier cannot be definitely refuted, we think them on balance implausible. Instead, it is our belief that we were studying a group of families that had established successful "fits" between their temperamental family interaction styles and the drinking patterns of their alcoholic members (including characteristic behavior when intoxicated). By suggesting that an alcoholism ←→ family environment fit existed in the families we studied, we are in no way implying that family temperament "causes" a particular drinking pattern to express itself in an alcoholic individual. Nor are we contending that a drinking pattern "creates" a particular family temperamental style. However, it is surely the case that a fine-tuning process does occur in which alcoholism parameters and family temperamental characteristics mutually influence one another and induce those subtle alterations that make for the stable fit between family behavior and the alcoholism behavior we observed in our study.

At a number of points, as we have attempted to describe the process that most likely leads to the formation of an Alcoholic Family, we referred to an interactive process that occurs between the emergence of alcoholic behavior and the evolving nature of family regulatory processes. At one point we noted that the family's response to alcoholism is both a reactive and a proactive one. That is, the family tends both to accommodate its behavior to the exigencies of alcoholism and to attempt to shape and delimit the effects of drinking to preserve important family functions. By the time the Alcoholic Family reaches middle phase, this process is far advanced. For the middle-phase family, the priority placed on internal stability means that regulatory behaviors have been organized around the primary goal of maintaining constancy of the family's internal environment.

The different patterns of drinking behavior used to categorize families in our home observation study carry with them very different types of challenges to this internal family stability. The stable wet pattern is quite predictable in its impact. Yet, at the same time, it presents the family with an almost constant challenge. It would appear to have the potential to wear the family down; it never goes away. The alternator pattern, in contrast, is highly unpredictable. The episodic nature of on-again, off-again drinking associated with this pattern presents the family with sudden destabilizing challenges. Yet it also allows for extended periods of sobriety, periods when the family can presumably turn its undivided attention to other matters. And, as paradoxical as it may at first glance appear, the stable dry pattern has its own set of challenges (challenges that become more apparent when we discuss some of the issues associated with loss of alcohol in chapter 9).

The relationship between the drinking pattern variable and the home behavior variable is the clearest example we have to date of the link between an individual-level property and a family-level property. Here is a clear view into the unfolding struggle between the needs of alcoholism and the needs of the family. The findings of the home observation study indicate that by the time the Alcoholic Family has reached middle phase, alcoholism and family behaviors fit together like an assembled jigsaw puzzle.

Although we are not yet able to substantiate it with firm data, it is our speculation that the Alcoholic Family only reaches middle phase if such a "goodness of fit" between fundamental regulatory processes and specific characteristics of alcoholism exist. That is, if a particular family is not temperamentally suited to deal with, say, the unpredictable nature of an alternator alcoholic member, then something must give. In such a situation, it is likely either that the alcoholic member will be forced to change his or her drinking behavior, that this person will be extruded from the family, or that the family will itself split up.

Looked at from another vantage point, one of the reasons why the families we have been describing seem to be so stable despite the challenges of alcoholism is that they have all already entered middle phase with their alcoholic identities intact. Thus when we visit them in their homes, what we find are a group of families whose patterns of daily routines and patterns of drinking behavior fit together in an intricate, coherent, and mutually reinforcing fashion.

CHAPTER 8

Alcoholism and Family Ritual Disruption

IN THE FIRST two chapters of this section we have dealt with two different types of regulatory behaviors that shape and conserve important organizational and identity issues for the family. We saw how the existence of chronic alcoholism in the family can alter these regulatory behaviors—short-term problem-solving strategies and daily routines—in order to maintain drinking behavior. And once altered, these behaviors reinforce a tendency in the family to organize itself around alcohol as a core identity issue. Thus the short-term problem-solving behaviors and daily routines serve to maintain overall stability in the Alcoholic Family, although often at the expense of normative growth and development.

In this chapter, we turn to the third category of regulatory behaviors we have identified as reflective of underlying morphostatic forces in middle-phase families—family rituals. Like the daily routines described in the last chapter, family rituals are behaviors of central importance in regulating family life. And like daily routines, they become preeminent in the middle phase of family development, playing a central role in giving color, substance, and style to family life during this period. Family rituals also mark off one family from another, giving each a special character. Finally, like daily routines, family rituals can be *invaded* and *permeated* by alcohol, with major consequences for family development.

Yet despite these similarities to daily routines, family rituals have their own unique properties. Thus, their study and the study of their relationship to alcoholism gives us a powerful new tool for understanding the Alcoholic Family and the distortions in its development.

220

The potential power of family rituals as regulatory behaviors in middle phase is illustrated in the following vignette:

A couple in their mid-forties, Fred and Claudine Fain, were interviewed by a researcher about their family life in their home. Fred worked as a mid-level government administrator. He had been a serious alcoholic for years. Fred's family, including his father, had a history of alcoholism; Claudine's family did not. Claudine was a registered nurse but gave up her career to raise four girls, now teenagers.

About midway through the interview, the couple began to describe a part of their family life that filled them with the greatest sense of pride, satisfaction, and enthusiasm: how they celebrate Christmas. What was especially meaningful to them was their own family tradition of hanging stockings. Claudine recalled that stockings were a big part of her family's Christmas celebrations when she was a child. She remembered that there was more excitement among the children about the stockings than about any other aspect of Christmas. When she was growing up, her mother made candy or gingerbread cookies for the stockings. Sometimes home-made toys were put inside. Each was individually wrapped and each opened with great glee.

When Fred and Claudine had had their own children they had resumed hanging stockings. At first Fred was reluctant, but after several years got caught up in the tradition. Claudine had remained the persistent and enthusiastic stocking filler; at times she too had made candy or cookies for them. More recently, Fred had been adding his own little gifts—toys he made himself—to the stockings. Beaming, her eyes filling with tears, Claudine told the interviewer, "and this year the children started to put presents in themselves—entirely on their own."

Although the couple did not seem aware of it, the interviewer was impressed with the timing of the children's initiative in becoming stocking fillers. It was shortly after Fred's mother died. After hearing about this important tradition, and noting silently its relationship to issues of family continuity, the interviewer asked, "Was there drinking during Christmas?"

Fred answered, with determination, "I never got smashed on a holiday. I never screwed up on a holiday."

With a steely but unmistakable anger, Claudine added, "I would have killed him if he did."

In our years of work with families—those with alcoholic members and those without—we have come to recognize the importance of family stories like the one told by Fred and Claudine Fain, stories centering on those discrete, patterned, and symbolic behaviors we have called family rituals. In some families we observe these rituals in the special modifications the family makes in their own celebrations of traditional holidays—Christmas, New Year's, Thanksgiving, Passover, and others. This is the case for the Fains. But rituals can also develop around more particular and idiosyncratic family traditions. And finally, rituals are developed around more routine family events such as dinnertime or the visits of relatives. In Alcoholic Families, the relationship of alcohol to these precious moments of family life is a major issue.

Families vary tremendously in the degree to which they develop and maintain rituals in the three areas noted above—celebrations, family traditions, and patterned routines. The importance of such rituals for a particular family depends on many factors, for example, the way rituals were treated in their families of origin, the presence and age of children, and ethnic ties. But for those families that are drawn to the power and symbolism of ritual behavior, such behaviors become important surface manifestations of underlying regulatory forces acting to conserve core identity issues for the family.

It is for this reason that ritual behaviors take on such potential importance for the middle-phase Alcoholic Family. The central issue is what happens to such rituals when the family is faced with the challenges associated with chronic alcoholism. The family must decide what stance to take when it is forced to choose between maintaining its ritual behavior or changing it to accommodate the unique needs of its alcoholic member. It must decide whether to place highest priority on family cohesiveness and include the alcoholic member in holidays and family traditions, or to concentrate on the preservation of the ritual itself, excluding the alcoholic member when his or her intoxicated behavior becomes disruptive. Because such rituals so clearly reflect underlying identity issues within the family, they are ideal for observing middle-phase identity struggles within the Alcoholic Family.

It is hardly surprising that alcohol abuse has the potential to alter family rituals, since its repercussions are felt in all the events and situations that engage family members as a group. As the family's customary leisure time or dinners or holiday celebrations are marked, more and more, by intoxicated interactions, they have no choice not to respond in some way.

What is of direct interest to us, however, is that careful examination of such reactions indicates that they take one of three very distinct forms. Some families rigorously exclude drinking from family rituals or isolate the drinker from them. The Fains are clearly among this group. Others make adjustments in order to accommodate the drinking and the drinker, thus tolerating the alcohol abuse in their midst. Still others allow alcohol to disrupt and destroy their established routines to become a central organizing principle of life.

It appears that the family's response pattern is a critical marker of the degree to which it is accepting or resisting an alcoholic identity. Thus we can say that clinical evidence of the extent to which alcoholism has *invaded* family ritual life is an unusually clear indicator of the extent to which the middle-phase Alcoholic Family has succumbed to alcoholism as the central organizing principle in its life. To use an analogy from individual ego psychology, the status of family ritual behavior reflects whether alcoholism is an egosyntonic or egodystonic issue for the family.

Earlier in the book, we focused attention on family rituals, when, in chapter 5, we described a research study that tracked the process of identity formation in early-phase families. By carefully reviewing how newly married couples had attempted to copy or veer away from the ritual practices in their families of heritage, we were able to elucidate the different pathways followed by early-phase families with alcoholic heritages.

In this chapter, our interest is in ritual as a regulatory behavior that has a differential effect on how alcoholic behavior will affect the family during middle phase. Just as was the case in early phase, families differ dramatically in the degree of resolve, of *deliberateness,* with which they approach the preservation of important rituals in the face of alcoholic challenges. In addition, the choices the family makes have profound consequences for the issue of intergeneration transmission of alcoholism as it is played out in the late-phase family. In this chapter, however, we focus on what is happening to family rituals in the middle-phase family, picking up the transmission story when we move on to a discussion of the late-phase family in part five.

Characteristics and Categories of Family Rituals

The importance and power of rituals in primitive societies or in religious groups is well-known. Rituals reinforce the shared beliefs and common heritage of those who take part in them. With their prescribed form and unchanging content, rituals help those who perform them make sense of their particular universe. But the family as a context for ritual had received little attention before 1950, when Bossard and Boll published *Rituals in Family Living,* a landmark study of ritual behavior in nearly two hundred families, based on published autobiographies and on reports written by college students about the rituals in their families of origin. Bossard and Boll came to some dramatic conclusions regarding the importance of family rituals, proposing that these repetitive and symbolic occasions were "the core of family culture," an index to the level of a family's integration. Bossard and Boll saw the ritual as a process that transmitted the family's enduring values, attitudes, and goals.

Over the past ten years of our work on the impact of alcohol abuse on family life, we have interviewed members of well over 150 families about the rituals practiced in their homes when they were growing up. Like Bossard and Boll, we have noted that families frequently describe themselves by the rituals they keep. In the carrying out of their rituals, members learn crucial family rules as well as the family's myths about its history.

Ritual behavior in families is patterned—it is repetitive, stable with respect to roles, and continued over time—and these patterns have meaning beyond their practical outcome or functional purpose. In the home— just as in a tribal gathering or religious context—ritual has the power to enhance affect and thus to intensify the emotional interaction of the participants. Ritual puts family members in an altered state of mind in which their awareness and sense of purpose are heightened. It affords them a means of symbolic communication through the use of "props" or significant objects and the "script" that they follow. Finally—and most important for our thinking about families in the middle phase of their development—ritual serves the function over time of stabilizing the feelings and actions of members of the group.

In our conception of family process over time, the long middle phase of development is best characterized by orderly growth and increasing equilibrium. This is the time when family functions such as the nurturing of children and the facilitating of relationships with the outside world acquire a certain predictability, and there is an expectation that the family will meet its members' needs in a similar fashion time after time. Family members can anticipate that tomorrow will very likely be more like, than different from, today.

In the prior phase, when the family was just getting established, ties to the previous generation played a major part in the formation of the young couple's identity. It was a time of adaptation and change, with the young couple—or young family—more vulnerable to external influences than they will ever be again. But as family life becomes more regulated by the internal processes described in earlier chapters, there is more resistance to change and a steady, slower kind of growth prevails. Family rituals make a major contribution to stability and continuity during these years.

Characteristics of Family Rituals

Family rituals, along with daily routines and short-term problem-solving strategies, are major behavioral regulators of stability in the middle-phase family. It stands to reason, therefore, that just as was the case for the other regulatory behaviors, family rituals have a major effect on the subtle relationships between alcohol use and ongoing family life in the Alcoholic Family. However, the specific area of influence for family rituals differs somewhat from the other regulatory behaviors. In large part, this difference can be attributed to five characteristics that distinguish family rituals from the problem-solving strategies and daily routines we have described earlier.

Bounded. Family rituals are bounded behaviors. That is, they are endowed with a sense of specialness and importance, are conducted with as little interruption as possible, often have a clear beginning and a clear end, and finally, and perhaps most important, often involve preparation. The preparation creates a sense of anticipation and, in effect, elevates the ritual by putting it on a pedestal.

Self-aware. Because of their importance and their boundedness, ritual practice is, in part, self-aware. Families can describe quite clearly the main lines of organization and the patterning of their rituals (although they may not be able to report critical details). This means that we can learn about family ritual via interviews with family members—to learn about problem-solving and daily routines we had to directly observe these behaviors.

Preemptory. Family rituals are compelling. A family will feel quite keenly their absence if they are not followed and will make strenuous efforts to keep them going or at least institute a semblance of the usual ritual if circumstances prevent its full or more complete replication.

Symbolic. Detailed studies of family rituals reveal the intricate symbolic processes inherent in their development and practice. Family members are often only dimly aware of these processes, but they seem to know—on some level—that they are symbolic. In describing rituals, families typically talk possessively of them. This is the way "we" do it; this is "our way" of celebrating.

Organizing. Many of the features of rituals we have described lead to another distinguishing characteristic: their capacity to organize or "entrain" other family behavior. Because family rituals are conspicuous, self-aware, symbolically rich, and preemptory, they come to play a special role in the organization of family behavior. Further, rituals are for the most part practiced by all members of the household. In fact, in some families, rituals may provide the only opportunity for face-to-face contact among family members. Thus, rituals provide a particularly central opportunity for a broad range of family behavior to be recalibrated, coordinated, planned, terminated, or delegated.

For these reasons, family rituals are in many ways quite different from the other regulatory behaviors we have dealt with earlier in the book. Their distinctive characteristics, especially their bounded, preemptory, and symbolic qualities, help us understand how they are capable of carrying out their most important and unique function—their central role as *conservers* and *transmitters* of the family's core identity issues.

As preemptory and repetitive episodes of family behavior, expressing and reaffirming central ideals and standards of the family's life, rituals conserve over time a broad range of its patterns. When fully established, no other form of family behavior has the same capacity to sustain unique values, standards, role prescriptions, and perceptions. Rituals thus serve over time as a prime source of stability for the central and distinctive features of family life.

Second, rituals are memorable. The main lines of rituals can thus be remembered by new generations and, in countless families we have observed, are remembered and reenacted with greater or less precision. But rituals are not, as we have explained, just gestures. They are behavioral sequences rich in meaning. A new generation cannot reenact a ritual without the symbolic reaffirmation (transmission) of values, affects, and perspectives of the previous generation.

We have thus been able to identify five characteristics that serve as core descriptors of family rituals and to point to two critical functions that rituals play in family life—conservators of family identity and transmitters of family values, affects, and perspectives.

Level of Ritualization

While the functions of family rituals are quite clear-cut, rituals are not used by all families for these purposes. We have found that families vary dramatically in the degree to which they enact rituals (level of ritualization) and in the importance they place on their form, substance, and reproducibility.

In some families, rituals have only a modest place in family affairs. The family is flexible about the timing of these rituals and even about their form. These low ritual families tend to be egalitarian, allowing all members to make changes in rituals, to modify or even to create new patterns in them.

In sharp contrast are families in which rituals are conspicuous, are practiced in precisely the same ways at the same times, and in which little change or deviation is tolerated. In these high ritual families, role relations tend to be hierarchical and rigid. The parents act as family priests, insisting on the rigid maintenance of particular practices and ordaining who shall and who shall not participate and precisely what roles they may play.

In between are a third group of families that share features with both the other groups. On the one hand, rituals are important and conspicuous. The family attaches great importance to their practice and exhibits great pride and feelings of accomplishment at their conclusion. On the other hand, flexibility is permitted and at times encouraged. Rituals may be modified or, on occasion, even set aside. As children grow or as parents' occupational status changes, or as new members are added to the family or as friendships develop, rituals are altered to reflect and even capitalize on these changes.

Alcoholic Families, despite their relative rigidity and intolerance for uncertainty, are not in our experience restricted to the "orthodox" subgroup. The important issue for the Alcoholic Family is not the degree or relative orthodoxy of ritual practice, but rather the specific role alcohol and the Alcoholic Family member come to play in the enactment of rituals. Thus the crucial issue is the relationship between alcoholic behavior and ritual behavior as the family moves through middle phase.

Types of Family Rituals

Family rituals can be classified into three main categories: family celebrations, family traditions, and ritualized routines. All three categories share the general features we have just described. However, ritualized routines come closest to the daily and nonritualized routines described in chapter 7.

Family celebrations are those holidays and occasions that are widely practiced throughout the culture and that are special in the mind of the family. To this category belong rites of passage, such as weddings, funerals, baptisms, and bar mitzvahs; annual religious celebrations, such as Christmas, Easter, the Passover Seder; and secular holiday observances, such as Thanksgiving, New Year's Day, or the Fourth of July. Celebration rituals are characterized by their relative standardization across most

American families, by the fact that they are usually specific to the subculture in which they are observed, and by the universality of the symbols that pertain to each of them. It is the atypical family that would not list a series of such occasions as part of its ritual legacy.

These holidays and occasions offer members the opportunity to clarify their status within the family and to assert their group identity as a family. This type of ritual also has a function unique among the three groups: it clarifies and expresses the family's perceived connection to wider ethnic cultural and religious communities. And through repetition over time, the family's ritual observances contribute to its stability. Rites of passage have their own important functions for the family: they help to define its membership (baptisms, weddings, funerals) and they signify the developmental phase of the family (bar mitzvahs, confirmations, graduations).

Family traditions, as a group, are less culture-specific and more idiosyncratic to the family. They do not have the annual periodicity of holidays or the standardization of rites of passage, though they recur in most families with regularity. They are only moderately organized in comparison to the rituals included in family celebrations.

Each family describes its own set of traditions, commonly including summer vacations, visits to and from extended family members, birthday and anniversary customs, parties of various kinds, and special meals. Participation in annual community events and in regular activities with kin—such as family reunions—are also mentioned. While the culture makes a contribution to the shaping of these traditions—birthday cards and birthday cake, for example—the family itself chooses the occasions it will embrace or emphasize as traditions. Perhaps this element of choice contributes to the high degree of meaning family members generally attribute to their traditions, and the attachment they exhibit to their continued observance. Family traditions seem to say, "This is what is unique or special about our family."

The least deliberate and most covert of family rituals are ritualized routines. Among rituals, these are the ones most frequently enacted, but they are the ones least consciously planned by the participants. To this category belong rituals such as a regular dinnertime, bedtime routines for children, the customary treatment of guests in the home, or leisure time activities on weekends or evenings. In some families, the discipline of children or everyday greetings and good-byes are considered rituals. Whatever the patterns, these interactions help to define members' roles and responsibilities; they are a means of organizing daily life.

We have been impressed by the near universality of rituals from all three categories—celebrations, traditions, and patterned family interactions—in the lives of the families whose members we interviewed, in spite of the differences in their socioeconomic background and their ethnic orientation. Nearly all families acknowledge and celebrate holidays or rites of passage. Similarly, most families we have studied reported traditions that symbolically represent their family; these traditions may be a response to the needs, and a reflection of the desires, of the family's present members, but are frequently influenced by the practices of the previous generation. And most families reported ritualized routines in everyday life; these are the rituals most idiosyncratic to the nuclear family in which they occur.

Rituals in the Alcoholic Family

Let us begin our consideration of ritual in the Alcoholic Family by examining a family's struggles to protect a critical holiday ritual in the face of severe drinking by the father.

When describing their most cherished family times in childhood, Sue Lawton and her brother Tom both referred to their annual summer vacation pilgrimage to a lakeside cottage resort. They were a working-class family struggling to make ends meet; their week at the lake meant a lot. Then mother and father, with the two children helping, would pack up the old station wagon on a Friday afternoon late in July, and like so many other families, spend an intense, but informal ten days together.

Although no one said as much during those growing-up years, the Lawton family's annual vacation at the lake was a true ritual. It was repeated time after time, with the same script and the same roles. There were many highly symbolic aspects to it and there was, crucially, a shared sense of its value. The family would stay at the same cottage year after year, eat in the same restaurants, and play the same card games in the evening. Perhaps they even discussed the same hopes and plans for the future.

When Sue, who was two years older than her brother Tom, turned fifteen, her father had already developed a serious drinking problem. Although a heavy drinker for many years, Alan Lawton had never missed work or been hospitalized for alcoholism. During this year, though, his level of functioning had dramatically deteriorated, and while he continued to work regularly, there were serious doubts as to his ability to handle the week at the lake. He spent most days, after work, at the bar. In fact, even at his job, where he worked as a mechanic, Mr. Lawton was undoubtedly intoxicated most of the day. Certainly he was physically addicted.

As a result, that year the family found itself openly discussing the question of how to manage the summer vacation. Detailed planners that they were, the Lawtons, found themselves focusing almost immediately on the dilemma of how to organize a vacation without forcing a confrontation about the alcohol issue. Two "practical" issues had surfaced. First, there was the driving. Their customary vacation site was a full day's drive from their home. Alan Lawton could no longer be relied upon as a driver. The second issue was the effect of Alan's drinking on his ability to participate in family activities during the vacation itself. As they went through the list of usual activities—hiking, fishing, water sports—it seemed clear to them that not only could he no longer participate in many of these activities but that his drinking made them potentially quite dangerous.

The solution arrived at was a conscious family decision to radically alter their customary vacation plans in order to facilitate Mr. Lawton's explicit need for alcohol. Their account of this change was both graphic and disturbing. They chose to vacation at a local seaside resort located within several hours of their home. The resort was chosen not only because of its proximity, but also because of its reputation as a "watering hole." On the appropriate Friday, Alan Lawton was packed, already drunk, into the rear cargo area of the family station wagon. A new bottle of whiskey was placed beside him for his use during the trip.

The rest of the vacation followed a pattern clearly presaged by what had occurred during the trip. Mr. Lawton was continually drunk. He seemed already intoxicated when the family awoke in the morning and spent most of his day in one of several bars close by the house they had rented. His wife, Jean, would set the rest of the family up at the beach, then make periodic forays to these local bars to monitor her husband's status. If he seemed able to remain at the bar (that is, if he hadn't passed out or created a disturbance), Jean would return to the beach. If she was told by the bartender that he should leave, she would bring him home and attempt to put him to sleep.

Although a semblance of daily routines was attempted, the family was increasingly obliged to adjust its schedule to deal with the events related to Alan Lawton's binge drinking. Jean Lawton, rather than feeling refreshed by the vacation, was understandably exhausted. Rapidly exhausted as well, were the family's vacation funds. By the end of the first week of a planned two-week vacation, Alan Lawton's drinking had doubled the estimated expenses. The family therefore found itself back on the road, heading home, one week early and with Alan Lawton once again stretched out in the back of the station wagon, sleeping off his final night's binge.

This dramatic and pointed story cannot help but evoke strong feelings in a listener. If one is hearing the story from the vantage point of the children in this family, one experiences outrage, apprehension about the future, and perhaps even a sense of hopelessness. If one is identifying with Jean Lawton, the feelings might include pity and anger at her victimization, tinged with annoyance at her complicity in this affair. If one is trying to understand Alan Lawton's behavior, the typical emotions often are a paradoxical mixture of sympathy and concern mixed with disgust and condemnation.

Our vantage point, however, is the family. From this perspective, what we have heard is an account of a family adjusting one of its most important rituals, the family vacation, to accommodate the drinking behavior of one of its members. In the process, both the form of ritual and its symbolic meaning had been substantively changed as well. It had been altered from a positive event that sustained and rejuvenated the family as a group to an event tinged with failure and disappointment. The family returned from this vacation emotionally and physically exhausted. The important sense of closeness, cohesiveness, and warmth that characterized prior vacations had disappeared, in effect dissolved in alcohol.

The Lawton family vacation is therefore an example of a process we have come to recognize as the confrontation between important family rituals and the maintenance of drinking behavior. What is at stake in such confrontations is nothing more or less then the critical decision about whether family identity is to be firmly organized around alcoholism, or the individual alcoholic is to be forced to subordinate his or her drinking to the family identity. We have highlighted the important role of family rituals both in symbolically expressing important aspects of a family's sense of self (its identity) and in preserving this identity. Although the form this confrontation takes is often more diffuse, more gradual, and significantly less dramatic than the distortion in vacation plans experienced by the Lawton family, its impact, we would argue, is no less significant. The family is faced with a crucial decision about the extent that the shape and form of family life is going to be *allowed* to change in the face of the mounting practical, physical, and emotional demands of alcoholism. Either the alcoholic member is going to have to accommodate his or her drinking to the family ritual, thereby preserving its sanctity and meaning for the family, or the ritual is going to have to bend, thereby elevating alcoholism to a dominant status in family life.

The family, of course, rarely makes a specific and clearly articulated decision to protect or sacrifice an important ritual when challenged by alcoholic behavior. Instead, it is a process that can be seen clearly only in retrospect. Months or years later, the family, in reviewing the events of these years, is able to appreciate the extraordinary efforts it expended to protect its basic rituals, or can see the insidious erosion of these rituals in the face of mounting alcoholism. However, the consequences of the decision to protect or to sacrifice family rituals, even if not explicitly stated, are profound.

Thus, although in the Lawtons' case it might at first glance appear that they had successfully "cut the difference" by altering the ritual to accommodate Alan Lawton's alcoholic needs, their decision was, in fact, an a priori commitment to the priority of including an alcoholic family member and his alcoholism in family rituals. Rather than being a reflection of family flexibility, sensitivity, and cohesiveness, the Lawtons' behavior demonstrated their willingness to subsidize alcoholic behavior, even to the point of altering a cherished component of family life. Although Mr. Lawton was in fact present at a vacation ritual, and although the ritual was preserved, its form and symbolic meaning had been so altered (disrupted) that the result was no longer an occasion when the members could share closeness, warmth, and their special sense of family.

Maintaining Family Rituals: A Basic Choice for Alcoholic Families

The dilemma faced by the Lawton family was a particularly dramatic and clear-cut one, and their solution was also quite dramatic. The image of Alan Lawton stretched out in the back of the family station wagon, nursing his bottle, as the family drives off to its beach cottage is one of those scenes that only a real family can invent. Yet, despite the extraordinary solution to their problem worked out by the Lawtons, the underlying problem was a quite common one. *All* middle-phase families with alcoholic parents have to make crucial decisions vis-à-vis their ritual behavior. Simply put, the family must take one of two paths. Alcoholic behavior can be kept out of family rituals and the alcoholic drinking kept relatively isolated from the critical components of the family's rituals. Or, alcohol is admitted into family ritual life, with drinking becoming part of the ceremony, holding a fixed and regular position in the standard and repeated sequences of these rituals. In extreme situations, the alcoholic behavior disorganizes and then destroys the family ritual. Ritual life itself becomes impoverished.

When the family opts for the first pathway, it must work to keep the alcoholic behavior out. As a consequence, the drinking member's role in ritual life may be diminished. He or she may have to be excluded from ritual practice in order to keep out the alcohol. Almost always, he or she has to be watched carefully and kept under family control. In either case, the alcoholic is no longer a full-fledged ritual celebrant. In the case of Fred and Claudine Fain (the Christmas stocking ritual), for example, Fred made a special effort to monitor his drinking, while Claudine remained coiled to spring if he touched a drop. Fred was never a full-fledged celebrant of the stocking routine—his status remained enduringly probationary.

When the family opts for the second pathway, in which alcohol is admitted into family ritual, the fundamental nature of the ritual is altered. It may either be made simpler and more rigid (e.g., a two-minute dinner-time) or more chaotic and unpredictable (e.g., the total loss of dinnertime). By admitting alcohol into this inner sanctum of family life, the family allows its identity to change. It comes to regard itself, in one way or another, as an Alcoholic Family. There is a subtle shift from pointing to the drinking member and saying "He (she) is alcoholic" to feeling the equivalent of, "We are an Alcoholic Family."

Thus the choice between maintaining ritual behavior versus altering rituals to accommodate alcoholic needs is not just one between two fundamentally different response patterns, but is also a reflection of the extent to which alcoholism has invaded core regulatory behaviors in the middle-phase Alcoholic Family. At one level, the state of family rituals is a concrete, easily measurable index of those more fundamental processes unfolding within these families during this phase of development. But at a second level, it is also a powerful transmitter of a message to all family members about the status alcoholism plays in their lives. And because of ritual's powerful role as conservator of family values and rules, this message about alcoholism is reinforced every time the ritual is reenacted.

Studying Family Rituals

We have already detailed, in chapter 5, an approach to the study of rituals that helped us track the crucial dimensions of identity formation in the early-phase Alcoholic Family. We described a method—the ritual interview—that, via conjoint family interviewing techniques and the use of a carefully designed semistructured interview schedule, could recreate the sum and substance of previously practiced family rituals. Further details regarding this method are provided in chapter 10.

In this chapter, however, we focus our attention on important parameters of ritual behavior in the middle-phase family. These parameters, as they have been outlined thus far, are (1) that alcoholic behavior is likely, in middle phase, to impinge upon (invade) important aspects of ritual performance in the three categories of rituals families engage in during middle phase—celebrations, traditions, and ritualized routines; and (2) that the family's response pattern to this invasion of rituals—especially how vigorously it defends its rituals from this intrusion by alcohol—is the single most important index of the relationship between alcoholism and this crucial type of regulatory behavior at middle phase.

Our conviction that this "invasion" process is a common feature of ritual life in the middle-phase Alcoholic Family, and that family response to this challenge can be characterized as the choice between protection versus disruption (accommodation) of ritual behavior initially arose from our clinical experiences with such families. However, it was subsequently substantiated by a research project that used the ritual interview method* to examine how those aspects of family living were altered—or not altered—in the face of moderate to severe alcohol abuse.

In this study, twenty-five predominantly middle- and upper-middle-class white families were questioned about the continuity of family heritage from the grandparents' generation into the current nuclear family and about six "areas of family life" during the children's growing-up years—dinners, holidays, evenings, weekends, vacations, and visitors in the home. As part of the coding system used to subsequently analyze these interview data, a coder was asked to focus on a comparison of family recollections about ritual behavior prior to, versus postonset of, the period of heaviest parental drinking. The coder answered a series of questions about the presence of the alcoholic parent, alcohol use, intoxication, the family's response to intoxication, changes in levels of participation in rituals, and the overall change in each family ritual.

Note that we did not explore some of the "rituals" traditionally associated with the use of alcohol, such as ceremonial drinking and its implications for introducing children to particular drinking styles or social drinking practices. Nor did we specifically investigate rituals associated only with alcohol misuse, such as a child's retrieval of his intoxicated father from the local bar every evening. Instead we attempted to identify the well-established rituals of a family's life and, next, to assess the impact of the alcoholic parent's drinking on those ritual activities or events persisting during midphase (defined in the study as the children's growing-up years). In short, we looked for changes in ritual life that are linked to increases in the frequency and severity of the alcoholic parent's drinking.

*The ritual interview method is described in greater detail in chapters 5 and 10.

Distinctive versus Subsumptive Rituals. As we have indicated, a systematic assessment of the response patterns of middle-phase Alcoholic Families suggests that two fundamentally different patterns of ritual behavior emerge in this period of development. (We are referring here to patterns of ritual behavior during the period when the Alcoholic Family member's drinking was heaviest compared with that prior to this period.) In the first pattern, little or no evidence of change in family rituals occurs between high and low drinking periods. This pattern we have labeled *distinctive,* to suggest that the family has managed to keep the drinking-related behavior "distinct" from ritual life. The second pattern, in which there was evidence of considerable impact, we labeled *subsumptive* (subsumed by alcohol).

Use of the term *distinctive* indicates that that there has been no notable alteration in the ritual. Drinking by the alcoholic parent that may go on during the ritual does not provoke change in the way the family enacts it. For example, if an alcoholic father's personality changes when he is drinking heavily and causes him to regularly berate a child at the dinner table— and the dinnertime atmosphere was previously calm—then the ritual has been altered. But if the alcoholic maintains his comportment during the meal and there are no other changes due to his drinking, the ritual is labeled "distinctive." This lack of change or impact may be purposeful (for example, the alcoholic parent may make a special effort not to drink on a holiday) or it may be accidental (the alcoholic parent's drinking pattern, times, and places of consumption happen to leave him or her sober at ritual times).

An occasional disruption does not necessarily mean the ritual has been altered; such breaches in the pattern may occur, but the event is still considered distinctive if there is evidence that what happened is considered highly unusual and will not be allowed to happen again.

Lack of availability of the alcoholic parent at ritual times can be a signal of change if that parent had been crucial to the celebration of the ritual before he or she began drinking heavily. However, if the alcoholic parent had never participated in the ritual or if the parent's participation was not central to it, absence due to drinking would not indicate a change in the ritual.

It is important that "distinctive" families not be seen as families in which there is less alcohol abuse behavior, or as families in which the alcoholic is simply not at home. "Distinctive" families can be exposed to a high level of alcoholism and still keep their rituals intact.

Subsumptive means that the ritual has been adapted to incorporate intoxication by the alcoholic parent, or, in more severe situations, disrupted. In the case of adaptation, the alcohol abuse behavior becomes part of the dinnertime and holiday ritual itself, either gradually over the years as the drinking increases, or abruptly during the heaviest drinking period. There is an adaptation by the family to the drinking, sometimes knowingly, sometimes not. While there is not necessarily any change in level or ritualization over the years, the family is unsuccessful at keeping the alcohol abuse behavior distinct from the rituals. In such families, you might find evidence of drinking rituals, some of which might become integrated into the ritual activities. In short, the alcohol abuse behavior becomes enmeshed in the activity itself.

In the case of ritual disruption, circumstances change either permanently or fluctuate so much from one time to the next, that the ritual is virtually lost under the influence of alcohol abuse behavior. In many families, the result is chaos or confusion. The family has given up one of its highly valued activities, and where there was once a tradition, a gap now exists.

Ritual Protection versus Ritual Disruption: Some Case Examples

No families in the study described earlier were unscarred by alcoholic disruption of rituals. There was, however, considerable variation from one family to another, in terms of ritual protection versus ritual disruption. Of the three principal ritual areas covered in the ritual interview—holiday celebrations, traditions, and patterned routines (i.e., a regular dinnertime)—holidays seemed to be the most vigorously protected. Dinnertime was the most likely to have been disrupted by alcoholism. Traditions, like the Lawton's beach vacation, were also highly susceptible to disruption.

Let us look at a representative example of this process in action for each of the three types of family rituals. Each example focuses on a segment from the ritual interview transcript of one of our subject families, a segment chosen to highlight the distinctive-subsumptive dichotomy we have been focusing on in this chapter.

Holiday Celebrations

December twenty-fifth comes every year, with a presence and power few families can resist. Some families, of course, choose not to acknowledge the religious content of the day. Yet the pressure of the culture is felt by all, including the nonreligious family that devises its own customs and carries them out with no less vigor than the "believing" family. It appears to be almost impossible for a family not to observe this day in some regular form.

Of the families we studied, most put their strongest group efforts into protecting their holiday rituals from the consequences of alcohol abuse behavior. Even in the most alcoholic families, fond memories of Christmases past persisted, seemingly beyond reason. Each year, Christmas would be anticipated with optimism, and in spite of the drinking, holiday celebrations *were* frequently unchanged and intact, in comparison to other areas of family life.

Even when holiday customs were altered as a result of the parent's intoxication, the impact might be purposely moderated by insistence that the drinker take his or her usual role in the ritual—a calculated risk on the part of the family. Relatives might take turns keeping a watchful eye on the drinker, discreetly monitoring the intake. Occasionally the alcohol abuser would take the responsibility on him- or herself, as if saying, "this is the one time of year too important to ruin." Our intuition that celebrations had more immunity from the invasive effects of alcohol abuse than other types of rituals was substantiated when we rated the families' descriptions of their ritual events according to our designations—distinctive versus subsumptive—and found that family celebrations were more apt to be labeled "distinctive."

The Barkers: A Distinctive Christmas Ritual. Several families from our group described their Christmases as still free from alcoholism even after their lives had been otherwise quite destroyed; it was the last family ritual to go under. For them, the disruption of the most cherished holiday represented a true family crisis. The Barker family was one that had withstood the disruption of many areas of family life over the years, but when their Christmas celebration was threatened, their strongest protective instincts were aroused. Robert and Marian Barker, at that time in their sixties, had raised seven children in the suburbs of a large eastern city. We interviewed the parents and four of their children, Ted, twenty-seven; Judy, twenty-five; Marian, twenty; and John, eighteen. Our questions focused on the period when Robert Barker was drinking most heavily, when the children were in their teens and early twenties.

All family members described their family as a close, cohesive unit despite the long-standing problem with alcohol. Everyone agreed that

Robert had drunk to excess daily for many years. He drank at home, during and after dinner, and was regularly intoxicated on weekends. When he drank, his personality seemed to change, the children reported, and he became more and more dominating. At mealtimes he would virtually rule all conversations, with loud, sarcastic, and hostile attacks against his wife and children. Because he had frequent blackouts, Robert could provoke the family into the same battle repeatedly. On other occasions, he would stay out at a local bar, singing and playing music until Marian sent one of the children to bring him home.

This pattern continued for several years. No ritual activities were actually eliminated, but several were altered in an effort to keep the family together during the stressful period (for instance, their dinnertime rituals were labeled "subsumptive"). But as the entirety of family life was affected to some extent, the family began to show the strain. This normally cohesive family was gradually coming apart. At several special family get-togethers, the children complained about their father's behavior. Other relatives became involved, since it was during these holiday times that the extended family visited the Barkers.

Finally, there was a blowup on Christmas—a Christmas that would be the last "wet" holiday in the Barker household. Some four years after this incident, the parents looked back at it (and we labeled it "distinctive"):

ROBERT: This is an unusual family in the sense that the nuclear family was very close and still is. Always the traditional things have been practiced in this family. So far it sounds very utopian, I'm sure of that. But the family was preserved through my drinking years.

MARIAN: At Christmas in 1975, Judy said that she would not be back that following Christmas if Dad is continuing drinking. And Warren [a family friend] said he was ashamed of you. Even when you started to drink, you were the kind that likes to monopolize a conversation, but [later] you became the *whole* conversation.

ROBERT: Rather obnoxious, as most alcoholics can get. I was oblivious to the fact that at Christmas I was obnoxious. I thought I was quite sober, quite controlled, but obviously everyone felt I wasn't. And I did not want that. I really didn't want that.

JOHN: Christmas has always been the most important holiday in our family, especially Christmas Eve. First we used to go down to my folks for dinner, and open up their gifts. Then over to the Barker grandparents and open gifts, and then back here.

ROBERT: And that tradition held, ironically, even when the older kids were older and doing their own thing. It never failed, never once, they would all be here. The preparation is probably the thing I've always looked forward to, it still is, a lot of preparation. All the children would be shattered if it were otherwise. [*To his wife*] When you were in the hospital, we brought you home Christmas Eve day and the girls postponed, literally, everything—it was that important. [To interviewer] The only time there was any dissension was the year that—and this had a lot to do with me quitting drinking—when they told Marian that I was obnoxious and they would not continue if I didn't change. Which I did change.

INTERVIEWER: Were there any other years when your drinking seemed to affect things at Christmas time?

ROBERT: Not to my knowledge.

Marian: That was the only time I was aware of.

Ted and Judy gave their impressions of the same events:

JUDY Christmas was the most important holiday in our family. Putting up the tree, kids preparing our presents, dinner at the grandparents' Christmas Eve. I loved the tree and the manger, the preparing, the feeling of Christmas, the spirit. Usually there wasn't a lot of conflict, people were more mellow. Father would be in good holiday cheer, but only that one year was it a big problem.

TED: I don't think drinking affected Christmas. Dad held it real well I thought. So I don't associate the drinking with holidays.

JUDY: The last year Father drank, four years ago, he had made a big issue to have other relatives over and it was a bad Christmas. He drove everyone out, even my uncles. We went and left early. Dinner was Christmas Day, the buffet was the part that was the same as always. Father was gung ho about playing the piano and wanted us to sing carols—something we'd never done. He had such great expectations and it turned out so terrible. People gradually left, one by one. Really embarrassing. Usually they stayed late. Father seemed oblivious to it, even afterwards. When he found out next month how we felt, he stopped drinking.

Family Traditions

When a mother gives her daughter the treasured family china platter, a tradition is handed across the generations. Family customs and expectations for behavior are usually associated with such an object, and are conveyed right along with it. An example on a larger scale is a family's vacation cabin in the mountains or at the shore. Even if a middle-phase family had other ideas for spending their vacation, the combination of financial pressures and the repeated "suggestions" of the grandmother may make it difficult to devise an alternative. Thus another family tradition— spending two weeks in July at Lake Crystal—lives on. This kind of desire for continuity is a primary motivation for ritual formation and perpetuation during the middle phase of development.

But another and very different set of influences is also at work during these years. This is the time when the family encounters a variety of stresses in the community and in the workplace, many of which are potentially divisive. The family's urge to protect itself—its cohesiveness and stability—in the face of these pressures provides an impetus for the establishment of "new" traditions. When father's work schedule becomes hectic and encroaches on the family's leisure time, the creative family responds by inventing and protecting special "family only" occasions. A big breakfast on Sunday morning or a weekly dinner out can help members preserve their sense of attachment and connectedness to each other. Even events shared with select friends and neighbors can take on special significance for a busy middle-phase family, if these are valued as family activities; participation in neighborhood ball games, school plays, or community barbecues can easily evolve into family traditions. Unfortunately, the very fact that these rituals arise as a response to the family's specific needs at a particular time makes family traditions especially susceptible to fragmentation and modification when drinking problems invade family life.

We noticed that the traditions of Alcoholic Families in our study group were altered more frequently than were the rituals in the celebration category. Several characteristics of "family traditions" help to explain this outcome. The boundaries and rules for performance of family traditions fall in the middle of the spectrum—they are neither as formalized as celebrations, nor as permeable as the patterned interactions of everyday life. They are under the family's control more than holiday rituals. Traditions are engaged in or acted out more often than celebrations, which are apt to be staged annually; they tend to be embraced a little less tightly than celebrations. Perhaps this is why the family's traditions were less often maintained in the face of alcoholic drinking.

For example, it is hard to imagine a family carrying out its traditional "family council" meetings without alteration. Even if the alcoholic parent took part, the meeting would have the characteristics of "wet" rather than "dry" family interaction; if the alcoholic parent were not present, major shifts in the roles normally taken by family members would follow. It is not surprising then that, in our sample, fewer family traditions remained distinctive during the period of heaviest drinking; in the majority of cases, they were subsumed.

The Schoenbecks: A Subsumptive Family Tradition. Alcohol abuse had a major impact on the Schoenbeck family's annual church retreat, according to our subsumptive designation. Previous to the time of heaviest drinking, this social ritual had been part of the family's life for many years. It was an important event for both parents, Sam and Laura, and for their two children, Margaret and Lon, who were adolescents at the time we interviewed Sam and Laura. Alcohol had always flowed freely at these weekend outings, opportunities for Sam to get drunk with his oldest friends and neighbors. This was challenging their marriage, reported the parents, and interfering with the discipline of their children, since Sam could not participate in any family discussions when he was drinking heavily. We asked them to tell us what happened—to them, and to the ritual.

LAURA: Last year we had some real conflict over our church's summer conference because I was so angry about Sam's drinking at the one before that. I was thinking about not going and then when I said, well maybe I won't go, he said, well maybe *he'd* just stay home, and we got into one of those things—I had felt for several years that Sam really avoided me at the conference, because he knew how I felt about his drinking. I didn't feel like we had to be together the whole time, but I felt very clearly avoided, this past year even more so. Friday night he drank very heavily and I don't remember what time he came in, but he slept through pretty much of Saturday and on Saturday night was gone until all hours. There was a crisis that came up with our daughter and he wasn't there to help me cope with that so I turned to another friend, and when he finally did come in, I had gone to bed and he came in and got some cigarettes and went out on the porch and he just said he was going out. I didn't know where.

INTERVIEWER: Did it lead to an argument?

LAURA: I told him the next morning, "You know how I felt last night," and that's where it stayed. We didn't say a whole lot more about it.

INTEVIEWER: Is that how you usually acted when you were upset about his drinking?

LAURA: I'd withdraw.

INTERVIEWER: And then you felt better about talking with him you would confront him to some extent, alone?

LAURA: Sometimes, yeah. Alone. That particular Sunday morning, it wasn't that I felt better. I felt awful, but I just felt I couldn't go on without saying something. I was furious, and very worried. But my behavior is pretty much a withdrawal, avoidance. Then tension would build up and I'd erupt and sometimes in a way that we could talk about it, sometimes not.

INTERVIEWER: But then you eventually said, "We're not going to go on this weekend."

LAURA: I said I'm just not going to go and then he responded, well he wouldn't go either. Well, we finally both went.

INTERVIEWER: So that even though it was a time of great concern for you, eventually you two got together and decided to go again.

LAURA: I really wanted to, I was really torn, I really wanted to go. This is a fun time, and a neat place to be and, the kids wanted to go.

SAM: It's a lot of small group work and it tends to be a very personal depth level and I get really hyped and it is one time of the year that I feel I have space and time to be with people on a very intense level. Laura, classically, her internal clock says it's time to go to bed and she does want me to go with her. And sometimes even there I'll go to bed and lay there for a while and finally get up and go out. So I guess I'm being a little defensive because [to his wife] you have said several times that I see it as license to drink more. I don't feel like it was, but I have used it as a license to do my own thing and to be with other people.

INTERVIEWER: And drinking was part of that?

SAM: Yeah. I just have to say that for a couple of years there or more, drinking was part of almost everything I did.

INTERVIWER: Is your family planning to go this June?

SAM: Can you imagine?

Patterned Family Interactions

All families establish routines that help to order their lives, but some of these everyday interactions have more significance to the family than others. When the dimension of meaning is added to some otherwise ordinary sequences or patterns of behavior, another kind of family life ritual has been created. For example, all of our families underscored the importance of regular family dinners. They reported how valuable it had been to sit together for mealtimes, how this ritualized routine restored the family's cohesiveness after the daily dispersion outside. In addition to its functional purpose—to organize family members for eating—the dinner gave them other forms of nourishment. It was through this patterned family interaction that family rules and values were transmitted; it was through this shared experience that the entire group affirmed its identity.

A variety of patterned interactions were described by the families we interviewed. While dinnertime was the ordinary activity most frequently identified as a ritual, other mundane activities were considered special in different family contexts. Most of them were associated with weekday evenings (TV watching, game playing, homework, car washing, socializing, churchgoing, Sunday brunches). Some important rituals surrounded child rearing: discipline practices and bedtime routines with small children were rituals—sometimes elaborate ones—for many families.

The Jarrells: A Disrupted Dinnertime Ritual. The disruption of patterns of behavior is a common experience for the Alcoholic Family. During the period of heaviest drinking, most families with an alcoholic parent were forced to modify or even abandon several of their daily routines. Dinnertime would be modified, for example, when the oldest daughter in a family took on her alcoholic mother's preparation chores. When an alcoholic father stayed out late at the bar night after night, the traditional family custom of gathering at the television set might well be ended, especially if the children were sent out to bring Dad home on a regular basis. In our experience, it was rare for a family to remain untouched in the area of patterned family interactions.

The Jarrell family's "subsumptive" dinnertime is a good example. The family was representative in its rage, disappointment, and sense of help-lessness as family members watched their mealtime washed away by their father's abusive drinking.

In the Jarrell family, the father's problems with alcohol began when the oldest son was sixteen and the youngest son eleven. Prior to that time, the boys described family life as enjoyable, with close relationships and good times. The boys were attached to their father, but when his drinking became heavy, they put distance between them and him and began to protect their mother. The family had started a rapid downhill slide. Ed Jarrell lost his job in Ohio and moved the family to Pennsylvania. The family's regular, cohesive life together was ended—there was little contact with their extended family, little time spent with immediate family members, and a loss of pride in family accomplishments.

Routine family dinnertime changed greatly as a result of Ed's alcohol-ism. The two sons, Larry and Don, could recall the changes most vividly:

DON: [Dinnertime had been] very important, time whole family was together, learned a lot. I remember back on it. When does [the] whole family sit down? It was very important to us [even if we didn't] always like the food. . . . In early years, we had to be there or have a good excuse. . . . Mother spent a lot of time preparing, my sister helped. My brothers washed dishes and set table. . . . Father fixed certain meals. . . . [We talked about the] usual events of the day, school. When drinking started, dinnertimes did stop. Not a time to look forward to. . . . It was relaxed and friendly except for the rougher times of his drinking. . . . [Many] changes related to drinking. It [became] a hurry-up affair. [He] drank in a beer joint . . . and we worried about him. It would make Mother mad.

LARRY: We were lucky to get something to eat when Dad was drinking—prior to that time [it was] very different. . . . [Dad] would come in long enough to eat [only a sandwich] and be off again. Never knew when we would see him again. We still ate together; had to live our lives too. It was as if he were dead. Two or three nights he was home; the rest of the nights he was away.

DON: If father didn't come [for a dinner], we'd spend the night looking for him. . . . When drinking started, dinnertimes weren't, they stopped. Mother would have dinner for my brother and whoever was there to eat. *Just a matter of eating, not a time to look forward to.* . . . Very little conversation, not a joyous occasion.

LARRY: He'd sit down and eat, but we didn't like it because he hadn't put the food on the table. Me and Donnie and Mom had put our money together to get the food and he was eating it. . . . He'd pick a fight and it would be all three of us against him. I felt helpless against him. . . .

LARRY: At that time, Donnie took the job at the drugstore, I was bricklaying, mother was working. [Larry had dropped out of school and rushed into a marriage to leave home.] *There really wasn't any dinner!*

Conclusion

In reviewing the major characteristics of family rituals, describing their role in the middle phase of family development, and examining the unique relationship between rituals and development in the Alcoholic Family, we emphasized two key functions that rituals play in the middle-phase family—their role in conserving the shared beliefs, central norms, perceptions, and values of the family; and their role as transmitters of core identity issues for the family. Both these functions are part and parcel of the role of rituals as one of the regulatory behaviors used by families to maintain stability during middle phase.

For the Alcoholic Family, the crucial issue proves to be the way alcohol and alcohol-related behaviors are handled whenever family rituals are enacted. Just as was the case for short-term problem-solving behaviors and home routines, family rituals can be *invaded* by alcohol. And just as was the case for the other two types of regulatory behaviors, when this invasion process occurs, it is highly likely that the overall course of family development will be distorted.

Family rituals are important at all phases of development. During early phase, they become part of the process by which the new couple marks out its distinctive identity. By enacting certain rituals carried over from one or another family of origin and ignoring others, the early-phase family endorses some values and perspectives from the prior generation while leaving others behind. During the late phase, rituals play a central role in what values and perspectives are to be transmitted from the aging family to the next generation. But it is during middle phase that rituals play their most important role—that of enacting, in symbolic form, the dynamic balance between accommodation and stability that all families struggle to achieve at this point in their development. When this balance is achieved, it not only leaves ample room for systemic maturation to proceed but it allows for the incorporation of individual developmental needs as well.

In the Alcoholic Family, however, this dynamic balance proves very difficult to achieve. The family is already likely to be suffering from the developmental consequences of the thematic overspecialization that has emerged during early phase. Further, the response patterns manifested during middle phase have led to a hypertrophying of regulatory behaviors in the service of maintaining stability while alcoholic behavior is in evidence. Thus for these families, the enactment of rituals during middle phase is a deadly serious business.

Although rituals always have a serious, as well as an enjoyable, side to them, the consequences of the decisions made by the Alcoholic Family vis-à-vis ritual enactment are particularly telling. For if the family takes a casual attitude toward the form and substance of its ritual behavior, it is more likely than not to find itself gradually accommodating rituals to ensure the inclusion of its alcoholic member. On the other hand, efforts to protect rituals from alcohol invasion require continual vigilance. The bottom line here is that rituals are protected, but at considerable cost to overall energy supplies. It is also likely that the form of ensuing versions of rituals will be more rigid than would otherwise be the case. Thus efforts at protecting rituals from alcoholism divert family resources from other equally compelling developmental issues and contribute to a heightening of rigidity or regulatory behavior during middle phase.

Thus, whichever choice it makes regarding ritual behavior, the family is likely to suffer considerable negative consequences. If it takes a laissez-faire, passive attitude, the likelihood that it will evolve into a subsumptive family is heightened. If it takes an active stance in excluding alcoholism from rituals, it will sap energies from other important issues and will intensify rigidity of ritual performance. This is the irony of the choices available to the Alcoholic Family.

However, of the two choices, the impact of alcoholism on family development must be considered more profound when alcohol is admitted into family rituals. For in this circumstance, it is not only possible for rituals to become co-opted and modified to meet the needs of alcoholism, it is also possible for them to become disorganized or, in the most extreme instance, to be obliterated entirely.

In such instances, the family has lost a valuable resource. For rituals not only provide the family with a strong sense of unity and reinforce shared values and beliefs, they also help to reiterate the complexity and subtlety of identity issues. By conveying these issues in a bounded, concisely packaged form, they allow for the efficient reiteration and reinforcement of the full range of identity issues. Without this vehicle available to it, the family is likely to be inappropriately influenced by one or two issues that command inordinate time and resources. Alcoholism is just such an issue.

Hence, when alcoholism disrupts, disorganizes, or obliterates ritual performance in the middle-phase family, the likely result is an even more skewed Alcoholic Family identity. And this now reinforced, powerful and hypertrophied alcoholic identity, in turn, dramatically heightens the skew within the family toward regulatory rigidity and away from coherent middle-phase development.

PART V

THE LATE PHASE
OF DEVELOPMENT

I N THIS SECTION of the book, we move from a description of the middle phase to a discussion of the late phase of development of the Alcoholic Family. Here two new issues come into play as foci for family development. The first of these is the distillation and clarification of identity issues within the family. The second is the transmission of these identity issues to succeeding generations.

In contrast to the middle phase—in which stability, regularity, boundary maintenance, and orderly integration of life themes and regulatory behavior are the norm—the late phase is again a phase of systemic expansion, of boundary redefinition, of transient, if not long-term, instability, and of systemic reorganization. Once again the family is in a phase of major systemic changes—a high-oscillation phase.

Since the early and late phases are mirror images of one another, many of the issues that dominated the early-phase family again emerge at late phase—for example, the need to draw clear family boundaries so that all know who is in and who is out; the need to identify those life themes that are most important to the family; the need to protect the family against the implosion of new ideas and new people. If left to run their own course, these late-phase issues could easily bury the family under their weight and competing demands, leaving the family largely unrecognizable and unable to function as an integrated, coherent unit.

Thus, as is the case in early phase, the degree of initiative manifested by the family now will be as important as the direction taken in shaping the course of development. The main difference between the early- and late-phase family, however, is that in late phase, the family is in the position of *defender* rather than *initiator* of family themes and boundary properties. The late-phase family characteristically sees as its primary task the protection of core aspects of its life themes and the defense of a set of organizational imperatives that have shaped family life during the most productive periods of its middle phase. Now it is challenged by the possibility that these themes and unique organizational characteristics will become lost or diffused in the next wave of systemic expansion. The key people whom the family has influenced (usually its children) will be participating in new families of their own.

The late-phase family must have a prominent role in this expansion process or it will wither on the vine, and which course it follows will be largely determined by the permutations and combinations that occur around the two major late-phase processes just noted—the clarification of core family-identity issues and the transmission of these identity issues to new-early-phase families.

In chapter 9 we take up the first of these issues—the identity clarification process. The chapter is organized around the construct of the *alcoholic family identity*. Families have four fundamentally different options from which to choose as they consolidate the alcohol-centered aspects of their family identity. Each of these options, when they are put into play, lead to very different pathways of development during late phase. We will illustrate each pathway by providing clinical vignettes shared with us by a number of the Alcoholic Families we have studied.

In chapter 10 we will deal with the second developmental issue of late phase—the intergenerational transmission of family identity and organizational properties. Here we will focus explicitly on the intergenerational transmission of alcoholism as the core issue of concern and will discuss at length the findings from a research study designed to examine the role of family environmental factors in the transmission process.

CHAPTER 9

Late-Phase Options for the Alcoholic Family

FAMILIES immersed in the middle phase of development, often feel that time is standing still. Some events, of course, bring with them a sense of rapid change; a feeling that each new day seems to bring surprises and challenges. But more often, changes are perceived only when large blocks of time are compared to one another. It is as if family growth during middle phase can only be felt when divided into time blocks analogous to those in adult development that Levinson (1978) has called "eras" (each approximately a decade in length). There is a regularity to life during the middle phase, a sense of orderliness and purposefulness—we have used the term "coherence"—that is the dominant characteristic of life during these years.

Most families experience this sense of coherence as comforting and soothing. Individual challenges at work, in school, and with friends are taken on in part because of the sense of support derived from the internal stability of the family environment during these years. Although occasional cries of woe about the boredom and meaninglessness of life can be heard emanating from the suburban houses of middle-phase families, most of the time it feels good to come home to familiar faces and known routines, to a place where one knows the rules of the game, even if occasionally it proves to be a potentially dangerous game.

For many middle-phase Alcoholic Families, on the other hand, coherent themes are often harder to identify. Instead of projecting a sense of purpose, these families seem at first glance to be drifting aimlessly about. Family behavior and major family decisions seem capricious or impulsive; the family appears to have lost its bearings rather than to have consolidated its options and prioritized its major life themes.

But such a picture is illusory. It is merely that these families are organized around a different life theme. Instead of being organized around work-, child-, or social–role-oriented themes, these families are organized around alcohol-related issues. Coherence only emerges when alcohol is taken into account. As we underscored in earlier chapters, life in the middle phase is almost totally dominated by an adherence to daily routines, by predictable and repetitive patterns of short-term problem-solving tied to the sobriety-intoxication cycle, and by alcohol-dominated family rituals.

For all middle-phase families, a shifting of the morphogenetic-morphostatic balance toward greater emphasis on regulatory processes is a necessary component of this phase. But in the Alcoholic Family, this shift is dramatic rather than subtle. Alcohol-infested family regulatory mechanisms reign supreme, a process we have called the "tyranny of the routine" or the "rule through morphostasis." By comparison, life in the average nonalcoholic middle-phase family seems wildly unpredictable. Yet, as much as this tyranny of the routine leads to a narrowing, an arresting of development in the middle-phase Alcoholic Families, for families who have an abhorrence of surprises, a profound sense of dysphoria when dealing with the unpredictable, day-to-day life organized around a chronic behavioral disorder like alcoholism can be surprisingly reassuring. Even when the alcoholic makes everyone in the family tense, it's a predictable feeling of tension. Even if everyone feels intense anger, it is anger expressed through known and familiar channels, hence safe to feel, safe to give in to.

For the normative family, the "eras" of the middle phase are demarcated by anticipated biological events (births and children's developmental milestones when spouses are in their twenties and thirties; changes in physical and psychological activity and preferences when the spouses are older), and by anticipated changes in social, family, and work relationships. These changes, orderly but significant, contribute to a sense of family maturation that is a dominant feature of the successful middle-phase family, perhaps analogous to Erik Erikson's (1963) concept of generativity as the critical task of adult development. As these eras build one upon another, the family becomes increasingly specialized in its commitments. The life options it has chosen become strengthened, flower and, it is hoped, bring the family recognition and satisfaction.

But for the Alcoholic Family, the area of specialization is the nurturance and maintenance of a social environment receptive to, compatible with, and in turn sustained by the continuance of alcoholic behavior. This is not to say the individuals in Alcoholic Families are not also concerned with work issues, children's performance in school, and the nature of their friendships and relations with extended family. But these other areas are pursued only insofar as they are compatible with the family's commitment to alcoholism. That is, the dominant theme in family life is the theme of alcoholism. The family's sense of itself is built around this theme, and family life is consequently distorted by the demands of this chronic psychopathological condition.

Yet life for the middle-phase Alcoholic Family, although not necessarily pleasant, is nevertheless predictable and, in its own way, coherent. In this sense, the Alcoholic Family is comparable to its nonalcoholic counterpart; for it too, the developmental conversion from middle to late phase of development takes place against a background of relative predictability, of relative coherence of family behavior, brought about by a balanced interplay of growth and regulatory forces within the family. Therefore, for alcoholic and nonalcoholic families alike, as the late phase of development gradually evolves, the family moves from a phase of relative stability to one of considerable instability. Whereas the emphasis in the middle phase was on the consolidation and maintenance of newly formed family structures, rules, and priorities; in the late phase, as opportunities for systemic expansion again arise, these very aspects of the family come under challenge and must be defended or changed in the face of these new challenges.

Normative Late-Phase Development

The Middle- to Late-Phase Conversion

Whereas the movement from the early to the middle phase of development represented a change from a time of transgenerational conflict to a time of relative orderliness, commitment, and peacefulness, the movement from the middle to the late phase is a conversion from a time of relative peace (low oscillation) to a return to a time of relative turmoil (high oscillation). During the early phase of development, the tensions that rapidly develop between families of origin and the new family, the need to hammer out the basic rules for behavior in the family, and the uncertainty about the family's relative strengths and weaknesses (including its survival power), all provide pressures that force the family to attempt to resolve these many outstanding issues. Insofar as the middle phase of development is a natural consequence of this earlier resolution process, one might say that the family, during this period of development, is an advocate for growth, a party interested in resolution, in movement forward.

But the move from the middle to the late phase is very different. During the middle phase, in even the "healthiest" of families, the dominant theme is the theme of commitment and orderly routine. As we have repeatedly emphasized, during the middle phase, morphostatic principles tend to take precedence over morphogenic forces. The middle to late switch therefore occurs only when events arise that are so disruptive in their consequences as to *force* the family to take on the major developmental tasks of late phase. In a family committed to routines (the middle-phase family), any event capable of irreversibly disrupting these routines can become a precipitant that, in retrospect, places in motion the developmental alterations that ultimately propel the family into late phase.

Most families at first tend to resist these developmental pressures. The current way of life is simply too entrenched. The movement into the late phase is therefore rarely an explosive or sudden one. But, over time, pressures continue to build until they reach an intolerable level. At this point, routines and existing regulatory mechanisms can no longer go on unaltered, and the family must take a stance.

There are two types of events that characteristically challenge the status quo in middle-phase families, irreversibly disrupting family coherence. The first is a series of *major losses* suffered by the family. Deaths of important people—a spouse; a spouse's parent; a close family friend—are perhaps the most obvious such losses. For families with children, the emergence of children into adulthood and their subsequent departure from the nuclear family is an equally important loss that must be dealt with. Retirement or the fading of a successful career can propel the work-centered family into the middle to late transitional period.

But families at this stage of development are also being challenged by a second type of event, the pressures of new members and new ideas. In particular, children are bringing in new people (either those with whom they are involved romantically or close friends "adopted" by the family). These new "family members" tend to challenge the family's ways of doing things and to raise questions about family priorities and values. The family is then forced to reexamine itself against these new and often unfamiliar standards.

As these two types of challenges mount in number and intensity—major losses on the one hand, and the demand to incorporate new members and ideas on the other—family routines and rituals are increasingly undermined. Because the middle-phase family, like the middle-aged adult, is far less flexible than it was at the time of its last major transitional period, it will only reluctantly rise to meet the many challenges it finds itself facing. The middle-phase family needs to be pushed by its individual members or by the outside world before it will take action. In this sense, it is very different from the early-phase family that is itself the major instigator of change in its intergenerational struggles with its family of origin. Nevertheless, the middle-phase family is inexorably pushed to deal with the mounting pressures associated with the growing challenges to its status quo. It begins, however reluctantly, to deal with the changing priorities in developmental functions that accompany the movement into the late phase of development.

As the family reaches this phase of development, it has come full cycle from an early phase in which the central task was separating from its two families of origin in order to establish itself as a unique group, to a middle phase in which options are selected and the emphasis is on stability and management of normative transitions, and finally to a late phase in which it becomes future-oriented. This is now a family with a history—a "life story" so to speak—a family with an attic full of mementos and a vested interest in seeing these important mementos effectively used in the future.

The family's interest is increasingly focused on its impact on the future, an impact that is most characteristically played out in the intergenerational issues emerging at that time between parents and children. However, it is a developmental process not necessarily restricted to parent-child interactions; the same themes might arise in the positions families take vis-à-vis their extended family network, their social network of friends and relationships, their community involvement, and even their work involvement. Our central contention, however, is that in all cases, the family's shifting attention to a concern about its "place in history" is stimulated by a series of important losses.

There are many terms that could be used to capture the flavor of the task faced by the late-phase family—a *summing up,* a *life review,* a *distillation* of life themes. But each of these terms attempts to convey the flavor of a family being challenged to clarify its priorities, its rules, its way of doing business; a family being challenged by a sense of diffusion that has built up as its membership and boundaries begin to erode in the face of a return to a time of systemic expansion.

Not all families rise to these challenges by turning their sights on the future. Some families resist these developmental pressures mightily. Instead of gradually beginning to focus on a life review and on the changes that must be made to accommodate the expansion process of late phase, these families impose on all their members an even stricter version of middle-phase priorities, routines, and rituals. If carried to its extreme, such behavior can effectively stave off the middle to late phase conversion entirely. In such instances, families become in effect *developmentally arrested*. When changes in family membership occur within such a family at this period of development, the family is likely to suffer a mortal blow. Young members are forced to sever ties entirely if they want to expand the family's boundaries. The family they leave behind merely plays itself out, withers, and dies. There is no intergenerational continuity, no continuity of family growth, and no development across time.

Thus it is entirely possible that a family will never move into late phase. How many families truly become arrested at this point in development is hard to estimate. Because the middle to late phase conversion is gradual rather than sudden and because families characteristically evidence at least a transient period of rigidity, one might decide that a family is arrested, only to find several years later that it had been merely "blowing off steam" before getting down to its late-phase business.

But developmental arrest *is* clearly one of the options families choose at this point, and it is one chosen by many Alcoholic Families. Most families, however, face up to (or succumb to) the march of time and move on to late-phase issues. Propelled by a need to contend with the disruptive forces unleashed by losses and the pressures of new members and ideas, families increasingly attempt to deal with those tasks that are at the core of late-phase development.

Late-Phase Developmental Tasks

We have proposed that the various developmental tasks associated with the three major phases of family development can be conveniently grouped under three main headings:

1. Those having to do with family membership (these are the people who are *in* our family—those other people are *not* in our family)
2. Those having to do with major life themes (these are the priority areas to which our family is committed, those areas of concentration around which family life is organized)
3. Those having to do with family values and family heritage (these are our shared views and values, which must clearly reflect the kind of family we are)

Although these various developmental tasks are continuous, as the family moves from one phase to the next, the relative importance of the three types of tasks shifts. For example, tasks associated with the prioritizing and consolidation of major life themes, although surely present during early and late phases, tend to be background issues at these junctures. But during middle phase, the need to select a finite number of options (areas of concentration) around which to organize family life, moves to the fore and becomes the top-priority developmental issue.

On the other hand, the developmental tasks faced by the late-phase family parallel those being undertaken by the early-phase family. But this time the generational position is reversed. For example, for the early-phase family, the issue is the establishment of new boundaries that separate it from its families of origin. For the late-phase family, the issue is how to allow this same process to occur without disrupting intergenerational contact. If for the early-phase family the issue is what aspects of prior family heritage should be incorporated or rejected into its own family identity, for the late-phase family the issue is what to transmit, what is to be the family's "place in history." But because both early and late phases involve family expansion, they are concerned with the same developmental issues, albeit from very different perspectives.

The tensions and fireworks that are often part and parcel of the late phase are most easily conceptualized as products of the tensions over membership issues that arise during this high-oscillation, expansion phase. This process is most clearly seen in the intergenerational struggles that occur when children get married. What status is the new spouse to have in the family? Is this fledgling marriage to be an extension of the late-phase family or is it to be granted independent status? What rights do parents have vis-à-vis children-in-law? Do power structures remain intact with the only structural change being an expanded family boundary that now incorporates the new marriage? Or is the child now fully independent, an extruded family member shot out like a spore to form a new and totally self-sufficient plant? These are developmental issues that deeply concern many families.

But as tempestuous as these membership issues can become, the developmental issues that prove ultimately compelling for late-phase families are those having to do with family values and family heritage. Because the core developmental issue for the late-phase family is its place in history, the ultimate direction and success of this phase will be largely determined by (1) the family's ability to distill out the most important aspects of its values and sense of itself (its family identity) in a form that clarifies the shape of this identity; and (2) the family's ability to transmit this clarified identity to subsequent generations. Hence our focus on the distillation-clarification process in this chapter and the transmission process in chapter 10.

The ultimate direction that these two tasks take is not solely determined by events occurring during the late phase of development. Family development is a continuous process, upon which we impose an externally constructed model built around a concept of developmental phases with associated developmental tasks. But we also appreciate that this model is not meant to be applied literally and that because the overall course of family development is epigenetic in nature, early- and middle-phase behavior will play prominent roles in determining what happens in late phase. Nevertheless, it is in late phase that the family is propelled into a period of intense concern around identity issues.

We have used the terms *distillation* and *clarification* to depict the behavior that one sees in the family at this time. Other terms—for example, *consolidation* or *condensation*—convey somewhat different aspects of this same process. What is most important here, however, is that it is a process that has as its ultimate product, a version of the family's identity that we might think of as the family's "last will and testament."

Thus what we are looking for are a set of statements by the family (both verbal and behavioral) reflecting a distilled (condensed) and clarified version of key identity issues. Do all families arrive at such a juncture? Probably not. Just as many individuals never write a will, so too, many families never reach a level of resolution about family identity sufficient to qualify as a "last will and testament." (We use the word *resolution* here as one would use it in describing a photograph.) But even those families that in late phase evolve a distilled and clarified version of key identity issues, do so with varying degrees of resolution. In one family, the shape of the "last will and testament" is crystal clear; in another family, it looks like a fuzzy photograph in which the setting is recognizable, but facial details are blurred, making interpretation of expressions (and perhaps even identification of people) chancy at best.

To extend this metaphor, in one family, the definition and prioritizing of values is apparent to all members. In another family, one has a general idea of what is important, but no clear idea of how to put it into practice. In the first type of family, one knows exactly what to do in order to carry on family traditions and preserve the family legacy as the family goes through its next phase of expansion. In the second family, mistakes can easily be made even if the intention is to accept and preserve the family heritage.

Thus we can see that once again the direction of family development is determined both by the actual choices made by the family and by the *style* the family manifests in making its choices (the analogy might be to the importance of both actual cognitions and cognitive style as determinants of behavior).

Late-Phase Development in the Alcoholic Family

Unique Conversion Factors

Against the above background of normative late-phase family development, how does the Alcoholic Family fare? The movement from middle to late phase in the Alcoholic Family is complicated (and often compromised) by two factors: (1) the degree of rigidity of regulatory processes manifested by the middle-phase alcoholic family; and (2) the singular importance of alcohol as a core component of family identity in these families.

The first factor increases the likelihood that these families will resist normative developmental pressures at this phase of the life cycle. The second factor raises the possibility that a decision to stop drinking will precipitate the developmental processes associated with middle to late phase conversion. That is, *loss of alcohol,* if and when it occurs, can well be the type of critical loss that propels the family into late-phase issues. Hence the task of reworking, condensing, and distilling core family identity characteristics may well center around a series of events set in motion not by the loss of children or parents or by retirement, but rather by the precipitous loss of alcohol.

Rigidity of Regulatory Processes. The rigidity of family regulatory processes in the middle-phase Alcoholic Family has been thoroughly documented in chapters 6, 7, and 8 describing short-term problem-solving styles, home routines, and family rituals. We concluded that these behaviors, as they became tied to alcoholism-related factors, were increasingly altered and redesigned to maintain family stability in the face of disruptive forces generated by the family's alcoholic member. If developmental priorities in late phase continue to support the structuring of regulatory behaviors in the service of alcoholism maintenance (i.e., drinking continues unabated in either stable wet or alternator patterns), then the family will continue to react to any disruptive event as a threat to family stability rather than as a potential for growth and change. That is, the family will continue to opt for short-term stability as its highest priority and will have a great deal of difficulty in allowing itself any perspective on its life themes.

In such cases, the distillation of family identity (the first developmental task of late phase) yields a product that is merely the perpetuation of family structure and behaviors organized around active alcoholism that existed in middle phase. Its inherent rigidity leaves little room for modification or new interpretations stimulated by the unique challenges of late phase and thus results in a developmental distortion that is best characterized as *developmental arrest.*

Loss of Alcohol. Loss of alcohol as a precipitating event for middle to late phase conversion in Alcoholic Families can produce yet another type of developmental distortion, *premature closure* regarding family-identity issues. That is, if loss of alcohol is the critical challenge that forces upon the family late-phase issues associated with identity distillation (in this case what stance to take about an alcoholic family identity), then the timing of this process may have little to do with normative developmental pressures within the family. Instead it may occur well before the family's natural maturing processes have prepared it for a comprehensive tackling of a clarification of central life themes.

For example, in one of the families we discuss at some length later in the chapter—the Nestors—the cessation of drinking occurred immediately following an incident in which Mr. Nestor was found by his young children lying on the bathroom floor, where he had passed out after an all-night drinking bout. He previously had confined his drinking to the basement family room. A family myth had built up that his alcoholism was therefore a "secret" affair, and of no consequence to others in his family. His children's questions about why he was "sleeping in the bathroom" shattered this myth, and abstinence immediately followed.

The family's stance vis-à-vis alcohol was now closed, but at a time well before the Nestors had any real comprehension of the role alcohol had played in their lives. In this sense, closure brought them not a three-dimensional appreciation of alcoholism and a fully textured clarification of this important issue in their lives, but rather a concrete, superficial stance about abstinence as necessary to wall the children off from the effects of alcoholism. As a consequence, the period of active drinking was subsequently seen as a puzzling but basically aberrant or unfathomable period, and therefore one not integrated or understood by the family. That is, the family had reached "closure" on the alcoholism issue not because it was developmentally prepared to tackle this issue but because a dramatic event prematurely precipitated a crisis that led to the family's taking on a late-phase issue when it was still in the beginning stages of its middle phase of development.

One can easily list other events that could precipitate premature closure in Alcoholic Families. In a work crisis caused by alcoholism-related absenteeism or performance decrement, the demand to face the alcoholism issue comes from *external* forces that have little appreciation of, or interest in, keeping a family's developmental patterns flowing in a synchronous fashion. The demand is that drinking stop, or else. Run-ins with the judicial system can have very similar effects. Thus, because these families often find themselves forced to resolve the most critical late-phase identity issue in their lives—the alcoholism issue—well before they are ready to move into late phase, premature closure of the identity issue is a frequent occurrence.

Management of Late-Phase Developmental Tasks

The two factors noted above—the rigidity of regulatory processes in middle-phase Alcoholic Families, and vulnerability to loss of alcohol as a late-phase precipitating event—when taken in concert often leave the Alcoholic Family ill-suited to manage the two critical developmental tasks of late phase (identity clarification and transmission). These by now quite rigid, highly specialized behavioral systems, whose organizational characteristics and behavior patterns have been dominated by a desire to maintain short term stability, are particularly ill-suited to deal with the developmental challenges posed by the movement into late phase.

Consider the first late-phase developmental task, the clarification of family identity precipitated by changes in family membership and boundaries. How does such a family deal with major losses? How can alcohol-invaded family rituals and daily routines help the family cope with the challenges of new ideas and new members? Obviously it cannot. The Alcoholic Family finds itself as compromised in meeting such challenges as was many an overly specialized and highly rigid ancient civilization in dealing with the challenge of outside ideas. Further, if the developmental challenge focuses on alcohol itself—that is, if there are demands by children or outside forces that alcoholism-related identity issues and regulatory behaviors be reexamined and modified or eliminated entirely—the family finds itself faced with a fundamental and often bitter choice. It must either try as best it can to keep these new challenges at bay, suffering the inevitable consequences of stagnation and continued developmental distortion or it must make an even more momentous decision, to give up alcohol.

And what about the transmission issue? Surely a family would be unlikely to have much flexibility about whether an alcoholic identity will be transmitted to the next generation when it already has for years been organizing important aspects of family behavior around alcoholic behavior.

The family's role in determining whether its sons and daughters are to "catch the disease" is probably largely determined by its behavioral patterns during *middle phase* (that is, of course, independent of whatever genetic influences may predetermine alcoholism). Children may decide "not to play the game," but (as we will see in chapter 10) it takes repudiation of the strongest type to overcome the influence of the forces already set in motion.

In some Alcoholic Families, the two late-phase developmental issues are closely linked with each another. For example, a reexamination of a stable wet family pattern might be stimulated by concerns about an emerging alcoholism problem in an adolescent. But it is also possible for them to be handled in a fashion and sequence largely independent of one another. For example, a family in which the husband-father is actively drinking is confronted with the news that an eighteen-year-old daughter is "in love" with a young man who has gotten drunk each time during the past month that they have spent an evening together. She is talking about marriage, and her parents must therefore struggle with what stance to take vis-à-vis alcoholism transmission (is the daughter also to be married to an alcoholic?) at a time when her father has no intention of stopping his own drinking and the family is not yet prepared to deal with their internal alcoholism problems.

Thus the separation we will be making between late-phase reworking of the Alcoholic Family identity, which will be dealt with in this chapter, and the transmission issue, which will be dealt with in the next chapter, will be, for some families, an artificial separation. But for other families, the separation will correspond to a developmental sequence that parallels the way they have handled these two tasks.

Four Late-Phase Pathways for the Alcoholic Family

One of the major themes stressed repeatedly throughout our book has been that Alcoholic Families come in many varieties. In discussing the early and middle phases of development, this theme was reflected in our emphasis on the different pathways Alcoholic Families can take at each phase.

In early phase, it was noted that an emergent family identity can be shaped around alcoholism as a core issue whether or not active drinking is at that time occurring. The crucial issues at this phase have to do with the decision about whether or not to incorporate aspects of family of heritage identities into the developing identity of the new family and with what degree of deliberateness to do so. One could therefore decide to continue an alcoholic heritage even though drinking is at this point controlled; to extend an active drinking pattern along the lines already demarcated by an alcoholic parent; to develop a new nonalcoholic identity; or to leave the issue unresolved.

In middle phase, those families that have by now fully elaborated alcoholic identities can still be meaningfully subdivided. This time there are crucial distinctions related to the drinking patterns evidenced by the alcoholic spouse. Thus at least three distinctive subtypes of families were identified in our studies of middle-phase families—the stable wet, alternator, and stable dry subtypes. Each of these were found to exist, *in stable form,* because of the "goodness-of-fit" that had emerged in middle phase between important aspects of family-personality determined dimensions of the family's internal environment, and the vicissitudes of drinking behavior.

Now, in late phase, we again find that Alcoholic Families move along not a single pathway but along one of several distinctive pathways. This time the different pathways are determined in large part by the family's response to the major developmental tasks of late phase. In particular, a set of crucial distinctions emerge as one tracks family behavior in regard to that late-phase task we have called the distillation-clarification of family identity. For the Alcoholic Family, the crucial issue (not surprisingly) is the family's stance vis-à-vis its *Alcoholic Family identity* as it turns to face the challenges that initiate movement into the late phase.

Answers to two questions prove particularly important in determining the different options available to the family at this point in development. The first is whether or not loss of alcohol has been one of the major precipitants initiating the onset of late phase issues. The second is whether, as a final product of the distillation-clarification process characteristic of this phase of development, the family has emerged with its alcoholic identity still intact, or, instead, has undergone a transformation into a changed, now nonalcoholic, family identity.

The answers to these two questions form the basis for identifying four fundamentally different developmental pathways evidenced by these

families during late phase. These four options—diagramed in table 9.1—
we call respectively: (1) the stable wet Alcoholic Family option; (2) the
stable wet or controlled drinking, nonalcoholic family option; (3) the stable
dry Alcoholic Family option; and (4) the stable dry nonalcoholic family
option.

Because two of these options are precipitated by a cessation of drinking,
while in the others drinking continues in much the same form that it has
during middle phase, the loss of alcohol will obviously create for the two
types of dry families a very different set of circumstances than the two
types of wet families will be dealing with. Similarly, a family that undergoes a major identity alteration as it moves into late phase will be
subjected to quite different experiences than a family for whom the late
phase of development represents a crystallization of lifelong themes.
Clearly, the four types of families delineated above will be following very
different pathways during late phase.

At the same time, within each pathway there can still be considerable
variation from one family to another. In particular, how stormy the middle-
to late-phase conversion is is not determined only by which pathway the
family is following, but rather by each family's unique life history and
personality. Further, within each pathway there are families that are taking
active and deliberate stances vis-à-vis the late-phase option they have
chosen, and other families for whom the pathway decision has been a
relatively passive one. This last group of families often appears not to have
made a decision at all, but merely to have followed the "pathway" of least
resistance. However, because the developmental tasks of late phase are not
ones that can be avoided (e.g., transmission invariably occurs even though

TABLE 9.1

The Four Late-Phase Options:
Postconsolidation Family Identity Theme

	Loss of Alcohol as Precipitating Event for Middle to Late Phase Conversion	
	Continued Drinking	Cessation of Drinking
Alcoholic	Stable Wet Alcoholic Family	Stable Dry Alcoholic Family
Nonalcoholic	Controlled Drinking or Stable Wet Nonalcoholic Family	Stable Dry Nonalcoholic Family

in some families it results in discontinuity of family identity), all Alcoholic Families, regardless of the character of their lives at this time in their life history, can be meaningfully compared along the two dimensions highlighted in table 9.1.

In describing the four different late-phase pathways used by the Alcoholic Family, we will cite as case examples families who participated in one of the several research studies discussed previously. These studies included opportunities for families to share with us the details of their experiences with alcohol and these interview data were instrumental in first suggesting to us the typology of late-phase options we are proposing here.

Option 1: The Stable Wet Alcoholic Family

The first option seems, at least at first glance, to call for the least amount of energy on the family's part. There are families that, according to the criteria that we have set up, reach the late phase of development without ever relinquishing either active drinking or their Alcoholic Family identities.

Although neither drinking behavior nor alcoholic identity have fundamentally changed, we know they have in fact reached the late phase of development because their discussion of alcoholism is replete with words, attitudes, and values that we associate with a family that has achieved late-phase clarification of an important family-identity issue. To all intents and purposes the family has taken a stance regarding the alcoholism issue; a conclusion has been reached, the family gives every indication that they anticipate a continuance of the stable wet pattern regardless of the consequences. Middle- to late-phase developmental challenges have emerged, but they *do not* include loss of alcohol as one of the precipitating events, and the family actively or passively opts for as little change as possible in its stable wet alcoholic identity. The distillation-clarification process results in a reaffirmation of the position that the family's alcoholic member will continue his or her drinking and that alcoholism will remain an organizing principle around which family life is to remain structured. The family has opted for the *stable wet Alcoholic Family* late-phase pathway.

Of course, from time to time, individual family members may challenge this way of life, question its wisdom, threaten to leave unless it is changed, or attempt to precipitate a crisis intended to force a cessation of drinking. For example, the deliberate disengagement of a young adult member from the family at this time, has been previously cited as one of the factors contributing to the development of a nonalcoholic family identity in the next generation (see chapter 5). But the family, as a group, will with firm resolve, fend off these challenges and reaffirm the family's commitment to active drinking.

In that the stable wet late-phase pathway entails neither a loss of alcohol nor a major alteration in the family's alcoholic identity, it would appear that this option is nothing more than a continuation of the behavior evidenced by the family during middle phase. Were there no other issues in the family at this time, this commitment to "business as usual" might in fact be effected with minimal expenditure of energy.

But two factors mitigate against this being the case. First, the alterations in family composition that are invariably occurring at this point in the life cycle and the corresponding implosion of new people and ideas introduces a degree of instability that cannot be easily countered simply by the Alcoholic Family doing just a little more of the same. If these challenges are to be neutralized, the family must act in a forceful way that leaves no doubt about its intentions. The movement for change within the family at this time (e.g., a newly married daughter makes parental sobriety the condition of her continued weekend family dinner visits), calls for a subjectively different response if the old order is to be reinforced than was the case during middle phase. Here the stakes are simply much higher.

The second factor is that the degree of rigidity that has characterized the middle phase in these families has already placed them in a highly compromised position. Many potential options for growth and change that might have been experimented with during middle phase have instead been prematurely closed by alcohol-based family regulatory behaviors. When one looks at day-to-day activity, there is the appearance of a great deal of action and movement. The sober-intoxicated cycle in particular, gives the illusion of instability, confrontation, conflict, and movement. But when one looks at the picture from a more macroscopic time frame, remarkably little change has been occurring from month to month, or even from year to year. It is analogous to a sailor who, attempting to sail upstream, feels he is making excellent progress as he looks over the side of his boat and sees the water rushing by, but when he looks over to shore, finds himself parallel with exactly the same landmark he spotted thirty minutes previously. Thus, a kind of developmental pressure has been gradually building up over years, a push toward growth that requires more and more energy to keep in check (if the status quo is to be maintained). The natural morphogenetic forces within the system have simply been held in check too long.

The singular emphasis on maintenance of short-term stability and the consequent flattening of the middle-phase growth curve for these families produces a numbing effect that has been amply illustrated in such families as the Pridgetts (chapter 6). These families seem to the outsider to be "burned out," to have lost the will to change. As much as they may engage in heated and affectively charged exchanges during periods of intoxication (such an exchange was described in our intoxicated interview with the Pridgetts), these exchanges follow preprogrammed scripts. Neither the outside observer nor the family believes that the outcome will be any different than that of past exchanges. It is as if the family has become paralyzed by the sheer weight of its repetitious behavior.

We know that these conditions exist in such families because one characteristically sees a profound sense of resignation at this time, especially on the part of family members who have a stake in the intergenerational transmission process that is reaching fruition. The mini-dramas that are still occurring within the family in which potential crises are neutralized via alcohol-based short-term problem-solving strategies are viewed with a sense of sadness rather than the old bitterness—intense disappointment rather than an energized sense of excitement.

At best, the response is a certain wistfulness for what might have been. The next generation's disengagement process (as children spin off to form new early-phase family groups) instead of being a highly charged, volatile process of intergenerational conflict and jockeying, is a tired, depressed process weighted down by the knowledge of the inevitable outcome of it all (at least with regard to the stance taken by the family of origin).

An example is an incident that occurred during our "intoxicated interview" with the Pridgett family. Midway through the interview, we learned that Mary, the Pridgett's twenty-year-old daughter, was engaged to be married. As she discussed her approaching marriage, she talked somewhat wistfully about her fantasies that she might have a "normal" wedding with a proud and clear-headed father to accompany her down the aisle. But now, following her father's latest return to drinking, she had, with very great sadness, relinquished this hope. It was a moving moment in the interview and Carl Pridgett, despite his growing mental confusion, seemed to sense it and tried his best to rise to the occasion. "Don't you worry," he told his daughter in his by-now-slurred speech. "I'll make it to the wedding sober. You mark my words, I'll make it sober."

It was a sad moment in the interview. No one in the family believed for a moment that Carl's prediction would come true. Here was an event that in many families would mark a transition, ultimately leading the family into the late phase of development. But the Pridgetts, much as they recognized the potential importance of the event, also sensed that it was insufficient to disrupt family homeostasis, insufficient to disrupt middle-phase behavior patterns.

Perhaps at some time in the future, the Pridgetts will face an event with a similar potential for triggering a major developmental conversion, and this time will succeed. But our suspicion is that this will not be the case. It is far more likely that the Pridgetts will deflect or neutralize each new developmental challenge, keeping it from provoking genuine changes in the family's way of doing business, and that the family will remain locked in what is effectively a state of developmental arrest.

A Case Example: The Callaghans.   An accurate flavor of what life is like in a stable wet late-phase Alcoholic Family is conveyed in a set of observations made of one such family during a celebration marking the sixtieth birthday of the family patriarch, who also was the identified alcoholic in the family. The family, the Callaghans, a working-class Irish-American family, had gathered at the parental home for an evening of eating, card playing, TV watching, and family conversation. A videotape recording of these activities allowed us to witness the following events:

The evening proved to be one not only of food and family entertainment, but also of almost constant consumption of alcohol by all the adult men (John Callaghan, his son, Danny, and his son-in-law, Paul). It started with whiskey mixed with early evening conversation, followed by wine served with dinner, and finished with after-meal consumption of whatever remained of the contents of two open bottles of whiskey placed on a coffee table in the living room, where the three men talked and drank for the remainder of the evening.

John Callaghan seemed to be drinking almost nonstop for the four hours we watched him. When he was not actually sipping, a glass of whiskey was always in his hand. After the meal, he sat down in his chair in the living room and seemed, from that position, to be orchestrating the almost continual supply and consumption of alcohol for the next several hours. In fact, we were hard-pressed to find a time when he was talking about anything else. He sat there, seemingly inattentive to the conversations going on around him, but as people moved in and out of the room, repeatedly asked them whether they needed a drink, whether they could bring another bottle, whether they liked what they were drinking, and so on.

Two of the large bottles of whiskey being consumed were the birthday presents his son and son-in-law had brought him for the occasion and had been presented to him when they first arrived. His wife, Sheila Callaghan, had made some remarks at the time about what "nice presents" they had brought.

As the evening wore on, John Callaghan not surprisingly became more and more drunk. If conversations had seemed somewhat peripheral to him several hours previously, he now clearly was unable to attend to what was going on around him. He seemed unable to get up from his chair and seemed confused by the level of noise, the simultaneous conversations, and the movements in and out of the room of his wife and children. But the family seemed quite aware of his presence and of his needs. Every ten minutes or so he would be asked "how he was doing," his whiskey would be checked, some comment would be made to him about what a nice birthday party it was.

At about 11:00 P.M., people began making preparations to leave. In the general milling about, with coats being put on and people gathering up their things and saying their good-byes, Mr. Callaghan's fifteen-year-old son, Gordy, walked into the living room, picked up the half-emptied whiskey bottle on the table next to his chair and walked out of the room with it. He watched him doing it and at first seemed startled and confused. He tried to get up from his chair but could not quite maneuver himself onto his feet and so, in a voice suffused part with rage, part with hurt, bellowed out, "He took my bottle. Gordy took my bottle. He took my birthday present. Bring it back, Gordy."

He looked around the room, appealing for help. It soon arrived. Sheila Callaghan, who had been talking with her son, abruptly left the room to find the whiskey bottle, while Danny went over to his father and reassured him with some pats on his shoulder and words like, "It's all right, Pop. Don't worry, Pop. Mom will get your birthday present."

And sure enough, Sheila Callaghan returned within a minute or so with his whiskey bottle, placed it in his lap, tousled his hair, and said, "It's okay now, John. Gordy doesn't understand. He didn't mean any harm, but he doesn't understand." John Callaghan, we see, is quickly mollified and the family returns to its parting rituals, bringing his sixtieth birthday celebration to a close.

Clinicians, looking at families like the Callaghans, view with considerable concern the family's entrenched commitment to alcoholism. Sheila Callaghan's collusion in her husband's drinking, the seemingly irrational behavior of his son and son-in-law in choosing his birthday presents, the family's catering to his every alcoholic whim, combine to make short shrift of his younger son's lonely challenge to his alcoholic drinking behavior. Our tendency is to view this as tragedy, a real-life drama in the finest Eugene O'Neill tradition.

Yet by looking at this occurrence from another perspective, one might reach a quite different conclusion. For example, a sociologist looking at this family would see no evidence of economic distress, no ostensible conflicts with society, and no mandatory need for medical services. An anthropologist would be impressed by the consonance between culturally determined values about alcohol and family attitudes toward its alcoholic member. Neither of these social scientists would feel that these findings lead directly to the conclusion that there is a tragic theme in what we have just witnessed. It is the clinically oriented researcher who wrings his or her hands when witnessing a ceremony like the Callaghans' birthday party.

Yet we must also note that it is families like the Callaghans that are least familiar to the clinician dealing with alcoholism. Our clinical intuition leads us to believe that the "wet Alcoholic Family" late-phase option is a negative one, that such families tend to be constricted in their behavior and perhaps significantly less adaptive in the long run than families who have not made this choice, but for the moment this judgment remains primarily a subjective one. The systematic studies done to date, our own included, have either focused on clinical populations (that is, families with an already manifest clinical problem) or families at the early and middle phases of development. Insofar as we have looked more directly at wet Alcoholic Families, our interest has centered primarily around the issue of transmission of alcoholism to the next generation. But even here, as we will detail in chapter 10, our data suggest that the mechanisms that either increase or decrease the likelihood of alcoholism being passed on to the next generation are those that occur primarily during the middle phase of development (detailed in chapter 8).

Just how many Alcoholic Families opt for the stable wet late-phase pathway is hard to estimate. The inherent rigidity of the middle-phase Alcoholic Family, its passionate commitment to the status quo, and its seeming resistance to any alteration in its way of doing business in the face of the kinds of challenges that often propel other families to consolidate and modify important identity issues as part of the middle- to late-phase conversion process, suggests that the number is quite large.

Most Alcoholic Families are experts at crisis management, having already experienced a wide-ranging series of "crises" that characteristically arise in conjunction with chronic alcoholism and having successfully neutralized them without making fundamental changes in family structure or behavior. Many Alcoholic Families have experienced medical crises like gastrointestinal bleeding secondary to ulcers, acute pancreatitis, or alcoholic hepatitis that have led to sudden hospitalization and warnings from physicians of impending doom if total abstinence is not strictly followed.

In the social sphere, deteriorating work performance, drunken excesses at formal social gatherings, traffic accidents and their legal consequences, and the terrifying psychological and social consequences often connected with alcoholic blackouts are all potential crises of the first order.

Nevertheless, Alcoholic Families often show remarkable resilience in the face of these crises. Short periods of sobriety, protestations that lessons have been learned, meek acceptance of mandatory referrals to treatment programs, short-term adherence to medical regimens, and temporary improvement in work performance all serve to reduce external pressures brought to bear on the family to change in a fundamental way. Six months later, we find the family back where it was, still very much organized around alcohol, still using sober-intoxicated cycling for short-term problem-solving, still engaged in the day-to-day routines supportive of a "stable wet" drinking pattern.

Thus many factors, both experiential and behavioral, existing in middle-phase Alcoholic Families reinforce the family's inclination to opt for a continuance of active drinking and a stable alcoholic identity into late phase. For now, let us therefore merely emphasize that the "wet Alcoholic Family" option is a very real one in the late phase of development, that it probably occurs with much higher frequency than is usually clinically appreciated, but that its consequences for the family are only poorly understood.

Option 2: The Stable Wet or Controlled Drinking Nonalcoholic Family

In this second late-phase option, the movement into late phase is accompanied by a change in the central role alcoholism had previously played as an organizing theme of family life. At the same time, this alteration in family identity is neither precipitated nor accompanied by an actual cessation of drinking. Thus the core feature of this late-phase option is the movement away from alcoholism as a family-identity issue. But it is a movement precipitated by developmental issues other than those associated with loss of alcohol itself. Loss issues still play a prominent role in the middle to late phase conversion for these families. But alcohol per se is not one of the losses involved.

For some families who follow this late-phase pathway, the movement away from alcoholism as a central family identity issue is accompanied by a significant reduction (although not a total cessation) of alcohol consumption. In such instances, Alcoholic Family members that had been repeatedly drinking to the point of intoxication will now engage in modest daily consumption of one or two drinks, or in occasional drinking at social functions. In other instances, quantity-frequency of drinking continues at levels comparable to those evidenced during the periods of heaviest drinking. What has changed, however, is that alcohol is no longer a central player in family regulatory behaviors; short-term problem-solving strategies are no longer built around the dichotomies of intoxicated versus sober behavior; daily routines are no longer organized around the exigencies of drinking patterns; family rituals are no longer structured to accommodate the needs of the family's alcoholic member.

In suggesting that a return to controlled drinking might be one possible drinking pattern associated with this second type of late-phase pathway, we are touching on a highly controversial topic in the alcoholism field. For those unfamiliar with this controversy, suffice it to say that a series of reports appearing in the literature of the 1970s purported to demonstrate a return to controlled drinking on the part of a substantial percentage of alcoholic individuals who had been patients in a wide variety of treatment programs. The best-known of these studies was the Rand Report, a large-scale survey of alcoholism treatment centers in the United States (Armor, Polich, and Stambul, 1978). A return to controlled drinking was also the explicit goal of a behaviorally oriented treatment program advocated by Mark and Linda Sobell (1978) who claimed considerable success for their program.

The combined weight of these various studies was compelling enough to lead some to question the prevailing view that total abstinence should *always* be the central goal of the alcoholism treatment program (Pattison, 1976). However, subsequent unsuccessful attempts to replicate the Sobells' findings (e.g., Ewing and Rouse, 1976), plus long-term follow-up of some of the research subjects used in these studies (Pendary, Maltzman, and West, 1982) raised doubts about the robustness and generalizability of findings suggesting that a return to controlled drinking is a feasible goal for treatment of alcoholism.

This view, that at most only a tiny percentage of alcoholic adults ever successfully revert to a pattern of stable, moderate (controlled) drinking, has also received strong support from a large-scale epidemiological study carried out by John Helzer and his colleagues (Helzer et al., 1985) at the Washington University School of Medicine. In this study, 1,249 former alcoholic patients were interviewed five to eight years after their initial treatment for alcoholism. Helzer employed the NIMH Diagnostic Interview Schedule, a highly respected epidemiological survey questionnaire to obtain data about current drinking practices. The findings indicated that although a substantial percentage (15 percent) of former patients continued to be abstinent at the time of follow-up, the vast majority of subjects who had returned to drinking were doing so at "heavy" or "alcoholic" levels. The figures were: 12 percent of the total sample had returned to heavy drinking, and 67 percent were "continuing alcoholics."

In contrast, only 2 percent of the sample were clearly moderate drinkers, by usual standards. Another 5 percent reported having had occasional drinks after treatment, but had been abstinent for a period of at least six full months prior to the follow-up interview. Thus the Helzer et al. study offers compelling data that controlled drinking is a highly infrequent resolution pattern in alcoholism. Nevertheless, the data also indicate that it does occasionally occur, and hence should be included in our schema for the sake of completeness.

For our purposes, however, what is most important is not whether or not "controlled" drinking has occurred. Rather it is the recognition that a family can, in late phase, move away from an Alcoholic Family identity without this change being necessarily accompanied by a complete cessation of drinking by the alcoholic member. Further, once the movement away from an alcoholic identity has occurred, the persistence and magnitude of alcohol use on the part of the identified alcoholic member of the family is no longer a core developmental issue for the family (although it might still be a powerful medical and/or psychological issue for the individual involved).

A Case Example: The Buchanans. The Buchanans, one of the families who participated in our home observation study, illustrate many of the important features of the stable wet, nonalcoholic late-phase pathway. Bernard and Florence Buchanan were a couple in their late fifties who, for most of their married life, had lived in a large house along with their only child, Joanna, and Naomi Alter, Mrs. Buchanan's divorced mother.

Those years were described as a time of constant tension and seemingly unending crises. Although the couple was able to point to specific events as precipitants of these crises, both husband and wife felt themselves to be living in a home situation that was always on the verge of exploding. This contentious atmosphere seemed most directly related to the intergenerational tensions that existed between the couple and Florence's mother, tensions that played themselves out around child-rearing issues, struggles over how to organize daily routines, and fights about boundary issues and rights to privacy. A tenuous power balance had been maintained over the years, but it seemed clear that alcohol-related behaviors had played a major role in maintaining this balance.

In this sense, life in the Buchanan family can be compared to those family situations described in some detail in chapter 6 in our discussion of short-term problem-solving in the middle-phase Alcoholic Family. Behaviors associated with the intoxicated interactional state led to an alteration in preferred interactional distance and affective tone within the family, thereby providing a short-term diffusing of what might have otherwise been a permanently disruptive breach in family cohesiveness.

The Buchanans were one of those families in which individual members tended to move to the four corners of a large, multilevel house and, within their territorial sphere of influence, would exist with very little interpersonal contact or emotional engagement. At least such was the situation during the sober interactional state. In conjunction with Bernard's drinking, however, the family would come together and attempt to "have it out" around whatever short-term issue had temporarily disrupted the tenuous balance of life within the family. Then, the situation having been diffused but not substantively resolved, family members would return to their prior state of emotional distance.

The situation was significantly altered when two major developmental losses occurred in close proximity to each other. Within the same year, first Naomi Alter died and then Joanna Buchanan left home for a college that, not surprisingly, had been selected in large part because of its geographical distance from the family home. Although Joanna continued to return home for major holidays, from the moment she left for college she effectively absented herself as a component member of family routines and problem-solving strategies. Even holiday rituals, for which she was at times present, no longer seemed to include her as an active participant. With Florence Buchanan's mother also no longer present, all of these aspects of regulatory processes within the family were substantively altered. Previously, family life—routines, rituals, and the like—had been subordinated to the pattern of Bernard's drinking. Now, very little relationship between these two types of behavior could be seen.

This is not to say that the family necessarily perceived the losses noted previously as major challenges to its way of doing business. This was not a family that was struggling with an attempt to clarify an Alcoholic Family identity in the face of major compositional changes. Rather, in a quiet but still significant way, alcohol and alcoholic behavior were no longer playing the central roles as organizers of family regulatory behavior that they had during middle phase. Thus, within the criteria we have established, we would judge the family to have been altered in the direction of a shift away from its middle-phase alcoholic identity toward a late-phase resolution in which alcohol was no longer a core identity issue.

Yet Bernard's drinking, although somewhat reduced, was still quite substantial. But now, even when he became intoxicated, the interactional and affective distance between him and his wife was unaltered. Whereas previously his drinking was accompanied by a heightened sense of engagement between the couple, now no perceptible change occurred. The sober-intoxicated duality typical of the middle-phase Alcoholic Family had simply disappeared. And with its disappearance went any semblance of marital cohesiveness. Although the couple remained married and continued to live together, they occupied different corners of the house (they actually lived on separate floors), ate separately, and had completely separate circles of friends and social activities. Thus the whims and vagaries of Bernard's drinking were no longer shaping family life in any way. Hence the label—stable wet, *nonalcoholic* late-phase family.

Option 3: The Stable Dry Alcoholic Family

The "wet" late-phase options previously discussed are developmental conversions that often can be seen only in retrospect. A subtle shift on the part of the family makes it clear that they have turned a corner and are now looking backward to share with us the resolution arrived at as they present a "final statement" about their family.

In a process of a very different nature, the precipitating event is a sharply demarcated one. For years, perhaps even decades, family life has been organized around alcohol consumption, intoxicated behavior, and its relationship to family regulatory mechanisms. Suddenly drinking has stopped, in some cases so quickly that it seems almost to take the family's breath away.

In the first of the "dry" late-phase options—the stable dry Alcoholic Family—the family negotiates the treacherous conversion to the dry state leaving its Alcoholic Family identity intact. How can a family be dry, yet still be called an Alcoholic Family? The answer lies in the concept of the alcoholic system. Alcoholic Families were originally so titled because of the critical role alcohol-related behaviors had come to play in their daily lives. However, it is possible for a family to continue to organize its life around alcohol even though its alcoholic member is no longer actively drinking.

That alcohol can play such a central role in family life during periods when active drinking is in full force is relatively easy for us to imagine. We have already documented at great length the relationships between alcohol consumption patterns and such critical components of family life as daily routines, short-term problem-solving strategies, and family rituals. What is not so readily appreciated is that for a significant number of families, the conversion to the dry state, although carrying with it a demand for substantive reorganization, still finds the family working out and resolving this reorganizational process around alcoholism as a core issue.

For some families, this process represents a logical extension of one initiated by the treatment program used during the transitional period. This is particularly true of programs that emphasize the value of long-term involvement in one or more of the various self-help groups so popular in the alcoholism field. Families might emerge from such a program having been introduced not only to Alcoholics Anonymous but also to Al-Anon, Alateen, or Alafam (the counterparts to AA groups for spouses, children, and whole families respectively). Involvement in these groups can become a very absorbing process. Not only is frequent attendance at meetings one of the requirements, but the groups also encourage veteran participants to assume responsibility for helping new members, a sponsorship program thought to be one of the reasons for the success of these groups.

Continued involvement in alcoholism-centered self-help groups is but one of several foci that keep alcohol center stage in these families. Reading material and family discussions recall the past difficulties related to alcoholism. Individuals within such families frequently have made substantive career changes that incorporate alcoholism as a work focus; for example, they have become alcoholism counselors or lobbyists involved in alcoholism activities on a community or national level. In many of these families, social life, family rituals, and vacation plans are all restructured to maintain the central role of alcoholism as a family life theme, albeit this time one organized to prevent slippage back to a wet stage.

There is nothing inherently good or bad, functional or dysfunctional, adaptive or maladaptive in a family's selecting the stable dry Alcoholic Family late-phase option. For one family this resolution option might represent the family's sense of mastery and control over its world, the importance it places on acknowledging its history and in sharing together its feeling of uniqueness that derives specifically from its experience with alcohol. Such a family might acknowledge that alcoholism has been a major stress in its life. It might even acknowledge that alcoholism has contributed to major distortions in the family's developmental history. But it might still feel, as it attempts to make a late-phase statement about this experience, that it has been pivotal, a challenge that has also increased the family's depth of understanding of itself and provided it with a sense of uniqueness and definition in the world.

Another family might have a very different view. For it, the dry Alcoholic Family resolution might stem from its fear that, without constant reminder, alcoholism might again engulf family life. Such a family might still feel that the comings and goings of periods of active drinking are as unfathomable as they ever were, and that they must therefore be constantly on guard against the unknown. Continuing reminders of its alcoholism as a core issue of family life keep the family on its toes against the ever-present danger of relapse.

Whether a dry Alcoholic Family is of the first variety or the second is therefore not a function of the specific late-phase option it has chosen, but rather a function of the family's personality. Just as was the case during the early and middle phases of development, it is the family's sense of itself and its world, combined with its temperamental disposition, that determines the ultimate adaptability, flexibility, and coherence of its late-phase resolution.

A Case Example: The Luries. George and Connie Lurie were a couple in the second decade of a marriage initially plagued by alcoholism. George, a forty-eight-year-old architect had been married once before; Connie, a forty-year-old housewife, had been married twice previously. Their household included four children—two from Connie's second marriage and two from the current marriage. In this sense, the Luries illustrated two aspects of family development that we have alluded to repeatedly—the difficulty of defining developmental stages according to age and family compositional factors; and the condensation process that often occurs in a blended family in which the spouse parents have been previously married. In the case of the Luries, although the marriage was just beginning its second decade, the family was already dealing with late-phase developmental issues.

This interesting family had an extremely complicated alcoholism history that can be most easily traced using Connie Lurie as the protagonist. Herself the product of an alcoholic father and a nonalcoholic mother, Connie was unaware of her father's drinking habits while she was living at home, only recently discovering that her father had "quite a problem with alcohol when he was younger." Connie herself had begun drinking as an adolescent, got drunk on numerous occasions, and had several episodes of blackouts. In her early twenties, she married a man who "drank too much" and became physically abusive when drunk. The first marriage ended in divorce after several years.

Connie remarried several years later, and her second husband also proved to have a serious alcoholism problem. This time, however, Connie also began drinking heavily and alcohol rapidly became a major part of their lives. Evenings always included drinking, and their social life seemed to revolve around drinking parties. As she remembered it, their behavior when they were with other people tended to be restrained, even when they were clearly drunk, but when they were drinking together at home, they would get into bitter quarrels. The verbal and physical abuse associated with these quarrels was a major precipitant of her second divorce, which occurred after three years of marriage. The two children born during this marriage seemed to have had little impact on the family's resistance to moving on to the middle phase of development. Commitments were never made, early-phase struggles dominated marital life, and this "second" family withered on the vine as a result.

Subsequent to her divorce from her second husband, Connie's drinking diminished dramatically. Nevertheless, shortly after she married her current husband, alcohol again became an issue. Although George had had no prior history of alcohol abuse nor was there alcoholism in his family of origin or in his first marriage, he was a social drinker accustomed to drinking wine regularly with meals and to going to bars and dancing clubs for entertainment. He brought these habits with him into his marriage and encouraged his wife to meet him several times a week for lunch, during which they would begin an extended drinking session that often continued into the late evening. As drinking increased, once again Connie found herself experiencing bitter feelings about her husband, and frequent verbal fights erupted at home.

As the contentiousness of their marriage gradually increased, George unilaterally decided to change the pattern of their lives. He reduced his own drinking and attempted to decrease the dependence of their social life on contacts outside the home, especially alcohol-centered activities. But Connie's response was to retreat into the solitude of her home, isolating herself and drinking almost constantly. Her drinking became more secretive and her quantity of alcohol consumption reached its highest point during this phase. Frightened by both the magnitude and consequences of her drinking—especially the fact that it was no longer being carried out in social settings where partying provided a convenient "cover"—she raised with her husband the possibility that she was an alcoholic. But he categorically refused to accept this conclusion.

Connie attended her first AA meeting at this point and initially remained sober for several months, but began drinking again during a reception following her son's marriage. She subsequently contacted her AA sponsor, was brought to an alcoholism treatment unit and detoxified, and was thereafter able to remain sober.

Here then is the precipitating event (loss of alcohol) that marks this family's entry into the late phase of development. The decision to stop drinking, a decision for which a period of hospitalization was needed in order for it to be solidified, left this family in a position to review its drinking history and prepare a summary statement about the meaning of alcoholism in its life. This statement, in turn, would form the core of the family's late-phase view of itself.

The initial attempts that George and Connie Lurie made in this regard reflected and mimicked the positions that they had taken earlier, during the family's middle phase of development. That is, Connie Lurie took the initiative in defining a position, a position her husband initially rebelled against but eventually came to accept, if perhaps in a slightly modified form. During the middle phase, her position had centered around her commitment to alcohol and her structuring of the couple's social life around alcohol-related activities. George initially "went along for the ride," then pulled back when frightened by the seriousness of his own drinking problem, but continued to deny the impact alcoholism was having on his marriage. This time Connie stated in explicit terms her concern about her alcoholism history and her need to protect herself against a recurrence of a serious drinking problem. Once again George went along, offering no direct objections to her involvement with AA, her decision to be hospitalized, or her refusal to start drinking again, but, at the same time, disparaging AA and her alcoholism treatment program openly, and alluding to her AA friends as "intruders" in the family. However, as the couple continued to work out their late-phase statement, George began attending Al-Anon meetings and started to openly acknowledge the family's past difficulties with alcoholism.

As the Luries late-phase position became clarified and began to take hold, Connie remained abstinent; George occasionally drank wine in moderate amounts; and both of them attended twice-weekly AA and Al-Anon meetings, respectively, at the alcoholism treatment unit attached to their community hospital. In addition, Connie regularly served as a sponsor for new AA members and talked warmly about her satisfaction with this role. She was continually on the phone talking to these people, making arrangements, helping them with transportation, and so on. For example, during our home observation study, which also included weekly multiple family discussion-group meetings held on alternating basis at the homes of the different families of the group, the Luries would regularly drive ten or fifteen miles out of their way to pick up one or two couples and bring them to the multiple family-group meetings. In describing these various alcohol-related activities, Connie talked about her involvement with AA and her "social work" role in dealing with other families in our study group as the closest analogy to a job or outside employment she had experienced in her adult life.

If one were to add up the number of hours devoted by this family to these activities and compare it to other social or community-related activities, we would see that alcoholism, while no longer being expressed in a traditional fashion in this family, was still very much the central organizing theme for the family's life in its community. It was a badge worn by the family; a way of introducing itself to outsiders; a component of family life that dominated the family's daily activities and discourse with outsiders.

A Second Case Example: The Piccas.   The Piccas, a late-phase stable dry Alcoholic Family with six members, had a very different history from the Luries. Not only had they been plagued by a long history of chronic alcoholism, but they had also been ravaged by one of the frequent concomitants of alcoholism, sexual abuse. In their case, this abuse took the form of multiple episodes of father-daughter incest, characteristically occurring during Robert Picca's (the identified alcoholic in the family) periods of heaviest drinking.

Robert and Anne Picca, a Spanish-Italian family, were both professionals working for a large multi-national corporation. During the first eighteen years of their marriage, Robert Picca, 62, (an economist), Anne Picca, 42 (a lawyer), and their four children lived in a series of African countries while on foreign duty assignments. Because of their differing job responsibilities, Irving and Sara experienced frequent and extended marital separation during these tours of duty. The family's "home bases" were a series of American compounds in the capital cities of the host countries to which they were assigned; the children attended English-language schools within these communities—in other words, a typical life-style for an American family abroad.

Throughout this time, Robert maintained a level of daily alcohol consumption that averaged one pint of whiskey per day. Although obviously affected in his work performance by this magnitude of drinking, because substantial alcohol consumption was almost a norm for professionals in the settings in which he worked, his behavior was rarely thought of as out of the ordinary. Thus he was neither confronted when he got drunk at social events, nor were his "morning blues" viewed with more than bemusement by his superiors.

Within Robert's family, however, a quite different drama was unfolding. Because of his irregular work schedule, Robert would frequently be at home alone with one or more of his daughters (there were three of them plus one son) while his wife was at work on a nine to five schedule. During these periods, he was also characteristically drinking steadily throughout the day. It was in this context that the incestuous behavior emerged and flourished.

The first episode of sexual abuse involved fondling and caressing his oldest daughter, Elena, around the time of her eleventh birthday. The frequency and character of sexual contact with his daughter increased dramatically over the next two years, however, culminating in sexual intercourse. Once initiated, intercourse occurred on a two-to-three-times-a-week basis whenever he returned home from one of his trips. As he and his wife had been sexually abstinent for some time, Anne Picca purported to be unaware of this dramatic turn of events in her family. Nor was she sensitive to her daughter's increasingly withdrawn behavior, declining school performance, unexplained outbursts of anger, or growing sense of isolation both within the family and among her peers.

The situation only surfaced when a school counselor pressed Elena because of her own growing concern about the teenager's obvious depression. The family members' reaction to the revelation of incestuous behavior was stereotypical. Robert denied that such behavior was occurring; Anne furiously accused her daughter of disregard for the family's reputation and of "pathological lying"; Elena's sisters and brother treated her as a pariah.

As verification of the incestuous behavior emerged, however, Anne Picca belatedly came to her daughter's defense and a set of fragile and tenuous bonds developed again between the three sisters. The marriage, obviously already shaky, was on the verge of breaking up. But a compromise was reached. On the promise that incestuous behavior would cease, both spouses agreed to work toward preserving the marriage in the service of providing a stable environment for their children. At no point, however, was a connection made between Robert's alcoholism and the emergence of sexual abuse within the family, and as a result a cessation of drinking was not made one of the conditions for the continuation of the marriage.

The explosive crisis now having been blunted, the family rapidly returned to its previous level of functioning and organizational characteristics. Robert and Anne's work schedules, the quality of daily routines, and the characteristics of Robert's behavior were all revived unchanged. And so, it turned out, was the incestuous behavior, although this time it involved Robert's next oldest daughter, Julie.

The unfolding of events around this second episode of father-daughter incest repeated, step by step, the process that had occurred within the family the first time. Again it was a school counselor who diagnosed the problem (as the family now lived in a different city, school officials treated this as a "new case"). Again the revelation came as a complete surprise to Anne, who initially expressed her disbelief because of her husband's earlier promises. And once again, the crisis was resolved by the establishment of a close and caring bond between Julie and the school counselor, which provided her some protection, and a reaffirmation on the parents' part that the marriage would continue only if Robert would pledge that incest would "never happen again." Again, of course, the alcoholism issue was ignored.

At this point, the family returned to the United States. Whether it was because of the change in living environment, with the concomitant increase in the complexity of the family's ties to outside individuals and agencies, or whether it was the fact that even within a family as rigid and impacted as the Piccas' a third episode of father-daughter incest could not possibly be dealt with in the same fashion as the first two, when a third round did occur (this time involving the Piccas' youngest daughter, Esther) there was finally a confrontation of Robert's alcoholic behavior.

Anne Picca, who shortly after coming to the United States had experienced a major depression, had been in ongoing psychotherapy after being hospitalized. Her therapist, on learning about the family history of incest, insisted on a series of meetings with the family to address this issue. It was in the context of these meetings that the recurrence of incest, this time involving Esther, was revealed. As a consequence, Robert was referred immediately for treatment of his alcoholism and was admitted to a residential program that included a heavy emphasis on participation in AA.

Drinking was thus precipitously halted, and Robert was rapidly immersed in a "total involvement" alcoholism treatment program that, post-hospitalization, centered around twice-daily AA meetings. Anne, her daughters, and her son were invited to a "family information session" as part of Robert's residential treatment program, and were encouraged to themselves attend Al-Anon meetings. They went to meetings once or twice a week for several months, but found them largely unsatisfying and gradually stopped going.

However, despite a successful conversion to the dry state, this family found itself even more emotionally estranged one from another than had been the case during the period of active drinking. Although they were now able to talk openly about the three episodes of incestuous behavior that had wreaked such emotional havoc on the family, little or no progress had been made in understanding either the psychological roots of this problem or in developing new strategies for turning the family into a more effective psychosocial environment for its members. Nowhere was this more evident than in the relationship between husband and wife. Both remained as ineffectual in their dealings with one another and as bitter about their lack of emotional support as they had ever been. And of equal importance, the absence of substantive change despite the sudden removal of alcohol from the family environment seemed to significantly increase the family's sense of resignation and despair. Thus, events in their lives seemed as unfathomable as ever.

This was a family that, on a concrete level at least, had undergone a process quite analoguous to that experienced by the Luries. The family was now dry. Continuing involvement in alcoholism-related activities—at least to the extent that family relationships and daily routines remained organized around AA—indicated that the Piccas also had opted for a stable dry Alcoholic Family late-phase pathway. But similarities clearly cease at that point.

The Luries, one could contend, saw themselves as being in charge of their lives, a confident and appropriately aggressive family, considerably strengthened by its mastery over a behavioral problem that might easily have ultimately destroyed the family. That this sense of mastery needed continual reenforcement through the family's replaying of the alcoholism theme in no way diminished the family's sense of confidence in the solidity of its resolution. As observers of this family in action, we were also left with a sense of admiration and respect for the solution they had arrived at.

In contrast, the Piccas' continued involvement in alcoholism-related activities reflected a timid and frightened world view. This family felt that it was living in a potentially hostile environment—an environment that might, in capricious fashion, suddenly rear up again to challenge family stability. The world (and, by extension, the family's internal environment) was thought of as populated with unpredictable and potentially malicious forces that had to be continually placated if the family was to survive.

An example is the very different attitudes toward AA and Al-Anon. The Luries thought of themselves as active participants in their respective groups, felt free to shape and direct the activities of the group, and easily moved into leadership roles vis-à-vis new group members. The Piccas, on the other hand, seemed to view AA and Al-Anon as magical entities. One senses that for them the quasi-religious character of these groups was one of the major attractions they held for both husband and wife. No one in the family could explain how the groups work; in fact, they were probably totally at a loss in this regard. But it did not matter; AA and Al-Anon involvement had somehow been associated with a cessation of drinking, so they saw no reason to ask questions about something that seemed to work.

In discussing the dry Alcoholic Family resolution option, emphasis has been placed on the striking continuity of alcoholism-focused activities despite the cessation of drinking. At the same time, it has been underscored that a life organized around alcoholism-related issues is not in and of itself a good or bad way for a family to structure life during the late phase. One family, the Luries, seemed masterful, aggressive, in charge; the other family, the Piccas, seemed defensive, apprehensive, bewildered. Both families had opted for the stable dry alcoholic pathway, but one senses that this same late-phase option had very different meanings for the two families and, by extension, in all likelihood, would have different consequences vis-à-vis the developmental themes of the late phase of family life.

The main point here is that it is another set of factors (not the specific resolution option itself) that is critical in determining the meaning and ultimate consequences to the family of a particular late-phase option. These are the factors we have subsumed under the terms *family personality* and *family regulatory mechanisms.*

Option 4: The Stable Dry Nonalcoholic Family

The final late-phase option available to the Alcoholic Family is the dry, nonalcoholic pathway. As the name implies, in this option, not only has drinking stopped, but the family has also given up its preoccupation with alcohol and alcohol-related issues. Why would a family be likely to choose the stable dry nonalcoholic family pathway? If drinking stops during early phase, it is easy to see how the family might conclude that its "alcoholism identity" was a false start, separate itself from this history, and move on to new issues. But what circumstances would lead a family to separate itself from an experience that was so pivotal a part of its life during the developmental phase when identity consolidation and boundary maintenance were the main developmental themes?

Once again (as with the stable dry Alcoholic Family resolution), there are two possible sets of circumstances. In the first, the family arrives at the dry nonalcoholic resolution as a *reaction* to developmental pressures created by the wet to dry conversion. It views this conversion with the same sense of bewilderment as it treated the previous long period of active drinking. In the second set of circumstances, the family arrives at this resolution as a product of a *proactive* response designed to master a developmental objective. There is an active process of family reorganization, largely shaped by the initiatives and experiments carried out by the family.

In the first instance, the conversion from wet to dry status tends to be followed by a reflexive but characteristically brief period of confusion and readjustment. But then a new phase of family life emerges, a phase no longer organized around alcohol. Yet the non-alcohol-centered reorganization arrived at by this first type of family is one reached more by default than by any deliberate decision. The critical feature of this type of reorganization is that the family seems strangely disconnected from its previous experiences with alcohol. Alcohol has been eliminated not only in a physical sense, but also as an emotional issue in the family's life (it is this latter feature that is, of course, the sine qua non of the nonalcoholic late-phase developmental option).

But it is not only that these families sense no ongoing commitment to alcoholism-related issues; they also evidence no interest in attempting to clearly understand what their experience with alcohol had meant for their lives. Even though it largely ruled their lives for many years, they never understood where it came from in the first place, and now they seem uninterested in why drinking has stopped. It is as if alcohol was an alien virus that invaded the family's inner world, infecting and influencing major family functions and thereby affecting all family members. But now it has been mysteriously "cured" and it makes little sense to the family to dwell on the issue any longer.

In the play, *Rosencrantz and Guildenstern Are Dead,* Tom Stoppard shows us how the central events in *Hamlet* might be viewed by two minor, peripheral characters. Over the course of two hours of alternatingly funny and sad dialogue, Rosencranz and Guildenstern share with us their struggles to comprehend events swirling about them. Though they seem continually bewildered, they are also subject to alternating periods of apprehension and efforts to analyze the facts and rumors that gradually emerge as they learn about some, but never all, of the tragic circumstances surrounding Hamlet and his troubled family. Since they are, after all, still characters in a play (and not even Stoppard's play at that), their ultimate fate is sealed. But one has the growing suspicion that no matter what information they would be privy to, the major events around them and their own decisions would still be very much the same.

It is precisely this type of response that one senses in this first type of dry, nonalcoholic family. Here also, family members seem to be wandering about the stage. Here too, if they engage in a dialogue about their past experiences with alcohol, it is a dialogue that leaves the observer with the impression of having watched confused and puzzled people struggling to understand events that they perceive to be somehow alien to their experience, even though their family life had been, for many years, organized around alcohol issues.

A Case Example: The Nestors.   The prototypical example of a "reactive" stable dry nonalcoholic family resolution was that manifested by the Nestor family cited earlier in this chapter. (This was the family in which Mr. Nestor's drinking suddenly stopped when his children found him passed out on the bathroom floor after a night of drinking.)

Bob and April Nestor and their children consistently conveyed the Rosencranz and Guildenstern sense of bewilderment and uncertainty about the relationship between their prior alcoholic state and their consequent dry nonalcoholic status (their status at the time they volunteered for one of our studies). Although it was widely acknowledged by all family members that the conversion from wet to dry status had been a precipitous one, they were unable to point with certainty to any factors or behavioral changes in family life that had accompanied it. Although there was general agreement that Bob Nestor's cessation of drinking was a positive step in the family's overall development, family members were hard-pressed to amplify on this relatively general and superficial statement.

In fact, quite to the contrary, there was evidence that important parameters of family life that seemed to be a product of Bob's alcoholism had survived intact. For example, patterns of daily home routines changed hardly at all after he stopped drinking. During his period of heaviest drinking (the period immediately preceding his precipitous conversion to abstinence), a typical evening for the Nestors would entail a family dinner without Bob, followed by an evening of school and housekeeping chores. April and the children would gather together in the ground-floor family room to carry out these chores.

Some time in the early evening, Bob would come home from work, eat by himself, and then retire to the basement for a postdinner evening of TV and drinking. Sometimes he would come upstairs to get a fresh supply of food and drink, but often he would not see his family again until the morning. In this way, the family myth that alcoholism was a sequestered event within the family, walled off from other family members and therefore of minimal consequence to them, was effectively maintained.

The "bathroom floor" episode was therefore read as evidence that this internal boundary was breaking down, and it was in this context that drinking precipitously stopped. But interestingly, although no longer drinking, Bob was as isolated at home as ever. That is, daily routines still included an early-evening meal for April Nestor and the children, but one only rarely attended by Bob. And postdinner activities again were carried out on several floors—April and the children on one floor; Bob on another.

Bob's TV watching and eating now occurred on the ground floor of the family home; the rest of the family had moved to the second floor where homework and housekeeping chores were now being carried out. Thus the basic interactional pattern within the family was essentially the same.

Family members had simply moved up one floor in the home to carry these patterns out. It was hardly surprising, therefore, that family members were hard-pressed to identify any changes in family life that had occurred as a result of the conversion from wet to dry status.

A second aspect of Nestor family behavior is also of interest to us. During a background interview, they described at some length a relationship they had developed with an across-the-street neighbor family. These neighbors had had a retarded child and their relationship with the Nestors had solidified around issues related to this child. The Nestor children had taken on caretaking roles for the child, and both Bob and April Nestor had encouraged inclusion of this child in their daily activities.

Our initial contact with the Nestors had occurred several months after the child had died. The Nestors had taken it upon themselves to build a handmade coffin for the child, and they described their project in considerable detail to us. We received a strong impression that their involvement with this other family, an involvement centering around their responsibilities for managing a chronic illness, filled a hole for them that had existed since the precipitous loss of alcohol several years before. We would argue that the Nestors were drawn to this situation in large part because of the confusion surrounding their resolution of the chronic alcoholism issue, a resolution that was largely reactive on the family's part and never really comprehended by them.

But there is a second group of stable dry nonalcoholic families—the "proactive" group and these families come to this resolution through a very different route. For these families, this late-phase option is not merely a resolution of active drinking issues, it is also a major family reorganization that, for many of them, occurs as a result of family-oriented psychotherapy. Not infrequently, the presenting complaint bringing the family to treatment is not the alcoholism issue at all, but is one of the other challenges characteristically faced by families at this stage in the developmental life cycle.

As has already been pointed out, distortions in family structure and functioning created by what we have called the Alcoholic Family identity places many of these families at high risk to experience severe stress as a consequence of normative developmental challenges. If, as a result of these stresses, the family seeks treatment and is fortunate enough to find a therapist sensitive to both family and alcoholism issues, then a treatment plan may evolve that leads ultimately to major "reconstructive surgery." In these cases, therapist and family work cooperatively to understand the role alcohol has been playing in family life and to work at restructuring family behavior around nonalcohol-related themes. A discussion with such a family about the changes that have occurred in their lives postcessation of drinking has a very different flavor from the one conveyed by the Nestors, as indicated in the following example.

A Case Example: The Moretts.   The Moretts were a couple in their late fifties with three adult children, none of whom were living at home. Phyllis Morett had had a serious alcoholism problem that had first surfaced when she was in her late thirties and had gradually worsened over a period of ten years. During this time she had become increasingly withdrawn, socially isolated, and dysfunctional at work. In addition, her role within the family had become more and more circumscribed, her daughters having increasingly taken over major responsibilities for housekeeping tasks and preparations for family social functions.

Despite her alcoholism's severe consequences in her work, social, and family life, Phyllis Morett had for many years seemed unable to halt the progressive advance of her drinking and its associated deterioration in her functioning. Although the severity of her alcoholism remained by and large unrecognized by her work colleagues and close friends, Phyllis's husband and children were well aware both of the seriousness of her symptoms and of the increasingly pernicious impact alcoholism was having on their family life. Family conferences, held when Phyllis was sober, led to a resolve on the family's part to seek active treatment for her drinking disorder. However, despite a number of attempts at residential treatment and participation in AA and Al-Anon programs, improvement in her level of functioning and ability to maintain sobriety was at best transient. Consonant with the increasing sense of pessimism the family experienced about Phyllis's alcoholism, a stable wet Alcoholic Family pattern increasingly took hold.

The break in this pattern occurred as a result of the confluence of two probably related events. First, the Morett's youngest child married and moved out of the family household; second, Wilbur and Phyllis Morett began seeing a family therapist with the goal not only of addressing Phyllis's alcoholism, but also of reassessing critical aspects of their marriage.

The first event precipitated major changes in family rituals and daily routines which, in turn, challenged family behavioral patterns that had to a large extent been shaped and determined by facets of Phyllis's drinking patterns. In other words, the Moretts were experiencing the first of a series of losses that served as precipitating events for the transition into late phase.

The therapy experience was important in two respects: It adopted as its primary focus a reexamination of the couple's marital relationship; and the therapist also was able to expose and effectively deal with links between Phyllis's drinking and underlying *chronic depression.* Although a cessation in drinking was still the therapy's primary goal, its ability to place drinking behavior within a family systems context and to provide a sophisticated assessment of the identified drinker's psychopathological status gave the work a distinctly different flavor from that of the residential alcoholism treatment programs the Moretts' had previously had experience with.

Keeping this background in mind, the Moretts' account of a family gathering provides a picture that might be viewed as representative of a *nonalcoholic family identity* that emerged in a family as it moved into the late phase of development.

The Moretts' most important holiday celebration was Christmas. For many years the family had engaged in a week-long series of ritualized dinners and outings over the Christmas vacation. As the children married and as grandchildren were born, this week continued to be set aside as the one time during the year when the "whole family" gathered together for shared activities.

In describing their experience of the most recent of these Christmas celebrations, Wilbur and Phyllis Morett had little difficulty in responding to a query about what changes they noted in family behavior for this "dry" gathering versus family life when she was still drinking. Three aspects were immediately pointed to: first, the children's increased level of participation in the planning and carrying out the week's activities (cited as evidence of increased role flexibility, of increased respect within the family for the views of the children, and of the increased diversity and range of activities tolerated by the family); second, the changed attitudes of both parents to their children's growing independence and competence (they found themselves struggling with the challenge of defining new ways of "contributing and being a part of the group," a challenge that initially made them feel anxious, but subsequently reenergized); and third, that the family seemed to have a new-found ability to withstand pressure for closure on an issue that hadn't yet been truly resolved (cited as evidence of the family's increased comfort with uncertainty).

These changes, we would contend, were not merely the inevitable outgrowths of an aging process in the family (children leaving home, new grandchildren, and so on). They also reflected fundamental characterological changes in the family's response patterns, internal relationships, and boundary characteristics. In this sense, the Morett family had undergone a systemic reorganization consonant with the cessation of drinking, a late-phase resolution quite different from that of the Nestors.

Conclusion

The tension that develops between family-level maturational issues and chronic alcoholism has been cited as a major factor in the process of developmental distortion that occurs in Alcoholic Families. Nowhere is this process more vividly illustrated than in the tensions that arise at the late phase of family development.

In this chapter we have described four different pathways available to Alcoholic Families as they move into late phase. Which pathway the family takes is determined by whether or not loss of alcohol was a major precipitant of the middle to late phase conversion and whether identity clarification resulted in an alcoholic or nonalcoholic late-phase family identity. Our discussion would have been made vastly simpler had we been able to conclude that some pathways are clearly more functional than others. But with the possible exception of the stable wet, Alcoholic Family pathway (which is almost always associated with developmental arrest), we were able to point to both functional and dysfunctional examples of each of the other pathways.

As for the stable wet option, the crucial idea here is that the late-phase consolidation process leads to a rigidification of middle-phase patterns and organizational principles, for example, a family that *must* be organized around a permanently disabled member who is supported in his invalidism (as in the Callaghan birthday party), or a family that will in perpetuity utilize the sober-intoxicated cycle to fend off and overreact to destabilizing events and to reinforce current organizational patterns (the Pridgetts).

In either case, the consolidation process reinforces a rigid and unidimensional family stance—the heritable family identity is to be transmitted as a total package, take it or leave it. No experimenting will be tolerated; the late-phase family will not alter its middle-phase commitments—the next-generation family must either accept a cloned identity or sever all meaningful ties (again remember the vignette of the Callaghan birthday party). And because in the stable wet option there is little shaping or alteration of family identity over time, we think of this option as associated with *developmental arrest*.

Thus it is hard to imagine a situation in which the stable wet pathway would not hamper normative family development. For the other pathways, however, the story is somewhat different, because the pathway itself does not determine the level of family functionality in late phase. Instead, two other factors prove to be critical: the first is the timing of the precipitant for middle to late phase conversion, whether the timing is synchronous with the overall pacing of systemic maturation in the family, or is premature. The second is the level of integration of identity clarification occurring as the family moves into late phase, whether the late-phase clarification of the family's alcoholic identity is clearly understood or remains fuzzy and diffuse. These are the two factors—timing and clarity—that determine whether major development distortions will occur in a particular Alcoholic Family's late phase.

In the normative family, the disruptive forces that characteristically occur toward the end of middle phase and that precipitate the onset of late phase impose themselves on a family that has had plenty of time to establish its routine and rules, to select and develop its priorities (life themes), and to order the pace of family growth. Although such a family might still object mightily to any disruption in this ordered existence, the system is well positioned to carry on with the life reviews and thematic clarifications that are a necessary component of late-phase identity resolution issues.

In the Alcoholic Family, on the other hand, a problem immediately arises in that alcoholism enters the equation both as the central identity issue for the family and as a potential precipitating event (loss of alcohol) initiating the middle to late phase conversion. It is the fortunate family (and probably the rare one as well) that finds itself able to deal with alcoholism resolution at a time when other developmental themes are also being resolved. As has been pointed out, the more frequent situation is one in which external events (job difficulties, medical consequences, societal sanctions) impose themselves on the family, creating irresistible pressures for resolution of the alcohol issue. The conversion from wet to dry status, when it is stimulated by such external pressures, is only partly a family-generated resolution. More often than not, the family seems to be mightily resisting facing a problem that no longer can be ignored. If alcohol must be given up as a result of an externally imposed crisis, the family seems to be dragged, kicking and screaming, to such a conclusion.

Middle-phase families are faced with such problems all the time. Geographical relocations, alterations of roles within the family, major illnesses—these events all create structural and functional pressures within the family and demand attention even from the most resistant of families. One might be tempted to add alcoholism to this list and to argue that the wet to dry conversion is yet another example of such a mini-crisis in the family's life. But such a position ignores how absolutely central a role alcoholism-related behaviors play in the middle-phase Alcoholic Family.

A fundamental identity issue is at stake here. It is therefore virtually impossible for the family to deal with this crisis via a simple midcourse correction, as it often can with other externally imposed middle-phase challenges.

But if the wet to dry conversion occurs when the family is developmentally unprepared to tackle resolution issues, what occurs is a *premature resolution* of a major family-identity issue. A family without a fully shaped, distinctive sense of itself is forced by external events to arrive at a "resolved" position regarding its most crucial identity issue. It is not hard to imagine that such a family would feel ill-equipped to deal with this challenge and that a "rush to judgment" would be the most likely outcome, as the family carries out a late-phase developmental task when, developmentally, it is still in the middle phase of development.

It is not surprising, then, that such a family should feel itself largely at the mercy of external events. And it is also not surprising that when other late-phase issues arise, especially the issue of intergenerational transmission of family identity, the family's position and behavior will be heavily influenced by its need to prematurely resolve the central identity issue of alcoholism.

CHAPTER 10

The Intergenerational Transmission of Alcoholism

THE TRANSMISSION of alcoholism across generations has traditionally been approached from two different perspectives—a genetic one and a cultural one. The genetic perspective holds that alcoholism is a biologically determined condition, that a predisposition toward alcoholic behavior is encoded in a person's genetic material, and that this predisposition can therefore be transmitted to subsequent generations via an alcoholic "gene." The cultural perspective holds that a society's attitudes, values and behavioral priorities—for example, those related to alcohol use—are transmitted from generation to generation via a process of socialization of children. The family has traditionally been proposed as the group responsible for carrying out this socialization process.

But of equal importance is the transmission of personal values, values that we might more appropriately call family, rather than societal or cultural. Although societal values regarding alcohol use clearly affect family and individual behavior, for our purposes the more interesting focus has to do with the family's unique perspective regarding alcohol. That is, for us the more interesting question is how values and behaviors related to alcohol use are incorporated within the *family culture*, and then transmitted to children. Thus when we talk about transmission of alcoholism across generations, it is primarily this family perspective that we will be taking.

The Genetic Perspective

The interest in transmission across generations as an important aspect of alcoholism has been stimulated by an impressive set of findings regarding familial incidence of chronic alcoholism (Cotton, 1979). As demonstrated now in many studies, children with alcoholic parents exhibit a vastly greater probability of developing alcoholism as they move into adulthood. For example, a frequently cited figure is that sons of alcoholic fathers have a four times greater likelihood of themselves becoming alcoholic than sons of nonalcoholic fathers (Cotton, 1979; Midanik, 1983).

Two recent studies have provided up-to-date statistics for the incidence of familial alcoholism in American society. McKenna and Pickens (1981) reported that among female alcoholics, 41 percent have fathers and 8 percent have mothers who are also alcoholic. While parental alcoholism is also high for alcoholic males, its incidence is not quite so high: 28 percent with alcoholic fathers and 5 percent with alcoholic mothers.

Midanik (1983) similarly noted the differences between men and women with respect to the extent of familial alcoholism. Based on the National Drinking Practices Survey, data are reported for the population in general as well as for respondents who indicated that they have alcohol problems of their own. For the population at large, 1010 women reported the following incidence of familial alcoholism: 14.3 percent with alcoholic fathers; 4.4 percent with alcoholic mothers; 14.4 percent with alcoholic brothers; and 4.6 percent with alcoholic sisters. The percentages for the 762 males surveyed were all lower: 10.2 percent with alcoholic fathers; 2.5 percent with alcoholic mothers; 12.7 percent with alcoholic brothers; and 1.7 percent with alcoholic sisters. Approximately 25 percent of the sample overall reported alcoholism or problem drinking among any first-degree relatives, 29 percent for women and 20 percent for men (p. 136).

Among those surveyed who indicated that they experienced either loss of control due to drinking or dependency on alcohol, women also reported higher percentages of familial alcoholism. For the 64 women who indicated that they themselves had such a positive indicator of alcoholism, 19.9 percent also indicated that their fathers were problem drinkers or alcoholics; 18.8 percent, mothers; 13.8 percent, brothers; and 10.5 percent, sisters. Among the 116 males indicating alcohol problems of their own, 12.5 percent indicated that their fathers were problem drinkers or alcoholics; 4.3 percent, mothers; 16.0 percent, brothers; and 1.9 percent, sisters. (p. 138).

Research into the genetic perspective has attempted to understand these data via the implementation of a series of studies designed to tease out biological from environmental variables. Three basic strategies have been employed.

In the first strategy—the genetic marker studies—the investigator first identifies a trait known to be inherited (such as blood groups or color blindness), and then looks for the incidence of this "marker" trait in alcoholic versus nonalcoholic subjects. If more alcoholic subjects have the marker trait than would be expected by chance, this finding is thought to support a genetic basis for alcoholism. Thus far, however, the genetic marker strategy has been largely unrewarding, yielding either inconclusive or contradictory results from one study to another and one type of marker to another.

The second strategy—twin studies—focuses on the coincident appearance of alcoholism in monozygotic versus dizygotic twins. Since monozygotic twins share the same genetic material, greater concordance for alcoholism among identical versus fraternal twins is interpreted as supportive evidence for the genetic hypothesis. Although here again studies have yielded equivocal findings, the results deserve more detailed discussion.

In the most frequently cited study, the one by Kaij (1960), a quite large sample of male twins born in southern Sweden and in which one or both twins had been reported to the local temperance board were interviewed to ascertain drinking habits and psychiatric status. A total of 292 individuals were interviewed and drinking status of each subject was classified according to a five-category system, ranging from abstainers and below-average consumers to chronic alcoholics. The main research strategy was then to determine the extent to which co-twins fell into the same drinking category as their proband sibling. Kaij reported that 25.4 percent of monozygotic co-twins had concordant drinking category classifications as opposed to 15.8 percent of dizygotic co-twins, a finding that was significant at the $p < .05$ level. Of equal, if not greater, import is the finding that if the comparison of monozygotic and dizygotic co-twins was made only for those cases in which the proband twin was classified as a chronic alcoholic, 71 percent of the monozygotic co-twins were also chronic alcoholics, compared with 32 percent of the co-twins of dizygotic probands.

At first glance, these findings are strongly suggestive of a genetic basis for the transmission of alcoholism. However, enthusiasm regarding these findings has been tempered by two factors. First, the study was carried out before widely accepted, standardized diagnostic criteria were available (the Research Diagnostic criteria and the subsequent *DSM-III*), and the robustness of Kaij's classificatory system has been challenged by other investigators. But of even greater concern, a more recent study by Gurling and his colleagues (1981) carried out at the Maudsley Hospital in England—this time using a standardized psychiatric interview, the Schedule of Affective Disorders and Schizophrenia (SADS–L)—has not been able to replicate the Kaij findings. Thus a cautious approach interpreting the twin study data as supporting the genetic hypothesis would appear to be warranted at this point.

On the other hand, the data generated by the third research strategy in this area—the adoption study approach—have been far more compelling. In this approach, comparisons are made between the adopted-out children of alcoholic biological parents versus adopted children with nonalcoholic biological parents. In the most widely cited studies of this type, those of Goodwin and his colleagues (1974, 1977) carried out in Denmark, the adopted-out male children of alcoholic biological parents were almost *four times* more likely to themselves become alcoholic in adult life. On the other hand, no differences were found for adopted-out female children of alcoholic versus nonalcoholic biological parents. This time, other adoption studies yielded findings largely consonant with those of the Goodwin et al. studies, leading Goodwin (1983) himself to suggest the following four "tentative" conclusions based on the data from the various adoption studies:

1. Male children of alcoholics are about four times more likely to become alcoholics than are children of nonalcoholics, whether raised by their alcoholic biological parents or by nonalcoholic foster parents.
2. These children's alcoholism develops at a rather early age, almost explosively in some cases.
3. The alcoholism is particularly severe.
4. The children are no more prone to other psychiatric disorder, including drug abuse, than are sons of nonalcoholics.

Despite the many concerns that have been expressed in various review articles about the validity of the above three "genetic" approaches (including the usual concerns about sampling, validity of diagnostic criteria used, statistical errors, and failure to appreciate the more subtle but potentially profound influence of environmental factors themselves on outcome findings), we nevertheless must be impressed with the overall evidence that at least some forms of alcoholism have a genetic predisposition (Goodwin, 1979).

However, it is also striking that the penetrance of this presumed genetic variable is relatively low. For example, even in the most compelling of the adoption studies—those carried out by Goodwin and his colleagues—only 10 percent of the adopted-out sons of alcoholic biological parents were themselves diagnosed as alcoholic (as compared to 5 percent of adoptees without an alcoholic biological parent.) Even if one combines the three alcoholism-related subcategories in Goodwin's diagnostic scheme—heavy drinker, problem drinker, and alcoholic—51 percent of male adoptees who had at least one biological parent hospitalized for alcoholism did *not* themselves fall into any of these three categories. In fact, it turned out that the adoptees *without* an alcoholic biological parent had a higher incidence of being classified as falling into one of the three alcoholism-related categories than the adopted-out sons of alcoholic biological parents (55 percent versus 49 percent).

The more recent work of Cloninger, Reich, and Rice at the Washington University School of Medicine in St. Louis and of their Swedish colleagues—Bohman and Sigvardsson—are examples of an epidemiological approach to alcoholism that espouses just such a multifactorial model of inheritance (Cloninger et al., 1979, 1981; Reich et al., 1981; Rice et al., 1978). Applying their model to samples in both the United States and Sweden in studies of alcoholism, antisocial personality, and criminality, they attempted to clarify the interaction between genetic and environmental contributions. They differentiated three types of models: (1) *polygenetic*, which does not take into account cultural influences on transmission; (2) *cultural*, which does not consider the genetic contributors; and (3) *multifactorial*, which encompasses the possibility of both genetic and cultural transmission (Rice, Cloninger, and Reich, 1978, p. 619).

Sex differences and assortative mating are a major focus of their studies. Reich and colleagues (1981) identified three kinds of assortative mating that might pertain to alcoholism etiology, as well as the "cultural" explanation for why couples drink similarly. *Social homogamy* stresses the inclination of people to marry from the same socioeconomic classes or groups. With respect to alcoholism, it may be that alcoholism or heavy drinking comes to the fore after marriage and that any similarities in a couple's drinking styles tend to have more to do with their common socioeconomic or cultural background than to specific selection around individual alcohol use preference. In *direct phenotypic assortative mating*, in contrast, certain individuals are drawn to each other and eventually marry because both have a particularly strong propensity to become alcoholic. Thus, it is common drinking styles that specifically attract the couple to each other. The final type of assortative mating is *contagion*, which places the emphasis on one mate influencing the other to drink excessively, thereby eventually leading to similar drinking styles (Hall et al., 1983; Reich et al., 1981).

The Washington University researchers have tested these three types of potential assortative mating with alcoholic and nonalcoholic American families in which both spouses were evaluated (see Reich et al., 1981). They found very high correlations between mates and concluded that, in fact, considerable assortative mating had occurred. In analyzing their data, they concluded that, of the three models, direct phenotypic assortative mating fit their data best. Furthermore, they found that when both spouses were alcoholic, there was significantly increased transmission to the offspring. From a multifactorial model of inheritance perspective, this increased transmission is most likely due to a combination of genetic and cultural factors. The researchers' work is ongoing and this model must, of course, be further tested. However, their position regarding the potential role of culture and genes in transmission is clear in the following quote: "Current etiologic theories must therefore take into account both genetic and nongenetic factors in alcoholism. Indeed, both types of factors are so closely intertwined that an understanding of one cannot proceed without an understanding of the other" (Reich et al. 1981, p. 146).

While this theoretical approach fits well into our own perspective on alcoholism transmission and we are pleased to see it being used by the St. Louis School, there are nevertheless major differences between the types of "environmental" variables we have been examining in our family studies and those addressed by researchers such as Cloninger and Reich. Whereas these other researchers frequently stress relatively discrete and usually more easily measured variables—socioeconomic class, religious affiliation, ethnicity, occupation—in our approach, we attempt to unravel and interpret some of the structural and processual dimensions of family life that affect the course of intergenerational transmission.

What these findings suggest, therefore, is that the final expression of the clinical condition (whether it be called alcoholism, problem drinking, or heavy drinking) cannot be predicted on the basis of biological predisposition alone, but appears instead to be the product of the complex interaction of multiple factors. This multifactorial hypothesis is not only more esthetically pleasing regarding the transmission of alcoholism data, it is also more keeping with the modern argument that genetic predisposition should be viewed as a *priming factor,* a necessary but not sufficient component of the complex process leading to the development of a behavioral disorder like alcoholism. The actual clinical expression of the condition is instead the product of the many interactions that occur between biological predispositions and subsequent environmental experience. It is the distinction, therefore, between factors accounting for the incidence of a particular condition versus factors determining prevalence of the condition.

Why is this distinction being made at the start of this chapter? Because it is important that the reader understand that the descriptions to follow of transmission of alcoholism across generations are not offered in opposition to a genetic argument about why alcoholism is a familial condition. Instead, what we will be describing are those factors within the family environment that serve to increase or decrease the likelihood of transmission of alcoholism to subsequent generations even in those cases in which the form of alcoholism in the parental generation may be genetically based.

The Psychosocial Perspective

To begin our discussion of the psychosocial perspective on transmission, two clinical vignettes provide snapshots of alcoholism transmission in process.

The O'Reillys were one of the families participating in our home observation study (see chapter 6), one component of which was a multiple family discussion group that met on a once-weekly schedule over twenty-four consecutive weeks. The meetings were held in the homes of the subject families, on a rotating basis.

During one of the meetings being hosted by the O'Reillys, seventeen-year-old Mary Beth O'Reilly shared with the group an experience she had had the previous night on a date with her nineteen-year-old boyfriend. After several hours of bowling and beer drinking, they had gone for a drive and had parked to talk. He had brought along a bottle of whiskey and they had finished it off between them over a period of several hours (she had a few drinks; he finished the rest of the bottle). About midnight they had dozed off and when she woke up a half hour later, she had been unable to arouse him to get him to drive her home. So instead, she had driven the car to her house and left it parked in the driveway with him asleep in the front seat. When she got up in the morning, the car was gone. Had she done the right thing, she was asking the group, in leaving him in the car? There is all that stuff about drinking and driving. Should she have driven to his house, or at least taken the keys so he couldn't use the car?

Some of the more aggressive adult members of the group, veterans of AA, began pressing her for more information. Was this a once-only episode? How long had she known this boy? What would she do if something like this happened again? Mary Beth let herself be drawn out on these issues, and although feigning reluctance, managed to share with the group that this was a several-month relationship, that her boyfriend had gotten drunk four of the last five times they had gone out together, but that she found herself extremely attracted to him and suspected that she was falling in love.

She rapidly became embroiled in a vigorous and heated debate with the adult members of other families in the group. Sitting on a couch in her own living room, she argued, in an impassioned tone, about all the positive things she saw in this man, of her fear of losing him if she confronted him about his drinking, of her thoughts about marriage, and of her belief that he was probably "just going through a phase." The more vigorous she was in taking these positions, the more adamant and heated the advice she received in return.

And what about her own parents? Her mother, Carol, said not one word as the discussion went on, instead moving back and forth between the living room and the kitchen getting coffee for group members, answering the telephone once or twice, and leaving her daughter to fend for herself. As for her father, Kevin—he had not even been in the room. Instead, he was at that moment passed out in an upstairs bedroom, hungover from a three-day drinking binge. Every member of the group knew where he was, and why. Yet no mention was made of it as this heated discussion about this seventeen-year-old's intense romantic attraction to her alcoholic boyfriend proceeded.

Our second vignette also is about a family from our home observation study, the Nestor family whom we previously met in chapter 9 in the section on the stable dry, nonalcoholic family resolution. Two years after their initial participation in the study, we interviewed them about how they had been coping during the ensuing two years as part of a protocol intended to collect extensive follow-up data from the families that had participated in the study. The Nestors were a five-member family—Bob, April, a nineteen-year-old daughter, Donna; a seventeen-year-old son, David; and fourteen-year-old son, Dan.

Donna, a junior at a local college, had not been told about the interview by her parents, although it would not have been difficult for her to come to the session. As the interview progressed, it became clear that the family's decision not to inform Donna about the interview was consistent with a more general strategy of excluding her systematically from family life. She was no longer being included in holiday celebrations; vacation plans rarely took her needs into account and therefore characteristically precluded her; her bedroom in the family home had been turned into a studio for April.

As you will recall from our prior description of the Nestors this also was the family in which the identified alcoholic, Bob Nestor, abruptly stopped drinking following an incident in which he was discovered by his children passed out on the bathroom floor after an all-night drinking bout. His own understanding of his drinking and subsequent sobriety was that alcoholism was a personal problem, tolerable only insofar as it did not affect his children. But as soon as they became aware of his drinking problem, it was precipitously stopped.

Now, many years later, the Nestors, in relating their experiences of the previous two years, revealed that the children in this family had not been as successfully protected as their parents had wished. Donna, we were told, had a by now long track record of periodic intoxication, uncontrolled drinking in social situations, and automobile accidents following drinking bouts. During her final two years of high school, her academic performance had become erratic, and confrontations with her parents around curfew limitations, socializing, and rules about driving increased in intensity. As a result, Bob Nestor told us, he became disturbed "to the extent that I was afraid the boys would get the idea that that was the way to do things." He went on, "In part that was the reason I was happy she decided to live in the dorm [at the local college] and not stay at home.... Once she got her driver's license and at some point got her own car [during her junior year at high school], our ability to control her comings and goings was nil. The boys would see her coming in at midnight or not coming in at all. I simply was not prepared to have the boys get the idea that that kind of behavior was the right thing to do. For them, their academic performance will be of more significance, so they can't afford to have that kind of life-style [presumably meaning alcohol abuse, although Mr. Nestor did not explicitly so state at this point in the interview]."

Yet, as the interview progressed, it became clear that this "containment" strategy for dealing with transmission of alcoholism, although seemingly ascribed to by all members of the family, had not been working. During a part of the interview in which disciplinary rules within the family were being discussed, an interchange between April and her older son, David, suggested that he also had been subject to bouts of excessive drinking, and that his parents seemed to have no clear-cut and decisive strategy for dealing with this turn of events. In this particular interchange, April Nestor alluded to an episode of curfew violation following a weekend party when her son seemingly failed to show up at home all night long. In fact, he had made it as far as the front door, "but it turned out he had taken a little nap on the front porch." Disciplinary consequences were supposed to include "grounding him" for the next week, but the plan fell apart when Bob and April needed his help in chauffeuring Dan to several events and allowed the sanctions about socializing and use of the car to slide away as well. But of particular import for our current discussion, the possibility that their son had passed out on the front porch because *he had been drunk* following a late-night party (incidentally paralleling the father's passing out on the bathroom floor many years previously), although it was recognized by both Bob and April Nestor and discussed between them, was never brought up in their discussions with their son.

Both these clinical vignettes deal with the drama of intergenerational transmission of alcoholism in the Alcoholic Family. It is a very real drama, being played out in episodes of considerable poignancy and emotional distress. Although genetic factors may be predisposing these families to deal with this particular drama, its form and content takes its shape from the unique character and social environment of the families themselves. The decisions made by the individual actors in these dramas—Carol O'Reilly's decision to serve coffee and answer the telephone while her daughter was, seemingly desperately, seeking adult guidance about an alcoholic boyfriend; Bob and April Nestor's decision to conceptualize alcoholism as an infectious disease and to extrude a family member who they felt had caught the illness in order to protect the remaining children—are decisions that are difficult to attribute to genetic predisposition per se. Thus what we see here is the family's response to its genetic vulnerability. It is this process—the response pattern—that is the family environmental component in this drama, a component that obviously has great variance across families.

Suppose we were to attempt to predict which of the adolescent children in these two families would at some time in the future be diagnosed as having an alcohol abuse or alcohol dependent disorder. Since in both instances the male parent met the Goodwin et al. criteria for alcoholism (the criteria set used by Goodwin and his colleagues in their adoption study), a presumed genetic predisposition exists in both cases.

What psychosocial environmental factors should we then look to as predictors of the clinical condition in the next generation? The personality characteristics of the individuals involved? Or the birth order of the children in the family, presupposing that this factor presents the child with a unique perspective and developmental history that consequently predisposes them to alcoholism (Blane and Barry, 1973)? Or what about cultural factors and their effects on attitudes toward alcohol use (Bennett and Ames, 1985)? In fact, all of these have been suggested as explanatory factors in the transmission process.* Our own perspective, however, is a *family systems* one, and we therefore limit our discussion of the transmission process to that perspective alone.

The Family Systems Approach to Transmission

The family systems view of intergeneration transmission of alcoholism requires that the transmission process be looked at from two different perspectives. On the one hand, we have the *transmitters*—the Alcoholic Family struggling with the issue of continuity versus discontinuity of this important aspect of its family identity. But on the other hand, we have the *receivers*—usually children within the family who have already, or will in the future, become participants of new family groups and in the process of identity formation associated with these new families have to deal with whether or not to organize their new families around Alcoholic Family identities. Because alcoholism is a condition that often develops insidiously, and the age of maximal risk is characteristically young adulthood, transmission of alcoholism may not become apparent until these new family units have already formed (that is, postmarriage of the children in the original Alcoholic Family). But it is also possible that the transmission issue is already being played out during adolescence, or even at the time of latency. From a family developmental perspective, therefore, transmission is best viewed as a continuous process, a process that is occurring in all three phases of family development.

At the same time, it is characteristically the case that it is during the late phase of development that the transmission process, which may have remained relatively subtle and largely unconscious to this point, becomes more overt and more clearly expressed. It is at this time of development that family identity becomes more sharply defined and that the family attempts to impose its will on its offspring in an effort to ensure intergenerational continuity of this identity. The transmission process, therefore, not only becomes overt at this time, but also takes on dramatic proportions. The stresses and strains that often occur between newly formed families and their families of origin during the early phase (as described in chapter 4) are, at their core, conflicts over the transmission of the family identity. For the early-phase family, the issue is which family of origin to emulate (one, both, or neither) as it shapes its own identity. But for the late-phase

*See the chapter by Steinglass and Robertson (1983) for a comprehensive review of this work.

family, the question is whether or not an already established family identity is to be preserved.

Yet despite the intense struggle that often characterizes the transition between the old and new families around family-identity issues, more often than not the outcome of this struggle has already been greatly influenced or even precluded by what has come before. Just as some churches claim that if they are "given a child until age six" they "will have that child for life," so too is it probably the case that the ultimate outcome of the overt struggles regarding identity witnessed during the late phase of development has been in part determined by factors occurring at a more covert level during the middle phase of development.

This is the perspective we bring to the family environmental component of the transmission phenomenon. We believe that the transmission of alcoholism from one generation to the next involves the whole family system over time. The context for transmission is the sum total of interactions, attitudes, and beliefs that define the family. The process is ongoing and dynamic, and has no particular beginning, end, or pivotal event. And it often goes on outside the awareness of the participants involved, the "senders" as well as the "receivers."

The Importance of Family Rituals. Because our developmental model suggests that it is during middle phase that the crucial seeds of the transmission process are being sown, it also instructs us to direct our attention to those family regulatory processes that play such a prominent role during middle phase—short-term problem-solving, daily routines, and family rituals—to see this process in bold relief. That is, we would expect to see that the extent to which each of these areas is shaped by and organized around alcoholism as a central thematic issue in a particular family, may well presage the extent to which alcoholism is or is not transmitted to subsequent generations of that family.

What does it mean, for example, to find oneself living in a family system that handles important internal and external conflicts via intoxication-induced interactional behavior? What is the lesson learned by the child who comes to associate heightened affective expressiveness or increased physical contact with drinking? Similarly, might we not hypothesize that a family whose daily routines are to a significant degree organized around alcohol is a family more likely to transmit alcoholism to the next generation?

Yet of the three different family regulatory processes noted earlier, the one that conceptually seems most closely linked to the transmission process is that of *family rituals.* Because we believe that rituals contribute so directly to the establishment and preservation of the family's collective sense of itself (the family identity), and because the concept of intergenerational transmission is so intimately linked with the notion of continuity-discontinuity of family-identity issues, it follows that rituals are the regulatory processes most pertinent to focus on as we attempt to track the alcoholism process from a family systems perspective.

A useful way to appreciate how family rituals help us track the process of intergenerational transmission of family behavior pattern is to use, as a metaphor for family transmission, the familiar biological process of cell division. During the initial stages of cell division, genetic material, which is ordinarily dispersed throughout the cell nucleus in strandlike structures called chromatin, gradually condenses and becomes organized as a series of discrete, bounded masses of DNA we call chromosomes. There is, of course, no change in either the total amount of DNA or in the location and sequencing of base pairs along DNA chains associated with this process. That is, the underlying genetic composition of the cell (the "regulators" of cell behavior) remains unchanged. But the organizational characteristics of this genetic material, which previously had been obscure, are now aggregated in clearly discernible clusters. Furthermore, this structural aggregation of chromatin appears to be a necessary prerequisite for successful cell division (mitosis) to occur because as the next state in mitosis, there is an elegant chromosomal dance in which chromosome pairs line up on either side of a dividing line, subsequent to duplicating themselves, and then rapidly separate as the nucleus and cell then divide.

It is a similar process that we are suggesting happens when families go through their version of cell division. In family terms, the issue is also transmission of information to the new cell and it is possible that families also need to package "family DNA" in some discrete way as a preliminary step in the orderly process of "family mitosis." That is, some version of *identity clarification* must occur if family mitosis is to be accomplished, and we would expect to see such a clarification process occurring whenever transmission issues emerge as important developmental themes for the family.

One of the ways of understanding the way family rituals fit into this picture is precisely as a vehicle for packaging, in clearly perceived and bounded terms, critical components of family identity. In this more sharply defined "package," the process of transmission is facilitated in the same way that the packaging of chromatin in chromosomal bodies seems to facilitate successful mitosis. Thus we would expect that the relative importance of family rituals, especially as regards functional relevance, is directly related to the importance of transmission issues at any particular point in family development.

The clearest example of this phenomenon occurs at times when individual family members spin off from the family of origin to form their own nuclear family. Here the actual physical separation ("division") of the family heightens the importance of remaining family rituals. But there are other times during the course of family development when transmission issues also are dominant developmental themes, even though physical separation has not yet occurred. For example, when young children are first being exposed to school situations and peer-group settings that rival the family in determining value systems and moral behavior, greater emphasis on structured family activities, including family rituals, provides a heightened definitional sense of values critical to the family's sense of itself. In this sense, transmission of family identity from one generation to another is clearly occurring and one can therefore see the behavioral concommitants of this process.

Over the past several years, we have carried out two research projects—both focusing explicitly on family rituals as the regulatory behavior of interest—that were designed to test the hypothesis that events or occurrences in the middle phase were predictive of the transmission of drinking problems to the children in these families. In both studies we began with the premise that the middle phase of family life is characterized by relatively stable and accepted family rituals. We then examined how these areas of regular family life were altered—or not altered—in the face of moderate to severe alcohol abuse. Again as in our previous studies, we did not explore some of the "rituals" traditionally associated with the use of alcohol, such as ceremonial drinking, and its implications for introducing children to particular drinking styles or social drinking practices. Nor did we specifically investigate rituals associated *only* with alcohol misuse, such as a child's retrieval of his intoxicated father from the local bar every evening. Instead we attempted to identify the well-established rituals of a family's life and, next, to assess the impact of the alcoholic parent's drinking on those ritual activities or events persisting during midphase (defined in the study as the children's growing-up years). In short, we looked for changes in ritual life that were linked to increases in the frequency and severity of the alcoholic parent's drinking.

One of these studies—the "Heritage study" (described in chapter 5)—examined this question from the perspective of the *receiver* generation. Specifically, its goal was the identification of specific factors in the behavior of the fledging family that might change the pathological potential from the prior generation. The second study—the "Transmission study"—which has not yet been described—examined a parallel question, but this time from the perspective of the *sender* family. The question was: What aspects of the psychosocial environment of the sender family influence the likelihood of alcoholism transmission?

Thus, to explore the question of how family environmental factors increase or decrease cross-generational transmission of alcoholism, we now return to our extensive data base regarding the relationship between family rituals and alcoholism to see whether or not the family's ritual behavior during middle phase is in fact a marker of its success in delimiting the perpetuation of an Alcoholic Family identity.

Family Rituals and the Alcoholism Transmission Process

There are two kinds of hypotheses about the relationship between family rituals and intergenerational transmission of alcoholism—"mechanism" hypotheses; and "marker" hypotheses. A *mechanism hypothesis* proposes that family rituals are actual vehicles for the transmission of an Alcoholic Family identity from one generation to the next. For example, it might be proposed that children *learn* about the important role alcoholism plays in the family's perception of itself when important family events like holidays and vacations are to a significant degree constructed around alcohol use. Such a hypothesis suggests that rituals, because of their condensed and bounded nature and their ability to symbolize important family characteristics, serve to teach and reinforce for family members the critical components that make up a family's unique identity. In this sense, rituals are the mechanisms by which important parameters of family identity, including alcoholism, are conveyed to family members. If alcoholism is an important component of these family rituals, the message to children growing up in such families presumably is that the continuance of family identity in subsequent generations can only be ensured if alcoholism is itself perpetuated.

Marker hypotheses, on the other hand, see the family ritual not so much as the transporting mechanism responsible for transmission of alcoholism across generations, but rather as a product of family identity. It is an accurate and measurable *reflection* of the family's sense of itself. The marker hypothesis takes no specific stance as to whether family rituals are the actual mechanism of transmission of family identity. But whether or not the ritual has this functional parameter, it nevertheless can, according to this hypothesis, be used as a convenient and reliable measure of important parameters of family identity.

In our discussion in chapter 5 of the factors determining the development of an Alcoholic Family identity in the early-phase family, we presented data from a study designed to investigate a "mechanism" hypothesis of alcoholism identity formation (the Heritage study). Extensive historical data was gathered from alcoholic and nonalcoholic siblings and their spouses. The critical design feature was that all siblings came from families that had at least one alcoholic parent.

The central question being asked was why it was that one sibling had developed alcoholism while another had not, even though both had grown up in the same alcoholic family environment. The original hypothesis of the study was that the explanation would lie in the factor we called "family of heritage." That is, each sibling and the sibling's spouse had presumably been engaged, during the early phase of their marriage in a process of identity formation, one component of which was the decision about continuity of the family identities of their two families of origin. It was thought that if this new family organized its identity in a fashion similar to that of the index sibling's family of origin (the family with an alcoholic parent), that sibling would her- or himself be more likely to develop alcoholism as she or he reached the age of highest risk. If, on the other hand, the couple chose to emulate either the spouse's family of origin or to develop an entirely new set of parameters in shaping their family identity, then the transmission of alcoholism would be less likely to occur.

We call this study an example of the investigation of a mechanism hypothesis because it was assumed that the best index of the continuity of family identity would be a comparison of ritual behavior in the newly formed family versus that in the two families of origin. That is, our detailed family-ritual interview would allow us to specify whether the new family had incorporated rituals from the index sibling's family of origin, the spouse's family of origin, both or neither. This determination would in turn, it was speculated, be the best predictor of why the index sibling had or had not developed alcoholism.

The underlying assumption here is that by choosing to continue the ritual pattern of one's family of origin, one indicates that one has learned, incorporated, and accepted the underlying family identity that these rituals reflect. Failure to continue the same pattern of family-ritual behavior in one's own family means that the lesson has never been learned, or has somehow gotten lost, or perhaps has even been deliberately rejected.

Whatever the reason, the proposal nevertheless remains the same—namely, that *family rituals are, in effect, condensed, prepackaged training modules intended to convey to all family members the important facts about family identity.*

As to how this hypothesis held up in this study, you will recall that although specific ritual heritage selection did not prove to be a powerful discriminator of those siblings who had gone on to become alcoholic versus those who had not, a new factor—one we called *deliberateness*—proved to be a very powerful predictor of alcoholism transmission. Deliberateness refers to a conscious decision made by an index sibling to shape and organize his or her family rituals along very specific lines vis-à-vis the two families of origin (a selective disengagement from the family identity of a family of origin containing an alcoholic parent).

The notion that family rituals are the actual mechanisms of transmission of an alcoholic family identity across generations therefore seems unlikely. However, at the same time, the study supported our contention that *family identity* is a powerful explanatory construct. The best way to attenuate the intergenerational transmission of alcoholism was clearly to disengage from one's origin family identity and to develop a new model.

The Heritage study focused primarily on the "receivers" in the transmission process. That is, the critical question being asked was why some siblings received the alcohol "gene" while others did not. Perhaps that is why the behavior of these index siblings and their new families proved so powerful a predictor of the outcome of this process.

Suppose, however, we tried to view the same process from the vantage point of the "senders" (the task we were now setting ourselves). The overall question remains the same—what factors seem to increase or decrease the likelihood of transmission of alcoholism to the next generation. But this time we are interested not so much in what the receivers do to attenuate the potential impact of the risky family environment they grew up in, but rather in what factors in that environment may be more or less virulent regarding the potential transmission of alcoholism. When we looked at the receiver families, we found that deliberateness was the best predictor of the transmission-nontransmission outcome variable. Interestingly, when we turned to the transmission process from the perspective of the sender families, we found that an analogous variable proved to be an accurate predictor of future transmission-nontransmission. This variable is the *subsumptiveness-distinctiveness* dimension previously described in chapter 8.

Subsumptiveness-distinctiveness refers to the extent to which Alcoholic Families modify their family rituals during periods of heaviest drinking in order to accommodate the needs of their alcoholic member. In families in which this accommodation process occurs, family rituals become *subsumed* to the demands of alcoholism, reflecting a disseminated or diffused impact of alcoholism on family identity. In such families, it is to be assumed that alcoholism has invaded virtually every nook and cranny of family life, thereby blurring the limits of its influence and relevance to the family. In the *distinctive* family pattern, however, although alcoholism is still a core identity issue and families may still be organizing aspects of their lives around this issue, alcoholism remains compartmentalized and walled-off, very much like an abscess in the families' midst. In this sense, distinctive families are less "alcoholic" than subsumptive families (that is, according to our definition of the Alcoholic Family).

Chronic abscesses, although localized, are nevertheless serious conditions, often draining resources and energy. But the clinical pictures they present are very different from those of systemic diseases that affect multiple organ systems. As we look at the environments within the "sender" families, therefore, we might hypothesize that a distinctive response pattern, one that walls off and delimits the relationship between alcoholism and family identity, will be a less likely environment for the transmission of alcoholism than the subsumptive response pattern.

The Transmission Study

The Transmission study—the study not previously described—was intended to examine the above hypothesis. As with the Heritage study, the Transmission study used family-ritual behavior as its central behavioral focus.* But this time, family rituals were treated as a reflection of an underlying process rather than as a mechanism of transmission in their own right. Thus, in this instance, the design of the study utilized family-ritual behavior as *a marker variable* intended to reflect *underlying* response patterns existing between chronic alcoholism on the one hand and family behavior on the other.

The core question was whether subsumptiveness-distinctiveness of family rituals during the period of heaviest parental drinking was systematically associated with transmission-nontransmission of alcoholism in the child generation. That is, was the ability of the family to preserve the form and content of its rituals despite the presence of a heavily drinking alcoholic member (the definition of distinctiveness) associated with subse-

*Although we described the Heritage study first, it was actually carried out after the Transmission study had been completed and, in fact, was designed partly as a replication of the Transmission study. Hence the ritual interview described in chapter 5 was really a refinement of a procedure originally developed as a core method for the Transmission study.

quent nontransmission of alcoholism. And similarly, was the tendency to cave in to the demands of alcoholism and alter rituals to accommodate the alcoholic member (subsumptiveness), the historical pattern in families that subsequently proved to have transmitted alcoholism.

It was in this sense that the study's focus was on the "senders" side of the transmission process, on what relevance patterns of behavior in the middle-phase "sender" Alcoholic Family had for transmission of alcoholism, independent of the behavior exhibited by the new "receiver" family. Thus the study was designed around a sample of two-generational Alcoholic Families in which the identified alcoholic was always one of the parents in a family that included adult children. The alcoholism-nonalcoholism status of these adult children then became the major independent variable in the study design.

Therefore, the twenty-five families that were recruited for the study all included at least one parent who met Goodwin's criteria of an alcoholic or problem drinker. In eighteen of the families, the father was the identified alcoholic, in five it was the mother, and in two families, both parents were alcoholics. Families were located through a variety of sources: referrals from counselors in alcoholism treatment centers; private practitioners and members of Alcoholics Anonymous; advertising; and informal contacts. At the time of the interviews, several individuals were in treatment, attending AA meetings, or both. However, ongoing treatment was not a prerequisite for participation in the study. Four of the alcoholic parents had never received treatment for their problem and had never been active in AA.

Individual interviews were conducted with both parents and with as many grown children as were able to participate in the study. Two types of semistructured interviews were carried out with each family member. The first covered the interviewee's personal history, including sociodemographic characteristics, drinking history, and relationships with other members of his or her nuclear family and family of origin. The second interview—the "ritual interview"—concerned the continuity of family heritage from the grandparents' generation into the current nuclear family and sought detailed information about six areas of family life during the children's growing-up years—dinners, holidays, evenings, weekends, vacations, and visitors in the home. Using a standardized series of lead questions, each family member was systematically walked through each of the six areas of family life in which ritualization frequently occurs. For each area, the family member was asked to recall what life was like (a) prior to the time when parental drinking was at its heaviest; and (b) during the period of heaviest drinking. As the family was queried regarding each of the six family life areas, a series of vignettes was gradually built up, that were then available (after transcription from audiotapes of the interviews) as the raw data for subsequent coding.

Coding the Ritual Interviews. From a methodological point of view, the most important feature of the Transmission study was the attempt to systematically reconstruct, via individual interviews, an accurate picture of family ritual life during the family's period of heaviest drinking. But it was also critical that data from these interviews be subjected to systematic analysis if a reliable judgment about the quality of family-ritual behavior was to be made. Thus a detailed coding procedure was developed and applied to these data.

The procedure (which was quite similar to the coding procedure used for the Heritage study, as described in chapter 5) was as follows: All ritual interviews were read by a coder who was guided by a manual designed for the project. (All references to the children's drinking or drinking outcome were deleted from the transcripts.) The coder was asked to answer two main questions about each of the six areas of family life covered by the interviews with each of the twenty-five families: (1) What rituals, if any, did the families have in their lives? And most important, (2) what happened to those rituals during the period of heaviest parental drinking?

The answers to these two core questions were in turn determined by the coder's responses to a series of probe questions within each family life area. The first group of questions was designed to assess the extent to which the family's behavior at a particular time or occasion constituted a ritual. As we have defined it, patterned behavior is repetitive, stable with respect to roles, and continued over a long period of time. To qualify as a ritual, an area of family life must have several additional attributes. Family members must accept the continuation of the patterned behavior, and they must attribute symbolic meaning or purpose to its continuation.

While the ritual-related questions focused on family life prior to the period of heaviest parental drinking, the second set of questions concerned alcohol use and referred to the period when the alcoholic parent's drinking was heaviest. We sought information about the presence of the alcoholic parent, alcohol use, intoxication, the family's response to intoxication, changes in levels of participation in rituals, and the overall change in each family ritual.

In the analysis of each of the six family ritual areas, our coder was asked to examine the family's reported interaction in the period following the onset of heaviest parental drinking (using the second group of probe questions) and to discriminate between two possible outcomes. If there had been minimal change, the ritual was categorized *distinctive* (to suggest that the alcoholic behavior had been kept distinct from the ritual performance). When there was evidence of considerable change, an impact so great that the ritual was substantially altered, the label *subsumptive* (subsumed by the alcohol behavior) was applied. A family-level designation for each ritual area was made by taking a mean for all individual family member's codes.

Thus as the final product of the coding procedure, each family in the study had been placed in one of three different categories based on the coder's formal assessment of changes in family ritual behavior during the period of heaviest parental drinking.

1. *Subsumptive families* were those families in which all six possible ritual areas had been substantively and consistently changed to accommodate the families' alcoholic member.
2. *Distinctive families* were those in which no possible ritual areas were disrupted during the period of family life when heaviest drinking was occurring.
3. *Intermediate families* were those in which approximately half of the possible ritual areas had undergone substantive changes.*

The Analytic Strategy. Since the core objective of the Transmission study was to examine whether the family's adoption of a subsumptive ritual pattern was associated with any increased likelihood of intergenerational transmission of alcoholism, the basic analytic strategy entailed a comparison of the frequency distribution of the two variables of interest —ritual disruption and alcoholism transmission. If a systematic associative pattern was found between subsumptiveness and transmission, then the basic hypothesis of the study would be confirmed.

We have already noted that the ritual-behavior dimension was coded as a three-category variable—*subsumptive* versus *intermediate* versus *distinctive.* The transmission dimension was also coded as a three-category variable. For some families, the child generation already included at least one person who met the Goodwin criteria for alcoholic or problem drinker. Such families were labeled "transmitter" families. In other families, all children were either clearly social drinkers or abstainers regarding alcohol use. These families were labeled "nontransmitter" families. A third group of families, however, contained one or more children who reported histories of heavy drinking with signs that suggested that they might be on their

*Families ranged from having one to five areas of family life that, according to our criteria, constituted "rituals." On the average, each family had two to three such rituals.

313

way toward alcoholic or problem drinking careers. However, because these children had not yet passed through the age of highest risk for development of alcoholism (ages twenty-five to forty-five), it did not seem reasonable to make a presumptive judgment that these families would, at some point in the future, become transmitter families. Thus they were labeled "intermediate" families.

Our twenty-five-family sample proved to have reasonably even distributions along both dimensions of interest—the ritual-behavior dimension and the transmission dimension. Since the variable for the transmission dimension had been controlled for in the sampling process, a relatively even distribution had been assured. The actual figures were as follows: Twelve had no evidence of alcohol problems in the child generation and hence were labeled "nontransmitter" families; in seven families a child or spouse of a child showed some difficulties in the form of heavy drinking and they thus were labeled "intermediate transmitter"; in the remaining six families, clear-cut transmission had already occurred, with problem or alcoholic drinking of a child or married-in spouse, and these families were therefore labeled "transmitters."

The ritual-change dimension, in contrast to the transmission dimension, was not formally controlled for in the design of the study and thus could only be determined after the ritual interview had been completed and coded. However, the families in the sample proved to be fairly evenly divided along this dimension as well. Of the twenty-five families in the study, in eight families, ritual life remained essentially unaltered (distinctive); in ten families, approximately half the rituals were changed (intermediate); and in seven families, all their rituals were greatly modified or destroyed (subsumptive). This distribution means that alcoholism per se does not invariably lead to a degradation of family-ritual behavior. Nor is it invariably the case that families find themselves helpless to resist alterations or modifications of important aspects of ritual behavior in order to accommodate the alcoholic member. As was the case in the data generated by the Heritage study, families clearly have a range of options regarding the shape their ritual behaviors are to take. Thus an examination of the associated patterns between family environment type and transmission outcome becomes a meaningful one to undertake.

The Transmission Findings.   The core findings resulting from a comparison of ritual type with transmission outcome are summarized in table 10.1. The crucial finding reflected in this table is that all six of the transmitter families proved to be either subsumptive or intermediate subsumptive with regard to their family-ritual behavior. An equally striking parallel finding was that only one of the twelve families in the nontransmitter category was coded as subsumptive in their ritual behavior.

It should also be underscored at this point that although the Transmission study's small sample size surely dictates a cautious approach to interpretation, the findings of the Heritage study were entirely consistent with the data summarized in table 10.1. That is, the emergence of an Alcoholic Family identity in the early-phase families described in chapter 5 was related, in part, to the child of an alcoholic parent reporting subsumptive dinnertime behaviors during the parent's heaviest drinking period.

Thus the overall distributional pattern of the twenty-five families in the study suggests that, in general, the greater the change in family rituals during the period of heaviest parental drinking, the more likely the recurrence of alcohol problems in the children's generation. That is, substantial change in family rituals *is* significantly associated with transmission of alcoholism or problem drinking into the children's generation.

Exactly how much ritual change is required to permit a firm judgment that a subsumptive process is at work is hard to say, based on the data from the Transmission study. The fact that six of the ten intermediate ritual-change families were nontransmitters might suggest that dramatic rather than subtle changes in ritual behavior are required before the family environment becomes one that leaves children vulnerable to the cross-generational transmission of alcoholism. On the other hand, this initial attempt at developing a systematic method for coding ritual behavior may require further modification to improve its discriminatory capabilities. In other words, it may be best at this point to focus attention primarily on the four "extreme" cells in the above distributional table. Table 10.2 reflects this approach. As can be seen, the associative pattern between ritual change and alcohol transmission is reflected in bold relief in such a

TABLE 10.1

Ritual Change Type by Transmission Category
(N = 25 Families)

	Transmitter	Intermediate Transmitter	Nontransmitter	Totals
Subsumptive	4	2	1	7
Intermediate	2	2	6	10
Distinctive	0	3	5	8
Totals	6	7	12	25

SOURCE: "Disrupted Family Rituals: a Factor in the Intergenerational Transmission of Alcoholism," by S. J. Wolin, L. A. Bennett, D. L. Noonan, and M. A. Teitelbaum, 1980, *Journal of Studies on Alcohol,* 41, p. 210.

"refined" table. If such a pattern were to be replicated in a large-scale examination of alcoholism transmission, it would be powerful evidence indeed of the linkage between these two phenomena.

In introducing the study, we described it as one that used ritual behavior as a psychosocial marker of important underlying processes in the internal family environment. The basic notion was that ritual behavior, because of its condensed and structured characteristics, might serve as an effective "marker" index of a more fundamental and pervasive process going on within the family—a process centered around family efforts to protect important family behaviors and regulatory processes from being co-opted and distorted by the needs of the family's alcoholic member. Thus the key underlying issue is whether the family is actively behaving in a way that minimizes the potential damage caused by alcoholism. In effect, we are talking about a set of family defense mechanisms, analogous to individual psychological defense mechanisms useful for managing and neutralizing the impact of stressor events, or biological defense mechanisms useful in protecting the body from external pathogens. A careful assessment of family ritual behavior is one way to track this very important process.

The data generated by the Transmission study cannot provide a definitive answer to the questions of whether and how family environment influences cross-generational transmission of alcoholism. But it is instructive to look further at the behavioral characteristics manifested by transmitter versus nontransmitter families as a way of exploring this set of questions in a tentative way (see table 10.3). Suppose, for example, we focus on the issue of the family's stance towards its alcoholic member as a possible index of its relative ability to "protect" the family from potential challenges deriving from alcoholic behavior. Such an analysis yields the following interesting findings.

It turned out that *transmitter families*, reflecting back on family rituals

TABLE 10.2

Ritual Change Type by Transmission Category Without Intermediate Families

	Transmitter	Nontransmitter	Totals
Subsumptive	4	1	5
Distinctive	0	5	5
Totals	4	6	10

SOURCE: "Family Rituals and the Recurrence of Alcoholism over Generations" by S. J. Wolin, L. A. Bennett, and D. L. Norman, 1979, *American Journal of Psychiatry*, 136: 4B, p. 591.

TABLE 10.3

Family Characteristics (Alcohol-Related)
During Rituals, According to Transmission Category *

	Transmitter Families	Intermediate Transmitter Families	Nontransmitter Families
Alcoholic Parent Usually Present	x		
Alcoholic Parent Usually Drinking	x	x	
Alcoholic Parent Usually Intoxicated	x	x	
Family Acceptance of Intoxication	x		
Family Rejection of Intoxication			x
Change in Participation by Alcoholic Parent	x		
Family Acceptance of Change in Participation	x	x	
Overall Change in Ritual Areas	x		
Change in Dinnertime Ritual†		x	
Change in Holiday Ritual†	x		
No Change in Holiday Ritual†		x	x

*An "x" indicates that at least two-thirds of the families in that category conformed to the particular characteristic.
†Does not include families without dinnertime or holiday rituals.

during the period of heaviest drinking, usually recalled the alcoholic parent as not only being present in the home but as usually drinking, *and* as usually intoxicated. Furthermore, the family response to the presence of this intoxicated parent was most often one of acceptance. That is, as these subjects (who were themselves now either alcoholic or married to an alcoholic spouse) recalled what it was like growing up in their own families, they reported a predominant attitude of acceptance and tolerance of intoxicated behavior with few active or negative responses directed at the alcoholic parent.

Because intoxicated behavior was tolerated rather than challenged, a concomitant characteristic in these families was a clear-cut alteration in the alcoholic parent's level of participation in family rituals (usually a diminished one, but in some instances a more prominent role when he or she became more demonstrative with intoxication). The combination of changed level of participation and tolerance of intoxicated behavior invariably meant that some substantial alteration of family ritual behavior had to occur. Thus there was widespread change in the rituals of these transmitter families. Hence the subsumptive or intermediate label applied to all six families in this category.

How did these findings compare with those for the other two groups of

families—the intermediate transmitters and the nontransmitters? Not surprisingly, the intermediate transmitter families, as a group, had some of the
same characteristics as the transmitter families. During ritual times, the
alcoholic parent was usually drinking and was usually intoxicated, and
family members accepted whatever change in level of participation occurred on his or her part.

The nontransmitter families, on the other hand, shared *none* of these
characteristics with the other two groups of families. And the single trait
that most dramatically set these nontransmitter families apart from the
other two groups was their uniform overt rejection of the alcoholic member's intoxicated behavior whenever it occurred while a family ritual was
in progress. This rejection might take the form either of an open confrontation of the parent or of a private "disapproving" discussion among themselves. But whichever it was, the impact on the child was a strong one—
this intoxicated behavior was not to be passively accepted or quietly
tolerated by the family.

Families with different transmission outcomes also differed from each
other in respect to changes in their rituals. While holiday traditions often
were kept intact in both nontransmitter and intermediate transmitter families, holidays in the transmitter families were uniformly altered during the
period of heaviest drinking. Interestingly, the intermediate transmitter
families did not always extend such protection to their dinnertime rituals.
Even in the face of a serious alcohol problem, holidays were the family
ritual most likely to survive without disruption.

If these interpretations of the ritual interview data are correct, then the
key construct that seems to emerge is that of *protection.* Is the family environment being protected from the demands of alcoholism or is it being
altered to accommodate the needs and behaviors of the alcoholic member.
In the language and design of the Transmission study, the issue becomes
how forcefully and effectively the family works to protect rituals from
being co-opted by alcoholism.

When we looked at some attributes of the families in which rituals were
protected, we found a strong relationship between the following characteristics—which we label "protective"—and a lack of alcohol problems in the
offspring: (1) during ritual times the alcoholic parent was not usually
intoxicated; (2) when intoxication did occur, the family actively rejected
the behavior; (3) there was usually no change in the alcoholic parent's level
of participation in ritual life; (4) when there was such a change, the family
actively rejected it; and (5) there was no overall change in the ritual areas
during the period of heaviest parental drinking (see table 10.4).

Nontransmitter families evidenced the highest average number of pro-

TABLE 10.4

Percentage of Alcohol-Related Characteristics
Indicating Family Protection of Ritual Areas* (by Transmission Category)

	Number of Families	Number of Possible Characteristics	Percent Protective Characteristics
Nontransmitter	12	60	53
Intermediate Transmitter	7	35	34
Transmitter	6	30	13
Totals	25	125	36

*Each family contributes five characteristics derived by summarizing coder responses to the five alcohol-related questions applied to all that family's ritual areas. Those codes, designated as "protective characteristics," are:
  a. Alcoholic parent not usually intoxicated;
  b. Family rejection of alcoholic parent's intoxication;
  c. No change in alcoholic parent's level of participation in ritual areas;
  d. Family rejection of any change in alcoholic parent's level of participation in ritual areas;
  e. No overall change in ritual areas during alcoholic parent's period of heaviest drinking.

tective characteristics while the transmitter families had the lowest. The intermediate transmitter families fell in between the transmitter and nontransmitter families. Using Analysis of Variance, we found that the differences in mean number of protective characteristics among the three groups were statistically significant at below the .005 level. The Newman-Kuels test demonstrated that the specific means that differed were those of the two extreme groups (transmitters vs. nontransmitters), statistically significant at below the .01 level.

Conclusion

In this chapter we have addressed that most puzzling of clinical issues—how a psychopathological condition is transmitted from one family generation to the next. In focusing on this issue, we have paid particular attention to those variables most relevant to the family systems perspective. The task, as we have delineated it, is a straightforward one—we need to identify those components of a family's psychosocial environment that, when present, seem to increase the likelihood that alcoholic behavior will be repeated in the next generation.

We have tried to make it clear that this family systems perspective in no way denies the potential importance of genetic variables in the inter-generational transmission of alcoholism. Quite the contrary, our reading of the twin and adoption studies literature leads us agree with the prevailing view expressed by most investigators in this area—namely, that at least some forms of alcoholism (those associated with symptoms of dependence and of highly persistent and voluminous drinking patterns) might well have a genetic component.

However, at the same time it seems clear that much is still not explained by the genetic studies. That is, if there is a genetic basis for transmission of alcoholism, then the penetrance of these genetic factors must be considered at best modest. It is also the case that the populations studied by genetic researchers have thus far been highly selective ones that probably represent only a fraction of those people whom clinicians identify as alcoholic.

The bulk of our chapter has been devoted to a description of a study (the Transmission study) intended to evaluate the role played by the "sender" family in the transmission process. A complementary study (the Heritage study) examining the role of the "receiver" family was discussed in chapter 5. In both studies, however, the central focus was on the associative relationships between family ritual behavior and the transmission of alcoholism.

In discussing the Transmission study, we have been well aware that the study's small sample size, retrospective approach to the reconstruction of ritual behavior during the family's period of heaviest drinking, and nonexperimental study design all dictate a cautious approach to the interpretation of findings. Thus of two possibly hypotheses that we might have proposed in designing the study—that family rituals are the *mechanisms* by which alcoholism is transmitted from generation to generation; or that family rituals are discrete, behavioral *markers* of underlying processes within the family responsible for intergenerational transmission—we have conceptualized rituals as markers.

By doing so, we do not want to imply that we have rejected a mechanism role for rituals. But a hypothesis that family rituals play a causative role in intergenerational transmission of alcoholism simply cannot be adequately tested using a cross-sectional, correlational design (such as that employed in the Transmission study). The best we can say at this point is that there is a strong association between characteristics of ritual behavior and transmission-nontransmission status in the families we studied. At the same time, because rituals are such powerful and symbolically invested aspects of family life and have obvious clinical face validity, the associative data emerging from the Transmission study clearly deserves our attention.

The fact that the study also represented the first attempt to systematically assess family rituals using a detailed coding manual and "blinded" raters to do the assessments further enhances the importance of the findings.

The study's findings can be interpreted at two different levels. At the first level, there is the association between ritual subsumptiveness and alcoholism transmission. Those families that experienced a significant alteration of family rituals during the period of heaviest drinking were also those families in which transmission of alcoholism occurred. At this first level, the finding can be stated either positively or negatively. That is, one could either say that *subsumptiveness* is a *vulnerability factor* present in the family environment, a factor that places subsequent generations at risk to develop alcoholism. Or one could think of *distinctiveness* as a *protective factor*— a family characteristic that helps protect children from the negative consequences of a psychopathological condition in a parent.

Both the "vulnerability" and "protective factor" approaches, however, are statements made about a global assessment of family ritual behavior. Have rituals been altered as a result of accommodating the needs of the alcoholic member or have they continued largely unchanged despite the challenges attendant to active drinking? If the answer is that rituals have changed—that is, that alcoholism has invaded family behavior associated with holiday celebrations, vacations, and the like—then a judgment of subsumptiveness is made. If the reverse is true, the family is judged distinctive.

The second level of interpretation attempts to tease out those qualities of behavior that seem particularly important as contributors to the relative vulnerability-protectiveness of the family environment. From a clinical perspective, it is this second level that is the more interesting one. Here the findings help us identify specific behaviors carried out by nontransmitter families that, by inference, seem capable of protecting children who might otherwise be at risk to develop alcoholism.

In particular, findings point to a single characteristic of behavior as especially important—the families' acceptance-rejection of intoxication when family rituals are being carried out. It is this aspect of behavior that proved to be the single best discriminator of nontransmitter families. In these families, the intrusion of intoxicated behavior during times of ritual was clearly and definitively rejected. In striking contrast, both the transmitter and intermediate transmitter families were relatively pliable on this issue, that is, the Alcoholic Family member was not automatically excluded from participation in family rituals if he or she happened to be intoxicated at the time.

Parenthetically, most of the families who actively rejected intoxicated behavior during times when rituals were occurring were also families whose rituals remained largely unchanged during the period of heaviest drinking. But the second level of analysis suggests that nontransmitter families protected their rituals from the vagaries of alcoholism in a very particular way. The emphasis was not only on preserving the characteristics and continuity of ritual behavior, but was a specific statement, apparently consciously made, that *intoxicated behavior* would not be tolerated while rituals were being carried out. That is, even if circumstances arose in which an intoxicated alcoholic family member could be present at a holiday celebration without any changes in the form or substance of how the holiday celebration was structured being necessitated, such a situation was simply not tolerated by the nontransmitter families. To participate in the family ritual, the alcoholic family member had to be sober.

This characteristic—an active, forceful, apparently conscious strategy on the part of the family—seems quite analogous to the property of *deliberateness* that was discussed at great length in chapter 5 on the early-phase Alcoholic Family. This earlier discussion, which focused on the transmission process from the prospective of the receivers rather than the transmitters, also highlighted a finding suggesting that an active, conscious decision on the part of the family to sever any possible ties between alcoholism and ritual behavior also appeared to diminish intergenerational transmission of alcoholism.

In this earlier discussion, the findings centered on decisions made by the early-phase family regarding which family of heritage they would imitate in shaping their own nascent family rituals. But the qualitative characteristics of the construct of deliberateness (as manifested by the early-phase family) and the construct of rejection of intoxicated behavior (as manifested by the middle- or late-phase family) has much the same feel to it. In both instances, the family appears intent on protecting family rituals from contamination by alcoholism. And it is this determination on the part of the family that seems to be the single most powerful protective element that emerges in the systematic assessment of family rituals we used in both the Heritage and Transmission studies.

Another way to state these issues is to point out that ritual behavior may be as much a marker variable for the family as it is for the researcher. If the variables of deliberateness related to continuity-discontinuity of ritual patterns from families of origin and the variable of rejection of intoxicated behavior during ritual performance are accurate reflections of a family's core stance vis-à-vis alcoholism, then for the family as well, the playing out of family rituals represents a condensed, visible, and symbolic statement of its underlying determination to keep its important identity issues and regulatory mechanisms free of alcoholism. The family ritual, then, because it is so highly condensed and discrete, provides a vehicle for reinforcing, through repetitive reenactment, an overt, direct statement of this *sense of determination.*

Were we to ask families directly about their sense of commitment to the principle of an alcoholism-free family identity, some might be able to respond directly to such a question. But for many families it might prove a difficult question to answer—overly abstract, something they have never directly or consciously thought about, a way of describing their family that might seem somewhat foreign. But when we ask them instead what it was that was so important to them in the way Christmastime was celebrated in the family, or what memories of family vacations are particularly meaningful to them, or what aspects of family celebrations, dinnertime behavior, and vacations they intend to continue in their newly formed family, that same family is now able to respond with gusto and a sense of conviction.

This is the big advantage of our focus on family rituals as a marker of the important, but often only dimly perceived, underlying regulatory functions associated with the development and maintenance of family identity. Because family rituals are the surface behavioral manifestations of these underlying regulatory processes, we are able to ask straightforward questions about whether or not they are organized around alcoholism issues, whether they have changed to accommodate the needs of an alcoholic member, and whether a degradation process has occurred that may reflect a comparable degradation of a defuse and ill-formed family identity. Then, through a careful and systematic examination of these rituals, we emerge with a relatively clear-cut picture of what might be going on at a deeper level within the family.

If such a process has credibility and if findings comparable to the ones emerging from the Heritage and Transmission studies can be replicated in larger-scale investigations, we will have added a major new level of conceptualization to our understanding of how chronic psychopathological conditions like alcoholism are transmitted from one generation to the next. Not only will the role of the family environment in this process be substantiated, but specific aspects of family behavior will be pinpointed as risk factors and potential protective mechanisms in determining outcome of a transmission process. The ultimate payoff in such a process is the hope that, having been able to specify these mechanisms more precisely, we will be in a position to directly intervene to strengthen potential protective mechanisms and to advise families about potential risk factors, with the goal of increasing the family's capacity to attenuate the intergenerational transmission of alcoholism.

PART VI

TREATING THE
ALCOHOLIC
FAMILY

W E HAVE NOW completed our detailed description of the life history of the Alcoholic Family. In providing both clinical and research data about the unique aspects of the three major developmental phases experienced by these families, we have at numerous points alluded to their potential treatment implications. In this section, we take up this part of the story. However, it is not our intention to provide a detailed and comprehensive manual for the treatment of Alcoholic Families. Rather, we want to identify those aspects of the Family Life History model that provide the underpinnings for specific treatment approaches that might otherwise not have been undertaken or considered.

Four issues are central to our discussion of the treatment of alcoholism: First, we now know that families with alcoholic members are a highly heterogeneous group. We have been able to provide extensive clinical and research data to support this contention. Therefore it stands to reason that no single treatment approach will be applicable to every clinical situation.

Second, we have pointed out that not all families with alcoholic members go on to organize family life around alcoholic behavior, but for those who do, alcoholism is so central a feature of family life as to involve and affect every member of the family. It should be self-evident, therefore, that some sort of family-focused therapy must be a key component of the clinical approach to treatment of the Alcoholic Family.

Third, because of alcoholism's proclivity to invade family regulatory behaviors, these behaviors become ideal marker variables of the extent to which family life has been reorganized around alcohol. Thus these behaviors become important foci for clinical evaluation and diagnosis of whether or not one is dealing with an Alcoholic Family.

And f<u>ourth</u>, alcoholism's most profound impact on the family is its ability to distort normative family development. Thus in working clinically with an Alcoholic Family, a developmental perspective is invaluable not only in helping the clinician key in on critical evaluative issues but also in providing a useful framework for the overall design of the treatment plan.

As we discuss these four issues, we will focus our attention primarily on three facets of the treatment approaches for alcoholism: (1) the role of family therapy in the treatment of alcoholism; (2) how to use family regulatory behaviors in the evaluation and diagnosis phase of the work; and (3) how an appreciation of the Family Life History developmental framework informs both the diagnostic and therapeutic approach to the Alcoholic Family.

CHAPTER 11

Family Therapy Approaches to Alcoholism

DESPITE the dramatic growth of family therapy over the past three decades, alcoholism was for many years bypassed by traditional family therapists. Largely ignorant of the prevalence of alcohol abuse and alcoholism in the general population, and poorly trained in alcoholism history taking, family therapists were often unable to accurately identify this condition in their patients. That is, alcoholism often had to be self-identified to be brought to the therapist's attention.

Even when properly diagnosed, alcoholism was often still downplayed, or even ignored. If the patient insisted that alcoholism was the issue to be dealt with, the family might be politely but firmly referred to a special alcoholism program. This was particularly true in family service agencies geared to deal with child- and adolescent-oriented problems. In such settings, therapists often seemed unable to switch gears and focus on alcoholism in a parent rather than on the behavioral disorder in a child.

The ability of family therapists to isolate themselves from alcoholism issues was also furthered by a complementary attitude on the part of the traditional alcoholism treatment community, which viewed alcoholism as a disease of the individual (Jellinek, 1960). As a corollary to this view, it was also thought that family therapy had little relevance to alcoholism treatment. Therefore, when this attitude finally began to change, as compelling evidence of the importance of family factors in influencing the course of alcoholism began to emerge, neither family therapists nor alcoholism counselors were well positioned to introduce family systems based on therapy models into comprehensive alcoholism treatment programs.

For example, one of the first attempts to meaningfully involve family members in the treatment process was an effort at the Henry Phipps Clinic of the Johns Hopkins Hospital to evaluate the use of concurrent group meetings for male alcoholics and their wives (Gliedman et al., 1956). At the same time that alcoholic patients were undergoing a traditional residential treatment program centered around detoxification and group psychotherapy, a separate series of meetings were organized for their nonalcoholic wives. A comparable approach was advocated by Ewing and colleagues (1961) in another of the early studies of the "family therapy" approach to alcoholism.

(In retrospect, the lasting impact of these experimental programs was twofold: first, they convincingly demonstrated that inclusion of spouses increased the likelihood that alcoholic patients would complete their own treatment (in essence, improved engagement in treatment); and second, they appropriately expanded the criteria to be used for successful treatment outcome (previously, abstinence was the sole criterion of treatment success, but these studies included psychiatric and social functioning measures of both spouses as appropriate outcome criteria)[Pattison, 1976]).

(For our purposes, however, these programs illustrate a different point. At a time when alcoholism specialists decided that a family perspective would be a useful addition to their treatment programs, their instinctive solution was to develop a concurrent, but separate program for nonalcoholic spouses. A family systems therapist would have been unlikely to have made such a suggestion. For the family therapist, the appropriate starting point would be conjoint, not concurrent therapy. Alcoholism specialists, on the other hand, being unfamiliar with family therapy techniques, would understandably adopt a more cautious approach.)

By 1986, the alcoholism treatment community's attitude toward the family had undergone a very substantial change. A burgeoning interest in adolescent alcoholism and in adult children of alcoholic parents are just two examples of the way alcoholism treatment programs have expanded their natural constituencies to include the full range of family members and alcoholism-related family issues.

However, although one is hard-pressed these days to find an alcoholism treatment program that does not include family members in some part of the treatment process, it is also the case that the most prevalent approach to incorporating the family remains that of establishing a concurrent, but independent program for family members *ex* the alcoholic member (who is separately detoxified and treated in a behavioral or psychodynamically oriented program that relies heavily on AA involvement to achieve its ends). The popularity of Al-Anon groups, for example, underscores the prevailing feeling among traditional alcoholism therapists that the key to the family component of the treatment process is the psychological "detachment" of family members (often called "co-alcoholics") from the identified alcoholic (Ablon, 1982). Although such an approach is not necessarily incompatible with a family systems perspective, it is also the case that it has not been informed by systems thinking, and hence is not an outgrowth of mainstream family therapy approaches.

Family Therapy Outcome Studies

A review of the family therapy of alcoholism literature underscores the above points. Such a review indicates that although subsequent to the concurrent group therapy approach noted above, clinicians were experimenting with at least three additional approaches to involvement of family members in the treatment process (conjoint family therapy [Esser, 1968, 1971; Meeks and Kelly, 1970], multiple couple group therapy [Cadogan, 1973; Gallant et al., 1973; Steinglass et al., 1977], and conjoint hospitalization [McCrady, Paolino, Longabaugh, and Rossi, 1979; Steinglass et al., 1977]), a careful reading of this literature still supports the view that family systems approaches to alcoholism treatment have yet to fully mature.

To summarize this literature, four general conclusions seem warranted:

1. Both clinical reports and controlled studies are overwhelmingly favorable to the use of family therapy for the treatment of alcoholism. However, with rare exception, all studies published to date should be characterized as pilot in nature. Sample sizes tend to be small, random assignment of patients has been carried out in only a few studies (Cadogan, 1973; McCrady et al., 1986), and details regarding treatment programs and qualifications of therapists tend to be scanty. On the other hand, there are no reports in the literature suggesting that family therapy is either less effective than an alternative treatment approach to which it has been compared, or that inclusion of family members in a treatment program has had detrimental effects.
2. Of the wide variety of family treatment approaches that have been tried, all have been reported to be efficacious; none has occupied a dominant position in the field.
3. Compelling evidence does exist that involvement of a nonalcoholic spouse in a treatment program significantly improves the likelihood

hat the alcoholic individual will participate in treatment as well (Ewing et al., 1961; Smith, 1969). Although this finding would also benefit from large-scale replication, given the consistency of data from multiple studies, involvement of nonalcoholic spouses (at the very least) should be incorporated into all alcoholism treatment programs for patients still living in intact families. A program that chooses to treat only the alcoholic individual should, in the face of this evidence, have a clearly articulated reason for doing so.

4. There is little evidence in the treatment outcome literature that clinicians are approaching alcoholism with a sophisticated sense of family dynamics or family systems principles. Nor is there evidence that clinicians appreciate the heterogeneity of this interesting group of families. Instead, the dominant model in clinical practice remains heavily influenced by the AA/Al-Anon philosophy of "separate but equal" treatment. For example, it would be unusual to find an alcoholism treatment program that incorporates a sophisticated family assessment as a mandatory part of its workup. It is much more likely to find an alcoholic individual and family being pushed and squeezed to fit the preconceived notions, treatment schedule, and goals of an already established program.

Overall, therefore, although the alcoholism field is receptive to the notion that family intervention has an appropriate place in the treatment process, it is still struggling to define the scope and form this intervention should take. A number of detailed texts and articles about family approaches to alcoholism are now available (e.g., Davis, 1987; Kaufman and Kaufman, 1979; Lawson et al., 1983). However, it is also the case that these approaches have not yet been formally evaluated in research designs nor have they received widespread testing in clinical settings.

The Family Life History Model Applied to Treatment

How would a treatment approach based on the Family Life History (FLH) model differ from the more traditional approaches noted above? Although we might point to many different issues in this regard, two aspects of the treatment process best illustrate the differences between a family systems based approach and the more traditional, family-oriented approaches to alcoholism treatment. These are: the importance of differentiating the

Alcoholic Family from the family with an alcoholic member as the critical step in the diagnostic phase of treatment; and the implications of a family-level developmental perspective in the identification of treatment goals and the design of the treatment plan itself.

Diagnosing the Alcoholic Family

Thus far, we have described the life history of that subgroup of families dealing with alcoholism that we have labeled Alcoholic Families and have pointed out (1) that these families have a propensity to reorganize regulatory behaviors in a way that accommodates the needs of the alcoholic member (we have called this process the "invasion" of regulatory behaviors by alcoholism); and (2) that these families also manifest characteristic developmental "distortions" secondary to reorganization of family life around alcoholism as a central developmental theme and priority.

We have illustrated these issues by reviewing a series of clinical case histories and systematic research studies. However, implicit in these discussions was the assumption that the model being evolved also had important implications for treatment. One of the most important of these is the value of the model during the diagnostic phase of treatment.

In focusing attention on the Alcoholic Family, the FLH model suggests that this group of families can be meaningfully distinguished from another group we have called "families with alcoholic members." In that Alcoholic Families can be defined as those in which alcoholism and alcohol-related behaviors have become central organizing principles for family life, a treatment program that leads to a cessation of drinking on the part of the family's alcoholic member will, in such families, have profound implications at almost every level of family life. Thus in such situations, overall treatment success is likely to depend not only on efforts aimed at alcoholism per se, but also on a comprehensive approach to dealing with the family-level implications of the cessation of drinking.

For example, if the Alcoholic Family believes that short-term problem-solving strategies are dependent on the availability of the intoxicated interactional system (see chapter 6), a precipitous alteration in the *family's* sobriety-intoxication cycle is likely to initially have a destabilizing effect on family life. The therapist fully conversant with the FLH model would not only be able to understand why such a reaction on the family's part might occur, but would also be able to anticipate such a reaction and work with the family to attenuate its negative implications.

Of equal import here is the fact that the FLH model also suggests specific areas that can be used as focal points in the diagnostic process. We have repeatedly emphasized the usefulness of three surface-level regulatory behaviors in tracking the intricate relationships between alcoholism and family behavior in the Alcoholic Family. These same three behaviors— short-term problem-solving strategies, daily routines, and family rituals— could be used as invaluable aids in the diagnostic phase of treatment.

Just as we were able to point to specific ways in which alcoholism can invade and alter each of these regulatory behaviors (and detail the implications of such an invasion process), we can now hunt for evidence of this invasion having occurred by taking a detailed history from the family about its problem-solving, daily routines, and ritual behaviors. That is, a modified version of the very same dimensions we highlighted in our discussions of our research designs can now be used in the service of accurate diagnosis of the Alcoholic Family. Hence, during the diagnostic interview, not only is it critical to be taking a history from the whole family rather than from the alcoholic individual alone, but it is also crucial that the interview schedule include specific questions about the nature of family regulatory behaviors and evidence that these behaviors have been altered in fundamental ways during periods of heaviest drinking. (We provide examples of specific questions that might be asked during the diagnostic interview later in this section.)

Thus, the ability to distinguish during the diagnostic phase of treatment the Alcoholic Family from its counterpart, the family with an alcoholic member, gives the therapist important leverage not only in selecting an appropriate treatment plan, but also in being able to quickly focus on key areas where alcoholism may have invaded and distorted family life.

Implications of a Developmental Perspective

The FLH model hypothesizes that at different phases, the Alcoholic Family is dealing with profoundly different systemic tasks. Hence both the subjective and functional meaning of alcoholism for the family changes dramatically as it moves from one phase to another. Therefore both the timing of the request for treatment and type of clinical presentation will vary considerably from one Alcoholic Family to another, depending on their systemic maturational phase.

For example, in the *early-phase* family, because the central maturational task is the differentiation of the new family unit from its families of origin and the coincident development of a family identity, the family's reaction to the alcoholism issue can be largely understood in terms of its struggle to establish a solid family identity. Thus the early-phase family's tendency to over- or underreact to the potential hazards of alcoholism is, in large part, a function of the role alcoholism is playing in the identity-formation process. If the family is determined to establish an identity clearly separate from that of one of the families of origin that also contained an alcoholic member, one might expect it to seek therapy at the slightest hint that an alcohol problem is arising in one of the spouses. On the other hand, attitudes toward alcohol that are profoundly different from those of an abstinent or teetotalling set of parents would lead to exactly the opposite situation.

By way of contrast, in the *middle-phase* family (in which an alcoholic identity has already been established), the focus on short-term stability and the tendency to employ rigid homeostatic mechanisms that often incorporate alcoholic behavior as part of short-term problem-solving makes it unlikely that such a family will use the alcoholism issue as a presenting complaint in therapy. If it does, it is probably an indication that a crisis has arisen, generated either by external events (loss of job, drunk-driving arrests, etc.) or events internal to the family (violence associated with intoxication, physical deterioration, etc.). The more likely situation, however, is that the family will present with a presumably nonalcohol-related problem, and a fuzzy but suspicious history of abusive drinking might emerge in the initial sessions. In such a case, it is usually up to the therapist to decide whether or not to shift the focus to deal with alcoholism as the primary issue.

Then we have the *late phase*, when the central issue is often the transmission of values to the next generation (what we have called the family's "place in history"). Two common problems present themselves at this point: the drinking behavior of a child of a "recovered" stable dry alcoholic family, and a need on the part of children who are on the verge of leaving the family to bring resolution to the alcoholism issue before departing. In these instances, the therapist is often called upon to provide guidance about appropriate priorities for the family. For example, should the therapeutic goal be a successful separation of children from the Alcoholic Family system, or are all interests best served by focusing on the family as a unit even though it might be a time when individuals within the family are attempting to establish their own independence?

Clearly, a uniform treatment approach that "plugs" each family into a standard treatment package, (e.g., a period of detoxification, a mandatory residential treatment phase, and a fixed number of family interviews), would hardly be appropriate to all of the above problems. Therapy must therefore be designed to take account of both the developmental phase and of the unique developmental needs of each family *and* of each individual within the family.

The following clinical examples illustrate these points.

An Early-Phase Family. Jonathan Danbury, a twenty-nine-year-old employee of a large international corporation, called about a possible psychiatric consultation on the advice of his closest friend. In a conversation with his friend, Mr. Danbury had expressed concern about the fact that he and his wife were due to leave for a three-year overseas assignment in four months and he had learned that availability of medical services (especially psychiatric services) would be poor in the country to which he was being posted. A brief review of Jonathan Danbury's areas of concern, carried out by the psychiatrist during the initial phone contact, revealed some nagging doubts about "my pattern of alcohol consumption"—something Mr. Danbury wanted to have "checked out" before he left. The psychiatrist suggested that Jonathan and his wife come together for the initial assessment and Jonathan agreed to this recommendation.

The Danburys proved to be an engaging couple with many assets. Intelligent, attractive, and quite committed to each other, they had nevertheless experienced some major difficulties in their five-year marriage. These difficulties centered around two main issues (which were initially presented as unconnected)—sexual problems attributed to Marcia Danbury's "inhibitions," and Jonathan's drinking habits.

As the couple described their life together to the psychiatrist, it became clear that they had developed two very different time-dependent styles of interacting with each other. The first pattern—an avoidance pattern—occurred during weekday evenings. During these times, they often ate separately and managed their work schedules without checking with or informing each other. Thus they would frequently return home at very different times, have different plans for the evening, and make no effort at coordinating sleep schedules. As might be imagined, sex was infrequent, and unsatisfying when it occurred.

The second pattern—an engagement pattern—which was almost diametrically opposite—characteristically occurred only during weekends. Plans were always highly coordinated; the couple jointly prepared and took great pleasure in extravagant meals; and sex was also an integral part of this interaction pattern. The weekend pattern was also invariably associated with very heavy consumption of alcohol by both spouses, whereas during the week Marcia rarely drank; during these evenings, only Jonathan drank (although he was a heavy drinker during these times as well as during the weekends).

As described by the Danburys, the important characteristics of a typical weekend were as follows: The couple would begin drinking together upon their arrival home on Friday afternoon, and all weekend meals were accompanied by consumption of very considerable quantities of wine and beer. The couple was therefore invariably intoxicated when sex occurred, a factor that frequently interfered with the sexual performance of both partners. However, they seemed able to avoid arguments around sexual issues—arguments that had been a common occurrence during the early years of their marriage.

Thus we can already see in this couple clear-cut data about the emergence of an alcoholic identity in early phase. (A particularly clear picture emerged when the psychiatrist asked about the structure and quality of the couple's daily routines (further evidence of the value of focusing on the relationships between alcohol use and family regulatory behaviors as a crucial part of the evaluative phase of treatment). The dramatic contrast between weekday and weekend routines are of import in that they were so clearly organized around alcohol use. Further, we were hearing about two fundamentally different interactional states and it was the intoxicated interactional state (the one that emerged during weekends) that had served the purpose of blunting this couple's very substantial conflicts over sexual difficulties.)

Questions about the celebration of family rituals proved equally helpful in pinning down the diagnosis. For example, the couple reported that visits to her parents for holiday meals included a new dinner-table ritual. Her parents and siblings had always been very modest drinkers. A perfunctory bottle of wine had been served at meals, but was rarely consumed. Recently, however, a second bottle of wine had been added and was placed in front of Mr. and Mrs. Danbury's place settings. Invariably, the couple completely consumed both bottles by the time the meal was completed. (Answers to questions about how this new ritual had developed indicated that Marcia's parents seemed puzzled by the couple's drinking habits, but also seemed willing to accommodate their need for alcohol in order to include them at holiday meals. Although concern about the drinking was expressed, the position taken was that it was Jonathan and Marcia's problem and that they must work it out themselves. Thus in the area of family ritual practice as well, there was concrete evidence that this couple's alcoholic drinking behavior had invaded this form of family regulatory behavior.)

Thus, this is a couple that in the early phase of its marriage had clearly come to organize important aspects of life around alcohol use. At the same, however, two mitigating factors had helped to keep the couple from fully embracing an alcoholic identity. First, alcoholism was a novel event in the family's history, neither family of origin had had pathological family drinking histories. The couple's break with tradition was thus as clear to them as it was to their parents. Yet this was a couple that felt closely attached to both families of origin, and thus the desire to perpetuate rather than to break with long-standing family traditions was strong. In this sense, the emergence of alcoholism and the growing recognition of the extent to which it had invaded and altered family ritual practices was extremely disturbing and ego-dystonic for this couple.

Second, the couple had become acutely aware of their psychological dependence on alcohol. They reported that they found themselves increasingly impatient, during the week, for time to pass quickly and bring them to the weekend activities. For two young professionals who had previously taken great pleasure in their work, this increasing sense of depression and dysphoria associated with the sober interactional state was readily perceived as abnormal, and hence something they could acknowledge concern about.

Thus we could appreciate why the impending posting to a foreign country had brought the issue to a head and led to the request for a psychiatric consultation. That is, what posed such a threat for the couple was the impending separation from their two families of origin at a time when the they were attempting to understand what was happening to them as they gradually embraced an alcoholic identity. What had previously been only dimly perceived, perhaps because the family had adopted a strategy of accommodation rather than of challenging the couple's alcoholic behavior, was now seen in bold relief as the couple attempted to come to grips with the isolation from extended family influences attendant on the move to a foreign country. This type of clinical presentation, we would contend, is typical of the early-phase Alcoholic Family, and is quite different in flavor from that of the other families to be described.

A Middle-Phase Family.   Joseph and Olivia Scott, a couple in their early thirties, married seven years, sought help because of Joseph's drinking. A clinical history revealed that he began drinking heavily while still in high school, and had serious alcohol problems while in the military service, including recurrent drunkenness during military leaves and at least one documented blackout. Joseph's father also had had a history of chronic alcoholism that was resistent to multiple treatment efforts, but gradually diminished in his fifties, leaving him with some residual liver pathology. However, Joseph's parents remained married throughout his father's more than thirty years of serious drinking.

The couple was fully aware of Joseph's serious drinking problem before they decided to get married. He drank heavily throughout their courtship, on a number of occasions becoming quite intoxicated in his fiancée's presence. After they were married, Olivia assumed the role of primary wage earner, enjoying steady employment as a computer programmer. Joseph had numerous jobs, but his longest period of steady employment was seven months.

About three years ago (although it was never openly so stated), a semipermanent arrangement had been made for Olivia to be responsible for income generation, and Joseph to attend to the cooking and housekeeping tasks. During this period of time, Joseph had settled into a pattern of almost constant heavy drinking, daily periods of intoxication, and a highly irregular sleep and meal schedule. However, he had never needed to be hospitalized for detoxification and there had been no episodes of family violence.

Why then, given this multiyear history of chronic alcoholism, and the fact that the chief complaint here was drinking that had for many years seemed quite compatible with family rules and behavior, had this couple presented themselves for treatment at this particular time? The answer lay in a developmental event, *the impending birth of the couple's first child.*

The reason that this event posed a problem was because the couple had decided that after the child was born, Olivia was to return to work and Joseph was to continue to handle management of household tasks. Care for the baby, particularly during daytime hours when Olivia was at work, would be his responsibility. They liked this pattern of life and wanted it to continue. The drinking behavior, which previously not only did not interfere with this organizational structure, but might even have been thought of as supporting it, now presented the couple with the problem of how he could be trusted to take on *parental* responsibilities during the day if he was intoxicated.

A therapist who was oblivious to this developmental issue might easily have misinterpreted the couple's own therapeutic goal, which was to insure that the basic organizational structure of their marriage remain intact in the face of the birth of their first child. They had not come with a request to treat the alcoholism per se; if they could have found a solution for their problem without having to disrupt husband's drinking, they would have been more than happy to embrace it.

It would be particularly important that the therapist appreciate the developmental issues involved here, because a treatment program primarily directed at drinking behavior might have had, as one of its goals, the "vocational rehabilitation" of the alcoholic patient. This is not to say that such a goal would be an inappropriate one, merely that it was not the couple's goal when they initially presented for treatment. The therapy

(approach in this instance would therefore have to be primarily organized around helping the family to deal with a major developmental transition, and to shape the alcoholism treatment component to fit the primary goal.)

A Late-Phase Family.   Our third example is the Leighners, a family already discussed at some length in chapter 6. Henry and Joan Leighner and three of their children, ages twenty-eight, twenty-four, and eighteen, had been seen for a series of family therapy sessions. Both Mr. and Mrs. Leighner had been drinking at alcoholic levels since the early years of their marriage. The request for treatment, however, was initiated by their oldest son, Stephan. Now married, and himself the father of two children, he had been prodded by his wife to "do something about your mother."

With his wife acting as offstage director, Stephan had spoken to his two siblings and obtained their agreement (despite their considerable misgivings) to contact a family therapist. The presenting complaint was to be his mother's drinking (although it was freely acknowledged within the family that his father was, if anything, an even heavier drinker), on the assumption that if the therapist and children presented a united front, Joan would have to finally confront the consequences of her years of alcohol abuse.

As outlined in chapter 6, a course of family therapy meetings culminated in Joan's dramatic recounting of how alcohol had helped "save" her son, Michael, from possible death, an episode that said a great deal about this woman's perceived connection between alcohol use and short-term problem-solving.

Now, however, we want to focus on therapeutic issues and from this perspective, we must confess that were we to measure therapy against an outcome standard of change in drinking, this particular case would have to be judged a treatment failure. For Joan Leighner was drinking just as heavily at the close of a fifteen-session course of family therapy as she was when brought in by her children. Episodes of abusive interchanges with neighbors, with service providers in public settings (waiters, clerks, and others) and with her husband remained frequent whenever she had been drinking heavily.

But if we assess this case against the developmental parameters we have outlined in our theoretical discussions, the most important factor to keep in mind is that the Leighner family was in the *late phase* of family development. That is (the critical developmental issues centered around the nature of the ongoing relationship between the parental and child generations in this family, and this struggle was clearly centered around alcoholism as a core identity issue.)

The parental generation, with Joan Leighner acting as spokesperson but her husband clearly in concurrence, insisted that alcoholism remain a central organizing theme for family life (Not only was her drinking and her husband's to continue unabated, but their relationship with each other, and the relationship between the family and its external environment, was to be regulated to a significant degree by problem-solving strategies incorporating aspects of intoxicated interactional behavior.

As spokesperson for this position, Mrs. Leighner was, in effect, stating the family's "last will and testament," the family identity, to be passed on to succeeding generations. (But her children, the people presumably on the receiving end of this legacy, were unwilling to be the passive recipients of such an inheritance. In particular, Stephan, the oldest child in the family, now married and himself a father (and therefore simultaneously engaged in the early phase of development of this next-generation family) was having to negotiate inheritance issues not only with his parents and siblings, but also with his wife.

And this "new member" of the family had clearly brought with her a different set of rules and values concerning her in-law's drinking. Passive acquiescence and lack of clarity about late-phase resolution of the alcoholism issue was not acceptable to her. The issue had to be directly confronted and a conscious decision made about continuity-discontinuity. That is, if her husband's family of origin was to be included in the identity development of this next-generation family, the late-phase resolution would have to be a nonalcoholic family resolution. Otherwise, their family heritage would come from her lineage, not his.)

Of the two other children in the Leighner family present at the family sessions, Douglas, the youngest son, claimed to have made a total break from his parents. He had his own household, showed no evidence of alcoholic drinking, and on the surface appeared to have successfully separated himself from the more pathological aspects of his family environment. However, as part of the presenting history, we heard that he had been able to develop only superficial relationships with women, largely because he felt distrustful of intimate relationships and wary of any thoughts of marriage.

The middle child, Michael, (the son who was the subject of Joan Leighner's dramatic medical anecdote), continued to live at home with his mother and father. Although prodded by his brothers to get a place of his own (he had a full-time job and could easily have afforded his own apartment), he had been reluctant to leave home, feeling that to do so would leave his mother at the mercies of a destructive and perhaps even sadistic husband.)

Thus the developmental perspective suggested that the request for treatment had been stimulated primarily by a demand from outside the family (Stephan's wife) for a resolution of the alcohol issue. The Leighners, it would appear, would either have to switch from Alcoholic Family to nonalcoholic family status, or be excluded from the identity formation process going on in the next-generation family. That is, a precipitating event was occurring that was propelling the Leighner family from the middle phase to the late phase of development. Therefore, this was a request for treatment coming at a time of developmental crisis.

Using this perspective alters our thinking regarding treatment goals and outcome criteria. If the central issue is continuity-discontinuity of alcoholism heritage, and if a developmental analysis suggests that the Leighners, if left to their own devices, would remain arrested in the middle phase of development, an appropriate goal for treatment might have been to assist the family in making the critical transition into late phase, independent of the actual late-resolution choice they made. Treatment would then have been measured only partly in terms of drinking behavior. Additional criteria might be evidence that each of the children within the family was able to tackle an age-appropriate developmental task relevant to their own role within the family.

Thus the oldest son would be able to actively participate with his wife in identity formation issues associated with the early phase of their new family; the youngest son would be free to explore and develop intimate relationships and consider marriage as a viable alternative for his life; and the middle son would be able to successfully separate from his parents, establish his own household, and also allow himself to participate in intimate relationships.

A three-year follow-up of the Leighner family indicated that each of these outcome goals had been met, at the same time that Mr. and Mrs. Leighner's drinking behavior and interactional style had remained largely unchanged.

The Course of Therapy with a Typical Alcoholic Family

No two clinical cases are exactly alike. Nevertheless, it is possible, in family therapy with an Alcoholic Family, to identify four characteristic stages that invariably follow the same sequential order. Not all families complete the entire four-stage process, but with rare exception, it behooves the therapist to structure the course of therapy with the following sequence in mind.

Stage I. Diagnosing Alcoholism and Labeling It a Family Problem

During this first stage, the therapist, identified alcoholic, and family try to reach a common understanding about the problems at issue and their order of priority. (This stage, usually synonomous with an evaluation or assessment phase, includes careful history taking regarding drinking behavior, prior treatment contacts, family perception of alcohol consumption and its consequences, and coping behaviors used to tackle the problem)

(The main questions that must be answered during this first stage of therapy are: whether this is an Alcoholic Family or a family with an alcoholic member; whether alcoholism is the primary treatment priority; whether family therapy is appropriate here; and whether an acceptable treatment contract can be worked out with the family.)

Stage II. Removing Alcohol from the Family System

If an alcohol problem is identified, and the therapist and family agree to work together on this issue, then therapy moves to the second stage, the stage of "removing alcohol from the family system." Meaningful therapy with an Alcoholic Family cannot proceed if the therapist adopts a laissez-faire attitude about drinking behavior and acquiesces in a decision to allow the identified alcoholic to continue drinking. The therapist must take a firm stand on this issue at the start of therapy, while at the same time acknowledging that it may not be an easy task and that there may be a number of slips before abstinence is finally achieved)

This second stage of therapy is sometimes accomplished in short order, but more often than not is a difficult stage to maneuver. It is critically important that both therapist and family have the goal of this stage clearly in focus and not be diverted by other issues, no matter how compelling they may at the time appear) Contracting models (what Haley [1976] has called "problem-solving therapy") are particularly useful during this stage of treatment.

Stage III. The Emotional Desert

A wet Alcoholic Family that suddenly finds itself dry is in a highly unstable and tenous position. For an extended period of time, perhaps as long as husband and wife have been married, family life has been organized around the microscopic cycling and macroscopic phasing tied to the on-again off-again drinking patterns of the alcoholic member of the family. Short-term problem-solving has incorporated aspects of intoxicated interactional behavior. The family may have accommodated important aspects of family life, such as family rituals, to the needs of the alcoholic member. Alcoholism has become a familiar and predictable way of life for the family. Emotional and interactional distance in the family has been regulated by behavioral mechanisms that have become closely tied to alcohol-related behaviors.

Suddenly, drinking has stopped. Intoxicated behavior and the interactional state that accompanies it has ceased to exist. Most families, when they experience this sudden shift, have the sensation of having been cut adrift, loosened from their familiar moorings, lost in a desert without any landmarks upon which to focus to regain their bearings. This is particularly true of emotional life within the family. Rather than experiencing a sense of exhilaration that drinking has stopped, families instead experience a profound sense of emptiness. A depressing pall hangs over the family.

This is the third stage in the therapy process, a stage that has been called the "emotional desert."* It is a time of intense dysphoria for all family members, not only for the alcoholic member who has stopped drinking. Pressures to return to the old way of life will be intense. The family must be helped to tolerate this stage and to reestablish a sense of stability that, this time, will be achieved without the use of alcohol-related behaviors.

Stage IV. Family Restabilization Versus Family Reorganization

After the emotional desert has been weathered, therapy enters its final stage, a resolution phase. The sobriety-intoxication cycle has been broken and a new homeostatic level has been tentatively achieved. The family must now regroup around this still unfamiliar "dry alcoholic phase." Often, this process leads to a resolution that does not fundamentally alter a family's sense of itself.

As was discussed in chapter 9, many families achieve sobriety but remain focused on, and organized around, alcoholism issues. We called this type of resolution the stable dry Alcoholic Family, and it is perhaps the most common outcome of therapy for the middle-phase Alcoholic Family. It is a successful outcome, but its success remains tied to alcoholism as a core feature of family life. The basic relationship patterns within the

*We are indebted to our colleagues, Marion Usher, Jeffrey Jay, and David Glass for their contributions in identifying and carefully describing this stage to us.

family have remained by and large unchanged, but alcohol consumption and intoxicated behavior are no longer necessary components of the regulation of these relationships. For such families, the fourth stage of therapy centers around a process of "family restabilization.")

In other families, the first three stages of treatment precipitate a crisis, the resolution of which leads the family to achieve a fundamentally different organizational pattern. In such situations, the fourth stage of therapy might be called one of "family reorganization." In these cases, the third stage of therapy tends to be far more abbreviated. The tensions and pressures that build up in the family during the third stage create a sense of crisis that propels the family into first, a stage of functional disorganization and then a phase of reorganization. This process has been called "discontinuous" or "second-order" change in the family therapy literature (Hoffman, 1981; Watzlawick, Weakland, and Fisch, 1974). Often when family reorganization is the goal, this fourth stage tends to be one of marital, rather than family therapy.

A Clinical Case: Stages I and II in the Treatment of a Hypothetical Middle-Phase Alcoholic Family

The four-stage treatment model outlined above is most distinctive in its approach to diagnosis and detoxification of the Alcoholic Family. Although all four stages keep family systems principles firmly in mind, the model most clearly reflects these principles in its suggestions that: (1) a critical task of the first stage of treatment is the accurate diagnosis of the Alcoholic Family; and (2) for the Alcoholic Family, detoxification must be conceptualized as occurring at the *family,* rather than the individual, level.

To provide a better flavor of how these two stages of therapy actually unfold, we will now describe in detail how Stages I and II of treatment might go if one were treating a typical middle-phase Alcoholic Family. The "case" to be described is not based on a single family, but rather on a number of Alcoholic Families we have seen. Our composite case will not only allow us to illustrate in sharper fashion some of the critical issues we want to discuss, but will also afford us the opportunity to discuss a series of options open to the therapist at critical choice points along the way as therapy unfolds.

Stage I: The Labeling Process

The family we have in mind, the Browns, live in a medium-sized, industrial city and have been there for several generations. Michael and Bernadette Brown are in their early fifties and have two children, David and Kathy, both of whom still live with them. Michael Brown is a machinist; Bernadette Brown a part-time secretary. David, the older child, is twenty-five years old, has never married, and has tried unsuccessfully on several occasions to set up his own apartment or to live with friends (the last time this occurred was two years prior to our initial interview with the family). Kathy, the younger child, is seventeen and is the ostensible reason for the Brown family having contacted us.

We have been told, over the phone, by Bernadette, that Kathy has suddenly, within the last two months, been manifesting defiant and disturbing behavior, including probable promiscuity, repeated curfew violations, deliberate lack of attentiveness to family chores, and a sudden deterioration in schoolwork. Following the phone contact, the family was encouraged to come in together for an evaluation, a suggestion to which they readily agreed.

Thus far, the presenting picture is a familiar one. An adolescent family member suddenly manifests uncharacteristic behavior that leads the family to seek a consultation. Most family therapists, confronted with this chief complaint, would assume that Kathy's behavior is related to a disruption in the family's homeostatic balance and that attention to the family's structural and dynamic characteristics is the most efficient way to deal with it. However, they would be less likely to assume that the critical underlying issue is alcoholism and that Kathy's behavior is at least in part related to serious conflicts between family members about what stance to take regarding alcoholic behavior on the part of another family member.

The interview starts with Bernadette's review of her daughter's behavior, with emphasis placed on both its defiant quality and the dramatic shift in her daughter's mood and attitude over the past few months. As her mother talks, Kathy gesticulates, criticizes, shouts, looks and acts defiant, and seems in this fashion to be validating her mother's description of her. The family men watch this mother-daughter performance silently.

The therapist moves from one family member to another, asking each to make a brief opening statement about his or her version of the presenting problem. Kathy remains the focus of attention. All four family members talk only about her behavior as "the problem" but there is mild disagreement about the effectiveness of strategies used by the family to bring her back into line. So far, therefore, nothing was unusual.

The therapist makes his first intervention. He says that the Browns seem to him a family in which the mother takes her job very seriously, and is worried about her daughter. After suggesting that it is, after all, quite appropriate for mothers to worry about their children, he asks the family to describe ways in which other family members might also be helping mother to be a good mother by giving her cause to worry.

Those readers familiar with structural and strategic approaches to family therapy recognize in this intervention a typical "probe" by the therapist, intended to momentarily stress the family by disrupting its customary behavior, in this case the repetitive sequences of accusations and counteraccusations regarding Kathy's behavior that have thus far dominated the session. The therapist's "reframing" question, by suddenly changing the context of Kathy's behaviors, breaks into the family's rhythm for dealing with the session and tests the family's ability to change its way of looking at a problem—in effect, a testing of the family's relative rigidity versus flexibility.

The family is of course at first confused and startled by this question. But the Browns prove able to accept and deal with the challenge. David volunteers the information that in addition to his sister's behavior, Bernadette has been concerned about the difficulty Michael Brown has had in keeping a steady job. Queried about David's revelation, Michael admits that he has had a lousy employment record during the past ten months, having been transferred to four different units within the factory during this time. It is only his union seniority, his son adds, that has kept him from being fired outright. Does he "quit" or is he "fired," the therapist asks. He is always "fired," he replies, and the critical event is invariably an intense and verbally abusive argument he has with his immediate supervisor.

We are now at a critical turning point in the interview. Two facts have been revealed to the therapist that separately or in combination are highly suggestive that Michael Brown is drinking at abusive or alcoholic levels. We have been told first, that his employment record has deteriorated dramatically within the past year and second, that his work transfers are precipitated by a series of verbal confrontations with supervisors (behavior hardly in evidence during the consultation session in his manner of interacting either with the therapist or with other family members).
(Obviously neither employment difficulties nor verbal outbursts are pathognomonic of alcoholism. But both are strongly associated with problem

347

drinking. A therapist sensitive to these associations will, at this point of the interview, be suspicious of the existence of an underlying alcoholism problem and will shape the interview to ensure that such a possibility is thoroughly assessed. A therapist sensitive only to family pathology and ignorant of the typical presenting pattern of chronic alcoholism will, in all likelihood, ignore these "warning signs" and never learn that Mr. Brown already has a serious alcoholism problem.)

At this point, we ask Michael Brown to give more details regarding his confrontations at work. Does he find it easy to fight with his bosses or does he have to get himself up for the fight? He seems to the therapist to be a relatively mild-mannered man. It is hard for the therapist to imagine him "blowing his stack." Does he need some help to do that?

What does the therapist mean by "help," Michael asks. Some people, he is reminded, find it easier to state their mind after they have had a drink or two; people who ordinarily do not like arguments and tend to avoid confrontations. Is he one of those people? Sure, he replies, it is easier for him if he relaxes first by having a drink or two, but what does that have to do with anything?

(Such a challenge is a characteristic response from patient to therapist when the issue of alcohol is first raised. But it is central to the task of this first stage of treatment, the assessment of whether or not a serious alcohol problem exists in this family, that the therapist have available enough data to make a professional judgment regarding the presence or absence of alcoholism.)

Therefore, it is critically important that the alcoholism issue not be sidestepped or handled deferentially at this stage in the interview out of the mistaken belief that it is too delicate an issue to be confronted directly via specific questions addressed to family members. If the therapist has only a marginal suspicion that alcoholism is an issue in a particular case, then he or she will sample family opinion, ask a few questions about quantity-frequency of alcohol consumption and, if answers from all family members are uniformly negative, drop the alcoholism issue and return to the previous tack of the family interview. If, however, his or her level of suspicion is stronger (as is the case regarding Michael Brown's drinking), it will only be satisfied after a series of "target" areas that can be used to evaluate whether or not alcoholism is present have been thoroughly explored.

Examples of target areas that can prove useful at this point, of course, include such individual-level parameters as quantity-frequency of alcohol consumption, blackouts, evidence of physical addiction, hiding of bottles, evidence of intoxicated behavior, and so on. But this is also the time to investigate whether or not alcoholism has invaded family ritual practices and to look for evidence that short-term problem-solving strategies have begun to incorporate alcohol-dependent interactional behaviors. In other words, this is the time to look for family-level, as well as individual-level manifestations of alcoholism.

Our therapist tells the Brown family that it is important for him to learn the extent of Mr. Brown's drinking behavior and toward that end asks each family member in turn for his or her opinion. Responses from family members are mixed. Bernadette Brown downplays her husband's drinking, acknowledging that from time to time she worries about him, but that she is sure it is not a problem; she also denies overt evidence that would lead her to suspect an alcohol problem. David admits to genuine concern, but he expresses it in a tentative fashion with repeated glances at his father as he is talking.

Kathy, however, is another story. With only modest prodding from the therapist, she expresses profound concern about her father's drinking. He often seems drunk to her; she has on several occasions accidently seen him alone in the basement drinking directly from a bottle without having bothered to first pour the liquor into a glass; she once saw a half-dozen empty vodka bottles in the trash can; and she often hears him pacing in his bedroom late at night, mumbling to himself with words she cannot understand. He seems to miss many family meals, even though he is in the house at the time, and she does not understand why her mother "lets him get away with this." The therapist has hit pay dirt.

The Brown family is not an unusual clinical case. The most frequent reason why therapists, including family therapists, fail to identify a serious alcoholism problem is because they simply do not ask the right questions (or, for that matter, any questions at all) about alcoholism. Occasionally one will come across a clinical situation in which a family responds with anger to a therapist's queries about drinking behavior. But by and large, in those situations in which families come voluntarily for treatment, they experience a sense of relief when they find a therapist who is not only willing to talk with them about a drinking problem they have long suspected should be of concern, but who also talks knowledgeably about the alcoholism issue.

The therapist has now identified an alcoholism problem in the Brown family and has shared this information with them. This is only the first part of a two-step process, however. He must now determine whether the

Browns are an Alcoholic Family (that is, whether they have organized their lives around Michael Brown's alcoholic behavior, and whether alcohol-related behavior has become a critical component of family regulatory mechanisms).

As we pointed out in our earlier discussions, occasionally families view alcoholic behavior as an individual affair, a personal problem that might engender feelings of sympathy, sadness, or anger, one that is not a central issue in family life. However, it is more likely, when one is dealing with a middle-stage family, that alcoholism, if it has been around for some time, has been incorporated into family life. If the family chose not to take this course of action, then the likely outcome would have been the willful extrusion from the family of the alcoholic member, either through separation or divorce. Although the therapist can assume that a middle-stage family with a long-standing alcoholism problem is most likely an alcoholic system, because the alternative is also possible, the therapist must determine which of these two situations he or she is facing.

The reason that this is a critical issue at this point of the assessment process is that the therapy plan will be dramatically different in the two cases. If one is dealing with an Alcoholic Family, alcoholism must be the starting point for therapy. But if the Browns are not an Alcoholic Family, the treatment plan will in all likelihood be built around a family-level formulation of the adolescent developmental crisis that ostensibly brought the family to treatment.

How does the therapist make such a determination? Our earlier discussions have focused on the relationship between alcoholic behavior and family regulatory mechanisms in middle-stage Alcoholic Families. Three aspects of family behavior—patterns of behavior at home; short-term problem-solving; and family rituals—proved of particular value to the researcher in exploring the relationship between alcoholism and regulatory mechanisms. By extension, these same three aspects of behavior can now help our therapist answer clinical questions.

The Browns are now asked about their behavior when Michael is drinking. Can they pinpoint specific patterns of behavior that characteristically occur during times of heavy drinking? (Remember Alice Clarion's recollections of her family's "automatic pilot" behavior in chapter 6.) What the behaviors actually are is not for the moment the relevant issue. It is the existence of a nonrandom pattern of family behavior associated with Michael Brown's drinking that the therapist is interested in hearing about.

Similarly, he questions them about dinnertime behavior and recent holidays. How does Michael's drinking affect the family's mealtime behavior? Once again, the therapist is interested in whether the family has a systematic policy, a defined strategy regarding mealtime behavior. A response that the family insists on including Michael at family dinners whether or not he has been drinking, and will delay the time of the meal to give him time to sober up enough to come to the dining room, is as much a verification that we are dealing with an Alcoholic Family as is the information that the family insists on protecting the sanctity of the evening meal regardless of what Michael Brown's current state of mind and body might be.

Of course, in the first instance, we might conclude that the Browns are a "subsumptive" family, whereas in the second instance we would call them a "distinctive" family, and that distinction might be valuable in alerting us to the relative risks of alcoholism being transmitted to Kathy or David (see chapter 8). But both answers imply a defined policy, a systematic response to drinking, an organization of behavior around alcoholism.

Many such topics can be used to explore the "Alcoholic Family" question. We might ask about treatment of neighbors, friends, and relatives when Michael is drinking. We might ask about interaction rates and affective expressiveness. We might, if we are seeing a married couple without children, ask about sexual behavior in relation to drinking. The specific topic is adjusted to the particular family one is evaluating. But the central task is always the same. We are exploring the links between alcoholic behavior and family regulatory mechanisms. If such links can be established, we are about to treat an Alcoholic Family.*

The therapist has now completed taking a careful drinking history and has reached his initial conclusion. He is dealing with an Alcoholic Family. He must now share his findings with the Browns. How is this best done?

*In our description of the therapist's work thus far, we have given short shrift to assessment of nonalcoholism-related aspects of family functioning. Our condensed version of this initial session has focused instead on those aspects of the assessment process that relate directly to evaluation of alcoholism and techniques for successfully managing the "labeling process" with the family.

However, although we haven't so specified, our therapist is, at the same time, carrying out a comprehensive assessment of family organization and functioning including developmental appropriateness, clarity and effectiveness of communication patterns, strength of existing coalitions and alliances within the family, quality of boundaries between the subsystems of the family and between the family and its external environment, family problem-solving effectiveness, and the level and appropriateness of affective expressiveness within the family.

Each of these dimensions of family organization and functioning are as important in the assessment of the strengths and weaknesses of the Alcoholic Family as they would be in the initial assessment of any family seeking a consultation from a family therapist. But they are outside the main focus of this book and hence will not be discussed in any detail.

The preferable approach, not only for the Browns but for the vast majority of clinical cases, is to state one's conclusions as directly as possible. For example, the therapist might say, "We are dealing here with *alcoholism.*" Or, "The family is having a problem with *alcoholism.*"

If asked why he thinks this is so, the therapist should again be direct in sharing with the family his reasons for having reached this conclusion. There is nothing mystical here. He has heard about a series of specific behaviors all of which signal that alcohol abuse is present.

In the case of the Browns, the therapist is asked by David Brown why he calls Michael Brown's problem "alcoholism." Why not, David suggests, call it "heavy social drinking?" The therapist does not back down in the face of this testing maneuver. Instead, he continues to respond in a straightforward, factual manner. He tells David that the most widely used definition of alcoholism is that it exists when drinking continues in the face of clear-cut evidence that it is causing negative physical, social, family, occupational, and/or legal consequences. The therapist points out that the Browns have already shared with him ample evidence of such behavior on Michael's part. Hence his conclusion that the family is dealing with an alcoholism problem.

Although we are using a family systems model to guide our therapy, the language we use with the family at this point of the treatment process is that alcohol is a problem for the family, not that the family has an alcohol problem. Although the second phraseology is more consistent with our systems approach, it unnecessarily challenges the family's perception that only one person in the family is actually consuming the alcohol. Better, therefore, to phrase one's conclusions to the family in terms compatible with their perception of who is actually doing the drinking. The critical issue for the therapist is his willingness to take a stand regarding the alcoholism issue, to label it for what it is, to support his conclusion with specific data from the family interview and, in the process, to set the stage for the next phase of treatment, the removal of alcohol from the family system.

This leaves us with one last piece of unfinished business. The Brown family came to us originally because of Kathy's behavior. We are about to propose a treatment plan focusing on Michael Brown's drinking problems. We must remind the family that we have not forgotten about their initial concern, but that for the moment we are proposing to put it aside, to put it on the shelf, because, in our experience, we cannot do it justice until we first tackle the alcoholism problem.

The therapist therefore explains this to the Brown family and then, turning to Kathy, asks if he can have her agreement to participate in such a treatment plan. Her cooperation, he tells her, includes her agreement to avoid provocative, "worry-inducing" behavior for the next four weeks, at which point she will again be free to express herself. (The therapist has selected the four-week time limit arbitrarily, using as his guideline a rough estimate of how long it will take to complete the *second* stage of treatment, but he also believes that Kathy's behavior was largely a response to family stresses secondary to the fact that Mr. Brown's alcoholic behavior is now perpetuating, rather than temporarily solving, problems. He assumes that when these alcoholism-related stresses are dealt with, her own defiant behavior will die out of its own accord.)

The three goals of Stage I have now been achieved: (1) alcoholism has been identified via careful history taking; (2) we have determined that the Browns are an Alcoholic Family, and (3), the therapist has established that therapy will begin with a direct assault on the alcoholism problem. Everything else will be temporarily placed in the background. Family resources and the therapeutic sessions themselves will be mobilized to deal effectively with the alcoholism issue. Although we are still in the initial session with the Brown family, since our first set of tasks have been completed, we are ready to move immediately onto Stage II, and plan a strategy for detoxifying this family.

Stage II: The Removal of Alcohol from the System

It is foolhardy to believe, as some family therapists do, that one can alter drinking behavior by merely working on the dynamics of an Alcoholic Family system without directly addressing the drinking behavior itself. This might occur in a case or two, but the overwhelming evidence is that alcoholic drinking behavior, once it takes hold, plays a central role in family life. It is the dominant theme, it cannot be ignored. We have been detailing throughout this book the reasons why this is so. The obvious clinical extension of our research findings suggest that a therapist, to be consistently effective in his work with the Alcoholic Family, must first convert the family from the wet to the dry stage, and then work with this now dry family at changing basic patterns of behavior within the family. So we now have to get Michael Brown to stop drinking.

Although alcoholism is not necessarily always identified in the initial consultation session with the family (it might only surface once the therapist has gained the family's confidence), the first step in Stage II of the therapy should always occur in the *same session* that the labeling process occurs. The therapist must get across to the family that there is no issue more important at this stage of the work than the cessation of drinking, and that family and therapist must mobilize all resources toward that goal and that goal alone. (Allowing the family to leave the consultation room without a clear-cut contract regarding cessation of drinking undermines the therapist's position concerning the importance of this issue.)

At the same time, we fully appreciate the family's anxiety about the intractibility of alcoholism, especially if this is only the last of many previously unsuccessful contacts they have had with treatment programs. Because of the complexities involved, including the varied and intricate ways families may, despite their best intentions, resist the wet to dry conversion, it is preferable to use a relatively simple, straightforward approach to the task. A problem-solving approach, utilizing a contracting model is one such example and is the approach we describe at some length further.*

There are basically three options available to the therapist in approaching the issue of removing alcohol from the family system: (1) insisting on inpatient detoxification for the alcoholic member; (2) accepting, as an intermediate course, a delimited time period (not to exceed two weeks) for attempting detoxification on an outpatient basis, followed by inpatient detoxification if there have been by then no meaningful steps taken in the direction of removing alcohol; or (3) outpatient detoxification alone (detoxification is used metaphorically here since this option is usually taken *only* when evidence of physical addiction is minimal or absent).

The therapist chooses the *first option* when it is clear, based on the alcoholism history taken in Stage I, that as soon as the patient stops drinking, he or she will experience withdrawal symptoms of a magnitude as to make it highly unlikely that withdrawal can be successfully completed without medication. *A therapist, having such a conviction, should not agree to continue working with an Alcoholic Family that refuses to accept a recommendation of hospitalization for detoxification.*

It is possible, of course, that the family as a group might support such a recommendation, but that the alcoholic individual might still refuse hospitalization. In such an instance, the therapist might choose to continue working with the family, but to exclude the alcoholic individual not only from therapy sessions, but from being considered an official patient.

*The problem-solving approach in family therapy is thoroughly described by Jay Haley (1976) in his book, *Problem-Solving Therapy,* which relies heavily on principles drawn from two of the major schools of family therapy, structural and strategic family therapy. Gurman and Kniskern's *Handbook of Family Therapy* (1981) can also be consulted for more details about these approaches.

(This is not a therapeutic ploy. It is untenable for a therapist to enter into a contract with an Alcoholic Family or individual that in effect ignores clear-cut evidence not only of physiological addiction to alcohol, but of the serious physical consequences that will inevitably result from a continuation of drinking. Such a stand totally undermines the therapist's credibility regarding the seriousness of the condition. In such an instance, the therapist is being asked to participate actively in a course of action that in the long run can only be detrimental to the patient and family. It is foolhardy, if not unethical, to do so.)

The therapist chooses the *second option* in those situations in which there is doubt (but not conviction) about the ability of the family to accomplish removal of alcohol on an outpatient basis, but the family is highly resistant to a recommendation that hospitalization occur immediately. The therapist's skepticism could be based either on evidence of moderate physiological addiction on the part of the alcoholic individual, or on a judgment that the family, because of its poor problem-solving skills, is unlikely to be able to successfully manage detoxification on an outpatient basis.

If the therapist chooses this option, he usually begins the process by sharing openly with the family his skepticism, but expressing a willingness to be flexible and to allow the family to prove him wrong. He might ask the family how much time it would like to give an outpatient approach a fair trial. If family members respond that they would like to try it out for a month or two, the therapist must take a firm stand that such a time period is unacceptable to him. Negotiations with the family should lead to a contract in which the therapist agrees to go along with a trial period of outpatient detoxification of at most two weeks (or in unusual cases perhaps three weeks) on the condition that if the situation shows no sign of movement at that point, the family agrees to then support the therapist in a recommendation of hospitalization. The critical issue in the implementation of this second option, therefore, is the negotiation of a firm time limit.

In the second option, after the time limit has been settled upon, the therapist and family engage in an additional contracting process that parallels the one used for the third option. Since this *third option*—outpatient removal of alcohol—is the one the therapist chose in his work with the Brown family, let us return to the session at this point.

Mr. Brown is a binge drinker. Although his alcohol consumption during these binges is as high as one quart of 90-proof vodka per day, he suffers only modest withdrawal symptoms. It is therefore clear that tackling initial cessation of drinking on an outpatient basis is a viable option.

In working with an Alcoholic Family around the issue of outpatient removal of alcohol from the family system, it is critical that the therapist establish a clearly understood contract in which cessation of drinking is seen as a problem that the *family* must tackle and solve ("family" includes the alcoholic member, of course). Since it is a family problem (as the therapist has just told the Browns at the conclusion of Stage I), it must be dealt with via a family solution.

In establishing the detoxification contract with the Browns, the therapist starts with Michael, and easily obtains his agreement to stop drinking as of that moment. (There might be some surprise that he agrees so easily. Our experience, however, is that once the therapist has directly and in a straightforward manner labeled alcoholism within the family, it is in most cases relatively easy to obtain verbal agreement to stop drinking from the identified alcoholic.)

The therapist next asks Michael what tasks he feels other family members should take responsibility for as part of the family problem-solving venture. Michael replies that he is sure he can handle the whole thing on his own and could not think of anything that they might do to help. However, the therapist refuses to accept this altruistic offer, and now turns to other family members and begins engaging them in a strategy-generation process.

The details of the detoxification contract will be somewhat different with each family one sees in treatment. However, several issues and themes will in all likelihood come up with each case. For example, there is always the issue of rules regarding alcohol in the home. What is to be done with alcohol already there; what stance will the family take about bringing additional alcohol into the home? What rules are to be followed regarding drinking behavior of nonalcoholic family members? Should a family that prides itself on its epicurean habits continue serving wine with dinner? What is to be done about social entertaining? Should the family be serving alcoholic drinks at parties and offering drinks to friends when they visit? Is it better to simply impose a rule of abstinence on the whole family and let it go at that, or is a more flexible policy appropriate?

There are no hard and fast ways to answer these questions. The therapist must use clinical judgment in shaping a unique contract with each family. What is important, however, is that the contract be as clear as possible. All participants should have agreed-upon criteria to use for judging whether the contract is being adhered to or is being broken, and each family member should have a clearly defined set of tasks to carry out as part of the overall contract.

For the Browns, the important part of the contract is the decision to make the house an alcohol-free zone, to reinstitute family dinners (Michael had been absenting himself from many meals and the family dinnertime had pretty much fallen apart), and to have a fixed schedule for entertainment at home (Michael had complained about never knowing when people were coming over and about surprise visits by Kathy's and David's friends). Each of these "contractual" items is selected after a family discussion has identified it as an important issue and agreement has been obtained that it could contribute to maximizing success of the central goal, the removal of alcohol.

From the therapist's perspective, his job is to keep the discussion alcohol-focused. The family has to arrive at consensus about the strategy to stop Michael's drinking. So the therapist asks, as each suggestion is raised, how it would contribute to the central goal. And as the items of the contract are agreed to, he reviews them with the family, repeating his understanding of what each person's task is to be, and asking for verification of this understanding.

Clarity and simplicity are the goals. Complex tasks could easily be misinterpreted. The family needs a clearly defined set of criteria against which to measure its performance. Since in the next session the therapist will be reviewing with the family its record of accomplishments, he wants to avoid a situation in which violation of a contractual clause might reasonably be attributed to confusion about the task to be done.

The first session is now over. The "problem" has been identified, its family-level nature established, and a treatment plan has been reviewed with the family. For now, the sole focus of therapy is to be the "detoxification" process. It will be carried out on an outpatient basis and all family members have agreed to an initial contract that establishes a clear-cut strategy for removing alcohol from the family system. The family is sent home to carry out this strategy and is to return in four days to report on their progress.

The ease with which the removal of alcohol from the family system is accomplished will vary greatly from family to family. The very fact that a family can consult the therapist as a group often indicates that a great deal of preliminary work has already occurred. The family perceives itself to be in distress and, even if alcohol has not been consciously identified as the primary source of difficulty, has a shared perception that there is a family-level problem.

Family members may point fingers at each other and claim that it is one or another member of the family who is the culprit, but their acknowledgement that it is important for the family to come as a group to the therapist's office is an indication that the therapist will have little problem in couching both the presenting problem and the strategies for intervention within a family perspective. In such an instance, a statement that "alcohol is clearly a problem for the whole family," finds a receptive audience. By extension, such a family may have already gone a long way toward seeing the solution as well, namely, that drinking must stop and that it is the responsibility of the family as a group to work out a strategy for bringing this goal about.

But just as often, the therapist's introduction of the "Alcoholic Family" perspective meets with substantial "resistance" on the family's part. For some families, this resistance is direct and forthright. "How can this be so," the therapist might be aggressively asked by an adolescent in the family, "when it's my father who's downing the booze?"

"I don't see your point," is a gentle way it might be put. "You're crazy; that doesn't make any sense," is a more pithy way to say the same thing.

However, when challenged in this fashion, the therapist is able to answer because he can back up his diagnosis with a wealth of data about alcoholism-related distortions that have occurred in family life. That is, he has such data at his disposal if he has heeded our advice and taken an extensive and comprehensive alcoholism-family history during Phase I of the treatment process. Examples of changes the family has made in vacation plans, in how holidays are celebrated, in the specifics of their daily schedules, in their entertainment patterns, in the way they have become isolated from their extended families, can all be used to illustrate to the family that substantial changes have occurred in family life as a direct consequence of accommodation to alcoholic drinking patterns.

In other families, negative or skeptical reactions to the Alcoholic Family formulation are less direct. These families seemingly accept the family-level diagnosis of alcoholism as it emerges in Stage I. They also seem cooperative during Stage II in agreeing to participate in the detoxification task. Only when they return for follow-up visits does the therapist learn that specific aspects of the detoxification contract have either not been carried out or have been performed in distorted fashion.

Thus, just as receptivity to the "Alcoholic Family" formulation varies greatly from family to family, so too does the family's response to the task of removing alcohol from the family system. Occasionally, the therapist will find that this task is accomplished with breathtaking ease. The family has already completed 95 percent of the emotional work necessary to take on the task and needs only the therapist's support and conviction to finish the job. But often the task proves to be a tough one for the family. In a *moment we will be suggesting an approach for dealing with such "resist-ances."*

The Browns return for a follow-up visit four days later. The therapist immediately moves to review how much of the detoxification contract has been accomplished. He learns that the family left the initial therapy session quite buoyed by the experience. All members agreed that the family was finally dealing with an important issue that had been insidiously undermining family morale. Further, the family had a long and gratifying dinnertime meal and postmeal discussion lasting several hours in which many of the concerns about Michael's drinking were again reviewed.

Following the meal, the family successfully carried out the initial task of emptying the liquor cabinet and refrigerator of all alcoholic beverages. In addition, Michael reports that he has not had anything to drink since the last session (although he offers this information only in response to a direct question from the therapist), and other family members confirm the absence of any behavioral evidence that he has been drinking (Bernadette, in contrast to her husband, reports this information spontaneously and with enthusiasm bordering on exuberance).

The therapist, noting the contrasting affective tones associated with Mr. and Mrs. Brown's responses, asks whether they see the events of the last few days differently. Bernadette expresses confusion about the question, and continues to bubble about how well things have been going. Michael fails to respond. The therapist therefore turns to David and Kathy and asks for their observations, both about how the contract was carried out and about the different moods of their parents. Repeating the pattern of the first session, David denies any problems, but Kathy notes that, "Dad may be upset because when the Stuarts [family friends] came over on Sunday for dinner, Mom served them some wine with the meal."

The therapist follows up on this new information, using a matter-of-fact tone. He checks out the details with each family member and asks whether it was their understanding that wine at meals was acceptable under the terms of the detoxification contract. Bernadette, despite the therapist's nonjudgmental stance, immediately becomes defensive. She explains that it was her understanding that the contract only covered the things Michael usually drank—namely, his vodka and the beer in the refrigerator.

At this point Michael becomes quite animated and in an accusatory tone tells his wife, "He [referring to the therapist] specifically told you that we weren't supposed to serve alcohol when our friends came over. Not at parties. Not even if they just come over for a meal." Michael continues,

"He even said we were supposed to tell everybody exactly what was happening and why alcohol was off-limits in our house. You didn't do that either."

The therapist moves to defuse the situation by asking the family members if Michael's version of his instructions coincide with their own memories of the treatment contract. Both children agree, although with differing levels of enthusiasm. Bernadette, however, becomes increasingly defensive. She thinks that Michael's drinking problem is a private matter and she doesn't understand why friends have to be told that the family is seeing a therapist for an alcohol problem. Besides, she also read in a magazine article that alcoholism is not caused by emotional problems in the family, and that what is most important for family members is *not* to feel that it is their responsibility to somehow get the alcoholic to stop drinking.

The therapist handles the situation by repeating again his understanding of the detoxification contract and of the importance of working toward making the family environment alcohol-free. Further, he compliments the family on their very considerable success thus far in achieving most of the goals of the contract. Regarding the incident of serving wine to friends, he describes this as "evidence that we didn't get the contract exactly right," adding, "It looks like we got the overall plan about 75 percent correctly. That's pretty good for a first pass. Why don't we go back and see if we can pin down the last 25 percent."

Here we have a representative example of the types of "resistances" that families engage in when attempting to carry out a family-level detoxification contract. Although families can be quite inventive in the forms these "resistances" take, they usually fall into one of three different categories: (1) situations in which the identified alcoholic stops drinking, but other family members fail to adhere to their tasks as detailed in the contract (the situation that occurred with the Browns); (2) situations in which the identified alcoholic sharply reduces his or her drinking to the point that intoxication is no longer occurring, but clearly defies the instruction to maintain abstinence; (3) situations in which the therapy sessions are directly undermined (e.g., the identified alcoholic member comes to a subsequent session intoxicated, or family members fail to attend a session, offering a reality-based excuse for their behavior).

These different categories of behavior might at first glance appear to be more or less serious as challenges to the therapeutic plan. More likely, however, they merely represent different stylistic approaches used by families. The emergence of any of these behaviors represents a challenge to the detoxification contract, a testing by the family of the limits of the contract. Therefore, whenever one or more of these behaviors surfaces as Stage II of treatment unfolds, the therapist must address it directly and forthrightly, reaffirming the critical importance of the family's adhering to the detoxification contract as written.

However, the attitudinal stance taken by the therapist in reviewing these issues with the family can still be one of curiosity about the behavior and empathy about the difficulty families experience initially in carrying out these contracts. The therapist therefore treats such behaviors as evidence that "although we got most of the contract right, it seems we need to re-review it to improve those aspects that we didn't get quite right, as evidenced by your not being able to fully achieve the goals we agreed would be important to work toward."

That is, the therapist must always keep in mind how anxiety provoking this phase of treatment is for a family whose life has for years been organized around a familiar (even if distressing) pattern of alcohol abuse. Such a family is obviously now contemplating a dramatic change in its way of life. Fantasies abound: "Will we be able to actually do it?" "Is he or she going to start drinking secretly? If so, what should we do about it?" "How can we ever face our friends again?" And sometimes there are even more dramatic concerns: about family secrets suddenly becoming public knowledge; or about a chronic susceptibility to severe depression becoming worse and thoughts of suicide arising.

What is being urged, therefore, is that until proven otherwise, the therapist should assume that family resistance is a product of anxiety about change. Thus, as Phase II unfolds, it is extremely useful to reframe difficulties experienced by the family in carrying out its assignments as "reasonable concerns" about disruption of the delicate balance achieved by the family over the years to deal with the alcoholism issue.

The rest of the session with the Browns is taken up by a careful re-review of the detoxification contract. The family is encouraged to brain-storm other areas that might be potential weak points in the contract and to pre-emptively suggest ways to avoid these pitfalls. Throughout this discussion, the therapist positively supports the family's efforts at problem-solving and reiterates his optimism about their being able to work out successful strategies for effecting the wet to dry conversion.

During subsequent sessions (still considered part of Stage II), the focus gradually shifts away from the details of the detoxification contract per se, and moves to discussions with the Browns about the quality of family interactional behavior and affective tone during this immediate postwet transitional phase.

The length of time necessary to engineer this transition will obviously vary from family to family. However, it is particularly useful during this phase to explore with the family any examples of issues that they feel are now being handled differently than they were when drinking was occurring. In particular, any opportunities to point out examples of issues that would have somehow been "easier" when drinking was going on, but are now more complicated (essentially an identification of aspects of family life in which adapted consequences of alcohol use might have held sway), should be taken.

It is also extremely useful to warn the family that, contrary to what they might anticipate, they may well find that after an initial period of positive feelings related to the cessation of drinking, they may begin to experience a sense of emptiness and depression. They should be told that such feelings are part of the normative recovery process and hence evidence that the conversion from wet to dry status is taking hold. A straightforward discussion with the family about the reasons for this "emotional desert" reaction is, in most cases, also extremely useful at this point.

Concluding Therapy

We will stop at this point in the treatment of the Browns. As we have already indicated, the main responsibility of the therapist during Stage III of treatment is to provide a "holding environment" as the family reacts to the major disruptions and changes in interactional and affective patterns associated with removal of alcohol from the family system. Most families tend to be extremely jittery and labile during this stage. They are on very new and unfamiliar ground, and the pull back to the old way of doing things seems irresistable. The therapist, by anticipating with the family the emergence of such reactions, and by providing a psychoeducational framework within which to understand and help family members appreciate what they are experiencing, can obviate impulsive behavior.

However, if slips do occur at this point and drinking resumes, neither the family nor therapist should panic. Instead, reiteration of the difficulty of the task, reminders about the chronicity of alcoholism, and emphasis on the length of time sobriety has been maintained can be used to encourage the family to return to the detoxification contract and reinstitute sobriety.

By restricting our detailed comments in this case to the first two stages of treatment, we do not mean to imply that Stages III and IV are any less important to the overall success of therapy, or that they are less complex than Stages I and II. Rather, they are being given abbreviated treatment for two reasons. First, because of their significantly longer duration (Stages I and II are usually completed within six sessions; Stages III and IV may extend over several months), they are hard to describe in a single chapter. Second, in that these later stages of treatment draw more heavily on traditional family therapy techniques and issues, they are less unique to alcoholism per se than are the diagnostic and detoxification phases of therapy.

It should be underscored, however, that because Stages III and IV of our proposed treatment model rely so heavily on traditional family therapy techniques and conceptualizations, the therapist attempting to use it must attain mastery of these skills.

Conclusion

In this chapter we have proposed a four-stage treatment model based on a family systems understanding of chronic alcoholism. Although the treatment model shares many aspects with traditional alcoholism treatment (e.g., insistence on cessation of drinking as the first step in treatment), it is unique in other aspects—especially in its approach to diagnosis, an approach that emphasizes the distinction between an Alcoholic Family and a family with an alcoholic member; and in its proposal that in treating the Alcoholic Family it is the whole family, not the alcoholic individual alone that must be "detoxified."

In reviewing this treatment model, we have demonstrated that the FLH model of the Alcoholic Family also has clear-cut and distinctive *therapeutic* implications. It should also be clear that the model is one that makes most sense when the case at hand is an Alcoholic Family. (That is, we are not proposing that a family systems-based therapy approach is the treatment of choice for every case of chronic alcoholism—clearly it cannot be successfully implemented when family members are not available.)

Nor does it make sense to us to undermine a previously successful treatment approach that has either been entirely individually based or has relied on Al-Anon groups to involve family members in their own component of the treatment while the alcoholic individual is in a traditional program. For example, several of the case histories presented in chapter 9 detailed instances in which engagement in traditional AA-affiliated treatment programs had resulted in highly adaptive and successful outcomes (e.g., the Luries, the stable dry Alcoholic Family).

However, we also described instances in which individually based treatment programs had been imposed on Alcoholic Families and the therapists had been unaware that though their interventions were seemingly leading to a positive therapeutic outcome for the alcoholic individual, they were having a profound *and negative* effect on the family as a group.

Thus we conclude this treatment chapter with the same caveat we used when we were discussing research data and clinical case material related to the developmental course of the Alcoholic Family—this is a highly heterogeneous group of families we are talking about. It is no more credible to propose that a single treatment approach will make sense for each and every Alcoholic Family than it is to assume that all Alcoholic Families follow comparable developmental courses or manifest the same personality features. The challenge in treatment is to develop a sophisticated appreciation of the factors and dimensions that distinguish one Alcoholic Family from another and to understand what it is that makes the Alcoholic Family unique.

References

Ablon, J. (1976). Family structure and behavior in alcoholism: A review of the literature. In B. Kissin and H. Beglieter (Eds.), *The biology of alcoholism: Vol. 4. Social aspects of alcoholism.* New York: Plenum Press.

Ablon, J. (1980). The significance of cultural patterning for the "alcoholic family." *Family Process, 19,* 127–144.

Ablon, J. (1982). Perspectives on Al-anon family groups. In N. J. Estes and M. E. Heinemann (Eds.), *Alcoholism: Development, consequences, and interventions,* (2nd ed.). St. Louis: C. V. Mosby.

Ablon, J. (1984). Literature on alcoholism and the family. In M. Galanter (Ed.), *Recent Developments in Alcoholism* (vol. 2). New York, Plenum Press.

Ablon, J. (1985). Irish-Americans in a west coast metropolitan area. In L. A. Bennett and G. M. Ames (Eds.), *The American experience with alcohol: Contrasting cultural perspectives.* New York: Plenum Press.

American Psychiatric Association (1987). *Diagnostic and Statistical Manual of Mental Disorders* (3rd ed., rev.). Washington, D. C.: American Psychiatric Association.

Ames, G. (1977). *A description of women alcoholics' behavior as affected by American sociocultural attitudes.* Unpublished master's thesis, San Francisco State University.

Ames, G. (1982). *Maternal alcoholism and family life.* Unpublished doctoral dissertation, University of California Medical Center, San Francisco.

Ames, G. (1985). Middle-class protestants: Alcohol and the family. In L. A. Bennett and G. M. Ames (Eds.), *The American experience with alcohol: Contrasting cultural perspectives.* New York: Plenum Press.

Armor, D. J., Polich, J. M., and Stambul, H. B. (1978). *Alcoholism and treatment.* New York: John Wiley and Sons.

Bailey, M. B. (1961). Alcoholism and marriage: A review of research and professional literature. *Quarterly Journal of Studies on Alcohol, 22,* 81–97.

Barnhill, L. R., and Longo, D. (1978). Fixation and regression in the family life cycle. *Family Process, 17,* 469–478.

Baumrind, D. (1971). Current patterns of parental authority. *Developmental Psychology Monograph, 4,* (No. 1, Part 2).

Bennett, L. A., and Ames, G. M. (1985). *The American experience with alcohol: Contrasting cultural perspectives.* New York: Plenum Press.

Bennett, L. A., and McAvity, K. J. (1985). Family research: A case for interviewing couples. In G. Handel (Ed.), *The psychosocial interior of the family* (3rd ed.). New York: Aldine.

Bennett, L. A., Wolin, S. J., Reiss, D., and Teitelbaum, M. (1987). Couples at risk for alcoholism recurrence: Protective influences. *Family Process, 26,* 111–129.

Berger, P., and Kellner, H. (1974). Marriage and the construction of reality. In R. L. Coser (Ed.), *The family: Its structures and functions.* New York: St. Martin's Press.

Berry, R. E., Jr., Boland, J. P., Smart, C. N., and Kanak, J. R. (1977). *The economic costs of alcohol abuse and alcoholism—1975* (Final Report to National Institute of Alcohol Abuse and Alcoholism under Contract No. ADM 281-76-0016). Boston: Policy Analysis.

Birnbaum, I. N., and Parker, E. S. (1977). *Alcohol and human memory.* Hillsdale, NJ: Lawrence Erlbaum.

365

Blane, H. T., and Barry, H., Jr. (1973). Birth order and alcoholism: A review. *Quarterly Journal of Studies on Alcohol, 34,* 837–952.

Bossard, J., and Boll, E. (1950). *Rituals in family living.* Philadelphia: University of Pennsylvania Press.

Bott, E. (1971). *Family and social network* (2nd ed.). New York: Free Press.

Bradley, R. H., and Caldwell, B. M. (1976). Early home environment and changes in mental test performance in children from six to thirty-six months. *Developmental Psychology, 12,* 93–97.

Breunlin, D. (in press). Oscillation theory and family development. In C. Falicov (Ed.), *Family transitions: Continuity and change over the life cycle.* New York: Guilford.

Browning, D., and Boatman, B. (1977). Children at risk. *American Journal of Psychiatry, 134,* 69–72.

Cadogan, D. A. (1973). Marital group therapy in the treatment of alcoholism. *Quarterly Journal of Studies on Alcohol, 34,* 1187–1194.

Cahalan, D. (1970). *Problem Drinkers.* San Francisco: Jossey-Bass.

Cahalan, D. (1982). Alcohol use in American life. In E. L. Gomberg, H. R. White, and J. A. Carpenter (Eds.), *Alcohol, science and society revisited.* Ann Arbor: University of Michigan Press.

Cahalan, D., Cisin, I. H., and Crossley, H. M. (1969). *American drinking practices: A national study of drinking behavior and attitudes* (Monograph no. 6). New Brunswick, NJ: Rutgers Center of Alcohol Studies.

Cahalan, D., and Room, R. (1974). *Problem drinking among American men* (Monograph no. 7). New Brunswick, NJ: Rutgers Center of Alcohol Studies.

Cannon, W. B. (1939). *The wisdom of the body.* New York: W. W. Norton.

Carter, E. A., and McGoldrick, M. (1980). *The family life cycle: A frame-work for family therapy.* New York: Gardner Press.

Chafetz, M. E., Blane, H. T., and Hill, M. J. (1971). Children of alcoholics: Observations in a child-guidance clinic. *Quarterly Journal of Studies on Alcohol, 32,* 687–698.

Clark, W. B., and Midanik, L. (1982). Alcohol use and alcohol problems among U.S. adults. In National Institute on Alcohol Abuse and Alcoholism, *Alcoholic consumption and related problems* (Alcohol and Health Monograph no. 1). Rockville, MD: NIAAA.

Clark-Stewart, K. A. (1973). Interactions between mothers and their young children: Characteristics and consequences. *Monographs of the Society for Research in Child Development, 38,* 1–109.

Cloninger, C. R., Bohman, M., and Sigvardsson, S. (1981). Inheritance of alcohol abuse: Cross-fostering analysis of adopted men. *Archives of General Psychiatry, 38,* 861–868.

Cloninger, C. R., Rice, J., and Reich, T. (1979). Multifactorial inheritance with cultural transmission and assortative mating: II. A general model of combined polygenetic and cultural inheritance. *American Journal of Human Genetics, 31,* 176–198.

Cohen, J., and Cohen, P. (1983). *Applied multiple regression/correlation analysis for behavioral sciences.* Hillsdale, NJ: Lawrence Erlbaum.

Cotton, N. S. (1979). The familial incidence of alcoholism: A review. *Journal of Studies on Alcohol, 40,* 89–116.

Davis, D. I. (1987). *Alcoholism treatment: An integrative family and individual approach.* New York: Gardner Press.

Davis, D. I., Berenson, D., Steinglass, P., and Davis, S. (1974). The adaptive consequences of drinking. *Psychiatry, 37,* 209–215.

Derogatis, L. R., Lippman, R. S., and Conti, L. (1973). SCL-90: An outpatient psychiatric rating scale. Preliminary report. *Psychopharmacology Bulletin, 9,* 13–28.

Duvall, E. M. (1971). *Family development.* New York: Lippincott.

Edwards, G., Gross, M. M., Keller, M., et al. (1977). *Alcohol-related disabilities* (WHO offset publication no. 32). Geneva: World Health Organization.

Edwards, P., Harvey, C., and Whitehead, P. C. (1973). Wives of alcoholics: A critical review and analysis. *Quarterly Journal of Studies on Alcohol, 34,* 112–132.

Erikson, E. H. (1950). *Childhood and society.* New York: W. W. Norton.

Erikson, E. H. (1959). Identity and the life cycle. In *Psychological Issues,* (No. 1). New York: International Universities Press.

Erikson, E. H. (1968). *Identity, youth and crisis.* New York: W. W. Norton.

Esser, P. H. (1968). Conjoint family therapy for alcoholics. *British Journal of Addictions, 63,* 177–182.

References

Esser, P. H. (1971). Evaluation of family therapy with alcoholics. *British Journal of Addictions, 66,* 251–255.

Ewing, J. A., and Fox, R. E. (1968). Family therapy of alcoholism. In J. H. Masserman (Ed.), *Current psychiatric therapies* (vol. 8). New York: Grune and Stratton.

Ewing, J. A., Long, V., and Wenzel, G. G. (1961). Concurrent group psychotherapy of alcoholic patients and their wives. *International Journal of Group Psychotherapy, 11,* 329–338.

Ewing, J. A., and Rouse, B. A. (1976). Failure of an experimental treatment program to inculcate controlled drinking in alcoholics. *British Journal of Addictions, 71,* 123–134.

Feighner, J., Robins, E., Guze, S., Woodruff, R., Winokur, G., and Munoz, R. (1972). Diagnostic criteria for use in psychiatric research. *Archives of General Psychiatry, 26,* 57–63.

Ferreira, A. (1966). Family myths. *Psychiatric Research Reports, 20,* 85–90.

Firth, R., Hubert, J., and Forge, A. (1970). *Families and their relatives: Kinship in a middle-class sector of London. An anthropological study.* New York: Humanities Press.

Fischer, J. L., and Fischer, A. (1966). *The New Englanders of Orchard Town, U.S.A.* New York: John Wiley and Sons.

Flanzer, J. (1981). The vicious circle of alcoholism and family violence. *Alcoholism,* (January–February), 30–32.

Ford, F., and Herrick, J. (1974). Family rules: Family life styles. *American Journal of Orthopsychiatry, 44,* 61–69.

Freed, E. X. (1978). Alcohol and food: An updated review. *International Journal of Addiction, 13,* 173–200.

Gallant, D. M., Rich, A., Bey, E., and Terranova, L. (1970). Group psychotherapy with married couples: A successful technique in New Orleans clinic patients. *Journal of the Louisiana Medical Society, 122,* 41–44.

Gans, H. (1962). *The urban villagers.* New York: Free Press.

Gelles, R. J. (1974). *The violent home.* Beverly Hills, CA: Sage Publications.

Gelles, R. J., and Straus, M. A. (1979). Determinants of violence in the family: Toward a theoretical integration. In W. R. Burr, R. Hill, F. I. Nye, and I. L. Reiss (Eds.), *Contemporary theories about the family* (vol. 1). New York: Free Press.

Gliedman, L. H., Rosenthal, D., Frank, J. D., and Nash, H. T. (1956). Group therapy of alcoholics with concurrent group meetings with their wives. *Quarterly Journal of Studies on Alcohol, 17,* 655–670.

Gomberg, G. S. (1975). Prevalence of alcoholism among ward patients in a Veterans Administration hospital. *Journal of Studies on Alcohol, 36,* 1458–1467.

Goodwin, D. W. (1971a). Is alcoholism hereditary? *Archives of General Psychiatry, 25,* 518–545.

Goodwin, D. W. (1971b). Is alcoholism hereditary? A review and critique. *Archives of General Psychiatry, 25,* 545–549.

Goodwin, D. W. (1979). Alcoholism and heredity: A review and hypothesis. *Archives of General Psychiatry, 36,* 57–61.

Goodwin, D. W. (1983). The role of genetics in the expression of alcoholism: Overview. In M. Galanter (Ed.), *Recent developments in alcoholism* (vol. 1). New York: Plenum Press.

Goodwin, D. W., Schulsinger, F., Knop, J., Mednick, S., and Guze, S. B. (1977). Alcoholism and depression in adopted-out daughters of alcoholics. *Archives of General Psychiatry, 34,* 751–755.

Goodwin, D. W., Schulsinger, F., Møller, N., Hermansen, L., Winokur, G., and Guze, S. B. (1974). Drinking problems in adopted and non-adopted sons of alcoholics. *Archives of General Psychiatry, 31,* 164–169.

Gray, W., and Rizzo, N. D. (1969). History and development of general systems theory. In W. Gray, F. J. Duhl, and N. D. Rizzo (Eds.), *General systems theory and psychiatry.* Boston: Little, Brown.

Gurling, H.M.D., Clifford, C. A., and Murray, R. M. (1981). Genetic contributions to alcohol dependence and its effect on brain function. In L. Gedda, P. Parisi, and W. A. Nance (Eds.), *Twin Research* (vol. 3). New York: Basic Books.

Gurman, A. S., and Kniskern, D. P. (1981). *Handbook of family therapy.* New York: Brunner/Mazel.

Haley, J. (1973). Uncommon therapy. *The psychiatric techniques of Milton H. Erikson.* New York: W. W. Norton.

Haley, J. (1976). *Problem-solving therapy.* San Francisco: Jossey-Bass.

Hall, R. L., Hesselbrok, V. M., and Stabenau, J. R. (1983). Familial distribution of alcohol use: 1. Assortative mating in the parents of alcoholics. *Behavior Genetics, 13,* 361–372.

Handel, G. (1967). *The psychosocial interior of the family.* Chicago: University of Chicago Press.

Hansen, C. (1981). Living in normal families. *Family Process, 20,* 53–75.

Helzer, J. E., Robins, L. N., Taylor, J. R., Carey, K., Miller, R. H., Combs-Orme, T., and Farmer, A. (1985). The extent of long-term moderate drinking among alcoholics discharged from medical and psychiatric treatment facilities. *New England Journal of Medicine, 312,* 1678–1682.

Henry, J. (1967). *Pathways to madness.* New York: Vintage Books.

Hill, R., and Rodgers, R. H. (1964). The developmental approach. In H. T. Christensen (Ed.), *Handbook of marriage and the family.* Chicago: Rand McNally.

Hindman, M. (1977). Child abuse and neglect: The alcoholic connection. *Alcohol Health and Research World, 1,* 2–7.

Hindman, M. (1979). Family Violence. *Alcohol Health and Research World, 1,* 1–11.

Hoffman, L. (1981). *Foundations of family therapy.* New York: Basic Books.

Howell, J. T. (1972). *Hard living on Clay Street: Portraits of blue collar families.* New York: Anchor Press, Doubleday.

Jackson, D. (1957). The question of family homeostasis. *Psychiatric Quarterly Supplement, 31,* 79–90.

Jackson, D. (1965). Family rules: The marital quid pro quo. *Archives of General Psychiatry, 8,* 343–348.

Jacob, T., and Seilhammer, R. (1987). Alcoholism and family interaction. In T. Jacob (Ed.), *Family interaction and psychopathology: Theories, methods and findings.* New York: Plenum Press.

Janna, V., Winokur, G., Elston, R., and Go, R.C.P. (1977). A genetic linkage study in support of the concept of depression spectrum disease. *Alcoholism: Clinical and experimental research, 1,* 119–123.

Jellinek, E. M. (1960). *The disease concept of alcoholism.* New Haven, CT: College and University Press in association with New Brunswick, NJ: Hillhouse Press.

Kaij, L. (1960). *Alcoholism in Twins.* Stockholm: Almqvist and Wiksell.

Kantor, D., and Lehr, W. (1975). *Inside the family: Toward a theory of family process.* New York: Harper & Row.

Kaufman, E., and Kaufman, P. N. (1979). *Family therapy of drug and alcohol abuse.* New York: Gardner Press.

Kempe, H. C., and Helfer, R. E. (1972). *Helping the battered child and his family.* New York: J. B. Lippincott.

LaRossa, R. (1977). *Conflict and power in marriage: The first child.* Beverly Hills, CA: Sage Publications.

Lawson, G., Peterson, J. S., and Lawson, A. (1983). *Alcoholism and the family: A guide to treatment and prevention.* Rockville, MD: Aspen Publications.

Lazarus, R. S., and Folkman, S. (1984). *Stress, appraisal, and coping.* New York: Springer.

Levinson, D. J. (1978). *The seasons of a man's life.* New York: Random House.

Lewis, J. M., Beavers, W. R., Gossett, J. T., and Phillips, V. A. (1976). *No single thread: Psychological health in family systems.* New York: Brunner/Mazel.

Lewis, O. (1959). *Five families.* New York: Basic Books.

Lytton, H. (1971). Observation studies of parent-child interaction: A methodological review. *Child Development, 42,* 651–684.

McCrady, B. S., Noel, N. E., Abrams, D. B., Stout, R. L., Nelson, H. F., and Hay, W. M. (1986). Comparative effectiveness of three types of spouse involvement in outpatient behavioral alcoholism treatment. *Journal of Studies on Alcohol, 47,* 459–467.

McCrady, B. S., Paolino, T. J., Jr., Longabaugh, R., and Rossi, J. (1979). Effects of joint hospital admission and couples treatment for hospitalized alcoholics: A pilot study. *Addictive Behavior. 4,* 155–165.

McKenna, T., and Pickens, R. (1981). Alcoholic children of alcoholics. *Journal of Studies on Alcohol, 42,* 1021–1029

Meeks, D. E., and Kelly, C. (1970). Family therapy with the families of recovering alcoholics. *Quarterly Journal of Studies on Alcohol, 31,* 399–413.

Mello, N. K. (1972). Behavioral studies of alcoholism. In B. Kissin and H. Begleiter (Eds.), *The biology of alcoholism: Vol. 2. Physiology and behavior.* New York: Plenum Press.

References

Mello, N. K., and Mendelson, J. H. (1978). Alcohol and human behavior. In L. L. Iversen, S. D. Iversen, and S. H. Snyder (Eds.), *Handbook of psychopharmacology* (vol. 12). New York: Plenum Press.

Mendelson, J. H. (1980). Biological concomitants of alcoholism. *New England Journal of Medicine, 283,* 24–32, 71–81.

Mendelson, J. H., and Mello, N. K. (1979). *The diagnosis and treatment of alcoholism.* New York: McGraw-Hill.

Midanik, L. (1983). Familial alcoholism and problem drinking in a national drinking practices survey. *Addictive Behaviors, 8,* 133–141.

Miller, J. G. (1965). Living systems: Basic concepts. *Behavioral Science, 10,* 193–237.

Minuchin, S. (1974). *Families and family therapy.* Cambridge, MA: Harvard University Press.

Myers, J. K., Weissman, M. M., Tischler, G. L., Holzer, C. E., Leaf, P. J., Orvaschel, H., Anthony, J. C., Boyd, J. H., Burke, J. D., Kramer, M., and Stoltzman, R. (1984). Six-month prevalence of psychiatric disorders in three communities. *Archives of General Psychiatry, 41,* 959–967.

Olson, D. H., McCubbin, H. I., Barnes, H., Larsen A., Muxen, M., and Wilson, M. (1983). *Families: What makes them work.* Beverly Hills, CA: Sage Publications.

Paolino, T. J., Jr., and McCrady, B. S. (1977). *The alcoholic marriage: Alternative perspectives.* New York: Grune and Stratton.

Patterson, G. R. (1982). *Coercive family process.* Eugene, OR: Custasia.

Patterson, G. R., and Reid, J. (1969). Reciprocity and coercion: Two facets of social systems. In C. Neuringer and J. Michael (Eds.), *Behavioral modification in clinical psychology.* New York: Appleton, Century, Crofts

Pattison, E. M. (1976). On abstinence drinking goals in the treatment of alcoholism. *Archives of General Psychiatry, 33,* 923–930.

Pendery, M. L., Maltzman, I. M., and West, L. J. (1982). Controlled drinking by alcoholics? New findings and a reevaluation of a major affirmative study. *Science, 217,* 169–175.

Pokorny, A. D. (1978). Sleep disturbances, alcohol and alcoholism: A review. In R. L. Willin and I. Karsean (Eds.), *Sleep disorders: Diagnosis and treatment.* New York: John Wiley and Sons.

Polich, J. N., Armor, D. J., and Braiker, H. B. (1980). *The course of alcoholism: Four years after treatment.* Santa Monica, CA: Rand Corp.

Reich, T., Cloninger, C. R., Lewis, C., and Rice, J. (1981). *Some recent findings in the study of genotype-environment interaction in alcoholism* (National Institute on Alcohol Abuse and Alcoholism Research Monograph no. 5).

Reiss, D. (1981). *The family's construction of reality.* Cambridge, MA: Harvard University Press.

Reiss, D., and Elstein, A. S. (1971). Perceptual and cognitive resources of family members: Contrasts between families of paranoid and nonparanoid schizophrenics and nonschizophrenic psychiatric patients. *Archives of General Psychiatry, 24,* 121–134.

Rice, J., Cloninger, C. R., and Reich, T. (1978). Multifactorial inheritance with cultural transmission and assortative mating: 1. Description and basic properties of the unitary models. *American Journal of Human Genetics, 30,* 618–643.

Riskin, J. (1963). Methodology for studying family interaction. *Archives of General Psychiatry, 8,* 343–348.

Robins, L. N. (1982). The diagnosis of alcoholism after DSM-III. In E. M. Pattison and E. Kaufman (Eds.), *Encyclopedic handbook of alcoholism.* New York, Gardner Press.

Robins, L. N., Helzer, J. E., Croughen, J., and Radcliff, K. S. (1981). National Institute of Mental Health Diagnostic Interview Schedule. *Archives of General Psychiatry, 38,* 381–389.

Robins, L. N., Helzer, J. E., Weissman, M. M., et al. (1984). Lifetime prevalence of specific psychiatric disorders in three sites. *Archives of General Psychiatry, 41,* 949–958.

Robins, L. N., West, P. A., and Murphy, G. E. (1977). The high rate of suicide in older white men: A study testing ten hypotheses. *Social Psychiatry, 12,* 1–20.

Russell, M., Henderson, C., and Blume, S. B. (1985). *Children of alcoholics: A review of the literature.* New York: Children of Alcoholics Foundation.

Scheflen, A. (1971), Living in an urban ghetto. *Family Process, 10,* 429–450.

Schuckit, M. A., and Morrisey, E. R. (1976). Alcoholism in women: Some clinical and social perspectives with an emphasis on possible subtypes. In N. Greenblatt and M. A. Schuckit (Eds.), *Alcoholism problems in women and children.* New York: Grune and Stratton.

Sharma, S., Ziedman, K., and Moskowitz, H. (1977). Alcohol effect on behavioral performance. In K. Blum, D. L. Bard, and M. G. Hamilton (Eds.), *Alcohol and opiates: Neurochemical and behavioral mechanisms*. New York: Academic Press.

Singer, M. (1985). Family comes first: An examination of the social networks of skid row men. *Human Organization, 44*, 137–142.

Smith, C. J. (1969). Alcoholics: Their treatment and their wives. *British Journal of Psychiatry, 115*, 1039–1042.

Sobell, N. B., and Sobell, L. C. (1978). *Behavioral treatment of alcohol problems*. New York: Plenum Press.

Spitzer, R., Endicott, J., and Robins, E. (1975). Clinical criteria for psychiatric diagnosis and DSM-III. *American Journal of Psychiatry, 132*, 1187–1192.

Stack, C. B. (1974). *All our kin: Strategies for survival in a black community*. San Francisco: Harper and Row.

Steiner, C. M. (1969). The alcoholic game. *Quarterly Journal of Studies on Alcohol, 30*, 920–938.

Steinglass, P. (1976). Experimenting with family treatment approaches to alcoholism, 1950–1975: A review. *Family Process, 15*, 97–123.

Steinglass, P. (1979). The Home Observation Assessment Method (HOAM): Real-time naturalistic observation of families in their homes. *Family Process, 18*, 337–354.

Steinglass, P. (1980). A life history model of the alcoholic family. *Family Process, 19*, 211–225.

Steinglass, P. (1981a). The alcoholic family at home: Patterns of interaction in dry, wet and transitional stages of alcoholism. *Archives of General Psychiatry, 38*, 578–584.

Steinglass, P. (1981b). The impact of alcoholism on the family: Relationship between degree of alcoholism and psychiatric symptomatology. *Journal of Studies on Alcohol, 42*, 288–303.

Steinglass, P., Davis, D. I., and Berensen, D. (1977). Observations of conjointly hospitalized "alcoholic couples" during sobriety and intoxication: Implications for theory and therapy. *Family Process, 16*, 1–16.

Steinglass, P., and Robertson, A. (1983). The alcoholic family. In B. Kissin and H. Begleiter (Eds.), *The biology of alcoholism: Vol. 6. The pathogenesis of alcoholism: Psychosocial factors*. New York: Plenum Press.

Steinglass, P., Tislenko, L., and Reiss, D. (1985). Stability/instability in the alcoholic marriage: The interrelationship between course of alcoholism, family process and marital outcome. *Family Process, 24*, 365–376.

Steinglass, P., Weiner, S., and Mendelson, J. H. (1971). A systems approach to alcoholism: A model and its clinical application. *Archives of General Psychiatry, 24*, 401–408.

Swenson, W., and Morse, R. (1973). The use of self-administered alcoholism screening test (SAAST) in a medical center. *Mayo Clinic Proceedings, 50*, 204–208.

Tamerin, J., and Mendelson, J. H. (1969). The psychodynamics of chronic inebriation: Observations of alcoholics during the process of drinking in an experimental group setting. *American Journal of Psychiatry, 125*, 886–889.

Thomas, A., and Chess, S. (1979). *Temperament and development*. New York: Brunner/Mazel.

Tislenko, L., and Steinglass, P. (unpublished manuscript). The relationship between sex of the alcoholic and patterns of interaction in the home.

Vaillant, G. E. (1983). *The natural history of alcoholism*. Cambridge, MA: Harvard University Press.

Van Bertalanffy, L. (1962). General systems theory: A critical review. *General Systems Yearbook, 7*, 1–20.

Watzlawick, P., Weakland, J., and Fisch, R. (1974). *Change: Principles of problem formation and problem resolution*. New York: W. W. Norton.

Whalen, T. (1953). Wives of alcoholics: Four types observed in a family service agency. *Quarterly Journal of Studies on Alcohol, 14*, 532–641.

Whitefield, C. O., and Williams, K. (1976). *The patient with alcoholism and other drug problems*. Springfield, IL: Southern Illinois University of Medicine.

Winokur, G. (1974). The division of depressive illness into depressive spectrum disease and pure depressive disease. *International Pharmacopsychiatry, 9*, 5–13.

Winokur, G. (1979). Alcoholism and depression in the same family. In D. G. Goodwin and C. K. Erickson (Eds.), *Alcoholism and affective disorders: Clinical, genetic and biochemical studies*. New York: SP Medical and Scientific Books.

Wolin, S. J., and Bennett, L. A. (1984). Family rituals. *Family Process, 23*, 401–420.

Wolin, S. J., Bennett, L. A., and Noonan, D. L. (1979). Family rituals and the reccurrence of alcoholism over generations. *American Journal of Psychiatry, 136:4B*, 589–593.

Wolin, S. J., Bennett, L. A., Noonan, D. L., and Teitelbaum, M. A. (1980). Disrupted family rituals: A factor in the intergenerational transmission of alcoholism. *Journal of Studies on Alcohol, 41,* 199–214.

Wolin, S. J., and Steinglass, P. (1974). Interactional behavior in an alcoholic community. *Medical Annals of D.C., 43,* 183–187.

Woodruff, R. A., Gruze, S. B., Clayton, P. J., and Carr, D. (1973). Alcoholism and depression. *Archives of General Psychiatry, 28,* 97–100.

Young, M., and Willmott, P. (1957). *Family and kinship in East London.* London: Routledge and Kegan Paul.

Index

Ablon, J., 8, 180

Abstinence, 260; alcoholic family identity maintained in, 275–89; as treatment goal, 272–73, 330, 343, 353–61; *see also* Loss of alcohol

Activity level, 204; and sobriety-intoxication cycle, 165–67, 172–73; *see also* Interactional rate

Addiction concept, 31

Adolescents, 28, 79, 91, 330; transmission issue and, 303

Adoption studies, 37, 39–40, 296–97, 320

Affect: and diagnostic phase of treatment, 351, 351*n;* in home interactions, 193–94, 199, 205, 209, 211–12; problem solving and, 47, 68; rituals and, 224; sobriety-intoxication cycle and, 165–67, 172–73

Alafam, 276

Al-Anon, 186, 276, 279, 282–83, 288, 330–32, 363

Alateen, 276

Alcoholic Family: chronicity factor and, 10–11; defined, 9*n;* developmental arrest in, 100–2, 256, 260, 268, 290; diagnosis of, 333–34, 343, 346–53; early-phase development in, 88–89, 107–40, 334–38; family identity of, 61, 107–40, 263–89; family systems theory and concept of, 44–48; growth and development in, 74–

102; late-phase development in, 94–95, 249–50, 259–91, 293–323; life history model of, 44, 48–102, 332–42, 362; middle-phase development in, 90–91, 143–75, 304, 335, 338–40, 349; predictability of responses in, 11–12, 154–55, 171, 183, 204–5, 218, 253; problem-solving styles of, 68–69; and psychobiological effects of alcohol, 11; regulatory mechanisms in, 47–48, 51–73, 100, 110, 272–73, 304–23, 333–34, 349–52; rituals in, 66, 229–36, 304–23; sobriety-intoxication cycle in, 11, 146–75; stress as experienced in, 15–19

Alcoholics Anonymous (AA), 186, 217, 276, 279, 282–83, 288, 299, 311; and traditional treatment of alcoholism, 330–32, 363

Alcoholism: definitions of, 30–32; as developmental life theme, 81; diagnosis of, 20–21, 30–40, 333–34, 343, 346–53; family ritual disruption and, 220–46; as functional for family life, 110, 162–75; genetic factors and, 37, 38–40, 88, 293–99, 302, 320; labeling, in therapeutic setting, 343, 351–52; life course of, 12; life impact study of, 13–19; prevalence of, 20–29; professional attitudes toward, 7–10; regulatory behaviors and, 69–73; therapists' failure to identify, 349; *see*